Panorama of Psychology

Vilen Vardanyan

authorHOUSE®

AuthorHouse™ UK Ltd.
500 Avebury Boulevard
Central Milton Keynes, MK9 2BE
www.authorhouse.co.uk
Phone: 08001974150

First published by AuthorHouse 1/5/2011.

ISBN: 978-1-4567-0033-1 (sc)
ISBN: 978-1-4567-0032-4 (e)

This book is printed on acid-free paper.

Dedicating to my parents

Contents

Introduction

One of the main goals of the history of Psychology is the examination of patterns of formation & development of views on the psyche based on the analysis of different approaches to the understanding of its origin & function. Psychology is closely associated & connected with different areas of science & culture. For many centuries psychology has been a part of philosophy. Its relationship with philosophy has not been interrupted during the entire period of existence of psychology as a science, although it weakened in the beginning of XIX century. The development of science & medicine played a major role in the development of psychological concepts. The history of psychology also examines various relationships with other sciences & their influence on each other. The sources for the history of psychology are primarily works of scientists, archival material, memories of their life and work, as well as analysis of historical and sociological materials, and even fiction to help recreate the spirit of time.

In its development, psychology has gone through several stages. The first, prescientific period ends in about VII-VI centuries B.C. prior to the objective, scientific research of psyche & its contents & functions. During this period the study of the soul was based on the many myths and legends, fairy tales & the original religious beliefs. Second, research period begins at the turn of the VII-VI centuries B.C. Psychology in this period developed in the framework of philosophy. In connection with the conventionality of periodization of development psychology, a natural for almost any historical research, there are some discrepancies in determining the provisional boundaries of individual stages. Sometimes the appearance of self-psychology is associated with a school of Wundt, i.e. the beginning of the development of experimental psychology. However, psychological science has identified as an independent much earlier, with the recognition of independence of its object, the uniqueness of its position in the sciences - the science & the humanities & natural at the same time, studies & internal & external manifestations of the psyche. Such an independent status of psychology was also observed with the appearance of it as an object of study in universities in late XVIII - early XIX century.

For a long time the subject of psychology was a soul. In ancient times the soul was understood as the fundamental principle of the body, by anal-

1

ogy with the notion of "Arche"-the essential foundation of the world, the basic building block from which is all that exists. In this case the main function of the soul was to assume a body activity, since, according to the first scientists-psychologists; the body was an inert mass. Gradually, the functions of soul added knowledge, & thus to the study of the activity was added the study of the stages of knowledge, which soon became one of the major problems of psychological science.

In the middle Ages the soul was being studied primarily for theology, which significantly reduced the possibilities of scientific knowledge. At the time regulatory functions, voluntary behavior & logical thinking were considered the prerogative of the divine will, rather than the material of the soul.

In modern times psychology got rid of the dictates of theology. Just like in Antiquity science tried again become an objective & rational discipline. With the development of biology & the discovery of evolution theory psychology began its departure from the philosophy. The most important stage in the development of psychology associated with the emergence of Wundt's experimental laboratory. But the use of those experiments & tests that have existed in psychology at the beginning of XX century was quite limited.

This has prompted scientists to look for a new subject & new methods of investigation of the psyche. The first school, which originated at the time, was short-lived. Soon began a period of pursuit of psychology that is adequate to the new situation & demands of the time. Thus, psychology was divided into several directions, each of which had its subject & method. In the second half of XX century new schools & directions arose, for example; humanistic psychology, genetic psychology & cognitive psychology.

Studies by many scientists have shown that the development of psychology as a science is influenced by several factors. One of them, the logic of psychological knowledge, was associated with the change of its subject, the influence of related sciences & the development of principles & categorical systems of psychology. Another more subjective factor is the influence of the social situation. The social & historical conditions can influence both scientific concepts & their distribution. The social situation may influence the development of science in several ways; it can create the conditions for the emergence of a conception.

No less important is another factor, the identity of the scientist, the creator of a psychological theory, its value orientation, cognitive style, strong-willed qualities, membership of a particular scientific school & etc. This factor reveals the internal vicissitudes of creative activity & sometimes emotional drama of the scientist. In this regard, may be interesting and the analysis of life, rich in vivid facts of active scientific struggle. However, despite the importance of the social situation and personality of the scientist, the leading factor is still the logic of psychological science, since this factor is closely linked with the development of the principles of psychology.

Just as the subject, the basic principles of psychology & its relation with other sciences have changed as well. In Antiquity psychology was focused primarily on the philosophy & level of development of philosophical knowledge. In the III B.C. there was a change of philosophical interest, due to the fact that the center the main focus of learning no longer laws of nature or society, but a man. This led to the emergence of new problems in psychology, raised questions about the nature of the features of the human psyche, the content of his soul. Changing the subject of psychology & its relations with other sciences raised meaningless substantive questions, for example, whether it is a natural science or humanitarian, or what should be its methodology - biology or philosophy. Analysis of the development of psychology shows that the uniqueness & value of it as a science lies in interdisciplinary nature.

There are three main methodological principles in psychology: determinism, the systems & development.

The principle of determinism implies that all mental phenomena have cause-effect relationship, i.e. everything that happens in our minds has some reason & because of this it may be identified & studied.

The systems principle explains the main types of communication between the different parties of psyche. It suggests that certain mental phenomena are intrinsically linked, forming the integrity & thereby acquiring new properties. Finally, the principle of development states that the most appropriate way to study the psyche is to study the laws of its genesis, its species & stages. There are two types of mental development - phylogenetic & ontogenetic, i.e., the development of the psyche in the process of the human race & in the process of life. Studies have shown that these two types of development are similar.

Antique Greek Psychology

The history of psychology as a scholarly study of the mind dates back to the Ancient Greeks, Egypt & India. Philosophers of those days considered important questions like what is free will, how does the mind work & what is the relationship of people to their surroundings. In Antiquity psychology was a part of the science that studies the general laws of society, nature & man. This science was called natural philosophy. For a long period of time, almost 20 centuries, psychology remained a part of philosophy. Another movement called Panpsychism considered the whole world to be animate & endowed with a soul. For several centuries the difference between the psyche of man & animals was treated as purely quantitative rather than qualitative.

The first theories of the soul, arising out of the early myths & religious beliefs, identified some of the functions of the soul, especially energy, which encouraged the body to the activity. These ideas formed the basis of studies of the first psychologists. The earliest studies were believed to have shown that the soul was not only activator but also the regulator or the activity of the individual, as well as a major tool in a process of understanding the world. These judgments about the properties of the soul became major objects of study. Eventually the analysis of the regularities of nature led thinkers of that time to the idea that the soul was material, i.e., consisting of the same particles as the surrounding world.

One of the earliest philosophical movements of the ancient Greece was Cynicism. It was a form of philosophy, primarily concerned with virtue, whose followers were known as "The Dog Philosophers." They believed that virtue was the only necessity for happiness & that it was wholly sufficient for attaining happiness. They followed this philosophy to the extent of neglecting everything that did not further their perfection of virtue & their attainment of happiness. Thus the title cynics, from the Greek word for dog, was assigned to them because they lived like dogs; neglecting society, hygiene, family, money, etc. The first philosopher to outline these themes was Antisthenes, who had been a pupil of Socrates. He was followed by Diogenes of Sinope, who lived in a tub on the streets of Athens. He took Cynicism to its logical extremes, & came to be seen as the archetypal Cynic philosopher. He was followed by Crates of Thebes who gave away a large fortune so he could live a life of Cynic poverty in Athens. Cynicism spread with the rise of Imperial Rome in the 1st century. It finally disappeared in the late 5th century, although many of its ascetic & rhetorical ideas were adopted by early Christians.

Another ancient Greek movement Hedonism was a school of ethics which argued that pleasure was the only intrinsic good. There were two types of hedonism: motivational, which held that only pleasure or pain motivates us & normative, which claimed that all & only pleasure had worth or value & all & only pain had disvalue.

Milesian School of Thought

Ancient Greek philosophers, from Thales (550 B.C.) through even to the Roman period, developed an elaborate theory of what they termed the psuche, from which the first half of "psychology" was derived. Thales of Miletus was the first to engage in such inquiry. The tradition claims that Thales predicted a solar eclipse in 585 BC introduced geometry into Greece from Egypt & produced some engineering marvels. Thales's interest in measuring & explaining celestial & terrestrial phenomena was as strong as his concern with the more abstract inquiries into the causes & principles of substance. Thales was the first to study the basic principles & the question of the originating substances of matter. He explored almost all areas of knowledge, philosophy, history, science, mathematics, engineering, geography, & politics. He proposed many interesting theories, like the ones of primary substance, support of the earth & the cause of change. Most of the biographical information about Thales came from the writings of Aristotle. Aristotle's comments do not sound as if they were based on first-hand knowledge of Thales' views, & the doxographical reports say that Thales did not write a book. However Aristotle was confident that Thales belonged to that group of thinkers that he called "inquirers into nature" & distinguished him from earlier poetical "myth-makers." Aristotle linked Thales' claim that the world rests on water with the view that water was fundamental principle. He suggested that Thales chose water because of its fundamental role in nutrition & growth, & claimed that water was the origin of the nature of moist things. The founder & followers of the Milesian School claimed that there was a single enduring material stuff that was both the origin of all things & their continuing nature. Therefore, when Thales said that the first principle was water, he should be understood as claiming both that the original state of things was water & that even now everything was really water in some state or another. The change from the original state to the present one involved changes in the material stuff such that although it may not now appear to be water everywhere there is no transformation of water into a different kind of stuff. For Thales water was the first principle because everything came from water. Water, then, was perhaps the original state of things for Thales, & water was a necessary condition for everything that was generated naturally. Thales may well have thought that certain characteristics of the original water persisted: in particular its capacity for motion, which must have been innate in order to generate the changes from the original state. This was suggested by Thales' reported claims that the lodestone (with its magnetic properties) and amber (which when rubbed exhibits powers of attraction through static electricity) have souls and that all things are full of gods. Thales identified soul, meaning that which made a thing alive with something in the whole universe, & so supposed that everything was full of gods. The reports about Thales showed him employing a certain kind of explanation: ultimately the explanation of why things were as they were was grounded in water as the basic stuff of the universe & the changes that it underwent through its own inherent nature. Thus, Thales marked a radical change from all other previous sorts of accounts of the world both Greek & non-Greek. Thales saw nature as a complete & self-ordering system. He had no reason to call on divine intervention from outside the natural world to supplement his account— water itself may be divine, but it was not something that intervened in the natural world from outside.

While the evidence for Thales' naturalistic account is circumstantial, this attitude can be directly verified for Anaximander. In fact the true history of written Greek philosophy started with Anaximander of Miletus in Asia Minor. He was believed to be Thales's disciple. Anaximander was known as the first thinker dared to write a treatise in prose, which has been called On Nature. Anaximander held that the universe had an orderly nature & that this order was internal rather than imposed from outside. A testimony about Anaximander from Pseudo-Plutarch says that "Something productive of hot and cold was separated off from the eternal at the genesis of this world and from this a sphere of flame grew around the air around the earth like the bark around a tree." Neither the cause nor the precise process of separation was explained, but it is probable that Anaximander would have thought of the original source of change as part of the character of the indefinite itself. Another passage from Simplicius shows that Anaximander did not held that the eternal indefinite stuff gives rise directly to the cosmos as we know it. Rather, the "apeiron" (which was the equivalent of matter) somehow generates the opposites hot & cold. Hot & cold are themselves stuffs with powers; & it was the actions of these stuffs/powers that produced the things that came to be in our world. The opposites dominated & contained each other, producing a regulated structure. This was a structured arrangement that Anaximander referred to when he spoke of justice & reparation. In addition Anaximander not only put forward the thesis that the Boundless was the principle, but also tried to argue for it. This early concept of the Boundless played a big role in Anaximander's account of the origin of the cosmos. According to several sources, the eternal movement of the Boundless was believed to have caused the origin of the heavens. Anaximander believed that the earth floated freely in the center of the universe. It is quite possible that he drew this bold conclusion from his assumption that the celestial bodies make full circles. His assumption was a correct one, more than 25 centuries later astronauts were able to observe what Anaximander knew. His observations led him to believe that the universe had depth. He was the first to introduce the idea that the celestial bodies lie behind one another.

The pattern that can be seen in Thales and Anaximander of an original basic stuff giving rise to the phenomena of the cosmos continues in the views of the third of the Milesians, Anaximenes. He lived in the mid 6th century B.C. & died around 528. He was the third philosopher of the Milesian School of philosophy & an associate, and possibly a student, of Anaximander's. Anaximenes replaced his teacher's "apeiron" with air, thus eliminating the first stage of the coming-to-be of the cosmos. Instead he returned to an originating stuff more like Thales' water. Anaximenes considered air to be the "arche," which was a Greek word used to describe primary senses, beginning, origin or first cause.

Anaximenes said that infinite air was the principle, from which things that are becoming, & that are, & that shall be, & gods and things divine, all come into being, & the rest from its product. It was believed to be in constant motion. For Anaximenes, all things came from air & ultimately were air. He held that air as the arche was infinite by which he meant unlimited or unconditioned & therefore unoriginate. Anaximenes did not accept Anaximander's view that the (first) principle, arche of all things could not be one of the elements which arise from it. He also introduced an interesting theory according to which the earth was formed from air by a felting process. Just like his teacher, Anaximenes used his advanced principles to account for various natural phenomena. For example lightning & thunder were believed to be a result of wind breaking out of clouds.

Early Idealistic Schools of thought

Socrates (469-347B.C.) is often considered one of the founders of Western Philosophy. He was an enigmatic & peculiar figure known mainly through the accounts of later classical writers. Despite his foundational place in the history of ideas, Socrates actually wrote very little. Most of our knowledge of him comes from the works of Plato (427-347), & since Plato had other concerns in mind than simple historical accuracy it was nearly impossible to determine how much of his thinking actually derived from Socrates.

The most accurate of Plato's writings on Socrates is probably the "Apology," which was Plato's account of Socrates's defense at his trial in 399 B.C. Socrates' method of philosophical inquiry consisted in questioning people on the positions they asserted & working them through questions into a contradiction, thus proving to them that their original assertion was wrong. Apparently Socrates himself never took any positions; in The Apology he radically and skeptically claims to know nothing at all except that he knows nothing. Socrates & Plato referred to this method of questioning as "elenchus," which meant "cross-examination." The Socratic elenchus will eventually give rise to dialectic. Dialectic was the idea that truth needed to be pursued by modifying one's position through questioning & conflict with opposing ideas. It was this idea of the truth being pursued, rather than discovered, that characterized Socratic thought & much of our world view today. The Western notion of dialectic was somewhat Socratic in nature in that it was conceived of as an ongoing process. The Athenians, of course with the exception of Plato, thought of Socrates as a Sophist, mainly because he was unconcerned with physical or metaphysical questions. For him, the issue of primary importance was ethics, living a good life. He seemed to tear down every ethical position he's confronted with; he never offered alternatives after he's torn down other people's ideas. He doesn't seem to be a radical skeptic, though. Scholars generally believe that the "Socratic paradox" was actually Socratic rather than an invention of Plato. The one positive statement that Socrates seemed to have made was a definition of virtue: "virtue is knowledge."

The most famous of Socrates's pupils was an aristocratic young man named Plato. He was born Athens between 429 & 423 B.C. After the death of Socrates, Plato carried on much of his former teacher's work and eventually founded his own school, the Academy, in 385. We know much about Plato's teachings, because he wrote dialogues between Socrates and others that would explore philosophical issues. Plato carried on the philosophy of Socrates, concentrating on the dialectical examination of basic ethical issues. He later began to develop his own philosophy, the fundamental aspect of which was the theory of "ideas" or "forms." Plato was stymied by the question of change in the physical.

He divided human beings up based on their innate intelligence, strength & courage. Those who were not overly bright, or strong, or brave, were suited to various productive professions, like farming & those who were somewhat bright, strong & especially courageous were suited to defensive & policing professions. The third category was intelligent, virtuous & brave, thus, suited to run the state. Finally the last category, lower end of human society consisted of an overwhelming majority of people in a state, which he called the "producers," since they were most suited for productive work. The best & the brightest were those who were in complete control of the state permanently. Plato called these people "Guardians." For Plato, human beings lived in a world of visible & intelligible things. The visible world was what surrounded us. The intelligible world was made up of the unchanging products of human reason: anything arising from reason alone, such as abstract definitions or mathematics, made up this intelligible world. According to Plato the intelligible world contained the eternal "Forms" of things; the visible world was the imperfect & changing. Later "Platonism" became a term coined by scholars to refer to the intellectual consequences of denying the reality of the material world.

Aristotle (384–322B.C.) was a student of Plato & a teacher of Alexander the Great. He was born at Stagira in northern Greece. Aristotle's writings covered many different fields, including physics, metaphysics, poetry, theater, music, logic, rhetoric, politics, government & ethics. He was the most notable product of the educational program devised by Plato. Aristotle spent twenty years of his life studying at the Academy & when Plato died, he returned to his native Macedonia, where he was supposed to have participated in the education of Philip's son, Alexander the Great. He to Athens in 335 & established his own school at the Lyceum. Aristotle radically transformed most areas of knowledge he touched. He wrote as many as 200 treatises majority of which was lost. Aristotle was the first to classify areas of human knowledge into distinct disciplines such as mathematics, biology, & ethics.

Aristotle's emphasis on good reasoning combined with his belief in the scientific method formed the backdrop for most of his work. For example, in his work in ethics & politics, Aristotle identifies the highest good with intellectual virtue; that is, a moral person is one who cultivates certain virtues based on reasoning. And in his work on psychology and the soul, Aristotle distinguishes sense perception from reason, which unifies & interprets the sense perceptions & is the source of all knowledge.

He was the first to develop a formalized system for reasoning. Aristotle observed that the validity of any argument can be determined by its structure rather than its content. A classic example of a valid argument is his syllogism: All men are mortal; Socrates is a man; therefore, Socrates is mortal. Thus, as long as the premises were true, then the conclusion was also guaranteed to be true. Aristotle's brand of logic dominated this area of thought until the rise of propositional logic.

Aristotle rejected Plato's theory of forms, which stated that properties such as beauty were abstract universal entities that existed independent of the objects themselves. Instead, he held that forms were intrinsic to the objects & could not exist apart from them. He also stated that such forms must be studied in relation to them, yet in discussing art, for some reason Aristotle rejected this, instead arguing for idealized universal form which artists attempted to capture in their work.

In Aristotle's writings logic & reasoning were the main preparatory instruments of scientific investigation. He used the term "logic" as equivalent to verbal reasoning. The "Categories" of Aristotle were basic classifications of individual words & include the following ten: substance, quantity, quality, relation, place, time, situation, condition, action, passion. They were arranged according to the order of the questions one would ask in gaining knowledge of an object. In Aristolte's opinion notions, when isolated did not in themselves express either truth or falsehood. It was only with the combination of ideas in a proposition that truth & falsity were possible. The elements of such a proposition were the noun substantive & the verb. He argued that the combination of words gave rise to rational speech & thought. Such thought could take many forms, but Aristotle's logic considered only demonstrative forms which expressed truth & falsehood. The truth or falsity of propositions was initially determined by their agreement or disagreement with the facts they represented.

For Aristotle, philosophy arose historically after basic necessities were secured. It grew out of a feeling of curiosity & wonder. Aristotle's subject of metaphysics dealt with the first principles of scientific knowledge & the ultimate conditions of all existence. More specifically, it dealt with existence in its most fundamental state & the essential attributes of existence. The latter differed from dialectics which was tentative & it differed from sophistry which was an imitation of knowledge without the reality. Aristotle was convinced that there were a handful of universal truths. He defended both the laws of contradiction & that of excluded middle.

The process of the development of potentiality to actuality was one of the most important aspects of Aristotle's philosophy. It was designed to solve the difficulties which earlier thinkers had raised with reference to the beginnings of existence & the relations of the one & many. The actual vs. potential state of things was explained in terms of the causes which act on things. There were four causes: material cause, or the elements out of which an object is created; efficient cause, or the means by which it is created; formal cause, or the expression of what it is & final cause, or the end for which it is. Aristotle held that God was the first of all substances, the necessary first source of movement who was himself unmoved.

In Aristotle's theory the universe was a scale lying between the two extremes: form without matter was on one end & matter without form was on the other end. The passage of matter into form was shown in its various stages in the world of nature. To do this was the object of Aristotle's physics, or philosophy of nature. The passage from form to matter within nature was described as a movement towards ends or purposes. Accordingly everything in nature had its end & function, & nothing was without its purpose. Motion was viewed as the passage of matter into form. There were four kinds of motion: 1. motion which affects the substance of a thing, particularly its beginning & its ending; 2. motion which brings about changes in quality; 3. motion which brings about changes in quantity, by increasing it & decreasing it; & 4.motion which brings about locomotion, or change of place.

Aristotle classified the objects of the senses three categories; 1 special, (such as color is the special object of sight, and sound of hearing), 2 common, or apprehended by several senses in combination (such as motion or figure), & 3 incidental or inferential (such as when from the immediate sensation of white we come to know a person or *object* which is white). Overall there were five special senses. Of these, touch was the most rudimentary, hearing the most instructive & sight the most ennobling. According to Aristotle, the organ in these senses never acted directly, but was affected by some medium such as air. Even touch, which seemed to act by actual contact, involved some vehicle of communication. He considered heart to be the common or central sense organ.

Aristotle also described the imagination as an active movement which resulted upon an actual sensation. Thus, it was the process by which an impression of the senses was pictured & retained before the mind. In his theory Illusions & dreams were both alike due to an excitement in the organ of sense similar to that which would be caused by the actual presence of the sensible phenomenon. Memory was defined as the permanent possession of the sensuous picture as a copy which represented the object of which it was a picture.

Aristotle rejected the definition of space as the void. To him, empty space was impossibility. He defined time as the measure of motion in regard to what was earlier & later. Time was dependent for its existence upon motion. He concluded, since the time was the measuring or counting of motion, it also must depend for its existence on a counting mind. If there were no mind to count, there could be no time.

Aristotle defined soul as the perfect expression or realization of a natural body. From this definition it follows that there is a close connection between psychological states & physiological processes. Metaphysicians before Aristotle discussed the soul abstractly without any regard to the bodily environment; this, Aristotle believed, was a mistake. At the same time, Aristotle regarded the soul or mind not as the product of the physiological conditions of the body, but as the truth of the body, meaning the substance in which only the bodily conditions gain their real meaning.

The Aristotelian soul had certain "faculties" or "parts" which corresponded with the stages of biological development. These were the faculties of nutrition, that of movement & that of reason. These faculties were similar to mathematical figures in which the higher includes the lower. As the subject of impression, perception involved a movement & a kind of qualitative change; but perception was not merely a passive or receptive affection. It acted & distinguished between the qualities of outward things.

One of the main issues for Aristotle was the question of character or personality, particularly what does it take for an individual human being to be good. In his theory every activity had a final cause, the good at which it aims. Since there cannot be an infinite regress of merely extrinsic goods, Aristotle held that there must be a highest good at which all human activity ultimately was aimed.

According to Aristotle, things of any variety had some characteristic functions that they were properly used to perform. The good for human beings, then, involved the entire proper function of human life as a whole. Thus, human beings should aim at a life in full conformity with their rational natures; for this, the satisfaction of desires & the acquisition of material goods were less important than the achievement of virtue.

Even more than twenty-three centuries after his death, Aristotle remained one of the most influential thinkers of all time. He was the founder of formal logic, pioneered the study of zoology & left every future scientist & philosopher in his debt through his contributions to the scientific method, but despite his numerous contributions many of his errors held back science considerably.

Atomistic School of Thought

The ancient Greek natural philosophers held that the universe was composed of physical 'atoms', the so called 'uncuttables'. Atomism as a philosophy originated with Leucippus (500-450B.C.). Democritus (470-400B.C.), his disciple, generally considered the father of atomism, as practically nothing is known of Leucippus. Later this theory was further developed by Epicurus (342-270B.C.) & Lucretius (95-51B.C.). These philosophers developed a systematic & comprehensive natural philosophy accounting for the origins of everything from the interaction of indivisible bodies, as these atoms—which have only a few intrinsic properties like size and shape—strike against one another, rebound & interlock in an infinite void. This atomist natural philosophy eschewed teleological explanation & denied divine intervention or design, regarding every composite of atoms as produced purely by material interactions of bodies, and accounting for the perceived properties of macroscopic bodies as produced by these same atomic interactions. In a sense, Atomism was one of the attempts by early Greek natural philosophers to respond to the challenge offered by Parmenides, who had argued that it is impossible for there to be change without something coming from nothing.

There is very little biographic information about Leucippus. According to several sources he was born in Elea. He lived during the fifth century B.C. The extent of Leucippus' contribution to the developed atomist theory is unknown. Most reports refer to the views of Democritus alone or to both atomists together.

Leucippus formulated his theory in response to the Eleatic claim that 'what is' must be one & unchanging, because any assertion of differentiation or change within 'what is' involves the assertion of 'what is not,' an unintelligible concept. He tried to formulate a theory that was consistent with the evidence of the senses that change & motion & a multiplicity of things existed in the world. In the atomist system, change only occurred at the level of appearances: the real constituents of being persist unchanged, merely rearranging themselves into new combinations that form the world of appearance. Leucippus also reportedly accepted the Eleatic Melissus' argument that void was necessary for motion, but took this to be evidence that, since we experience motion, there must be void.

The reason for positing smallest indivisible magnitudes was also reported to be a response to Zeno's argument that, if every magnitude could be divided to infinity, motion would be impossible. According to Leucippus atoms were always in motion.

In Leucippus' cosmology worlds were formed when groups of atoms were combined to form a cosmic whirl, which caused the atoms to separate out & sort by like kind. He also stated that worlds were formed, grew & perished according to a kind of necessity. Leucippus said that nothing happens in vain but everything from logos & by necessity. This has been found puzzling, since the reference to logos might seem to suggest that things are ruled by reason, an idea that Democritus' system excludes.

Democritus was born at Abdera sometime around 458 B.C. He was described as well traveled, probably visiting Babylon, Egypt, & Ethiopia. He spent all of his time on scientific & philosophical studies, teaching, and writing— some 60 works have been listed. Of his voluminous writings, only a few fragments of his ethical theory remain. His truly advanced atomic theory put him among the foremost thinkers of his time.

Democritus' theory of the atomic nature of the physical world was known only through the works of critics of the theory such as Aristotle & Theophrastus. It resolved the question of how a world evidently in a state of flux could nevertheless have an underlying nature that was eternal & unchanging. By positing infinitely small things that remained the same but formed different combinations with each other, Leucippus initially, & Democritus in greater detail, managed to answer the question in a way that has been subject to increasingly successful elaboration ever since.

Democritus was an original thinker in ethical theory, setting high standards of personal integrity and social responsibility, without invoking supernatural sanctions. Democritus argued that one's own consciousness of right & wrong should prevent one from doing anything shameful, not the fear of breaking the law or being vilified by public opinion. He thought that men fashioned an image of Chance as an excuse for their own stupidity, because chance rarely conflicts with intelligence and most things in life can be set in order by an intelligent farsightedness.

In Democritus' theory of perception images were presented as thin layers of atoms, constantly sloughed off from the surfaces of macroscopic bodies & carried through the air. These films of atoms had the capacity shrink & expand. Only those that shrink could be visible for the eye. It was the impact of these on our sense organs that enables us to perceive. Visible properties of macroscopic objects, like their size & shape, were conveyed to us by these films. The properties perceived by other senses were also conveyed by contact of some kind.

Democritus' account why things sometimes taste different to people who are ill depended on two factors, neither of which undercut the notion that certain atomic shapes regularly affected us in a given way. One was that a given substance like honey was not quite homogeneous, but contained atoms of different shapes. While it took its normal character from the predominant type of atom present, there were other atom-types present within. The other was that our sense-organs needed to be suitably harmonized to admit a given atom-type, & the disposition of our passageways could be affected by illness or other conditions. This was the Democrit's term that Aristotle had translated as 'position,' thesis, i.e. one of the three fundamental ways in which atoms can appear differently to us.

Democritus did not distinguish between touch & contact. According to Democritus & Leucippus thought, as well as sensation were caused by images impinging on the body from outside. Thus, thought & perception were dependent on images. In addition both were described as changes in the body. Democritus realized that his view gave rise to an epistemological problem: it took the knowledge of the world to be derived from sense experience, but the senses themselves were not in direct contact with the nature of things, thus leaving room for error. The idea that knowledge was based on the reception of images from outside was employed in Democritus' discussion of the gods. In it our knowledge of the gods came from giant films of atoms with the characteristics we attribute to the gods. Although atomism was often identified as an atheist doctrine in later times, it was not clear whether this was really Democritus' position. Democritus was the originator of an ancient theory about the historical development of human communities. He suggested that human life was originally like that of animals. Democritus' theory described the gradual development of human communities for purposes of mutual aid, the origin of language, crafts & agriculture. If Democritus is the source for this theory, it suggests that he took seriously the need to account for the origin of all aspects of the world of our experience. Human institutions could not be assumed to be permanent features or divine gifts. The explanations offered suggest that human culture developed as a response to necessity & the hardships of our environment. It has been suggested that the sheer infinite size of the atomist universe were important in the development of an account that can show how human institutions arise without assuming theological origin. Democritus' naturalistic ethics can be traced to his materialist account of the soul & his rejection of supernatural ideas.

Epicurus' philosophy conveyed the ultimate conviction that individuals can live in serene happiness, fortified by the continual experience of modest pleasures. He was born in the Greek colony on Samos, but spent most of his active life in Athens, where he founded yet another school of philosophy. Epicurus adopted the atomism of Leucippus & Democritus, maintaining that all objects, events & even human lives were in reality nothing more than physical interactions among minute indestructible particles. His philosophy was a complete & interdependent system with an empiricist theory of knowledge, a description of nature based on atomistic materialism, & a naturalistic account of evolution. Epicurus thought that, on the basis of a radical materialism which dispensed with transcendent entities such as the Platonic Ideas or Forms, he could disprove the possibility of the soul's survival after death, & hence the prospect of punishment in the afterlife. He regarded the unacknowledged fear of death as the primary cause of anxiety among human being. According to his theory, anxiety was the source of all extreme & irrational desires. Thus the elimination of the fears & corresponding desires would leave people free to pursue their physical & metal pleasures to which they were naturally drawn. Epicurus was convinced that deeply ingrained habits of thought were not easily corrected, & thus he proposed various exercises to assist the novice. His system included advice on the proper attitude toward politics, the role of sex, Gods, marriage & friendship.

Epicurus held that soul atoms were distributed throughout the body & it was by means of them that we have sensations & the experience of pain & pleasure. He further argued that body without soul atoms was unconscious & inert, & when the atoms of the body were disarranged so that it could no longer support conscious life, the soul atoms were scattered & no longer retain the capacities for sensation. He also described a part of the human soul that was concentrated in the chest. It was viewed as the seat of the higher intellectual functions. Epicurus concluded that the soul could not survive the death of the body, because its texture was too delicate to exist independently of the body that contains it. From this it followed that there could be no punishment after death, nor any regrets for the life that has been lost. He also maintained that the soul was responsive to physical impressions. In his theory no phenomena were purely mental. The elementary sensations of pleasure & pain, accordingly, rather than abstract moral principles or abstract concepts of goodness or badness, were the fundamental guides to what was good & bad. Even the function of the human mind was not to seek higher things, but to maximize pleasure & minimize pain.

Epicurus proposed a radically reductive hypothesis: just as sensations occur as a result of thin films emitted by objects that enter the appropriate sense organ, so too some of these simulacra are fine enough to penetrate directly to the mind (located in the chest), & that is how we imagine such objects. This process was invoked to explain not only dream images, but any kind of mental impression, including impressions constituting voluntary thought: the latter occurred when we attend to one or another of the exiguous physical films. Imagining a thing was thus nothing more than picking out the simulacra that have been emitted by it. In Epicurus' theory mental images had no privileged status, they were always true.

Epicurus offered an interesting classification of desires. In his theory some desires were natural, others were empty. The natural desires were of two sorts, those that were necessary & those that were merely natural. Natural & necessary were those that look to happiness, physical well-being, or life itself. Unnecessary but natural desires were for pleasant things like good-tasting food & drink. Empty desires were those that had as their objects things designated by empty sounds, such as immortality.

Epicurus developed a truly materialistic metaphysics, empiricist epistemology, & hedonistic ethics. He rejected the existence of Platonic forms & an immaterial soul, saying that Gods have no influence on human's lives. Epicurus also thought skepticism was untenable, & that one can gain knowledge of the world relying solely upon the senses.

Epicurus' disciple Titus Lucretius Carus was born at the very beginning of the first century B.C. These were bad times politically, life was insecure & the future uncertain; the old religion had largely faded, & for the first time the full force of the Greek philosophical tradition, especially the work of Epicurus, was available for Roman eyes. In such a world Lucretius came to maturity, soaked himself in volumes of Greek thought largely unavailable to us now, & put together in poetry of grand design & remarkable execution a major philosophical treatise. This was all the more remarkable because Romans generally had small patience for philosophy. His six-book Latin hexameter poem "De rerum natura" variously translated "On the nature of things" & "On the nature of the universe," survived virtually intact. It was a work of physics, written in the venerable tradition of Greek treatises "On nature." Nevertheless, Lucretius wrote as a complete Epicurean, offering his reader not just cosmological understanding but the full recipe for happiness.

According to Lucretius to fear a future state of death meant to make the conceptual blunder of supposing yourself present to regret & bewail your own non-existence. The reality was that being dead will be no worse than it was, long ago, not yet to have been born. This Lucretian symmetry argument which has enjoyed widespread discussion in the recent philosophical literature on death was found in company with a whole battery of further arguments for acquiescing in the prospect of one's own dissolution.

Lucretius was considered by Roman patristic thinkers like Lactantius to be the leading spokesman of the godless Epicurean philosophy. Lucretius was both, admired & imitated by writers of the early Roman empire but despite his extensive impact in literary & philosophical circles Lucretius struggled for two centuries to get rid of the label of 'atheist'. He became a key influence on the emergence of early modern atomism in the 17th century — a development above all due to Pierre Gassendi's construction of an atomistic system.

Lucretius opposed the supernatural explanations of phenomena, arguing that the world was not created by divine intelligence. Instead, it must be understood as an entirely natural phenomenon, the outcome of a random process. He viewed the various events in the universe not as the product of design, but as a part of an ongoing sequence of purely physical events.

Pythagoreanism

Pythagoreanism was a complex ethical, religious, & mystical system of teaching founded by Pythagoras in the sixth century B.C. The first school was established in Croton about 530 BC & by the fifth century B.C. Pythagoras denied equality of souls, believing that there was no equality in nature & among people. These differences, according to Pythagoras, were not hereditary. He sought to search for capable & wise people to specially train them to become leaders of society. The ideas of Pythagoras on the need for a class of rulers of the most wise & enlightened people have left their imprint on the theory of Plato's ideal society.

Pythagoras held that the world of mathematics, the world of perfect geometric & logical formulas was more important than the objective world of real objects. He was the first thinker to conclude that the soul could not die with the body of a particular person & that it must develop its own laws, respectively, of its purpose. This purpose, he believed, was the purification, i.e., the soul in the process of his life should become more perfect & clean. His concept left an imprint on the ideas of Buddhism & reincarnation of the soul, as well as the Orphic religion, which believed that after death the soul moves the body to another body, depending on the moral assessment of its existence.

Pythagorean societies in southern Italy had become involved in the fierce fighting between the aristocracy & the democratic forces of government. Eventually Pythagoreans separated into two distinct groups called the Acusmatici (meaning "oral precept") whose members emphasized the observation of the special Pythagorean way of life taught by the master himself & the Mathematici (meaning "students of theoretical subjects"), who were more interested in arithmetic, the theory of music, cosmology & astronomy. Later the Mathematici group became closely associated with the doctrine of Plato & his followers who established the Platonic Academy, whereas the Acusmatici became wandering ascetics finally joining the Cynics.Pythagorean thought was scientific as well as metaphysical & included specific developments in arithmetic & geometry, in the science of musical tones & harmonies, & in astronomy.

The number speculation perhaps was the most characteristic feature of

Pythagoreanism. In it things "were" number, or "resembled" number. Back then this concept meant that things were measurable & commensurable or proportional in terms of number. For some Pythagoreans even abstracted things "had" their number: "justice" was associated with the number four & with a square, "marriage" with the number five, & so on. Eventually the speculation on number & proportion led to an intuitive feeling of the so called "harmonia" of the "kosmos"& the application of the so called "tetraktys" to the theory of music. Pythagoreans thought that the distances of the heavenly bodies from the Earth somehow corresponded to musical intervals. This theory under the influence of Platonic conceptions later resulted in the famous idea of the harmony of the spheres.

As a school of thought the original Pythagoreanism was quite controversial, & the conglomeration of disparate features that it displayed was intrinsically confusing. By laying stress on certain inner experiences & intuitive truths revealed only to the initiated, Pythagoreanism represented a soul-directed subjectivism alien to the mainstream Greek thought. Unlike the Ionian naturalism, Pythagoreanism was akin to trends seen in mystery religions & emotional movements. Overall they accepted the essentially Ionian doctrines that the world was composed of opposites & generated from something unlimited.

Pyrrhonism

Pyrrhonism or Pyrrhonian skepticism was a school of thought founded by Aenesidemus in the first century BC. It was named after Pyrrho, a philosopher who lived from c. 360 to c. 270 BC, although the relationship between the philosophy of the school & of the historical figure was murky. Pyrrhonian skepticism differs from academic skepticism, because the latter is identified with the claim that no knowledge is possible, whereas the former argues for suspension of judgment on all questions concerning knowledge. Since Pyrrhonism is often associated with a technique of argumentation it is sometimes confused with relativism; but whereas a relativist would argue that there can be no grounds for comparing the merits or truth-values of competing systems of thought, the Pyrrhonist suspends judgment on such questions. Pyrrhonian skepticism became popular through the publication in 1562 & 1569 of Latin translations of Sextus Empiricus' works. The acceptance of Pyrrhonian ideas & philosophical practices became possible due to crisis in anti-intellectual movements of the late middle ages & by the various attacks on scholastic Aristotelianism. The Pyrrhonians believed that there were two potential sources of knowledge: perception & reasoning. When the results of perception were introduced to settle a non-evident matter—say the actual color of an object (as opposed to how it appeared to someone), they would point out that members of different species of animals probably perceive colors quite differently because their eyes are constructed differently, & also that members of the same species would have different perceptions of the color depending upon such things as the condition of their eyes, the nature of the medium of perception, & the order in which objects were perceived. Being reminded of the relativity of perception could incline a person to refrain from assenting to judgments of perception, when those judgments were about the "real" properties of the objects. The Pyrrhonians further held that there were modes which could induce withholding assent to the results of reasoning.

Stoicism

The name of this school came from the word porch in the Agora at Athens decorated with mural paintings, where the members of the school met, & their lectures were held. Stoicism was the relatively new philosophical movement of the Hellenistic period. Its founder was considered to be Zeno (336-264 B.C.) not to be confused with the Eleatic Zeno. He was quite impressed with the thought & character of Socrates. Zeno interpreted the Socratic model from the point of view of the Cynics, Antisthenes, Diogenes, & Crates of Thebes, who was his teacher at the time. For Stoics philosophy was a way of life. The Stoics of the Hellenistic period such as Cleanthes of Assos (331-233 B.C.) & Chrysippus (281-208 B.C.) developed Stoicism as a systematic body of doctrine, complete with a system of logic, epistemology, & cosmology. Chrysippus was recognized by his contemporaries as the equal of Aristotle in logic. Stoic epistemology was decidedly empiricist & nominalist in spirit. They rejected both Plato's & Aristotle's notions of form. There were no abstract universals, either apart from particulars, as Plato would have it, or in particular substances, as Aristotle held. Only particular things existed & our knowledge of them was based solely on the impressions they make upon the soul. Our knowledge of particular objects was therefore based on sense perception, as was our knowledge of our mental states and activities, our soul itself being a material thing.

Thus, metaphysically the Stoics were materialists. While all that existed was material, nevertheless there were two principles of reality. The passive principle was matter devoid of quality. Borrowing from Heraclitus, the Stoics identified the active principle of reality with the "Logos," Reason, or God. Unlike later Christian versions, the Stoic view of the "Logos" was both materialistic & pantheistic. It is safe to say that the Stoics were determinists, even fatalists, holding that whatever happens happens necessarily. They also held that all events were determined by prior events & that the universe was a precise & perfect, rational whole. Stoics maintained that the knowledge of nature was of instrumental value only. Its value was entirely determined by its role in fostering the life of virtue understood as living in accord with nature. This practical aspect of Stoicism was especially prevalent in the Roman Stoic, Epictetus (c 50-138CE), who was responsible for developing the ethical & religious side of Stoicism.

The Stoic movement persisted for some five hundred years in antiquity. While it differed from Christianity in fundamental ways (it was materialistic & pantheistic), nonetheless Christianity defined itself in an intellectual environment pervaded by Stoic ideas of the "logos." Stoic ideas regarding the natural order of things and of each rational soul as a divine element provided one basis upon which later ideas of natural law were erected. Kant's conception of the pre-eminent value of the Good Will & the moral indifference of external circumstances, though not entirely Stoic, showed the influence of Stoicism. In addition, Spinoza's conception of the promotion of the active over & against the passive emotions further reflects the pervasive influence of Stoic ideas.

The materialistic position of the Antique Greek thought was strengthened by the achievements of the antique doctors in the fields of anatomy & medicine. The first thinker to localize thought process in the brain was Alcmaeon of Croton. He was one of the most eminent medical theorists of antiquity. Very little is known about Alcmaeon's life. Despite the fact that he wrote mostly on medical topics there is some suggestion that he was not a physician but a philosopher of science. Alcmaeon has several significant writings in astrology & meteorology. Conducting surveillance on the disease & brain damage, he opened the main nerves of the sensory organs. Also in several essays Alcmaeon wrote about the development of the embryo in the womb. He became known in the history of psychology as a founder of the principle "nervism." Alcmaeon viewed the psyche & the work the brain & nervous system as a whole.

The practice of cross sections of bodies for scientific purposes allowed him to provide the first systematic description of the general structure of the body & the intended functions of the organism. In the study of individual body systems, including the brain & nervous system, Alcmaeon detected the presence of conductors running from the brain to the senses. He concluded that the brain senses & it's so called wires were both in humans & animals.

Just like Alcmaeon Hippocrates (460-377B.C.) held that the organ of thinking & sensation was the brain. He became known as the founder of medicine & was regarded as the greatest physician of his time. Hippocrates traveled throughout Greece practicing his medicine. He founded a medical school on the island of Cos, Greece & began teaching his ideas. He soon developed an Oath of Medical Ethics for physicians to follow. This Oath is taken by physicians today as they begin their medical practice. He died in 377 BC. Today Hippocrates is known as the "Father of Medicine".

Hippocrates based his medical practice on observations & on the study of the human body. He rejected the views of his time that considered illness to be caused by superstitions & by possession of evil spirits & disfavor of the gods. On contrary, he argued that illness had a physical & a rational explanation.

In addition Hippocrates held the belief that the body must be treated as a whole and not just a series of parts. He noted that there were individual differences in the severity of disease symptoms & that some individuals were better able to cope with their disease & illness than others.

Perhaps Hippocrates is best known for providing the field of psychology with the theory of the Four Humors, the first ever personality theory. According to this theory, the individual was made up of four humors, of which any one humor was perpetually dominant. This dominant humor affected the individual's personality & made him one specific 'type' of individual. The four humors were: 1.Sanguine (blood) characterized as a warm, outgoing personality. Rarely loses temper & is compassionate & loving by nature; 2. Phlegmatic (phlegm) is mainly lazy & laid-back personality. Phlegmatic is rarely bothered by carrying out jobs or work, & does not express many emotions; 3.Choleric (yellow bile) is described as an angry, aggressive personality. Is often loyal, but at the same time, has a very short fuse & is impulsive by nature; 4. Melancholic (black bile) is sad & despondent personality. Tends to display more reactions of negativity towards stimuli, & is often selfish & self-absorbed.

The antique medicine was markedly developed in Alexandria, where Herophilus (355-280B.C.) & Erasistratus (304-250B.C.) made several important discoveries. Herophilus made public dissections, comparing human & animal morphology. He viewed the brain as the site of intelligence. Herophilus also studied the spinal cord & distinguished between motor & sensory nerves. He also studied the eye, the alimentary canal, the reproductive organs, & blood vessels.

Erasistratus is considered by many to be the father of physiology. He accurately described the structure of the brain, including the cavities & membranes, & made a distinction between its cerebrum & cerebellum. Unlike the thinkers of the time Erasistratus viewed the brain as the source of intelligence. He also rightly concluded that a greater number of brain convolutions resulted in greater intelligence, as well as, accurately described the structure & function of the gastric muscles.

Erasistratus understood that the heart served as a pump, thereby dilating the arteries, and he found & explained the functioning of the heart valves. He held that the arteries & veins both spread from the heart, dividing finally into extremely fine capillaries that were invisible to the eye. After Erasistratus, anatomical research through dissection ended, due to the pressure of public opinion.

The anatomical & physiological data of the Hellenistic period was summed up & completed by a Roman doctor Galen (129-200). In 15 years, Galen began to study philosophy, but in 18 seriously engaged in medicine. In 150 he wrote a philosophical treatise on the medical experience, which is preserved in Arabic translation. Then he studied for some time at Smyrna, visited Greece, he went to study anatomy in Alexandria, the main center of Greek science & medicine, where the practice of the autopsy of human corpses began with the Greek Ptolemaic dynasty, ca. 300 BC. Some time Galen worked in Alexandria, perfecting his knowledge of medicine & paying special attention to the study of the human skeleton. After returning to Ephesus in 157, he became a doctor. After acquiring extensive experience in the practice of medicine & surgery, he began to conduct physiological experiments. Around 159 Galen discovered function of nerves that control the voice. Around the same time studied the complex structure and function of muscles involved in breathing. In the 162, already having a solid reputation, Galen left Pergamum to work in Rome.

Collected works of Galen, come down to our time, exceeds the volume of all medical works, written before him, for us they are - the main source of information on ancient medicine. Most of the works of that era, except for those that have come under the name of Hippocrates, were lost. Without a doubt, his writings greatly influenced the development of medicine. Galen's books on anatomy & physiology contain extensive factual material were closest to science. These works became the foundation of modern scientific medicine. Many terms of the modern medical language directly traced back to Galen or to the Latin translation of his works. Other essays were devoted to pathology, hygiene, dietetics, therapeutic issues & pharmacology.

Many of Galen's theories were closely linked to his religious beliefs. He firmly believed in the existence of air, the so called "Spirit" or "breathe of life". He believed that the world is full of air, which is when breathing is drawn into the body, as well as the fact that, when the world stops pneumatic inhaled a person or other creature dies. Galen believed in one God & all his scientific work was imbued with the consciousness of the divine creation of all nature & especially human. He believed that everything in the structure of the human body, down to the smallest detail, was created by God. Galen believed that the brain generated & transmitted a vital spirit through the (hollow) nerves to the muscles, allowing movement & sensation.

After Galen, experimental physiology & anatomical research ceased for many centuries. Galen's teachings became the ultimate medical authority, approved by the newly ascendant Christian church because of Galen's belief in a divine purpose for all things, even the structure & functioning of the human body.

The emergence of psychology in ancient Greece was related to the formation of an objective science of man that considered the soul is not based on fairy tales, myths, legends, & with the objective of knowledge (mathematics, medicine, philosophy), which arose in that period. At that time psychology was a science that studied the general laws of society, nature & man. This science was called natural philosophy, for a long period of time, almost 20 centuries psychology remained a part of philosophy.

For several centuries the difference between the psyche of man & animals treated as purely quantitative rather than qualitative. From the Philosophy the Psychology has taken important for any science position on the need to base their theory on the basis of knowledge rather than faith. Avoiding sacredness, i.e., the connection of faith with knowledge, not with the mind, the desire to prove the correctness of the views expressed & was the most important difference between scientific, philosophical psychology & the pre-scientific.

The principle of absolute immateriality of the soul was reintroduced by the Greek philosopher Plotinus (203 -269) who was also a founder of the Roman school of Neo-Platonism. He saw the basis of the existence of all bodily in an emanation (expiry) of the divine, spiritual ultimate beginning. Apart from the religious metaphysics, mysticism inspired, then applied to the progress of psychological thought in the representations of the soul of Plotinus contained new & important point. His psychology for the first time in its history has become a science of consciousness, understood as "consciousness itself". Turning to the study of internal mental life of man started in the ancient culture long before the dam. However, markedly increasing pressure in the Hellenistic period, the trend towards individualization, the prerequisites for the realization of the subject itself as the ultimate independent center of mental acts have not yet formed. These acts were regarded as derivative from the air by the Stoics, from atomic flows - from the Epicureans.

Plotinus taught that the individual soul comes from the world of the soul, to which it is oriented & that the other vector activity of the individual soul is directed to the world of sense. Plotinus himself highlighted another trend - namely, turning of the soul itself, self-invisible actions: it seems to be watching his work, becomes its "mirror". In modern times, when the existing real social basis for the assertion of the subject as an independent free person claiming to be the uniqueness of his mental being, re-flexion acted as a base & the main source of knowledge about this being. Such an interpretation contained in the first-generation programs in psychology, with its own object, which distinguishes it from other sciences. Indeed, no science is studying the capacity for reflection. Of course, emphasizing reflection as one of the activities of the soul, Plotinus could not consider the individual soul's own internal self-sufficient source of images & action.

The doctrine of Plotinus influenced Augustine (354-430), whose work marked the transition from the ancient tradition of the medieval Christian worldview. Augustine gave the interpretation of the special nature of the soul: the soul counting instrument which governs the body, he claimed that it forms the basis of the will, not reason. He thus became the founder of the doctrine, named after voluntarism. According to Augustine, the will of an individual depended on the divine & worked in two ways: controlled the actions of the soul & drew it to itself. All knowledge was believed to be inherent in the soul that lived & moved in God. The ground truth of such knowledge was the internal experience: the soul turning to itself, to grasp with the utmost reliability of its performance. The idea of inner experience was of theological significance to Augustine since it was assumed that the true gift came from God.

The writings of ancient Greek thinkers discovered many of the great challenges that today guide the development of psychological ideas. The explanations of the origin & structure of the soul was done in three main areas. The first area was the explanation of the psyche based on the laws of motion & development of the material world. Here the main idea was the decisive dependence of mental manifestations of the total order of things, their physical nature. The second line of ancient psychology, founded by Aristotle that focus mainly on wildlife, the starting point for it served as a contrast to the properties of organic bodies from inorganic. Since the mind is a form of life, bringing to the fore the issue was a major step forward.

The third direction viewed mental activity of the individual dependent on the forms that were not of physical or organic nature. The forms which played an important role in the structure and dynamics of mental processes were, however, beginning with the Pythagoreans and Plato, being alienated from the material world from the real history of culture & society are represented in the form of special spiritual beings.

In Ancient Greece there were three means of comprehension of a man

& his soul: religion, art & science. Religion was based on myth, art - the artistic image, the science - on the organized & controlled by the logical thought experiment. In the development of psychology antiquity glorified the great theoretical achievements. These include not only the discovery of the facts, creating innovative models & explanatory schemes. Classical first tried to answer the questions as to the relationship in a man body & spirit, thinking & communication, personal & socio-cultural, motivational & cognitive, rational & irrational, & much more, that was believed to be inherent human being.

Psychological Ideas in middle Ages

The middle Ages, which lasted for nearly ten centuries, had no history sufficiently clear periodization. This era began with the fall of the Roman Empire, i.e., the V century. At the same time, scientists note that the elements of the medieval ideology, just as medieval science, appeared much earlier, already in the III century. This is natural, since the emergence of such a significant culture change in the perception of the world & people cannot arise suddenly. The end of the medieval period is associated usually with the XV century, with the Renaissance art, secular science, the discovery of America. At the same time the first signs of a new ideology emerged by late XIV century. However, even in modern times scientists had to prove the possibility & necessity of separating science, especially the science of the soul - psychology from theology. The gradual development & fading characteristics of medieval philosophy in psychology clearly reflects the concepts of Avicenna & Francis Bacon.

In the beginning the influence of the ancient world was quite strong. Education was based on the study of classic authors, philosophers, & natural scientists like Hippocrates, Aristotle & Epicurus.

One of the major characteristics of medieval science, particularly psychology, has been its close relationship with religion. More precisely, non-theological, outside the Church of science at that time in Europe did not exist. It is an important feature in this period was the emergence of sacredness, of which psychology shedding in the transition from mythology to scientific knowledge in the VII-VI centuries B.C. Dependence on religion again raised the issue of communication & mutual knowledge & belief, which became important for scientists throughout this period. One of the typical stereotypes in the analysis of the middle Ages was the clear idea of the negative nature of the development of science & society as a whole in this period. The beginning of a new phase in the development of psychology was associated with the actual change in its object, as the official science of the soul was theology.

With the rise of Christianity most popular schools of thought were shut down & scientists, who kept the ancient knowledge of science, were forced to move to Asia Minor. One of the main reasons for the antagonism between psychology & theology was the incompatibility of knowledge of faith, which tolerated no dissent, no doubt in their dogma. Church at the time severely censured not only those who doubted its truth, but even those who tried to prove them something, believing that the desire to prove is a lack of faith.

After the initial stage of development psychology began to strive to find its place in the study of the soul, attempting to define a wide range of issues. This led in part to the revision of the object of psychology. The differ from the theology has led to the theory of two truths, which argued that truth was knowledge & truth of faith did not coincide & contradict each other, like two parallel lines. Soon a new direction of thought, deism emerged, which argued that there were two souls - the spiritual (it is exploring theology) & the body, which studied the psychology.

St. Augustine was born in Tagaste, Numidia in North Africa. His mother was a Christian, but his father remained a pagan until late in life. After a rather unremarkable childhood, marred only by a case of stealing pears, Augustine drifted through several philosophical systems before converting to Christianity at the age of thirty-one. At the age of nineteen, Augustine read Cicero's "Hortensius," an experience that led him into the fascination with philosophical questions and methods that would remain with him throughout his life. After a few years as a Manichean, he became attracted to the more skeptical positions of the Academic philosophers. Although tempted in the direction of Christianity upon his arrival at Milan in 383, he turned first to Neo-Platonism. During this time, Augustine fathered a child by a mistress. This period of exploration, including its youthful excesses (perhaps somewhat exaggerated) was recorded in Augustine's most widely read work, the "Confessions."

During his youth, Augustine had studied rhetoric at Carthage, a discipline that he used to gain employment teaching in Carthage and then in Rome and Milan, where he met Ambrose who is credited with effecting Augustine's conversion and who baptized Augustine in 387. Returning to his homeland soon after his conversion, he was ordained a presbyter in 391, taking the position as bishop of Hippo in 396, a position which he held until his death.

Besides the "Confessions," Augustine's most celebrated work is his "De Civitate Dei" (On the City of God), a study of the relationship between Christianity and secular society, which was inspired by the fall of Rome to the Visigoths in 410. Among his other works, many are polemical attacks on various heresies: "Against Faustus, the Manichean"; "On Baptism"; "Against the Donatists"; and many attacks on Pelagianism and Semi-Pelagianism. Other works include treatises "On the Trinity"; "On Faith, Hope, & Love"; "On Christian Doctrine"; & some early dialogues.

St. Augustine stands as a powerful advocate for orthodoxy and of the episcopacy as the sole means for the dispensing of saving grace. In the light of later scholarship, Augustine can be seen to serve as a bridge between the ancient & medieval worlds. A review of his life and work, however, shows him as an active mind engaging the practical concerns of the churches he served.

A study on the relationship between faith and reason in the soul of man has been continued in the works of John Scotus Eriugena (810-877). The name Eriugena means the same as Scotus, 'born in Ireland'. He was an Irish theologian, Neo-Platonist philosopher & a poet. He is best known for translating & commenting on the works of Pseudo-Dionysius the Areopagite. He helped to transmit Dionysian mystical theology to the Medieval Latin West. Though born in Ireland he later (in 845) moved to France, where he took over the school, the Palatine Academy, at the invitation of King Charles I. He remained in France for 30 years. In 858 at the request of the Greek Emperor Michael John undertook some translation into Latin of the works of Pseudo-Dionysius & added his own commentary. He was thus the first to introduce the ideas of Neo-Platonism from the Greek into the Western European intellectual tradition, where they were to have a deeply formative influence on Christian theology.

Advocating the importance of reason, Eriugena in his treatise "On Divine Destiny" argued that the knowledge acquired by man, was no less important authority than the divine revelation. On this basis were built his proof of freedom that man finds in the process of scientific activity. This treatise, as well as the subsequent work Eriugena, was condemned by church. Eriugena's writings eventually gained fame & served as a starting point for subsequent generations of scientists. Proving the fact that the general precedes the individual, Eriugena actually reproduced the arguments of Plato & laid the foundation for the discussion of the origin of universals. From his point of view since the "common" was preceded by things, then, consequently, it contained the essence & purpose. "Common" for Eriugena was like a "soul" for Plato. The concept of mind was of great importance in Eriugena's theory. He wrote that a man as a special world in its formation goes through the same stages as the world. However, in contrast to the biogenetic law establishing the natural world & man, Eriugena connected the three stages of human development with the stages of development of knowledge, calling them mind, intellect & inner feelings.

One of the main areas of study in medieval science was the process thinking & its relationship with speech. Analyzing the emergence of conceptual thinking, the scientists raised the question of the origin of the general concepts. For example realists (like Anselm of Canterbury) argued that all of the general concepts really existed before the things in the mind of God. This approach echoed the position of Plato, who claimed that the general concepts existed in the world-soul, as a model for real objects. On the other hand Nominalists (like William Ockham), believed that the general concepts did not exist in reality. The founder of Conceptualism (directions, abutting to nominalism) Peter Abelard argued that the general concepts existed outside of things meaning that the word was not only a sound but also the value, which remained in the names transmitted to humans. At the same time he was one of the first who defended the rule of reason over faith, saying that one should understand to believe. In examining the issues of cognition in late scholasticism & the Renaissance substantial work was influenced not only the ancient scholars, but also Arab psychologists who began to penetrate into Europe in the XII-XIII centuries.

The well-known scholar of the time of Ibn al-Haytham (965-1039) made several important discoveries in the field of psychophysiology of perception. He also made significant contributions to the principles of optics, as well as to physics, anatomy, astronomy, engineering, mathematics, medicine, ophthalmology, philosophy, visual perception, & to science in general. He was born in Basra, Iraq. Ibn al-Haytham is regarded as the "father of modern optics" for his influential "Book of Optics" which proved the intromission theory of vision & refined it into essentially its modern form. His natural-scientific approach to the organs of perception was the first in the history of psychological thought attempt to interpret functions, based on the laws of optics. It was important that these laws were available to experience & mathematical analysis.

Without limiting the general considerations about the dependence of phenomena on the physical (optical) factors & laws, Ibn al-Haytham studied such experimentally relevant phenomena as binocular vision & color mixing. He argued that for the full perception of objects certain eye movement, like the movement of the visual axes was necessary. As a result the body will automatically produce operations, which represent a various judgments about the whereabouts of the things perceived, their distance from the person & their relationship to each other. In the event when the impact of objects was short-lived, the eyes have time to properly absorb only the familiar objects that have left traces in the nervous system.

Of great importance to psychology was the work of another prominent Arab thinker; Abu Ali al-Husain ibn Abd Allah ibn Sina, known in west as Avicenna (980-1037). Avicenna was a Persian philosopher & physician & one of the main interpreters of Aristotle to the Islamic world. He wrote prolifically on science, religion, & philosophy, but many of his works had been lost. Although Avicenna has influenced a number of Muslim, Jewish & Western philosophers, among them Roger Bacon & John Duns Scotus his thoughts also have been much criticized. In his later years he tried to alter perception of Islamic speculative theology so that it would be treated as a demonstrative science. Going against the Islamic orthodoxy, he held that only the soul, not the person, is immortal.

Avicenna was born in Afshana, near Bukhara (now in Uzbekistan), the son of a provincial governor. In his childhood he made so rapid a progress in learning, that several tutors were engaged to instruct him until he surpassed his teachers. While still in his teens, he served as the court physician. Avicenna carefully studied works of Greek philosophers & mathematicians, including Aristotle's "Metaphysics." That is why later in his own works Avicenna combined Aristotleanism & Neoplatonic tradition with Islamic theology. His later writings showed Gnostic, Hermeneutic & mystical tendencies. Much of his life Avicenna spent travelling from court to court in Persia. At one point he became the vizier or prime minister to Shams al-Dawlah of the Shii Buyid dynasty. During this period he wrote "The Book of Remedy." Avicenna wrote some four hundred fifty books, about half of which still exists. After Shams al-Dawlah died, Avicenna was imprisoned. He fled from Hamadan & traveled to Esfahan (Isfahan), where he spent the last 14 years of his life. Avicenna served as physician & adviser to the local ruler, 'Ala' ad-Dawlah, & wrote most of his nearly 200 treatises. Avicenna died in Hamadan at the age of fifty-eight.

Avicenna was an encyclopedic; his creativity was not limited to medicine & psychology, although his greatest achievements were reached in these areas. In his philosophical writings of Avicenna developed a so-called theory of two truths, which was crucial for the development of not only psychology, but also other sciences in the medieval period. In psychology, this theory has helped to bring the subject of its study of the general subject of theology. The theory of two truths states that there are two independent parallels truths the belief & knowledge. Therefore the knowledge of the truth, without going into contact & conflict with religion, is entitled to its own area of research & methods of studying man.

Avicenna's study was not limited to the facts gleaned from practical study of the simplest reactions. He taught that by using these facts it was possible to explain such a complex phenomenon in mental life, as imagination. Avicenna's idea of the relationship of mental & physiological brought him a worldwide fame.

Avicenna was also a pioneer in the fields of psychophysiology & psychosomatic medicine. He was a proponent of physiological psychology in the treatment of illnesses involving emotions, & developed a system for associating changes in the pulse rate with inner feelings. Avicenna was reported to have treated a very ill patient by feeling the patient's pulse & reciting aloud to him the names of provinces, districts, towns, streets, & people. He noticed how the patient's pulse increased when certain names were mentioned, from which Avicenna deduced that the patient was in love with a girl whose home Avicenna was able to locate by the digital examination. Avicenna advised the patient to marry the girl he is in love with, & the patient soon recovered from his illness after his marriage.

In the "Canon of Medicine" Avicenna dealt with neuropsychiatry & described a number of neuropsychiatric conditions, including melancholia. He described melancholia as a depressive type of mood disorder in which the person may become suspicious & develop certain types of phobias. He also held that the first & most important sense in human beings was common sense, which fused information from the physical senses into an epistemic object. The second sense was imagination which processed the image of the perceived epistemic object. The third sense was the imaginative faculty which combined images in memory, at the same time producing new images. The fourth sense was estimation that translated the perceived image into its significance.

Ibn Rushd also known as Averroes of Cordoba (1126-1198) was an Andalusian-Arab philosopher & physician, a master of philosophy & Islamic law. He also has valuable writings in mathematics & medicine. He was born in Cordoba, Spain. Throughout his life he wrote extensively on Philosophy & Religion, attributes of God, origin of the universe, Metaphysics and Psychology. Averroes was most famous for his commentaries on Aristotle's works, which had been mostly forgotten in the West. The few existing Latin translations of Aristotle's works had been largely ignored by European scholars, & it was through the Latin translations of Averroes' work, beginning in the twelfth century, that the legacy of Aristotle was recovered. He attempted to reconcile Aristotelian philosophy with Islamic theology & to demonstrate that philosophy and theology were two different paths to understanding the same truth. Averroes' work on medicine called "Colliget" was used as a textbook throughout Europe until the advent of investigative science. He also wrote works on law and justice, & commentaries on Plato's work.

In 1160 Averroes was assigned a judge of Seville. Later he served in many other court appointments in Cordoba, & Morocco. Towards the end of the 12th century his political career was ended. He devoted the rest of his life to his philosophical writings. He died at the age of 72.

Averroes considered the study of the psyche as a part of physics, only because it was related specifically to the generable & corruptible union of form & matter found in the physical world. He divided the soul into five faculties: the nutritive, the sensitive, the imaginative, the appetitive & the rational. Averroes held that the primary psychological faculty of all plants & animals was the nutritive faculty, passed on through sexual generation. The remaining four higher faculties he saw dependent on the nutritive faculty. In his theory the nutritive faculty used natural heat to convert nutrients from potentiality to actuality, which were essential for basic survival. Such a faculty was almost like an active power which was moved by the heavenly body. The sensitive faculty, on the other hand, was a passive power divided into two aspects, the proximate & the ultimate. The rational faculty differed from the imaginative faculty, in that it apprehended motion in a universal way & separate from matter. Averroes thought that it had two divisions, the practical & theoretical. He believed that the rational faculty was the power that allowed humanity to create, understand & be ethical. The practical was derived from the sensual & imaginative faculties, in that it was rooted in sensibles & related to moral virtues like friendship & love. The theoretical apprehended universal intelligibles & according to Averroes did not need an external agent for intellectualization. In its effort to achieve perfection, the rational faculty moved from potentiality to actuality.

Averroes argued that it is necessary to study the inseparable connection between the functions of the organism & those sensations, feelings, thoughts, that person is experiencing as a process inherent in his soul. As a physician, he carefully studied the structure of the human body & its senses, showing the dependence of the perception of the world on the properties of the nervous system. Averroes concluded that after the collapse of the body of the individual, soul was also destroyed. He also held that the ability to think had a potential character. As the sun affects the eye, causing it to feel light, same is the universal mind acting on our potential ability & causing us to think.

In Averroes' theory the human soul was a separate substance ontologically identical with the active intellect. Thus, when this active intellect was embodied in an individual human it was the material intellect. He viewed the material intellect to be similar to prime matter. The human mind was a composite of the material intellect & the passive intellect, which was the third element of the intellect. The passive intellect, according to Averroes was identified with the imagination, which was the sense-connected finite & passive faculty that received sensual forms. When the material intellect was actualized by information received, it was described as the speculative or habitual intellect. When this speculative intellect moved towards perfection, having the active intellect as an object of thought, it became the acquired intellect. Averroes argued that the soul was a unique faculty that was similar to the focus of its intention. He also postulated that it was the Muslim doctrine of the afterlife that best motivated people to an ethical life. The Christian & Jewish doctrines, in his opinion, were too focused upon the spiritual elements of the afterlife. Averroes in many ways was able to provide a valid explanation of the human soul & intellect that did not involve an immediate transcendent agent. His philosophical writings appeared in Europe in the early thirteenth century through the Latin translations done by the German translator, Hermannus Alemannus. Roger Bacon studied extensively the Latin translations and commentaries & believed that the introduction of Averroes's Aristotle to the Christian West was responsible for important changes in the history of medieval thought. In the thirteenth century, Latin Averroeism, a controversial secular movement in Christian thought based on Averroes's philosophy, gained popularity but was bitterly refuted by some in the Church leaders.

Anselm of Canterbury (1033-1109) was most famous in philosophy for having discovered the "ontological argument." The latter was an argument for the existence of God, which attempted the method of a priori proof, using intuition & reason alone. The argument examined the concept of God, & stated that if we can conceive of the greatest possible being, then it must exist. His work covered many other important philosophical & theological issues, among which were the understanding the aspects & the unity of the divine nature & the extent of our possible knowledge & understanding of the divine nature. Anselm was born in Aosta, a Burgundian town on the frontier with Lombardy. Later in life Anselm moved to Normandy where his interest was captured by the Benedictine abbey at Bec. In 1060 Anselm entered the abbey as a novice. His intellectual & spiritual gifts brought him rapid advancement. Under Anselm's leadership the reputation of Bec as an intellectual center grew, & Anselm managed to write a good deal of philosophy. His works while at Bec include the "Monologion" (1075-76), the "Proslogion" (1077-78), & his four philosophical dialogues: "De grammatico" (1059-60), "De veritate," & "De libertate arbitrii," & "De casu diabolic" (1080-86). In 1093 Anselm was enthroned as Archbishop of Canterbury. His works as Archbishop of Canterbury include the "Epistola de Incarnatione Verbi" (1094), Cur Deus Homo (1095-98), "De conceptu virginali" (1099), "De processione Spiritus Sancti" (1102), the "Epistola de sacrificio azymi et fermentati" & so on.

In his "Monologion" Anselm wrote that there must be some one thing that was supremely good, through which all good things had their goodness. He also argued that things that were good through another could not be equal to or greater than the good thing that was good through itself. Anselm maintained that all existing things existed through some one thing. Thus, every existing thing existed either through something or through nothing. But naturally nothing existed through nothing, so every existing thing existed through something. In "Proslogion" God was something which nothing greater can be thought. God was so great & so full of metaphysical oomph that one could not so much as conceive of a being who would be greater than God.

Anselm thought that freedom of choice was the power to preserve rectitude of will for its own sake. In Anselm's theory truth was a broad notion, since he spoke of it not only in statements & opinions but also in the will, actions, the senses, & even the essences of things. His truth consisted in correctness or rectitude. Rectitude was understood teleologically; a thing was correct whenever it was or did whatever it ought. So Anselm held a correspondence theory of truth, but it was a somewhat unusual correspondence theory. Statements were true when they corresponded to reality, but only because corresponding to reality was what statements were for.

Anselm's patient approach to philosophical issues & his willingness to engage in debate with other thinkers who disagreed with the positions he defended were greatly influential on western culture. They helped give rise to the development of scholasticism, a process of intergenerational cooperation engendered by shared appeal to a common tradition of rational argumentation.

Anselm is considered to be one of the fathers of scholastic theology. As a philosopher, he was most often remembered for his attempts to prove the existence of god. Anselm held that all creatures owe their being & value to god as the source of all truth, to whom a life lived well is the highest praise. In the "Monologion" he described deity as the one most truly good thing, from which all real moral values derive & whose existence was required by the reality of those values.

Peter Abelard, real name Pierre du Pallet (1079-1142) was born at Palets, a Breton town near Nantes. Abelard from his earliest years showed an aptitude and inclination for an academic career, & as a young man entered the University of Paris, where he rapidly acquired a reputation for intelligence, wit, debating skill, arrogance, & embarrassing his professors. He worked as a lecturer, first at Melun & then at Corbeil.

Abelard went to Paris sometime between 1108 & 1113, (after a short period of being ill) & attended William of Champeaux's lectures. Later he entered a debate with his teacher over the problem of universals. Around 1113 Abelard decided to study theology; he sought out the most eminent teacher of theology of his day, Anselm of Laon (not to be confused with Anselm of Canterbury), & became his student. But Anselm's traditional methods did not appeal to Abelard &, eventually he returned to Paris to continue on his own. After his affair with Heloise, Abelard withdrew to the abbey of St. Denis, where he made his profession as a monk. Although he cared for regular discipline, he was too restless for the monastic life. His theological work, "On the Divine Unity and Trinity," was burned at an ecclesiastical council. Abelard founded the school of the Paraclete near Nogent-sur-Seine in 1125, left to become abbot of St. Gildas in Brittany, & returned to Paris to lecture at St. Genevieve. Abelard retired to Cluny, where the abbot, Peter the Venerable, extolled his piety, modesty & dignity & also reconciled him to St. Bernard.

Many consider Abelard's metaphysics to be the first example of nominalism in the Western tradition. He was an irrealist not only about universals, but also about propositions, events, & times other than the present, natural kinds, relations, wholes, absolute space, hylomorphic composites, & the like. Instead, Abelard held that the concrete individual was more than enough to populate the world. Abelard preferred reductive, atomist, & material explanations whenever possible; he devoted a great deal of effort to pouring cold water on the metaphysical excesses of his predecessors. Abelard defended his thesis that universals were nothing but words by arguing that ontological realism about universals was incoherent. Abelard concluded that universality was not an ontological feature of the world but a semantic feature of language.

Abelard postulated that collections were posterior to their parts & that the collection was not shared among its parts in the way a universal was said to be common to many. He also concluded that universality was merely linguistic & not a feature of the world. Much of Abelard's philosophy of language was in fact devoted to analyzing how a given expression or class of expressions functioned logically. Meaning what words were quantifiers, which implied negation & the like, so that the logic described above may be applied. When Abelard puts forward his claim that universality was only a linguistic phenomenon, so that universals were "nothing more than words," he raised the objection that unless common names were the names of common items, they will be meaningless.

In addition Abelard was the first to propose that the intentionality was a primitive & irreducible feature of the mind. He viewed different acts of attention to be intrinsically different from one another. Hence Abelard adopted what is nowadays called an adverbial theory of thought. Given that intentionality was primitive, Abelard adopted a contextual approach to mental content: he embedded these irreducible acts of attention in a structure whose articulation helped to define the character of its constituent elements. Abelard gave something very like a linguistic account of mental representation or intentionality. In a sense he embraced a principle of compositionality, holding that what an understanding was about was a function of what its constituent understandings were about. In Abelard's theory the understanding of a complex could be treated as a complex of distinct understandings, aggregated in the same thought. His acts of attention displayed the logical structure of the understanding they expressed, & thereby gave the semantics of written or spoken language.

Of great importance for the development of scholasticism & logic was the work of Abelard "Yes & no," in which he unfolded a picture of the dialectical judgments logically justifying & refuting the various judgments. In the theory of conceptualism Abelard returned to the forgotten idea of the meaning of the word, pointing out that the word was necessary to distinguish its physical nature (sound) & meaning, which, unlike sound, was not lost, but remained in the minds of people.

Throughout his life Abelard wrote & said many things which were open to objection from the point of view of orthodoxy. Abelard's influence on his immediate successors was not very great, owing partly to his conflict with the ecclesiastical authorities, but his influence on the philosophers & theologians of the thirteenth century was, however, very great. Despite his faults of character & mistakes of judgment, Abelard was an important contributor to scholastic method, an enlightened opponent of obscurantism, & a continuator of that revival of learning which occurred in the Carolingian age.

In 13-th century the reputation of the Catholic Church was beginning to crumble under the pressure from heretic movements. The struggle between the classes was becoming more & more intense. The socio-political changes paved the way for several new schools of thought. Around this time scientific activities develop in all areas of knowledge. Psychology in the middle Ages, took an ethical-theological & a phenomenological-mystical turn.

One of the founders of the so called classical scholasticism was Thomas Aquinas (1225-1274). He was born in Sicily. When he was only five years old, Aquinas began his early education at Monte Cassino. He also studied at the Studium Generale University in Napoli. From a very early age Aquinas was fascinated by subjective idealism. He especially liked the writings of Aristotle. During his study at Naples Aquinas was greatly influenced by a Dominican preacher (John of St. Julian) in Naples. He joined the Dominican order at the age of nineteen, but his family was against it. He was detained for two years in the family homes at Monte San Giovanni in an attempt to prevent him from assuming the Dominican habit. During his detention, Aquinas spent most of his time tutoring his sisters & communicating with members of the Dominican Order. Later, in 1244 he went to Naples & then to Rome to meet Johannes von Wildeshausen, who was the ruler of the Dominican order.

One year later Aquinas was sent to study at the University of Paris' Faculty of Arts. He taught in Cologne as an apprentice professor instructing students on the books of the Old Testament. He wrote several books in Cologne. In 1252 he came back to Paris to study for the master's degree in theology. In spring of 1256, Aquinas became a regent master in theology in 1256. Towards the end of his regency, Aquinas was working on one of his most famous works called "Summa Contra Gentiles." In 1268 the Dominican Order assigned Aquinas to be regent master at the University of Paris again. Constant disputes with some important Franciscans made his second regency much more difficult & troubled than the first. In 1272 Aquinas moved to Naples to establish an institution. He was desperately trying to unite the Orthodox churches with the Catholic Church.

Aquinas' philosophical thought has exerted enormous influence on subsequent Christian theology, especially that of the Roman Catholic Church, extending to Western philosophy in general. In his thought, the goal of human existence was union & eternal fellowship with God. Aquinas held that individual's will should be guided toward right things, such as holiness & peace. Being a subjective idealist Aquinas was convinced that in order to gain knowledge man needs divine help, & that the intellect was guided by God.

In his system Aquinas sought not only to systematize the accumulated knowledge, but also to reconcile theology with science, including the science of antiquity, especially with the theory of Aristotle. On this basis, He modified the Averroes' theory of two truths stating that in the event of contradictions true knowledge yields the faith. Proving the unlimited possibilities of the mind in the knowledge of the world, including in understanding the most complex of its laws, the divine Logos, Aquinas argued against the thesis of Averroes on the separation of soul from the mind. He argued that thinking is imminent & the main feature of the soul. Thus, he defended the idea of eternity of the soul, as well as the inability to explain all its laws without relying on theology. In Aquinas' theory the soul was not just reasonable, it was conscious & differed from the unconscious mind of animals.

The important point was sensationalism, which Aquinas regarded as the principal way of knowledge. He wrote that the experience should be the body, the organs of perception. He held that the mind cannot function normally without images of the surroundings. Therefore, bodily disorder inevitably leads to mental derangement.

Based on his approach to cognition Aquinas reconciled certain positions of nominalism & realism.

Although Aquinas' concepts were quite popular & widespread, but by the end of the 18-th century scholastic deficiencies were so obvious that a growing number of scholars have begun to consider it (and theology in general) as a brake on the further development of science.

Thomism

When Aquinas died he left no direct successor, but his system was adopted by various individuals, most notably by many of his confreres in the Dominican order. At the time there was still much opposition to his Aristotelianism on the part of church authorities, & in 1277 in Paris and Oxford several propositions derived from Thomas's teachings were condemned. It was primarily due to Dominican efforts that the system of Aquinas was not only eventually rehabilitated, but that he himself was canonized in 1323. After this Thomism became one of the several competing schools of medieval philosophy. It was opposing the classical Augustinianism with its reliance on Aristotle, most eminently by insisting on a unified anthropology whereby the soul was the form of the body.

One of the most famous followers of Thomism was Thomas de Vio Cardinal Cajetan (1469 - 1534). His unique brand of Thomism included the analysis of analogy, in which Cajetan argued that this concept was best understood as the proportionality of an attribute to two essences rather than as the predication of an attribute primary in one essence derived in a second. He also thought more in terms of abstract essences than his predecessors, who majored on existing substances. And finally he raised serious doubts concerning the provability of both God's existence & the immortality of the soul.

In the 16-th century Thomism became the leading school of Catholic thought. Several factors contributed to its ascendancy. The Jesuit order known for its aggressive teaching, aligned itself with Aquinas; also, the Council of Trent (first convened in 1545), switched to Thomistic phraseology.

Thomism was very popular in 17-th century as well. John of St. Thomas (1589-1644) was a creative teacher & interpreter of Aquinas's thought; he was a careful & compassionate official of the Spanish Inquisition; and he was an intimate advisor to King Philip IV. Thus in him the intellectual, theological, & political machinations of Thomism were brought to a focus. Eventually Thomism became too self-contained to cope with the rise of rationalism & empirical science. Thomism would not adapt itself; and so the alternatives left were obscurantism or non - Thomistic philosophy.

Consequently, though Thomism was still alive, primarily in Dominican circles, in the eighteenth century, it was essentially a spent force.

The main doctrines distinctive of Thomism (composed principally of Dominican writers) were the unity of substantial form in composite beings, applied to man, which required that for the soul to be the substantial form of the man & the real distinction between the essence & existence.

Despite the absolute dominance of religious thinking new schools of thought based on the observation of the natural phenomena began to emerge. Most of these schools were influenced by early Arabic philosophy.

In England, one of the most active followers of this new movement was Roger Bacon (around 1214-1292). He was born at Ilchester, England. Bacon studied & later became a Master at Oxford. He was mainly lecturing & reinterpreting the works of Aristotle. After Oxford he began to lecture at the University of Paris. Roger Bacon was a pioneer in the introduction of the study of Aristotle as interpreted by Averroes & Avicenna to the University. He had confronted & reviewed some of the major issues concerning Latin Averroism that lead to a major crisis at Paris in the period 1266-1277. Sometime in the late 1240s, Bacon ceased being a Master of Arts at Paris, became an independent scholar, & returned to England. He eventually became a Friar in the Franciscan Order. Bacon had been attracted to the Order by the philosophical, theological & scientific example of Grosseteste & Adam Marsh.

His polemical writings were describing the struggles in the Arts & Theology at Paris. The Pope instructed Bacon in 1266 to ignore the rules of his Order & to send him his remedies about a matter of some importance. It would appear from the context of Bacon's works for the Pope that the remedies had to do with educational matters at Paris, which at this time was the main University of the Christian Commonwealth. Because of this instruction, Bacon's later works, written in haste, consist of short treatises united by a self-conscious rhetoric for the reformation of education.

In Bacon's writings stochastic methods were substituted by science, which, according to Bacon, offered people direct benefits as opposed to fruitless arguments. In his writings he had stressed that the most dangerous for mankind was not the error but ignorance. He advocated the development of objective knowledge, proving that experience, experiment & mathematics should be the basis of all scientific disciplines. Drawing on the views of Aristotle, Bacon argued that the sensation was the leading mental process. Sensation was a material from which knowledge was born.

According to Bacon scientific knowledge was twofold: first, there was an innate, imperfect & confused knowledge by which the mind was inclined to the love of the good. Second, there was explicit rational knowledge. One part of this had to do with the knowledge of the principles of science; the other was the knowledge of conclusions. This latter was complete knowledge but it is not exhaustive. He also introduced the concepts of experimentia & experimentum. Experimentia (which all animal possessed) was considered to be the distinct knowledge of singular things, whereas experimentum that is, a science of principles based on experience was not typical for all animals. Thus, only humans & none other animals could have true experience.

Bacon had an interesting interpretation of the concept of matter. He offered six meanings of it; 1 Matter is the subject of action as when we say that wood is the matter for the action of the carpenter. 2 In the proper sense of the term, matter is that which with form constitutes the composite as in the case of every created substance. 3 Matter is the subject of generation & corruption and has the property of being an incomplete and imperfect thing in potency to a complete thing. 4 Matter is the subject of alteration since it receives contrary accidents. 5 Matter can be considered as an individual in relation to the universal, the latter being founded in its individual as in a material principle. 6 Matter is the name for that which is gross, as when we say that earth has more matter than fire. Bacon did not view matter as a mere potency, but rather as an incomplete substance. He also maintained that form had a certain priority to matter as the end of generation & as the perfection of the material principle. It was the principle of action & of knowledge.

In his early works Bacon introduced his unique versions of the concepts of universals & individuation. He distinguished the real universal from the mental universal. Thus, the universal as the ultimate basis of predication was not the species as mental intention. In Bacon's theory universals in the primary sense as the basis of scientific objectivity were extra-mental. He claimed that universal emerges from common matter & common form, therefore it has no need of being immediately individuated. Bacon was convinced that universal in & of itself was prior to the knowledge process.

He also stated that the so called particular nature is the directing power of the species with its individuals. This directing power was divisible into the directive power of the species & of the individual. He further distinguished the absolute nature of an individual as something absolute.

In his early writings Bacon described the soul as a spiritual substance in union with the body. The soul had two intellects, potential & agent. The former was directly connected with the sensitive powers & the object of this intellect was the singular material thing. On the other hand, the agent intellect was directed upward & knew spiritual beings in its own essence. He also identified the potential intellect with the intellective soul. It was considered to be both a spiritual substance & a form of the body. As a spiritual substance it had confused innate knowledge of spiritual substances, & as united with the body, it became an empty slate open to knowledge. It was helped towards new knowledge by means of impressed intelligible species given by the agent intellect.

In his famous "Opus Maius" Bacon criticized the scholastic practice of the universities of that time. He favored language study over "Sentence-Method." He advocated training in mathematics & the sciences as requirements for students in theology. Bacon was attempting to assemble a new, more efficient model of medieval philosophy. He took Aristotelian concepts & transcended them into Neo-Platonism. He reshaped metaphysics into a new form of moral philosophy. He was first to use mathematics in religion & theology. Bacon's views of psychology were largely based on Aristotle's system. Unlike the orthodox movements, Bacon viewed the soul as the unity of form & matter. Bacon also redefined the concept of perspective, in which he introduced his model for application of mathematics to the study of nature & mind. According to Bacon, vision took place when the crystalline humor was altered by the intromission of visual species from the object. This complex process was continued when the species proceeded through the vitreous humor to the optic nerve & through this to the common nerve. It was here that a common visual judgment was made. Thus Bacon introduced a geometrical account of radiation through the eye. Bacon's seemingly original theory of the eye was taken from the Galenic tradition handed on by Constantine the African's translation of Hunyan Ibn Isaq & from Avicenna & Ibn al-Haytham.

The new scientific approach to interpretation of various natural phenomena was continued by the new movement called "nominalism". Many considered nominalism to be the early version of materialism. Nominalists held that general or abstract terms & predicates definitely exist, while, abstract objects & universals which are sometimes thought to correspond to these terms, do not. It also opposed "realism," according to which universals existed over and above particulars. After Bacon the scientific approach to the interpretation of the psyche was continued by British nominalists, Oxford professors William Ockham (1288-1348) & Duns Scotus (1265-1308).

John Duns Scotus, also known as "the Subtle Doctor," was one of the most influential & prominent philosophers of the middle ages. Scotus was in fact his nickname; it meant that he was Scottish. His family name was Duns, which was also the name of the Scottish village in which he was born. He was ordained to the priesthood in the Order of Friars Minor at Saint Andrew's Priory in Northampton, England, on 17 March 1291. According to various sources Scotus began his formal studies at Oxford in October 1288 & finished them in June 1301. In 1298-99 he commented on the *Sentences* of Peter Lombard. A year later he was lecturing on the *Sentences* in Paris. In June 1303 Scotus was expelled from France along with eighty other friars for taking the Pope's side in a dispute with the king. They were allowed to return in April 1304. The same year Scotus was appointed the Franciscan regent master in theology at Paris. Eventually he was sent to the Franciscan stadium at Cologne. He died in 1308.

Scotus was the founder of Scotism, which is unique form of Scholasticism. His work was influenced by Aristotle's & St. Augustine's philosophy. Inspired by Aristotle, Scotus held that being in general the first object of the intellect. He considered metaphysics a real theoretical science, because it treated things rather than concepts. Scotus was focused on determining what the distinctive subject matter of metaphysics was. He concluded that metaphysics concerned "being *qua* being," meaning the metaphysician studied being simply as such, rather than studying, say, material being as material. The study of being included the study of the transcendentals, because according to Scotus, being itself was a transcendental category. In addition he distinguished an indefinite number of disjunctions that were supposedly coextensive with being & therefore counted as transcendentals. The doctrine of the univocity of being implied the denial of any real distinction between essence &existence. For example, Aquinas had argued that in all finite being, except God, the essence of a thing is distinct from its existence.

He also wrote that the material basis of mind brought people together in a common group, as the matter was something that all people & things in nature had in common. According to Scotus objects differed because of they had a form. Hence, the knowledge should be directed to the knowledge of the individual aspects, specific to each item. Such knowledge was based on sense experience. Scotus held that mind, continuing the process of comprehension of our surroundings summarizes the necessary data, transforming it into a concept. Thus, Scotus introduced into the psychology an important position on the active nature of sensations & their relationship.

Scotus saw matter as something that persists through substantial change & substantial form. He came up with three important theses that marked him off from some other philosophers of his day: he held that there exists matter that has no form whatsoever, that not all created substances were composites of form & matter, & finally that one & the same substance can have more than one substantial form.

Just like the rest of the medieval Aristotelian Scotus held that human beings, alone among the animals, have two different sorts of cognitive powers: senses & intellect. He recognized few differences between the two. For example the senses differed from the intellect in that they had physical organs; the intellect was immaterial. Hence, in order for the intellect to adopt sensory information it must somehow take the raw material provided by the senses in the form of material images &transform them into suitable objects for understanding. Latter process was known as abstraction.

In addition, Scotus comprehended intuitive cognition by way of contrast with abstractive cognition. The abstractive cognition involved the concept of universal, which in turn, shouldn't be exemplified. Sensory cognition, as Scotus recognized it, counted as intuitive cognition on this account. His much bolder claim concerned the so called intellectual intuitive cognition, with the help of which the intellect cognized a particular thing as existing at that very moment. Therefore, intellectual intuitive cognition did not require phantasms; the cognized object somehow just caused the intellectual act by which its existence was made present.

Scotus maintained that the human intellect was capable of achieving certainty in its knowledge of the truth simply by the exercise of its own natural powers. By making such a statement he opposed both skepticism, which denied the possibility of certain knowledge, & illuminationism, which insisted a person needed special divine illumination in order to attain certainty.

Duns Scotus caused serious damage to the idealistic thinking of his time by simply raising the question of matter's ability to think & process. Since then this question became one of the main subjects of study in materialistic movement. His work indeed contained many entirely modern ideas, such as the stress he laid on freedom in scientific & also in religious matters, upon the separateness of the objective world & of thought, the self-activity of the thinking subject, the dignity and value of personality.

William of Ockham joined the Franciscan order at a young age, the exact date is unknown. He is believed to have studied theology at the University of Oxford from 1309 to 1321. William of Ockham became a Franciscan at a young age. He is believed to have studied theology at the University of Oxford from 1309 to 1321. It is possible that he never completed his master's degree. In 1323 he was summoned to the papal court in Avignon to answer to charges of heresy. He eventually escaped from Avignon to avoid trial. Ockham spent the rest of his life in Munich as a political activist, writing treatises against religion. He died sometime between 1347 & 1349.

Being a nominalist Ockham denied the real existence of metaphysical universals. At times he was leaning more toward conceptualism than nominalism. Nominalists held that universals were merely names & words rather than existing realities, whereas conceptualists held that they were mental concepts, meaning the names were names of concepts, which do exist (although only in the mind). That is why the universal concept had for its object the internal representation which was a product of the understanding itself. Ockham was against the metaphysical realism. He found its principles to be simple & even naive. Ockham held that has realism been incoherent. However, he agreed with Aristotle that human beings were born blank states & that there were no innate certainties to be discovered in human mind. Ockham introduced a version of empiricism called "direct realism." He opposed the concept of intermediary between the perceiver & the world.

In Ockham's theory there were four steps of knowledge acquisition. The first step was sensory cognition: receiving data through the five senses (present in humans & animals). The second step, intuitive cognition, was uniquely human. Intuitive cognition was awareness that the particular individual perceived existed & had the qualities it had. The third step was called recordative cognition, by which one remembered past perceptions. Finally the fourth step was abstractive cognition, by which one placed individuals in groups of similar individuals. Ockham, as a follower of the so called mentalese philosophy compared thought to a machine ready to manipulate a vast quantity of empty boxes. In his theory mind was born without any knowledge, yet fully equipped with a system for processing perceptions. As we observe the world, perceptions are placed in the empty boxes. Then the machine sorts and organizes the boxes according to content. Two small boxes with similar contents might be placed together in a big box, & then the big box might be conjoined to another big box. Ockham's intuitive cognition provided a basis for a causal theory of reference in philosophy.

Ockham's so called Razor was the principle of parsimony or simplicity according to which the simpler theory was more likely to be true. For a long time the principle of simplicity implied that the world was maximally simple. Unlike the rest Ockham never made this assumption. For Ockham, the principle of simplicity limited the multiplication of hypotheses. He implied that theories are meant to do things, namely, explain & predict. The fascination with Aristotle's physics led Ockham to write several volumes dedicated to natural philosophy. According to his principle of ontological parsimony, people do not need to allow entities in all ten of Aristotle's categories. Hence we do not need the category of quantity, as the mathematical entities are not "real". He felt that mathematics must be applied to other categories, such as the categories of substance or qualities.

Illuminationism

Illuminationist philosophy got its name from the Arabic term "ishraq," meaning 'rising.' The term is also linked to the Arabic for 'East', & has come to represent a specifically Eastern form of philosophical thought. It was mainly used within the context of Persian poetic literature, to represent a form of thought which contrasted with cognitive reason. Illuminationist philosophy started in 12-th century Persia, & has been an important force in Islamic, especially Persian philosophy. It presented a critique of some of the leading ideas of Aristotelianism, as represented by the philosophy of Avicenna & argued that many of the distinctions which were crucial to the character of that form of philosophy were misguided. Illuminationists developed a view of reality in accordance with which essence was much more important than existence. They also held that intuitive knowledge was more significant than scientific knowledge. Illuminationists used the notion of light as a way of exploring the links between God, the Light of Lights, & his creation. The result was a view of the whole of reality as a continuum, with the physical world being an aspect of the divine.

The crucial notion for Illuminationist epistemology was knowledge-by-presence, which identified an epistemological position prior to representational knowledge. This has often been related to intuitive knowledge, & results in attempts to unravel the mysteries of nature not through the principles of physics but through the metaphysical world.

According to Illuminationist theory if existence had a reality outside the mind, then the real must consisted of the principle of the reality of existence & the being of existence, which required a referent outside the mind. Its referent outside the mind must also consist of two things, which could in turn be subdivided, & so on ad infinitum. Thus, if 'existence' denotes an existent, then there must be another 'existence' connected to it which makes it real, & if so then this would also apply to the second 'existence', which leads to a vicious regress.

In addition Illuminationist philosophy challenged the Peripatetic position of the absolute, unchanging & universal validity of the truths discoverable by Aristotelian methodology. Illuminationists also rejected Aristotle's theory of definition, arguing that there is no criterion for the parts of a definition. They maintained that some of the Aristotelian categories were superfluous, since action & passion were modes of motion, & possession & posture were kinds of relation. In the Illuminationist view of logic, a conclusion reached by using a formally established syllogism has no epistemological value as a starting point in philosophical construction. For a universal affirmative proposition to have philosophical value as a foundation of scientific knowledge, it must be 'necessary & always true'. Yet if we introduce the mode 'possibility' and give it extension in time as in 'future possibility', the universal affirmative proposition cannot be 'necessarily true always'. This is because of the impossibility of knowing or deducing all possible future instances.

The influence of Illuminationist philosophy on the Islamic world persists to this day. Many important thinkers including Nasir al-Din al-Tusi, Shams al-Din Shahrazuri, Qutb al-Din al-Shirazi, Jalal al-Din al-Dawani, the School of Isfahan &, right up to our own day, Ha'iri Yazdi, are clearly within this tradition of philosophy.

Averroism

The term Averroism was applied to two philosophical trends originating among European scholastics in the late thirteenth century, after the introduction of Averroes' interpretations of Aristotle. The three most important points of difference were the individual immortality of human intellectual souls, the attainability of happiness in this life & the eternity of the world. The Averroists held that philosophy leads to the conclusions that there was only one intellect shared by all humans & that happiness was attainable in earthly life. Thus, they have generally been credited with a 'theory of double truth', according to which there was an irreconcilable clash between truths of faith & truths arrived at by means of reason. Averroism had often been assigned the role of a dangerous line of thought, against which Thomas Aquinas opposed his synthesis of faith & reason.

Contemporaries were alert to the Averroistic theory's inability to explain how all humans can share an intellect without sharing all thoughts. However, to medieval thinkers the gravest objection against monopsychism was that it left no individual rational soul to carry responsibility for a deceased person's acts. Nor was it easy to see how an immaterial intellect could fail to be eternal, which was contrary to Christian doctrine that God creates new souls every day and that they are in principle perishable. Averroists have been credited with a theory of double truth, occasioned by the fact that when medieval thinkers saw a conflict between philosophy (science) & the teaching of the church, they could not simply reject Church doctrine. Instead, they could hold that philosophers had misinterpreted some of the information obtained by natural means, or they could hold that there was no way to detect any error in the derivation of the philosophical thesis.

The way to happiness was thought to consist in an intellectual ascent to the contemplation of ever higher beings, culminating in contemplation of the First Cause & the union of one's possible intellect with the source of intellectual understanding, the agent intellect; In this tradition, the agent intellect was thought to be a separate substance & not identical with God. This line of thought would seem to permit the construction of a naturalistic ethics with no need for either divine revelation or an individual life after death in order that human beings may reach their ultimate goal & happiness.

Scholasticism

The term Scholasticism comes from the Latin word scholasticus, which means translate as that which belongs to the school. This term was used to designate both a method & a system. Scholasticism is divided into three periods: medieval, second & Neo-Scholasticism. Medieval Scholasticism was extending from Boethius (5th-6th centuries) to the 16th century, with its Golden Age in the 13th century. Boethius was proclaimed the first scholastic mainly because he provided the first Latin translations of Aristotle's logic & other basic works used in the schools of the early middle ages as a prerequisite to understanding the Bible. In a stricter sense, scholasticism began with the Sentences of Peter Lombard, the Decretum of Gratian, & the flood of new Latin translations of classical philosophers, including all of Aristotle, made from Greek & Arabic throughout the second half of the 12th century. The Protestant Reformation in the 16th century stimulated a revival of theology by a return to the language of the Bible, the Fathers of the Church, & the great scholastics of the 13th century. This second scholasticism was aided by the founding (1540) of the Society of Jesus (the Jesuits) by Saint Ignatius Loyola with the approval of Pope Paul III. Early in the 19th century in Italy certain Catholic professors of philosophy began to see in Aquinas's teaching basic principles that might resolve the problems associated with Kantian & Hegelian Idealism, British Empiricism, current Rationalism, Skepticism, & Liberalism. By 1850, neo-Thomism or Neo-Scholasticism began to be heard through the writings of Gaetano Sanseverino in Naples, Matteo Liberatore in Rome, & the Jesuit periodical Civilita Cattolica founded in Naples in 1850.

Scholasticism primarily was the philosophy of permanent substantial being. They believed in the ontogenetic evolution of the human embryo from mere vegetative life to the life of a brute animal, & thence to the life of a rational being. Therefore in the generation of animal and man, these having the most perfect form, there occur many intermediate forms & generations, & consequently destructions, because the generation of one is the destruction of another. The vegetative soul therefore, which was first in the embryo, while it lived the life of a plant, was destroyed, & there succeeded a more perfect soul, which was at once natural & sentient.

Psychological Thought in the Epoch of Renaissance

The transitional period that signified the end of feudal culture & the beginning of bourgeois order became known as Renaissance. It was a cultural movement that spanned roughly the 14th to the 17th century, beginning in Florence in the late middle ages & later spreading to the rest of Europe. To some extent, the problems that arose before the psychology of the Renaissance, repeated the old, arising from the making of scientific psychology at the turn of the VII-VI centuries B.C. One of the most important features of the Renaissance was perhaps the rebirth of scientific disciplines. Finally the natural philosophy was able to partially free itself from the direct subordination of religion. During this period, the science was not born within the walls of universities, but in the workshops of artists, sculptors, engravers, architects, who were also engineers, mathematicians & technicians.

In Italy, Pietro Pomponazzi (1462-1525) was one of the major thinkers in the Aristotelian tradition of the first quarter of the 16th century. He introduced a reassessment of the "mortalist" interpretation of Aristotelian psychology & a radical critique of what were commonly thought of as miracles. Pomponazzi attempted redefine free will outside the deterministic framework of traditional philosophical systems. He was born in Mantua in 1462. Pomponazzi studied philosophical disciplines at the University of Padua. He later taught at Padua from 1488 to 1496, in the final year receiving a doctorate in medicine and writing the treatise "De maximo et minimo" ("On Maxima & Minima"), a polemical discussion of William Heytesbury's theories. He then spent three years teaching logic at the court of Alberto Pio, prince of Carpi. This was followed by another period of teaching at Padua (1499-1509). After briefly holding a post at the University of Ferrara, Pomponazzi was appointed professor at Bologna in 1511, remaining there until his death in 1525.

Before Pomponazzi the fundamental presupposition of every theory of immortality was that the soul can exist separately from the body. He maintained that person's soul was mortal in so far as it was inseparable from the body. By stating the latter he adopted the strategy of showing that the human soul can never performs its activities without bodily assistance. Hence, in order to preserve the unity of the individual, the separate existence of the soul cannot be maintained. Pomponazzi had a rather mortalist solution to the problem, which at least in part revived the thesis of the animal nature & thus the mortality of the human soul. He began with Aristotle's dictum which states "if knowing is imagination or not without imagination, the soul cannot be separated." Naturally thought does not depend on the body as its material or instrumental substrate; it receives from the body representational objects like images. Therefore, thought cannot continue to exist without the assistance of the body "as object" precisely because intelligible elements come to be known by our soul through images received by the senses.

According to Pomponazzi human knowledge can extend to the level of the universal, but only imperfectly, abstracting it from individual instances by means of discursive operations. Thus, even an analysis of the intellectual knowledge reveals our inability to escape from our material condition. Because of this philosophical arguments necessarily lead to the conclusion that, since our soul is never devoid of materiality, it must be mortal. This philosophical conclusion raised serious challenges at the anthropological, moral & religious level.

He saw the main precondition of human free will or free choice to be the contingency of the sublunary world. According to Pomponazzi if we draw the ultimate consequences from Aristotle's worldview, there appears to be a unified order of causes and effects in the universe, descending from God, who is the Unmoved Mover & First Cause. So if we accept this picture of a concatenation of causes & effects throughout the universe, we will be forced to rethink the role of chance & contingency. The fact that events often appear contingent to us, is merely because we are unaware of the causes which determine them. Pomponazzi maintained that to assert free will would imply an exception to the necessary character of divine providence: freedom of choice clashes with the universal government exercised by the First Mover, a cause which is always identical to itself and whose effects are determined. Regardless of anything, the philosophical system of the world seems to eliminate the indeterminacy required for us to be genuinely free, in our ethical deliberations, to choose between equally possible courses. Pomponazzi was convinced that our will was a cause moved by a series of superior causes.

In his later writings Pomponazzi presents pointed out that all human conclusions were merely conjectural, provisional & equal in degree of probability. He also stated that the greatest shortcoming of philosophy is uncertainty. He thought that philosophy would be beautiful, if it were as certain as mathematics, metaphysics & natural philosophy. Eventually this awareness of the shortcomings of philosophy undermined the possibility of building up a systematic body of knowledge & increasingly led Pomponazzi to conceive of philosophy as an analytical task. He was prepared to accept that human knowledge was limited because he compared it to God's absolute knowledge, in which there was no room for uncertainty.

Judah Abrabanel (1465-1523), a Jewish Portuguese physician, poet & philosopher, was a follower of the unique Renaissance schools; Platonism & Humanism. He was also known as Leone Ebreo. Abrabanel's magnum opus, the "Dialogues of Love" belonged to the genre of the treatise on love that was intimately connected to both the Renaissance & the development of the Italian vernacular. He was born in Lisbon, Portugal. Abrabanel went to Genoa, where he studied in an Italian humanist milieu & wrote the first two of his dialogues. In 1501 he became a servant of King Frederick of Naples. After two years he left for Venice, where he rejoined his father. While in Naples, Judah became the doctor of the Spanish viceroy, Don Gonsalvo of Cordoba.

In 1506 Abrabanel left Naples for Venice, where he dedicated himself to the study of philosophy. His most famous work, "Dialogues of Love" was probably written around 1501-02. Abrabanel was already dead when in 1535 his friend Mariano Lenzi discovered the manuscript & published his only famous book.

The tension between faith & reason existed in Jewish philosophy before Abrabanel. This antagonism between faith & reason was even present in Abrabanel's father's writings (philosopher Don Isaac Abrabanel), who constantly tried to uphold traditional Jewish belief against what he considered to be the onslaught of philosophical radicalism. In Judah's theory this "conflict" between the hitherto venerable antagonists virtually was not present.

In Abrabanel's theory concepts of beauty & love were presented almost like technical terms through which he examined virtually every traditional philosophical issue. Often his discussion of one of these terms was predicated on the existence of the other; as a result, beauty & love were inseparable. According to Abrabanel, without beauty the intellect was unable to desire something outside of itself &, thus, it was effectively unable to cognize. He also held that the lower senses such as taste, smell or touch could not grasp Beauty. Only the higher senses like sight & hearing, as well as imagination & the intellect were fit enough to comprehend Beauty. Moreover, since Beauty was mirrored throughout the universe, physical objects (notes, melodies, etc.) both participated in & pointed the way towards this incorporeal Beauty.

Although Abrabanel believed that there was an intimate connection between sensual & cosmic beauty it was by means of the latter that he framed his discussion of cosmology, ontology, & psychology. Beauty was something that inspired love & desire, & thereby connected all levels of the universe into an interlocking relationship.

In Abrabanel's theory the five external senses were divided into 1. Primarily material: touch, taste & smell; & 2. Spiritual: hearing & sight. It seemed that only the latter were able to penetrate behind the purely physical so as to abstract the spiritual from the corporeal. Central to the unfolding argument in the "Dialoghi" was the concept of ocular power. In the first dialogue, Judah described two modes of apprehending spiritual matters. The first was through the faculty of sight & the second through the intellect. For the eye, like the intellect, was illumined by means of light, thereby establishing a relationship between the eye, the object seen, & the space that separated them. Abrabanel distinguished between three types of vision. The highest type was that of God's visual apprehension of himself; following this was that associated with the angelic world, which saw God directly though not on equal terms; finally, there was human vision, which was the weakest of the three types. He also divided the human into a tripartite structure consisting of the body, the soul & the intellect. The soul was the intermediary between the body & the intellect. Although he did define the functioning of the soul in any detail, he did claim that it was indispensable to the proper working of the body & the intellect.

Abrabanel adopted certain concepts of medieval cosmology & psychology, combined them with Renaissance notions of beauty, & thereby created a full-blown aesthetics of Judaism. He viewed the universe as a living, dynamic structure, in which all levels shared in a symbiotic relationship. Abrabanel's emphasis, like that of many of his Renaissance contemporaries, on aesthetics & the phenomenal world eventually became an important dimension of 16-th and 17-th century natural philosophy.

The empirical-naturalistic movement of the 16-th century was founded by Bernardino Telesio (1509-1588). He was born at Cosenza, in Calabria to a noble & wealthy family. Bernardino was educated by his uncle Antonio Telesio, who was a humanist. He also studied in Rome & Padua. Telesio's studies included all the wide range of subjects like classics, science & philosophy. He spent several years in a Benedictine monastery (1535–44). In 1553 he returned to Cosenza where he was assigned a high ranking position at the Academia Cosentina. Telesio never held a salaried position. After the death of his wife in 1561, which marked the beginning of his financial difficulties, he seems to have spent some time in Rome under the patronage of Pope Pius IV. From 1576 on he was moving between Cosenza and Naples; in Naples he lived with the son & heir of Alfonso Carafa, Ferrante. Telesio died in Cosenza, in 1588.

Bernardino Telesio was one of the few truly materialist thinkers of his time. He rejected the previous metaphysical principles of matter and form, & opposed Aristotle's definition of the soul. In Telesio's theory the soul was a separate being & a specific part of the body. He defined it as an element coursing through the nervous system & having its main seat in the brain. Telesio's soul or spiritus was believed to be produced by the white semen. By ascribing psychic functions to a specific part of the body, Telesio rejected one of the main principles of the Aristotelian & Christian traditions, the difference between organic & inorganic life. According to Telesio, there was a quantitative difference here, which consisted in the higher degree of complexity & the higher degree of warmth that some physical bodies had. He also stated that there was no metaphysical difference between living & non-living bodies, & in addition he saw no qualitative difference between animals & humans.

In order to explain mental natural laws, Telesio organized the first society of scientists, which aimed to explore the nature in all its forms. Therefore, at the forefront of his vision came the doctrine of the driving forces as the source of energy for different forms of development. The main forms of development, according to Telesio, were heat, cold, light & darkness, as well as the ability to expand & reduce. These were supposedly in mutual penetration, creating new entities associated with the concentration of certain forces. The struggle of opposing forces was the source of all development.

Telesio also believed that the main purpose of nature was the conservation of the achieved state. Thus, we can say that in his concept was first introduced the idea of homeostasis, although described at the naïve level of science at that time. Telesio held that in positive emotions the strength of the soul manifests itself & in the negative - its weakness which hinders the self-preservation.

Telesio postulated that the functioning of an organic body cannot be explained by presupposing a plurality of rulers. He rejected the current Aristotelian & medical traditions. In asserting the unity of the spirit, Telesio relied on the findings of medical theorist Giovanni Argenterio (1513–1572), who defended the unity of the spirit. He also rejected the traditional concept of sense organs, replacing it with a mechanistic explanation of sense perception. In his opinion, to speak of sense organs is inappropriate, as the so-called sense organs are nothing else than parts of the body which are either more subtle or soft than others, or perforated & open. Telesio was the first thinker of his time to come so close to a neuronal explanation of sense perception, which is a mechanical process arising from the transfer of tactile impressions through the nerves to the brain. In his explanation of sense perception Telesio comes close to the Democritan theory which he combines with Stoic notions.

Telesio rejected the traditional distinction between sense perception & reason. He also denied that there exists something like a purely mental sphere & a corresponding intellect. By doing so he was defending an empirical approach in epistemology. In Telesio's theory understanding was a process which required sense perception & memory (which was not visual). He maintained that the ability of making rational conclusions consisted in comparing new experiences to old ones & in supplementing hidden aspects when referring them to former experiences.

Although Telesio maintained a purely scientific approach, he did not deny the existence of God & of the human soul. He compared God to a mechanic that creates an artifact which will work without interruption & default. Telesio accepted the existence of an immortal soul superimposed by God.

Telesio's cosmology signified the end of complicated, metaphysical interpretations of the various phenomena. He rejected the Aristotelian notion of a bipartite cosmos divided into a sublunary world, in which generation & corruption took place. In Telesio's opinion space was absolute. He did not agree with the concept of transcendent mind or idea. In Telesio's theory all things acted solely according to their own nature, starting from the primary forces of cold & heat. Thus, primary forces & all beings which arise through their antagonistic interaction must be able to sense what is convenient & what is inconvenient or damaging for their survival. Telesio's philosophy was a type of pansensism in which all beings, animate or inanimate, were believed to have the power of sensation. He was one of the most prudent critics of metaphysics in late Renaissance times.

In the beginning of the 16-th century the majority of scientific elite in Spain was busy combining theoretical knowledge with practical aspects of life in an attempt to mold an ideal, truth gathering version of science. One of those scientists was Juan Luis Vives (1493-1540). He was born in Valencia, Spain to a family of Jewish cloth merchants who had converted to Catholicism. He first studied at the University of Paris, & later settled at Bruges, which became his second fatherland, and which he left only for numerous journeys. Here he was introduced to Erasmus & appointed as tutor to the Flemish nobleman William of Croy. After Croy's death in 1521, Vives lived in Louvain & taught at the Collegium Trilingue, a humanist foundation based on Erasmian educational principles. In 1523 Vives was invited to England, where he worked as a tutor. He was made doctor of laws at Corpus Christi College, Oxford. In 1528 he lost the favor of Henry VIII & was placed under house arrest for a time, before being allowed to return to Bruges, where he published several of the works for which he is best known today. His writings & attitude eventually made him an object of suspicion during the so called wars of religion. He attempted to resume his lectures at Louvain, but he spent nearly all the remainder of his life at Bruges. Vives died when he was undertaking a general apology for Christianity.

Vives justified the new approach to psychology as an empirical science, based on the analysis of sensory experience. For the proper construction of the concepts he proposed a new way of synthesis of sense data - induction. Although operational-logical methods of the induction were later developed Francis Bacon, Vives was the founder of the proof of the possibility & validity of a logical transition from private to general. The basis of such transition according to Vives, were the laws of association. According to Vives associative impressions determined the nature of memory. On the same basis, simple concepts emerged, that gave the material for all subsequent work of intelligence. In addition to the sensory side of mental activity of great importance was its emotional aspect. Vives one of the first to conclude that came the most effective for the suppression of negative emotions was not its control or suppression of reason, but the displacement of it with the other, more powerful experience.

Vives tried combine the Aristotelian view of the soul as an organizing principle with the Platonic conception of the soul as an immaterial substance. His psychology was influenced by Galen's tradition, maintaining that person's mental capacities depend on the temperament of his body.

The soul was believed to be composed of a number of different faculties or powers, each directed toward a different object. In his writings Vives introduced the functions of the so called vegetative & cogitative souls. Vegetative soul was responsible for nutrition, reproduction & growth, whereas the cogitative soul was in charge of cognitive faculties, like, imagination, fantasy & the estimative power. According to Vives the rational soul possessed three faculties; mind, will, & memory. He considered the soul as the principal agent inhabiting a body adapted to life. Vives further postulated that the organs controlling rational functions consist of fine & bright spirits exhaled from the pericardial blood.

He described the branch of philosophy that provides a remedy for the severe diseases of the soul as the foundation of all morality. In Vives's theory emotions were defined as the acts of those faculties which nature gave to soul for the pursuit of good & the avoidance of evil. Emotions were also viewed as means lead toward the good & away from evil. Vives's "good" & "evil" mean, not what is in reality good or evil, but rather what each person judges to be good or evil. Hence, the more pure & elevated the judgment, the more it takes account of what is genuinely good & true.

Vives was the first Renaissance thinker to introduce psychological inquiry in his study of the human soul. His psychological principles in were complex, detailed & ahead of their time. He applied these principles not only to individual conduct & education, but also to professional practice, practical affairs & social reform.

Vives's Christian humanism & his overall philosophy were designed to transform society & mankind. He rejected Aristotelian principles leaning more toward Platonism & Stoicism, which he believed were more in line with Christian morality. For example, he saw self-knowledge as the first step toward virtue, which he regarded as the culmination of human perfection. He held that nothing can be called our own except for our soul, in which learning & virtue, or their opposites exist. The best way to reform a society, according to Vives, was through the moral & practical training of the individual. He viewed the development of society as a distinctly human achievement, based on the ability to profit from experience.

Vives saw knowledge as a kind of making or as a capacity to make. In his theory things had external & internal layers. External layers consisted in the sensible accidents of the thing, whereas internal layers were hidden essence of the thing. He also maintained that the genuine essences of all things were not known by a man in himself. Vives mainly agreed with the Aristotelian principle that all human knowledge has its origin in perception, yet at the same time stated that the human mind must realize that, since it is locked up in a dark prison & surrounded by obscurity, it is prevented from understanding many things. Vives argued that sensory knowledge must be transcended by means of reasoning.

Vives was a brilliant educational theorist & a humanist who strongly criticized dogmatic concepts of scholasticism, at the same time making his mark as one of the most influential advocates of early scientific & humanistic learning. By many Vives is considered the first scholar to analyze the psyche directly. His thought is eclectic & pragmatic, as well as historical, in its orientation. Vives taught monarchs. His idea of a diverse & concrete children's education long preceded Rousseau, & may have indirectly influenced Rousseau through Montaigne. Vives was closely associated with the humanistic movement of the Europe & maintained a friendly relationship with Thomas More.

In the second half of the 16-th century Spanish Absolutism was suffering a noticeable decline. Roman Catholic Church was strengthening its influence in the region. Around this time, in 1575 a Spanish doctor Juan Huarte (1529-1592) published his book called "Examen de ingenios para las ciencias"(The Examination of Men's Wits). He was born at Saint-Jean-Pied-de-Port around 1530. Huarte received his first education at the University of Huesca. He also studied at the University of Alcalá de Henares, where he received a degree in medicine.

"The Examination of Men's Wits" won Huarte a European reputation & fame. Huarte's treatise was historically significant as the first attempt to show the connection between psychology & physiology. Huarte's psychology dealt with the problem of the organic relations between the brain & understanding. His concepts accept the possible influences exerted by temper on the will within the field of the Neurobiology of Intelligence. Thus, over four centuries ago Huarte became the founder of Differential or Physiological Psychology. Huarte's writings played a major role in the history & development of the body of neuroscientific knowledge. In 1594, after his death, a second, revised version of his famous book was published. During the 16th, 17th & 18th century, the *Examen* was translated into six European languages: French, Italian, English, Latin, German and Dutch. Today Huarte is considered the patron of Spanish psychology.

Huarte's writings were the first psychological work, which set as a special task to study individual differences in ability to the professional selection. The basic human abilities, according to Huarte, were imagination (fantasy), memory & intelligence. Analyzing a variety of arts and sciences, Huarte assessed them in terms of which of the three skills they require. Huarte argued that physiological factors, namely nutrition play a major role in the process of shaping abilities. He also believed that it was especially important to establish the outer signs by which one could distinguish the quality of the brain that determined the nature of talent. Although his observations about the correspondences between bodily features & capabilities were very naive, the idea of a correlation between internal & external was quite rational.

During the Italian Renaissance, Francesco Patrizi (1529-1597) earned a reputation of the leading critic of the dominant Aristotelianism of the times. Patrizi worked on various philosophical, scientific, artistic & literary issues. Patrizi was born in Cherso (Croatia), then the territory of the

Republic of Venice. At first he studied economy in Venice, after which he moved to study in Ingolstadt under the patronage of his cousin. Later he went to study medicine & philosophy at the University of Padova. After graduation he lived in different cities in Italy: Rome, Bologna, Ferrara & Venice. He finally went to live in Ferrara, which at a time was a center of Platonism in Italy. Here he was appointed to the chair of philosophy at the University of Ferrara. Despite his opposition to Aristotelians Patrizi managed to make a comprehensive study of contemporary science, publishing in 15 books a treatise on the "New Geometry" (1587). He was subsequently invited in Rome by Pope Clement VIII in 1592, where he spent five years as the chair of Platonic philosophy. In his two works Patrizi developed the view that, whereas Aristotle's teaching was in direct opposition to Christianity, Plato, on the contrary, foreshadowed the Christian revelation & prepared the way for its acceptance. Patrizi died in Rome at age of 68.

According to his theory of the universe God created Light which extended throughout space & was the explanation of all development. Although this Light was not corporeal, it was the fundamental reality of things. He also held that from Light came Heat & Fluidity; these three together with Space made up the elements out of which all things were constructed.

Patrizi was one of the few thinkers of his time that attempted to incorporate a systematic account of the natural world within an overall methodological & metaphysical context, anticipating by doing so some of the defining characteristics of such thinkers as Galileo, Descartes & Leibniz. He tried to replace the four Aristotelian elements with his own alternatives – space, light, heat & humidity. Space, was viewed as preferable to the Aristotelian conception of "place" construed as the inner surface of the body surrounding given object. Space was believed to be construed as prior to all bodies, even light. In Patrizi's theory the universe consisted of three separate worlds: the "Empyrean", an infinite space filled with light; the "Aetheric", which contained all the stars & other heavenly bodies down to the Moon; & the "Elementary", which embraced the so called sublunar realm.

One of the brightest representatives of the Italian Aristotelianism was a philosopher & logician Giacomo Zabarella (1533-1589). He was an orthodox Aristotelian seeking to defend the scientific status of theoretical natural philosophy against the pressures emanating from the practical disciplines. Zabarella was born into in Padua to a noble family. He entered the University of Padua, where he received the doctorate in 1553. In 1577 he was promoted to the first extraordinary chair of natural philosophy. He published his "Opera logica," in 1578. In 1582 Zabarella published "Tabula logicae" in which he presented his commentary on Aristotle's "Posterior Analytics." In 1585 Zabarella obtained the second ordinary chair of natural philosophy, which he held until his death.

According to Zabarella the purpose of active philosophy was to remove hindrance to the acquisition of knowledge. Thus he held that contemplative philosophy was the master of all active philosophy. He further argued that in productive disciplines it was not necessary to define the objects under production as strictly as in the contemplative sciences. Science was designed to deal with what already existed, whereas art was concerned with creation. Zabarella thought that the subject-matter of a science was immutable, whereas the subject-matter of an art was viewed as the formation of things as yet non-existent. He insisted that the contemplative philosopher should not be interested in initiating anything, but rather must comprehend & arrange the forms of existing things. The ultimate purpose of the contemplative science was the sole pursuit of knowledge for its own sake.

Zabarella distinguished three contemplative or speculative sciences: divine science (metaphysics) mathematics, & natural philosophy. He maintained that each speculative science should demonstrate its own principles & not borrow them from other disciplines like metaphysics. In Zabarella's theory natural philosophy, which dealt with corporeal beings that have an inner principle of movement, differed from metaphysics (which contemplates being as being) & from mathematics (which deals with abstracted beings) in both ways. Thus he concluded that natural philosophy was autonomous & independent of both the other contemplative sciences. He also held that the science with a nobler subject-matter could be considered superior. In the contemplative sciences the nobility of the subject-matter should be considered superior to the causality of knowledge.

Zabarella rejected the definition of the science of the soul as a middle discipline between physics & metaphysics. In his opinion it was obvious that the science of the soul was the noblest part of natural philosophy. Zabarella held that the science of the soul was more exquisite & certain than all the parts of natural philosophy, because the causes of the science of the soul were more exact.

According to Zabarella the methods were intellectual instruments proceeding from the known to produce knowledge of the unknown. These methods had argumentative force dealing with specific problems of the disciplines instead of arranging the contents of a whole discipline. As with orders, Zabarella denied the possibility of more than two methods. He sought to prove that other procedures, like the composition & division used in the hunt of definitions as well as the so-called dialectical syllogisms were not genuinely productive of knowledge. In his theory Zabarella introduced two methods, which he labeled demonstrative & resolutive. Demonstrative method proceeded from cause to effect & involved demonstration of the reasoned fact. On the other hand, resolutive method proceeded from effect to cause &, despite its name, also involved demonstration. This demonstration of course was of an inferior kind. Related to this alter type of demonstration was the process of induction, which was helpful for discovering principles that were known naturally but were not immediately evident. By the force of induction, human intellect was capable of distinguishing the universal, which was hidden in particulars.

Zabarella was also known for being the first to discuss the relationship between the philosophy of nature & medical art. In his "De natura logicae" Zabarella criticized writers who put medicine alongside the philosophy of nature among the sciences. He insisted that no matter how valuable & precise medicine may be, it could never be a science because it is practiced not for the sake of knowledge, but for the maintenance or restoration of health. Zabarella stated that if knowledge of the human body was considered purely for its own sake, rather than for curative purposes, it should be called natural philosophy rather than medicine.

Although Zabarella's theory had a certain empirical basis, his natural philosophy was not concerned with experiment. Perhaps he did not use experiments in order to verify or falsify theories in the modern sense. Nevertheless Zabarella's theories had a large impact among Protestant Aristotelians in Germany & in the Low Countries during the late sixteenth century and first part of the seventeenth century. His systematic interpretation of Aristotle's logic & natural philosophy was used as a basis for numerous Aristotelian textbooks printed in Germany.

The emergence of new approaches to the construction of science in the 15-16-th centuries was associated with the pursuit of rationality & the conclusiveness of theoretical positions, ushered in a new stage in the process of psychology. The development of these approaches has been the main motive of scientists that developed the psychological concept in modern times. Psychology in this period, as well as in the early stages of development of ancient science, has strengthened its relationship with philosophy. This was due to the fact that, while remaining within the science of the soul, psychology had been more difficult to get rid of scholastic dogmas, separate from theology. However, the orientation of philosophy at the time narrowed the subject of psychology, which dealt mainly general patterns of development of the human psyche, not the living world as a whole. A close relationship with the philosophy did not mean that psychology at that time did not seek its own object of research. The questions about the content & functions of consciousness brought scientists to study its role in human life, therefore, in human behavior. On one hand psychology was methodologically limited to issues of consciousness & ways of its formation & on the other it was concerned with the study of content & functions of consciousness.

At the end of 16-th century the scientists were mainly focused on the problem of the subject of psychology, objective research methods in psychology & data analysis (which were central to the theories of Francis Bacon). The 17-th century established a new look at the universe & the nature in general as a giant mechanism. A similar approach was developed in the teachings about the human body, which had seen a kind of automatic machines, functioning according to the principle of any mechanism for the strict laws of physics. This new explanatory principle became known as mechanistic determinism.

Psychological Thought of the 17-th Century About Mechanistic Movement

The study of learning processes divided psychologists into two different directions. Some thought that the foundation of our knowledge was sensation, while others gave priority to thinking. These directions were called sensationalism & rationalism. Eventually the psychological thought of the seventeenth century was influenced by the new branch of philosophy: mechanistic movement. According to this movement the universe was a great machine with its constant laws & regulations. This idea originated first in natural philosophy (later known as physics) as a result of the work of Galileo & eventually Newton. The nature of all that existed was considered to be nothing more than particles of matter in motion. Thus, every physical effect followed from a direct cause was a subject to laws of measurement, calculation & prediction. The physical universe (believed to be designed by God) was considered lawful & predictable. The methods & findings of science were growing apace with technology during this time & the two meshed very effectively. Experimentation & observation came to the hallmark of science & were followed closely by measurement. It was believed that every function or phenomenon could be defined by a number. The barometer, thermometer, micrometer & other measuring devices perfected in this era served to further reinforce the notion that it was possible to measure all aspects of the mechanical universe. It was thought then that the nature of the man was also mechanical & therefore measurable.

One of the most famous proponents of empirical knowledge at the time was English philosopher Francis Bacon (1561-1626). He was born in London to a prominent & well-connected family. Bacon received his early education at home at the family estate at Gorhambury. At the age of twelve he entered Trinity College, in Cambridge. In 1576 Bacon began reading law at Gray's Inn. A year later he took a position in the diplomatic service in France as an assistant to the ambassador. After his father died Bacon returned to England & resumed the study of law. Bacon received his law degree in 1582. In 1584 he was elected to Parliament. In 1588 he worked as a lecturer at Gray's Inn. In 1589, he received the valuable appointment of reversion to the Clerkship of the Star Chamber.

Bacon's criticism of a new tax levy, in 1593, resulted in a major setback to his career expectations, the Queen taking personal offense at his opposition. But Elizabeth eventually relented to the extent of appointing Bacon her Extraordinary Counsel in 1596. After being knighted by the king, he rapidly ascended the ladder of state & from 1604-1618 filled a succession of many high-profile advisory positions.

Bacon divided human knowledge into three primary categories: History, Poesy & Philosophy. He was convinced that in order for a genuine advancement of learning to occur, the prestige of philosophy had to be elevated. Bacon thought he could accomplish this by making history a virtual sub-species of philosophy. Meanwhile, poesy was set off to the side as a mere illustrative vehicle. In addition the modern idea of technological progress, meaning the historical advance in applied scientific knowledge began with Bacon's "The Advancement of Learning." Knowledge was viewed as a driving force of the history.

He was also the founder of the doctrine of "idols," which he described as characteristic errors, natural tendencies, or defects that beset the mind & prevent it from achieving a full understanding of nature. According to Bacon recognizing & counteracting the idols was as important to the study of nature as the recognition & refutation of bad arguments was to logic. Incidentally, he uses the word "idol" – from theBacon introduced four different classes of idols: 1 idols of tribe, 2 idols of cave, 3 idols of market place & 4 idols of theatre. The idols of tribe were natural weaknesses & tendencies common to human nature. Unlike the idols of the tribe, which are common to all human beings, those of the cave vary from individual to individual. They arise from culture & thus reflect the peculiar distortions, prejudices & beliefs. Idols of market place were defined as hindrances to clear thinking. The main culprit here is language, though not just common speech, but also the special discourses, vocabularies & jargons of various academic communities & disciplines. He held that the idols imposed by words on the understanding were of two kinds: they were either names of things that did not exist or faulty, vague, or misleading names for things that did exist. The idols of theatre were culturally acquired. Bacon argued that these idols derive mainly from grand schemes or systems of philosophy, like sophistical, empirical & superstitious.

Francis Bacon's legacy remains controversial even today. People who share his view that nature exists only for human use & benefit generally applaud him as a great social visionary. On the other hand, those who view nature as an entity in its own right, a higher-order estate of which the human community is only a part, tend to perceive him as an evil originator of the idea of science as the instrument of global imperialism.

In 17-th century several valuable theories & concepts were introduced to accelerate the future development of psychology. One of the founders of such theory was English philosopher Thomas Hobbes (1588-1679). Hobbes was best known for his vision of the world that was at the same time original & relevant to contemporary politics. He was born in Wiltshire, England. His family was poor, but luckily enough his uncle was wealthy & willing to provide for his education. Hobbes received his first education at Oxford, after which he started tutoring the son of an important noble family, the Cavendishes. When the Civil Wars of 1642-46 & 1648-51 were about to begin, Hobbes felt forced to leave the country for his personal safety. He lived in France from 1640 to 1651. Here Hobbes focused his study on the physical doctrine of motion & physical momentum. He first worked out a systematic doctrine of body, hoping to demonstrate how physical phenomena were universally explicable in terms of motion, after which he singled out Man from the realm of Nature & plants. Then, in following treatise, he showed what specific bodily motions were involved in the production of the peculiar phenomena of sensation, knowledge, affections and passions. In his crowning treatise he considered how Men were moved to enter into society. Even after the monarchy had been restored in 1660, Hobbes's security was not always certain because of the powerful religious figures critical of his writings.

He returned to England in 1637 & in 1640 he wrote his famous "The Elements of Law, Natural & Politic." Without a doubt the social & political turmoil affected Hobbes's life & shaped his thought, but it never hampered his intellectual development. His early position as a tutor gave him the scope to read, write & publish. It also brought him into contact with notable English intellectuals such as Francis Bacon. Hobbes was known as a scientist, as a mathematician, as a translator of the classics, as a writer on law & as a disputant in metaphysics & epistemology. The English Civil War revitalized Hobbes's political interests. As a result his "De Cive" was republished & more widely distributed. In 1647 Hobbes was working as a mathematical instructor to the Prince of Wales Charles. The company of the exiled royalists led Hobbes to produce an English book to set forth his theory of civil government. In it the State was regarded as a great artificial man or monster (Leviathan), composed of men. He also he criticized religious doctrines on rationalistic grounds in the Commonwealth.

In 1647 Hobbes became serious ill. On recovering from this near fatal disorder, he resumed his literary task, & carried it steadily forward to completion by the year 1650. The same year a pirated edition of "The Elements of Law, Natural and Politic" was published. The work had immediate impact & Hobbes was more lauded & decried than any other thinker of his time. The first effect of its publication was to sever his link with the exiled royalists, forcing him to appeal to the revolutionary English government for protection. Hobbes returned to Britain in 1651 after the death of Charles I. In 1666 Parliament threatened to investigate him as an atheist. His works were considered important statements of the nascent ideas of liberalism. He died on Dec. 4, 1679, at the age of 91.

According to Hobbes human beings were physical objects & sophisticated machines all of whose functions & activities could be described & explained in purely mechanistic terms. Hobbes's concept of sensation involved a series of mechanical processes operating within the human nervous system. In his theory specific desires & appetites arose in the human body & were experienced as discomforts or pains. Thus, each of us is motivated to act in such ways as we believe likely to relieve our discomfort. Hobbes human volition was nothing but the determination of the will by the strongest present desire. He further maintained that human agents were free in the sense that their activities were not under constraint from anyone else. Therefore we have no reason to complain about the strict determination of the will so long as we are not subject to interference from outside ourselves. As Hobbes stated, this account of human nature emphasized our animal nature, leaving each of us to live independently of everyone else, acting only in his or her own self-interest.

Unable to rely indefinitely on their individual powers in the effort to secure livelihood & contentment, Hobbes supposed, human beings join together in the formation of a commonwealth. The commonwealth as a whole was designed to embody a network of associated contracts & provide for the highest form of social organization. According to Hobbes the formation of the commonwealth created a new, artificial person (the Leviathan) to whom all responsibility for social order & public welfare was entrusted. The commonwealth-creating covenant was not in essence a relationship between subjects & their sovereign at all. Rather, what counts was the relationship among subjects, all of whom agreed to divest themselves of their native powers in order to secure the benefits of orderly government by obeying the dictates of the sovereign authority. Despite his firm insistence on the vital role of the sovereign as the embodiment of the commonwealth, Hobbes acknowledged that there were particular circumstances under which it may fail to accomplish its purpose.

Hobbes sought to discover rational principles for the construction of a civil polity that would not be subject to destruction from within. Because virtually any government would be better than a civil war, and, according to Hobbes's analysis, all but absolute governments are systematically prone to dissolution into civil war, people ought to submit themselves to an absolute political authority. Continued stability will require that they also refrain from the sorts of actions that might undermine such a regime. Hobbes aimed to demonstrate the reciprocal relationship between political obedience & peace.

One of the most vital aspects of Hobbes's political philosophy was his treatment of religion. He progressively expanded his discussion of Christian religion in each revision of his political philosophy, until it came in "Leviathan" to comprise roughly half the book. In reality there was no settled consensus on how Hobbes understood the significance of religion within his political theory. Some commentators have argued that Hobbes was trying to demonstrate to his readers the compatibility of his political theory with core Christian commitments, since it may seem that Christians' religious duties forbid their affording the sort of absolute obedience to their governors which Hobbes's theory requires of them. Others have doubted the sincerity of his professed Christianity, arguing that by the use of irony or other subtle rhetorical devices, Hobbes sought to undermine his readers' religious beliefs.

During golden era of insights & discoveries many great thinkers helped to create the atmosphere in which the truly scientific inquiry flourished. One of them was Rene Descartes (1596-1650) who symbolized the transition from Renaissance to modern era of science. He was born in 1956 at La Haye in Touraine, France. From an early childhood Descartes was very fond of mathematics.

Rene Descartes was definitely contributing to the future development of psychology when he was attempting to resolve mind-body problem. In his theory the mind was no longer the master of two entities. The body, the material side of man was viewed in a new & more central manner, allowing certain functions previously attributed to the mind to be considered as bodily. Descartes was known for offering a physical-psychological approach to the mind-body problem. Before him, in the middle ages mind was held responsible not only for thought & reason, but for reproduction, perception & locomotion. Descartes dualism was designed to study mind with its mental operations as opposed to soul & its abstract sense. Methods of inquiry changed as a result from metaphysical analysis & deduction to induction & objective observation.

Descartes viewed mind & body as two distinct entities, claiming that the matter & the body are extended substances that operate by mechanical principles. The soul or mind was viewed as something free, unextended & insubstantial. Perhaps the most radical idea was that mind & body though totally separate & distinct are capable of interacting in the human organism. Thus the body can influence the mind & the mind can influence the body. It was believed that since the body is comprised of physical matter, it must share those characteristics common to all matter: extension in space & capability of movement. Since the body is matter, than the laws of physics & mechanics that account for movement & action in the physical world must also be applicable to the body. The body is like a machine apart from mind. Its operation can be explained by the mechanical laws of the movement of objects in space.

Descartes held that nonmaterial mind has the capacities of thought & consequently provides us with knowledge of the external world. It has none of the properties of matter. The most important characteristic of the mind is its capacity to think. Hence, if mind perceives & wills, it must somehow influence & be influenced by the body. Descartes recognized that when the mind decides to move from one point to another, for example this decision is carried out somehow by the nerves & the muscles of the body. Similarly when the body is stimulated in some fashion the mind recognizes & interprets these sensory data & makes a decision as to the appropriate response.

Eventually Descartes was led to formulate what is perhaps the most important part of his theory: the interaction of these two totally different entities. He was looking for a point of interaction where the mind & a body could engage in their mutual influence. Descartes was convinced that this point of interaction was somewhere within the brain. Clearly, then, the brain had to be the focal point of the mind's functions. Since the only structure of the brain that is single & unitary is the pineal gland, he considered it the only logical choice for a point of interaction.

Descartes also formulated the doctrine of ideas, which contributed a great deal to the development of psychology. He believed that the mind gives rise to two kinds of ideas: derived & innate. Derived ideas are those produced by the direct application of an external stimulus. These derived ideas are products of the experiences of the senses. The notion of innate ideas is more important, since these ideas are not produced by the objects in the external world impinging on the senses. The label innate describes their source. They develop out of the mind or consciousness alone. Their innate tendency is independent of sense experience, though it may e realized or actualized in the presence of appropriate sense experience. Some of these innate ideas are the ideas of the self, God, the geometric axioms, perfection, & infinity.

Although inaccurate, the works of Descartes served as a catalyst for many trends later prominent in psychology. His most important systematic conceptions are his mechanistic conception of the body, his mind-body theory of the interactionism, the localization of the mind's functions in the brain, & the doctrine of innate ideas.

Materialism, Positivism & Empiricism was the main philosophical foundations of the new psychology. At last the psychological phenomena were being viewed in the framework made up of factual, observational & quantitative evidence based on sensory experience. Of the three new traditions materialism & empiricism played a greater role in shaping the early development of the new science of psychology.

Empiricism was a theory of knowledge which emphasized those aspects of science that are closely related to experience. Empirical knowledge was formed through deliberate experimental arrangements. Empiricism grew rapidly since it seems to be the only discipline that provided psychology with both theory & a method. Unlike older speculative methods, empirical method relies only on objective observation. According to empiricist view human mind grows through the progressive accumulation of sensory experiences. This attitude is in distinct opposition to Descartes viewpoint of innate ideas.

The doctrine of Empiricism was first formulated by John Locke (1632-1704) in the seventeenth century. Locke argued that the mind is a "white paper" on which experiences leave their mark. John Locke studied at the Westminster & Oxford. He received his bachelor degree in 1656 & his master's degree soon after that. Locke's major work of importance to psychology is "An Essay Concerning Human Understanding" which was published in 1690. It marked the formal beginning of the British Empiricism. Locke was concerned primarily with the question of how mind acquires knowledge. In his pursuit he first denied the existence of innate ideas, claiming that man simply cannot be equipped with knowledge at birth. But later he admitted that certain ideas may appear to be innate because he has been constantly taught them from childhood & cannot remember any time when he was not aware of them. The innateness of ideas is explained by Locke in terms of learning & even habit. Locke maintained that mind acquires knowledge through emphatically, through experience. He also held that experience derives either from sensation or form reflection. Certain ideas originate from direct sensory input from physical objects in the environment. In addition to the operation of sensations upon the mind, however, the operation of the mind itself (reflection) can give rise to ideas. The ideas produced by reflection are based on those already experienced sensorially.

Sensations are the necessary precursors of reflections, thus they come first in the development of the individual. In reflection, individual is able to remember past sensory impressions combining them with various forms of abstractions & higher level ideas. All ideas arise from these two sources, but overall origin remains sense impressions or experience.

Locke also had an interesting definition for simple & complex ideas. Simple ideas, according to Locke, arise from both sensation & reflection & are received passively by the mind. On the other hand, complex ideas are compounded or comprised of simple ideas, & hence are capable of being analyzed or resolved into simple ideas. This notion of a mental combination of ideas marks the beginning of the so called mental chemistry that characterizes the notion of association. The unique decomposition of mental life into elements or simple ideas, & the compounding of these elements to form complex ideas subsequently formed the core of the new scientific psychology.

Locke treated the mind in accordance with the laws of the physical universe. The particles of mental world were the simple ideas. These simple ideas were analogous to material atoms in Newtonian mechanistic scheme. He also introduced an interesting notion of primary & secondary qualities as they apply to simple ideas of sense. Primary qualities exist in the object whether we perceive them or not. Accordingly, the shape & the size of the object are primary qualities, whereas the color & odor are secondary. Secondary qualities are not in the object; rather, they exist in one's perception of the object.

Far more advanced were the theories of Baruch (in some literature Benedictus) Spinoza (1632-1677). He was one of the most important & radical philosophers of the early modern period. His complex thought combined a commitment to Cartesian metaphysical & epistemological principles with elements from ancient Stoicism & medieval Jewish rationalism into a nonetheless highly original system. His purely naturalistic views served to ground a moral philosophy centered on the control of the passions leading to virtue & happiness. Of all the philosophers of the seventeenth-century, without a doubt none have more relevance today than Spinoza. He was born in Amsterdam, Holland. Spinoza initially received a traditional orthodox Jewish education, studying Talmud & Hebrew as a child and a young adult. At the age of seventeen, he was forced to cut short his formal studies to help run the family's importing business. Spinoza was very gifted. From a very young age he showed a facility for languages & eventually mastered Spanish, Portuguese, Dutch, German, Hebrew, Latin, & Greek. In 1656 Spinoza was expelled by his congregation on charges of atheism. For the next 4 years Spinoza worked as a teacher in a private academy in Amsterdam. His future interests in mathematics, physics, & politics stem from this period. From 1660 to 1663 he lived near Leiden among a free religious sect, who called themselves Collegiants, & there he wrote "Principles of Cartesianism," "Short Treatise on God, Man & His Well-being," & the first book of "Ethics." In fact his critical exposition of Descartes' "Principles of Philosophy" was the only work he published under his own name in his lifetime. In 1670 he anonymously published his "Theological-Political Treatise." In addition to these not very extensive writings, Spinoza conducted a large correspondence with various scientists & philosophers. Two of the most important were Henry Oldenburg, the first secretary of the British Royal Society, & Gottfried Leibniz. In 1673 Spinoza had declined a professorship at the University of Heidelberg in order to preserve his "freedom of philosophizing." His most scandalous work, the "Theological-Political Treatise" was published anonymously in 1670. When Spinoza died in 1677, he was still at work on his Political Treatise; this was soon published by his friends along with his other unpublished writings, including a "Compendium to Hebrew Grammar."

In Spinoza's writings the human mind (like God) contains ideas. Some of these ideas or sensory images were imprecise qualitative phenomena, being the expression in thought of states of the body as it was affected by the bodies surrounding it. In reality such ideas did not convey adequate & true knowledge of the world, but only a partial & subjective picture of how things appeared to the perceiver. He did not introduce a systematic order to these perceptions, nor any critical oversight by reason. Spinoza stated that as long as the human mind perceives things from the common order of nature, it does not have an adequate, but only a confused & mutilated knowledge of itself, of its own body, & of external bodies. The adequate ideas were believed to be formed in a rational & orderly manner, thus, were necessarily true & revelatory of the essences of things. The Reason, viewed as the second kind of knowledge after random experience, was the apprehension of the essence of a thing through a discursive, inferential procedure. Spinoza held that a true idea meant nothing other than knowing a thing perfectly, or in the best way. It involved grasping a thing's causal connections not just to other objects but, more importantly, to the attributes of God & the laws of nature that follow immediately from them. Thus, perceiving by the way of adequate ideas was the same as perceiving the necessity inherent in Nature.

Spinoza maintained that the senses present things only as they appear from a given perspective at a given moment in time. On contrary, an adequate idea by showing how a thing followed necessarily from one or another of God's attributes, presented it in its "eternal" aspects, without any relation to time. Overall Spinoza's conception of adequate knowledge revealed an unrivaled optimism in the cognitive powers of the human being.

Spinoza introduced a very detailed analysis of the composition of the human being because it was essential to his goal of showing how the human being was a part of Nature, existing within the same causal nexuses as other extended & mental beings. This had serious ethical implications. First, it implied that a human being was not endowed with freedom, at least in the ordinary sense of that term. Because our minds & the events in our minds are simply ideas that exist within the causal series of ideas that followed from God's attribute Thought, our actions & volitions were as necessarily determined as any other natural events.

Spinoza divided human affects into actions & passions. When the cause of an event is in our own nature—more particularly, our knowledge or adequate ideas—then it is a case of the mind acting. On the other hand, when something happens in us the cause of which lies outside of our nature, then we are passive & being acted upon. Usually what takes place, both when we are acting and when we are being acted upon, is some change in our mental or physical capacities. Spinoza called it "an increase or decrease in our power of acting" or in our "power to persevere in being."

According to Spinoza we naturally pursue those things that we believe will benefit us by increasing our power of acting & shun or flee those things that we believe will harm us by decreasing our power of acting because of our innate striving to persevere. This provides Spinoza with a foundation for cataloguing the human passions. Joy also translated as pleasure was viewed as the movement or passage to a greater capacity for action, while sadness or pain on the other hand, was the passage to a lesser state of perfection. All of the human emotions, in so far as they are passions, are constantly directed outward, towards things and their capacities to affect us one way or another. Aroused by our passions & desires, we seek or flee those things that we believe cause joy or sadness. Our hopes & fears fluctuate depending on whether we regard the objects of our desires or aversions as remote, near, necessary, possible or unlikely. But the objects of our passions, being external to us, are completely beyond our control.

Spinoza's ethical theory was slightly Stoic. He postulated that the mind's intellectual love of God was our understanding of the universe, our virtue, our happiness, our well-being & our salvation. Spinoza's "free person" was one who bared the gifts & losses of fortune with equanimity. Such a person did only those things that he believed to be the most important in life. The free person neither hoped for any eternal, otherworldly rewards nor feared any eternal punishments. He knew that the soul was not immortal in any personal sense, but was endowed only with a certain kind of eternity. Spinoza argued that the more the mind consisted of true & adequate ideas, the more of it remained after the death of the body. This understanding of his place in the natural scheme of things brings to the free individual true peace of mind.

He further concluded that free human beings will be mutually beneficial & useful, as well as tolerant of the opinions & the errors of others. But naturally human beings do not generally live under the guidance of reason. The state therefore, is required in order to insure that individuals are protected from the unrestrained pursuit of self-interest on the part of other individuals. The transition from a state of nature, where each seeks his own advantage without limitation, to a civil state, in Spinoza's theory, involved the universal renunciation of natural rights.

Spinoza saw god as a being with infinitely many attributes, each of which was itself infinite & upon which no limits of any kind could be imposed. He argued that infinite substance must be indivisible, eternal, & unitary. There could be only one such substance, "god or nature," in which everything else was wholly contained. Thus, Spinoza was an extreme monist. He considered god to be an extended as well as a thinking substance. He also stated that god was perfectly free. Of course it would be incorrect to suppose that god had any choices about what to do. Everything that happened was not only causally determined but actually occurred by logical necessity from immutable laws. But since everything was merely a part of god, those laws themselves, & cause & effect alike, were simply aspects of the divine essence.

Substance, in Spinoza's theory, was defined not only as existing in itself but also as "conceived through itself." This statement limited the possibility of interaction between things, since he declared that causation was a relation of logical necessity. Since causal interaction is impossible between two substances that differ essentially, & no two substances can share a common attribute or essence, it follows that no substance can produce genuine change in any another substance. Each must be the cause of its own existence & since it cannot be subject to limitations imposed from outside it, must also be absolutely infinite.

Another famous philosopher of the 17-th century was Gottfried Leibniz (1642-1727). He also was a mathematician, historian & jurist. Leibniz was a contemporary of Newton with whom he feuded bitterly over the invention of calculus. Although Gottfried Leibniz left behind no philosophical magnum opus, he is still considered to be among the giant thinkers of the 17th-century. Leibniz believed in "pre-established harmony" between the outer world & mind, & developed a philosophy of Rationalism by which he attempted to reconcile the existence of matter with the existence of God.

He was born at Leipzig on June 21, 1646. By the time Leibniz was 12 he had taught himself to read Latin & had begun Greek. He entered the University of Leipzig at age 14 & completed a Bachelor's degree in philosophy. By the time he was 20 he had mastered the ordinary text-books on mathematics, philosophy, theology & law. In 1666 Leibniz published his first book titled "On the Art of Combinations." The first part of this book was also his habilitation thesis in philosophy. Tense & jealous atmosphere in Leipzig made Leibniz leave & enroll in the University of Altdorf. He obtained a license & doctorate in law in November of 1966. He then declined an offer of academic appointment at Altdorf, & spent the rest of his life in the service of two major German noble families. After completing his philosophical & legal education, Leibniz spent several years as a diplomat in France, England, & Holland. He became acquainted with the leading intellectuals of the age. He then settled in Hanover, where he devoted most of his adult life to the development of a comprehensive scheme for human knowledge, comprising logic, mathematics, philosophy, theology, history, & jurisprudence. Although his own rationalism was founded upon an advanced understanding of logic, which Leibniz largely kept to himself, he did publish many less technical expositions of his results for the general public.

He invented the differential & integral calculus in 1674, but the earliest traces of the use of it in his extant note-books do not occur till 1675, & it was not till 1677 that we find it developed into a consistent system; it was not published till 1684. Most of his mathematical papers were produced within the ten years from 1682 to 1692, and many of them in a journal, called the "Acta Eruditorum," founded by himself & Otto Mencke in 1682.

Most of Leibniz's philosophical writings were composed in the last twenty or twenty-five years of his life; & the points as to whether his views were original or whether they were appropriated from Spinoza, whom he visited in 1676, is still in question among philosophers. He regarded the ultimate elements of the universe as individual percipient beings that he called monads. According to him the monads were centers of force, while space, matter, & motion were merely phenomenal; finally, the existence of God was inferred from the existing harmony among the monads.

In 1700 he helped to create the academy of Berlin. On the accession in 1714 of his master, George I., to the throne of England, Leibnitz was thrown aside as a useless tool; he was forbidden to come to England; & the last two years of his life were spent in neglect. He died at Hanover in 1716.

Leibniz was one of the great philosophers of the age of Rationalism & the last major philosopher who was also a first rate, indeed a great, mathematician. His system, especially as developed by Christian Wolff (1679-1754), established the basic form of metaphysics in German universities, providing the philosophical starting point for Immanuel Kant. Leibniz's metaphysics was most profitably contrasted with that of his near contemporary Baruch Spinoza, since the two of them come down on exactly opposite sides of many important issues. Leibniz's system was also to be compared with the natural science of Isaac Newton who became Leibniz's bitter enemy, not just in metaphysics, but in the argument over who had priority for the development of calculus.

Leibniz agreed with Aristotle that every event has a final cause. This puts him at odds with Spinoza, who denied that there are any final causes, even for God. It also puts him at odds with most subsequent philosophy & science, which has gravitated in the direction of Spinoza's view. Even the rather common sense idea today that beings with intelligence and intention have purposes & ends has been called into question by philosophers like Gilbert Ryle & psychologists like B.F. Skinner, who thought that everything about human behavior was causally determined.

Leibniz's theory of truth owed a great deal to Aristotle. We understand the nature of things, according to Aristotle, by the abstraction of the forms of things into the mind, which then become concepts. The thing then has an "intentional" existence in the mind. For Leibniz, a Monad, which is like an Aristotelian form, contains its entire history & so everything that is true about it. God thinks every Monad clearly & distinctly, which means that everything he would think about each Monad is already contained in the concept that he possesses of it. According to Leibniz's theory all truth was analytic. We do not always appreciate this because our knowledge of things does not reflect the complete history of each Monad. As truth emerges in our minds, it is because we have learned more about the nature of things.

Leibniz remained opposed to materialism throughout his career, particularly as it figured in the writings of Epicurus & Hobbes. By opposing both materialism & dualism, Leibniz carved himself an interesting place in the history of views concerning the relationship between thought & matter. Most of his arguments against materialism were directly aimed at the thesis that perception & consciousness can be given mechanical explanations. His position was that perception & consciousness cannot possibly be explained mechanically. Leibniz rejected materialism on the grounds that it could not, in principle, ever capture the "true unity" of perceptual consciousness, that characteristic of the self which can simultaneously unify a manifoldness of perceptual content. Leibniz's rejection of materialist conceptions of the mind was coupled with a strong opposition to dualistic views concerning the relationship between mind & body, particularly the substance dualism that figured in the philosophy of Descartes. According to this dualism, the world fundamentally consisted of two disparate substances: extended material substance (body) & unextended thinking substance (mind).

According to Leibniz, bodies (qua material) were aggregates, & an aggregate, of course, was not a substance on account of its lack of unity. The claim in the above passage is that whatever being, or reality, an aggregate has derives from the being & reality of its constituents. Thus, Leibniz thought that if a body had any reality at all, if it was more than a mere "phenomenon, lacking all reality as would a coherent dream," then it would ultimately be composed of things which were real beings. Atoms, he claimed, were unfit for this role, because they were themselves extended beings, & for Leibniz, divisibility was of the essence of extension. Leibniz held a special position with respect to the history of views concerning thought & its relationship to matter. He rejected the materialist position that thought & consciousness can be captured by purely mechanical principles. But he also rejected the dualist position that the universe must therefore be bifurcated into two different kinds of substance, thinking substance, & material substance.

George Berkeley, (1685-1753) Locke's immediate successor was one of the metaphysician-idealist philosophers of the early modern period. He was a deeply religious man & at the age of 24 was ordained a deacon in the Anglican Church. Later he published a series of philosophical works that were to exert an influence on psychology: "An Essay towards a New Theory of Vision," (1709) & "A Treatise Concerning the Principles of Human Knowledge" (1710).

Berkeley agreed with Locke that all knowledge of the external world comes from experience but disagreed with his doctrine of primary & secondary qualities. Berkeley held that there are no primary qualities in existence. To Berkeley all knowledge was a function of the experiencing or perceiving person. Later this position was labeled "mentalism" to denote Berkeley's emphasis on purely mental phenomena.

According to Berkeley perception is the only reality of which we can be sure. Thus, a person cannot know with certainty the nature of physical objects in the experimental world; all he knows for sure is how he perceives the objects. Berkeley thought that physical objects are nothing more than accumulations of sensations. Hence, if we take away the perception, the quality disappears. Berkeley was not exactly stating that real objects exist in the material world only when they are perceived; he was rather arguing that since all experience is within ourselves we can never know with certainty the nature of real objects. At the same time he recognized a certain degree of independence, consistency & stability of objects in the real world & he had to find some way of accounting for this. Unfortunately he did so by invoking God. He made God a permanent perceiver of all objects in the universe. Further he invoked the theory of association to explain our knowledge of objects in the real world. This knowledge is a construction of mental elements held together by the mortar of association.

Berkeley's views were idealistic & naïve. His only true contribution to psychology was his attempt to explain purely psychological process in terms of association of sensations.

Movements of the 18-th Century

The development of psychology in the 18-th century, in contrast to the previous century, was closely associated with rationalism. The writings of Francis Bacon, Descartes and other scientists of the 18-th century proved the necessity of constructing an objective science, built on reason & independent of faith. At the same time, the rapid development of industry & new social conditions demanded a study of psychological mechanisms of mental adjustment, analysis of ways of influencing the minds & consciousness of man & his ability to adapt to new conditions. The rapid development of science gave rise to the idea of progress, the idea that everything in the world develops from simple to complex.

"British" Empiricism was a philosophical movement in 18-th century that originated in Great Britain. Empiricists maintained that all knowledge comes from experience. Continental Rationalists held that knowledge comes from foundational concepts known intuitively through reason, such as innate ideas. Other concepts were then deductively drawn from these. British Empiricists staunchly rejected the theory of innate ideas, yet they did not reject the notion of instinct or innateness in general. Indeed, we have inborn propensities which regulate our bodily functions & produce emotions. What Empiricists denied, though, was that we are born with detailed, picture-like, concepts of God, causality, & even mathematics. They also moved away from deductive proofs & used an inductive method of arguing which was more conducive to the data of experience.

David Hume (1711-1776) was the last of the classical British empiricists. He was born in Edinburgh. Hume became a student at the University of Edinburgh when he was only twelve years old. His first choice was a career in law, but later he turned to philosophy. In 1734 Hume went to La Flèche in Anjou, France, where he had frequent discourse with the Jesuits. Here he wrote his famous "A Treatise of Human Nature." In 1744, despite the criticism of his previous work Hume wrote "Essays Moral & Political." During the 1745 Hume began tutoring the Marquis of Annandale, & at the same time writing his great historical work "The History of Great Britain." From 1746, Hume served for three years as Secretary to Lieutenant-General St Clair. Around this time he wrote "An Enquiry Concerning Human Understanding."

In 1737 Hume returned to England to prepare his "Treatise" for the press. Book I, "Of the Understanding," & Book II, "Of the Passions," was published anonymously in 1739. Book III, "Of Morals," appeared in 1740. An offer to serve as Librarian to the Edinburgh Faculty of Advocates gave Hume the opportunity to work steadily on another project of "The History of England."

In 1763 Hume served as a Private Secretary to Lord Hertford, the Ambassador to France. Three years later Hume returned to England accompanied by Jean-Jacques Rousseau, who was then fleeing persecution in Switzerland. After a year (1767-68) in London as an Under-Secretary of State, Hume returned to Edinburgh to stay in August, 1769. He built a house in Edinburgh's New Town, & spent his autumnal years quietly and comfortably, dining & conversing with friends.

Hume held that there was a secret union among particular ideas, which caused the mind to conjoin them more frequently together. He also argued that a science of human nature should account for these connections. Hume stated that, although "it will be too obvious to escape observation, that different ideas are connected together; I do not find that any philosopher has attempted to enumerate or class all the principles of association." His introduction of these "principles of association" was the other distinctive feature of his empiricism.

In Hume's theory human perceptions were divided into two classes: ideas & impressions. Ideas were the less lively perceptions, of which person was conscious when he reflected on his sensations. All the materials of human thinking were derived either from outward or inward sentiment; the mixture & composition of these belonged alone to the mind and will. Or, in other terms, all our ideas or more feeble perceptions were copies of our impressions or more lively ones. According to Hume even the idea of God arose from reflecting on the operations of our own mind.

Hume's "experience" refuted the dualism of will & physical agencies, at the same time, destroying the dualism of reason & instinct. We learn many things from experience, & infer that the same events will always follow the same causes. By this principle they become acquainted with the more obvious properties of external objects, & gradually, from their birth, treasure up a knowledge of the nature of fire, water, earth, stones, heights, depths, & etc. Hume emphasized Locke's notion of the compounding of simple ideas into complex ideas, at the same time developing & making more explicit the notion of association. He agreed with Berkeley on nonexistence of the material world except when it is perceived, but he made some changes of his own. He abolished mind as substance claiming that the mind is secondary quality, like matter. Hume defined mind as a flow of sensations, ideas & memories. He drew a clear distinction between the two kinds of mental contents: impressions & ideas. Impressions are the basic elements of mental life & are closely related to sensation & perception today. An idea is the mental experience we have in the absence of stimulating object; the modern equivalent is "image." Hume failed to define these two mental contents either in physiological terms or in reference to any external stimulating object. He was careful not to assign any stimulating causes to impressions. These two mental contents differ not in terms of their source or point of origin, but in terms of their relative strength or vivacity, meaning impressions are strong & vivid, whereas ideas are weaker. Hume called the ideas weak copies of impressions. It is obvious that both of these mental contents can be simple or complex, with a simple idea resembling its simple impression.

Complex ideas are compounded from simple ideas by association & Hume's ultimate laws of association are resemblance & contiguity in time or place. Thus, the more similar & contiguous are two ideas, the more readily they will be associated. According to Hume the law of association of ideas was the mental counterpart of the law of gravity in the physical world; that is, a universal of the operation of the mind.

David Hartley (1705-1757), a philosopher, scientist is best known for writing famous "Observations on Man, His Frame, His Duty, & His Expectations."His work inspired social & religious radicals in 1700's, & led to the school of "Association Psychology" in the 1800's. Hartley was a son of a minister preparing for a career in the church, but because of the doctrinal difficulties he turned to medicine. David Hartley was born in the vicinity of Halifax, Yorkshire to a family of an Anglican clergyman. He was first enrolled at Bradford Grammar School & Jesus College, Cambridge, of which society he became a fellow in 1727. Hartley practiced medicine in Bury St. Edmunds (1730-35), London (1735-42), & Bath, where he died on 28 August 1757.

As a matter of method, Hartley proposed the scientific investigation of "man." He wrote that the body's "component particles" were "subjected to the same subtle laws" as are all other material entities. Hartley also presented a "theory of vibrations" that explained, in detail, how the "component particles" that constitute the nerves & brain interacted with the physical universe suggested by Newton. In Hartley's theory the starting point was the living organism, & specifically the physical "vibrations" present in brain & nervous system. From this starting point, two important considerations followed. The first was that sensations & ideas were products, not givens, & their "generation" & "raising" required explanation. The second involved the recognition that organisms were active beings.

Hartley was convinced that all people will ultimately become "partakers of the divine nature." He sought to show that the gathering together of all humanity into the "mystical body of Christ" was a process inherent in our nature: the psychological dynamic of association, which generated our ideas & perfected our secondarily automatic movements. He also maintained that a seemingly inert particle of matter contained within itself forces of attraction & repulsion in a dynamic equilibrium. Supposedly in such particles concretions & dissolutions occurred continuously, causing the materials within the bodies of living things to form, dissolve, & form again. In addition Hartley offered an original model of psychological development, in which the various emotional states, like pleasures & pains were subdivided into "six classes": imagination, ambition, self-interest, sympathy, theopathy, & the moral sense. These in turn, formed two groups of three, each consisting of two basic orientations & a means of regulating them. The first group consisted of imagination, the orientation toward objects as sources of pleasure or displeasure, & of ambition. The second group combined sympathy, the orientation of personal inter-subjectivity, & theopathy, the person's relationship with the divine. In fact the term "Theopathy" was Hartley's invention. He calls the moral sense the "monitor" of sympathy & theopathy. Although Hartley identified "sympathy" & "theopathy" as basic orientations, the orientations did not necessarily have a positive content.

Hartley's model of the self in terms of imagination, ambition, & self-interest, & then of sympathy, theopathy, & the moral sense, was dynamically quite complex. In his moral psychology, emotions were similar to electrical charges that easily jumped from one object, symbol, word, or thought to another. Through such "transferences" of emotion, the six orientations developed content; like physical concretions, they coalesced, as emotional energies were bonded together. And when the energy in one was sufficiently strong, the orientation became the person's "primary pursuit": it demanded accretion of pleasure.

Hartley was considered important for the great clarity & precision of his organization & systematization of the previous work. The basic premises of this doctrine were certainly not new with Hartley, but he served the very important function of bringing together the earlier threads of thought. His fundamental law of association was contiguity, by which he attempted to explain memory, emotions, reasoning & both voluntary & involuntary action. Ideas that recurred together became associated. Thus, repetition in addition to contiguity was necessary for the formation of associations. Hartley argued fully with Locke that all ideas & knowledge were derived from sensory experience; there were no associations present at birth. As the child grew & accumulated a variety of sensory experiences, connections & trains of association of greater & greater complexity were established. This way, higher systems of thought were developed by the time adulthood was reached. Higher order mental life was capable of analysis or reduction to the elements or atoms from which it was formed through the mental compounding associations. Hartley was the first scientist to explain the various types of mental activity with the help of association.

Hartley attempted to explain psychological processes in mechanical terms. He used Newton's vibratory theory to explain the operation of the brain & nervous system. Vibrations in the nerves transmit impulses from one part of the body to another. The vibrations in the nerves set up smaller vibrations in the brain, which he considered to be physiological counterparts of ideas. It was yet another attempt to use the principles of mechanical universe as a model for understanding the nature of man.

James Mill (1773-1836) was a political philosopher, psychologist, historian, educational theorist, economist & a reformer. Mill's range of interests was remarkably wide, extending from education & psychology to political economy. He applied the notion of mechanism to human mind with a directness & comprehensiveness not shown by his predecessors. His intention was to destroy the idea of subjective, physical activities & show that the mind of man was nothing more than a machine. Mill was born at Northwater Bridge, in the parish of Logie-Pert, Angus, Scotland. He first received education at the parish school, after which he entered the Montrose Academy. Originally intending to become a minister of the Church of Scotland, Mill received his M.A. in 1794. Mill left Edinburgh in 1797, with a license to preach but gradually lost his faith. He worked for a while as an itinerant tutor in Scotland until 1802, when Stuart invited Mill to join him in London. He tried his hand at journalism, landing a steady job at the "Literary Journal" & feeling confident enough to marry Harriet Burrow in 1805. However, the journal folded in 1806, & soon enough Mill's only source of income was as a writer of hack articles, editorials and essays for a wide assortment of newspapers and journals.

In 1808, Mill forged long-lasting friendships with two very influential men: David Ricardo & Jeremy Bentham. Ricardo would provide him his economics; Bentham would guide his political & social philosophy. Interestingly, the two doctrines seemed to never have met each other in the mind of James Mill. In 1817, Mill introduced his "History of India," which he had been working on the side for many years. Its analysis was clearly inspired by the conjectural histories typical of the Scottish Enlightenment. The success of his History led him to be hired by the London office of the East India Company in 1823, which provided him with financial security for the remainder of his life. He rose gradually through the ranks until he was appointed head of the examiner's office in 1830. Mill's writings & his personal connections with radical politicians helped determine the change of view from theories of the rights of man & the absolute equality of men, as promulgated by the French Revolution. His "Elements of Political Economy" (1821) summarized the views of the philosophical radicals, based primarily on the work of the economist David Ricardo. In this work Mill maintained that the main problem of political reformers was to limit the increase of population, on the assumption that capital does not naturally increase at the same rate as population.

Mill felt that others, in arguing that the mind was like a machine in its operations, had not gone far enough. The mind was a machine that functioned in a same mechanical way as the clock; set in operation by external physical forces & run by internal physical forces. Mill viewed mind as something passive, able to act upon only when the external stimuli is present. The individual simply responded to these stimuli & was not able to act spontaneously. Obviously, then, there was no such thing as freedom of the will. This point of view persisted in the forms of psychology had derived from the mechanistic spirit. Mill believed that the mind must be studied through its reduction or analysis into basic elementary components. This was a strong tenet of mechanistic spirit. To understand complex phenomena, it was necessary to break them down into smaller component parts. He held that sensations & ideas were the only two kinds of mental elements. In the empiricist-associationist tradition all knowledge started with sensations, from which were derived the higher level complexes of ideas through the process of association. Association was a matter of contiguity that could be either synchronous or successive.

According to Mill the mind had no creative function because he felt that association was a purely passive process. Sensations that had occurred together were in a certain order were mechanically reproduced as ideas, & these resulting ideas occurred in the same order as their corresponding sensations. Association was thus treated in very mechanistic terms, with the resulting ideas being merely the accumulation of the individual elements.

Empiricism contributed very little to the future of science, except philosophy begun to turn away from its older tradition of dogmatism & rationalism with the rise of this new movement.

 The increasing interest of a large group of French scientists to the problems of content & structure of personality led them to the investigation of the role of culture & social environment in the process of the development of psyche. One central issue was the relationship between the conscious & unconscious in the psyche, namely the impact of unconscious motives on human actions. Naturally, the first research, which analyzed the nature of hypnosis & suggestion, attracted the attention of scientists to anomalous phenomena. Increased attention to the study of the role of suggestion & hypnosis is associated with the work of Franz Anton Mesmer (1734-1815). Mesmer was born in Iznang, Germany. At the age of 25 he enrolled at the University of Vienna to study law. Eventually he switched to medicine, earning a medical degree in 1766. In his doctoral dissertation Mesmer described his theory of "animal gravitation," in which health in humans was supposedly affected by the gravitational pull of the various planets. He also held that there was a specific fluid-like substance occurring in nature that channeled this gravity. In the 1770s he carried out dramatic demonstrations of his ability to "mesmerize" his patients using magnetized objects. Accused by Viennese physicians of fraud, he left Austria & settled in Paris (1778), where he also came under fire from the medical establishment. Mesmer retired to Switzerland at the beginning of the French Revolution in 1789, where he spent the remaining years of his life. The study of hypnotic phenomena attracted not only physicians but also psychologists. These studies made it possible to study the field of unconscious phenomena, which was out of reach for ordinary experiments. Of equal importance was the study of factors influencing suggestibility, showing the degree of hypnotic depending on age, individual characteristics & mental state of man. Around the turn of the century the study of the role of hypnosis in France attracted two schools at once - Paris & Nancy.

Psychology of Abilities

The unstable social & political climate of the 18-th century was hindering the further progress of capitalism in Germany. During this time many new psychological movements emerged. One of the most popular of those was the psychology of abilities founded by German scientist, philosopher Christian Wolff (1679-1754).

He was born in Breslau, Silesia into a middle class family. His early education involved studying mathematics & physics at the University of Jena. Wolff later switched to philosophy, which he found more suitable in for his pursuit if the truth. In 1703 he became a Privatdozent at the University of Leipzig. He stayed at Leipzig until 1706, when he was called as professor of natural philosophy & mathematics to the University of Halle. Wolff attempted to base theological truths on mathematically certain evidence. Because of his unconventional methods Wolff was ousted in 1723 from his first chair at Halle. When Wolff died he was a very wealthy man, almost entirely due to his income from lecture-fees, salaries & royalties. His school, the Wolffians, was the first school, in the philosophical sense, associated with a German philosopher. Wolff's philosophical thought held almost undisputed leadership in Germany until it was displaced by the Kantian movement.

Wolff's philosophy combined the determinism & optimism of Leibniz. He attempted to make the principle of contradiction the fundamental principle of philosophy. Wolffian philosophy was a science of the possible. It was divided in accordance with the two faculties of the human individual; theoretical & practical. Wolff held that logic formed the introduction to both of these faculties. His theoretical philosophy had for its parts ontology, rational psychology & natural theology. Wolff further divided Practical philosophy into ethics, economics & politics. His moral principle was the realization of human perfection.

Wolff postulated that human knowledge should be understood primarily as an ability or disposition of the human mind to perceive facts about reality. He thought that there are facts of reality & that person can be certain that he perceives these facts as facts. In his theory human consciousness was the starting point from which Wolff established his entire system of human science. Wolff was convinced that we reveal the intuitive knowledge, natural to all humans upon recognizing our own existence as conscious souls.

He stated that self-discovery affords knowledge of the truth. The knowledge of the truth supposedly was helping us to attain certainty in our beliefs. Thus, when humans recognize a particular fact of reality as a fact, they have knowledge of the truth. Wolff identified three facts that people know intuitively from the experience of self-discovery: they exist as a souls/minds; other, material things exist outside of them; & they are certain of their existence & the existence of other things.

Wolff stated that the artificial logic could provide the rules for reaching reliable conclusions in scientific disciplines, i.e. artificial logic differs from the natural way of thinking only insofar as the former is a distinct explanation of the latter. That the rules governing people's natural way of thinking can be made explicit & formalized in an artificial logic is significant in two different respects. First, it implied that the logical principles needed for formulating sound judgments were already built into the very structure of the human understanding, & second the ability to make explicit an artificial logic allows for a reliable method to be employed in all areas of human inquiry.

Wolff viewed knowledge in a continuous state of progress. He firmly believed in intelligible order & interconnectedness between all the different disciplines. Wolff, however, did not distinguish between the understanding & reason. So by stating that science was a habit of the understanding, he actually meant to claim that human reason can discern groups of facts, establish a certain order & interconnectedness between these facts. To him Individual sciences such as philosophy, cosmology, or psychology, were simply the various sets of demonstrable facts. Naturally Wolff's system of human science was constructed according to a notion of rational order. He held that certain sciences whose subject matter was more basic & which ultimately stood as the foundation for other sciences had a more valid, specialized focus.

In Wolff's opinion the main objective of the philosopher was to provide the manner & reason of their possibility, because by sufficient reason one understands that, from which it is understood why something is or can be. He considered the notion of sufficient reason to have a much broader scope of application to include the set of all possible objects. The idea that everything has a sufficient reason was presented formally by Wolff as the Principle of Sufficient Reason (PSR), which was considered to be an innate principle of the human mind & a self-evident logical axiom. The self-evident nature of PSR becomes apparent, argued Wolff, when we consider three specific aspects of our rational/conscious experience. First, PSR is never contradicted by experience; the second is that we can recognize singular instances, or examples, of it in our experience of the world, & the third is that we have an inquisitive attitude toward our future life & our surroundings. He saw these characteristics as a necessary presupposition to be a part of our conscious experience.

Wolff postulated that the world was an extended whole that was composed of a finite number of interacting physical bodies. The conclusions that Wolff drew regarding the wholeness of the world were simply extrapolated from his analysis of physical bodies, which was given from two different perspectives. First, bodies were defined as aggregates of simple substances & second, the reality of bodies was explained in terms of interacting primitive.

Wolff's lifelong commitment to empirical knowledge from a rationalistic standpoint was epitomized in his approach to psychology. He was willing to establish a set of principles about the soul based on observation & experience, after which he was planning to give an account of why & how the human soul was the way that it was. The empirical knowledge of person's consciousness was viewed as a special case of knowledge. For Wolff it provided the starting points for both proving the existence of the human soul & identifying its principal operations. In Wolff's opinion empirical psychology was the science of establishing through experience the principles from which a reason was given of those things which occur in the human soul. On the other hand the rational psychology was considered to be the science of those things which were possible through the human soul. In the empirical approach, the content of introspective experience allowed for the construction of a nominal definition of the soul. Wolff's psychology was also concerned with the discussion of the mind-body problem, in both the empirical & rational treatments of the subject.

Wolff was often regarded as the central historical figure, which linked the philosophical systems of Leibniz & Kant. Despite the fact that his influence was largely isolated to German schools & universities during & shortly after his lifetime, he did receive some international acclaim.

A different version of the psychology of abilities was being developed by the so called Scottish school. In order to protect the religious dogmas of the time they criticized the materialistic view of the sensual experience, as well as idealistic sensualism & associationism of Berkley & Hume. The founder of the above mentioned Scottish school was Thomas Reid (1710-1796). He was born on of Strachan in Kincardineshire, Scotland. Reid's father was a Presbyterian minister. He received his early education at Kincardine parish school & later in Aberdeen Grammar School. At the age of 12 Reid enrolled in Marischal College, in Aberdeen. Here he studied arts, later switching to the study divinity. Reid graduated in 1731, after which he was admitted to the ministry of the Church of Scotland. He also worked as a librarian at the Marischal College from 1733–36. In 1740 Reid married his cousin Elizabeth Reid, & during their long life together they raised nine children. In 1752 he gave up his ministry at New Machar to become a professor of philosophy at King's College, Aberdeen. He continued teaching until he retired at the age of 71. For the remaining 15 years of his life Reid published extensively. The two most important works of this period were "Essays on the Intellectual Powers of Man" (1785) & "Essays on the Active Powers of Man" (1788). Reid died on Oct. 7, 1796.

Reid's theory of conception is at the heart of faculty psychology. In it, conception lies at the heart of the operations of the intellectual faculties because they provided the intentional content to mental states. Reid thought that the mind has an irreducible capacity for intentional conception. He developed his account of the objects of conception by describing three different types of conceptions, each of which had an analogue in painting. First, he held that one can conceive of fanciful creatures and unreal beings, which do not represent something in the world. These were like paintings of fantastical places & creatures. In the second group of conceptions were copies of originals, which were similar to pictures taken from life. Third kind of conception was identical to the copies which the painter makes from pictures done before.

Reid held that people knew what the intentional contents of their thoughts were. But the Way of Ideas jeopardized Reid's commitment to the obviousness of our introspective ability to identify what we are thinking about. Like the veil of perception created by the representational role of ideas, there was also a veil of conception. The seed of Reid's argument was in Hume's remark that mental events appear entirely loose & separate. According to him Hume's causal explanation of reverberating impacts on impressions in the mind did not explain the content of our thoughts, since he described his theory of thought as corpuscular because impressions were atomic, separable mental states without any determinate intentional link to anything else. As with Reid's appeal to the irreducible intentionality of conception, Reid's position regarding the conception of non-existent objects has proven inaccurate & difficult to explain. Though his commitment to the importance of self-knowledge & the transparency of thought was obvious, Reid risked his allegiance to common sense by asserting that people think of non-existent objects directly & without thinking of a mental intermediary.

Reid developed a direct theory of memory according to which the objects of memory were events in the past. He tried to provide sufficient continuity of the self through time to ground sameness of person without lapsing into Hum's skepticism about the self. In Reid's theory memory was a faculty of its own & the objects of memory were viewed as events in the past. Memories were accompanied by their own phenomenology & sensory experience.

In Reid's theory there were two types of memory; distinct & indistinct. He stated that distinct memories were "real knowledge" & indistinct memories were not. He postulated that memory was always accompanied with the belief of that which we remember, as perception is accompanied with the belief of that which we perceive. He further held that in mature years, & in a sound state of mind, every man feels that he must believe what he distinctly remembers, though he can give no other reason of his belief, but that he remembers the thing distinctly.

Reid's moral philosophy was quite diverse, composed of several core theses. These include: 1 that human beings have an active power that is not causally determined by prior causes, laws of nature, or the conjunction of the two; 2 that moral statements were to be interpreted as propositions with subject/object content; 3 that truth makers for moral statements were non-natural & independent of the mental states of human beings; & 4 that moral knowledge was produced in a way structurally similar to knowledge of the external world through perception. Obviously Reid's moral philosophy was influenced by his belief in a benevolent, just, Christian God, although he did not endorse divine command theory.

Thomas Reid was one of the founders of the "common sense" school of philosophy. He viewed common sense as those tenets that we cannot help but believe, given that we are constructed the way we are constructed. Reid was also known for his epistemology of sensation. He held that sensations served to make us directly aware of real objects without the aid of any intervening medium. He criticized Locke's view of personal identity & Hume's view of causation. However, Reid also wrote on a wide variety of other philosophical topics including ethics, aesthetics & various topics in the philosophy of mind.

Another Scottish philosopher Dugald Stewart (1753-1828) was a successor & active supporter of Reid's theories. He was born in Edinburgh. Stewart's father was professor of mathematics in the University of Edinburgh. First Stewart was educated in Edinburgh at the Royal High School followed by the University, where he took mathematics & moral philosophy. In 1771 he went to Glasgow, where he studied under Thomas Reid. After a short stay in Glasgow Dugald Stewart was summoned by his father, whose health was beginning to fail, to conduct the mathematical classes in the University of Edinburgh. After acting three years as his father's substitute he was elected professor of mathematics in conjunction with him in 1775. In addition to his mathematical work, he delivered an original course of lectures on morals. Stewart's course on moral philosophy was unique, because it embraced lectures on political philosophy. From 1800 onwards a separate course of lectures was delivered on political economy, then almost unknown as a science to the general public. In 1792 he published the first volume of the "Elements of the Philosophy of the Human Mind." The second volume appeared in 1814 & the third in1827. In 1810 Stewart published his "Philosophical Essays", in 1814 the second volume of the "Elements", in 1811 the first part & in 1821 the second part of the "Dissertation" written for the Encyclopedia Britannica Supplement, entitled "A General View of the Progress of Metaphysical, Ethical, and Political Philosophy since the Revival of Letters." In 1827 he published the third volume of the "Elements, & in 1828, a few weeks before his death, "The Philosophy of the Active and Moral Powers."

Stewart noted that there is a lack of direct evidence for the origin of language. He also used the term 'conjectural history' for the sort of history exemplified by the earlier accounts of the origin of language. Thus, conjectural history worked against the illegitimate encroachment of religion into the lives of people who were too quick to reach for God as the solution to a problem. As regards the credentials of Stewart's 'incontrovertible logical maxim', if the claim that human nature is invariant is an empirical claim, it must be based on observation of our contemporaries & on evidence of people's lives in other places & at other times. Of course we can go back so far that we have no facts beyond the generalities that we have worked out in the light of our experience, but to rely on conjecture in order to support the very principle that forms the first premise in any exercise in conjectural history is to come suspiciously close to arguing in a circle. The incontrovertible logical maxim of Dugald Stewart should probably be accorded at most the status of a well-supported empirical generalization. Indeed, he was responsible for making the "Scottish philosophy" predominant in early 19th-century Europe. In the second half of the century, as with so much of Enlightenment thought, it came to be seen as superseded, & Stewart's work as merely the reproduction of his teacher Reid. He upheld Reid's psychological method & expounded the "common-sense" doctrine. Perhaps the part of his originality lay in his readiness to depart from the pure Scottish tradition & incorporate elements of moderate empiricism.

The Study of Neuro-Psychological Functions & the rise of Materialism

Albrecht von Haller (1708-1777) was one of the most famous physiologists of the 18-th century. He was born at Berne. Haller was very gifted as a child, for instance at the age of four he used to read & expound the Bible to his father's servants. According to various sources, when he was ten he had prepared a Greek & a Hebrew vocabulary & compiled a collection of two thousand biographies of famous people. At fifteen he was an author of numerous metrical translations from Ovid, Horace & Virgil. Haller finished medical school at Leiden when he was 19. Then he went back to Bern. He tried to find a professorship in history & rhetoric. He did some lecturing on anatomy. He also walked the mountains writing poetry. Haller published his book of poems when he was 40. The medical school at Göttingen finally gave Haller a position. He stayed there 17 years. It was there he rewrote physiology.

Haller is best known for revolutionizing the theories of blood flow & heart action. He redefined the relation between respiration & blood flow, explained nerve action in muscles & gave new precise insights into human reproduction. In 1766 Haller published his "Physiological Elements of the Human Body," in which he described the advances in physiology made since the time of William Harvey, enriched with his own conclusions. Prior to Haller, physiology was based on the views of René Descartes, who held that bodily systems were essentially mechanical. Haller opposed Descartes stating that muscular irritability was inherent in the fiber & not caused by external factors.

Haller's research was concentrated on two specific reactions: irritability & sensibility. He defined irritability as the contraction of a muscle that occurs when a stimulus is applied to the muscle. Haller also concluded that irritability increases when the stimulus is applied to the nerve connected to a muscle. He further discovered that ordinary tissue does not respond to stimuli, but that nerves do. He was able to demonstrate that stimuli applied to nerve endings traveled through the body, into the spinal column, & eventually into the brain.

In the beginning of the 18-th century French materialistic movements supporting the idea of empirical knowledge were becoming popular than ever. The main critics of scholasticism & metaphysics were Francois Voltaire (1694-1778) & Etienne Bonnot de Condillac (1715-1780). Condillac was born at Grenoble, France.

He received education in Paris at the Sorbonne & at St-Suplice, where he was ordained a priest in 1740. Condillac later abandoned priesthood to become a writer. He was influenced by John Locke's psychology & empiricism & by Newton's search for fundamental principles.

Condillac's writings in fact were similar to Locke's principles, except they reduced the operations of human understanding to one principle, sensation. He viewed reflection as a sequence & comparison of sensations. In Condillac's opinion language was the source of man's superiority to animals. In his "Traité des sensations" (1754) Condillac demonstrated how ideas originate through sensation. The work stressed the integration of man's senses & noted that the higher forms of understanding develop from mere animal sensation. Condillac opposed Descartes' view of animals by declaring that man was in many ways similar to animals.

Condillac moved to Parma in 1758 to tutor Louis XV's grandson. Here he wrote a 16-volume "Cours d'études pour l'instruction du Prince de Parme". Nine years later he returned to France. Condillac refused to tutor the Dauphin's sons & retired instead to a quiet life of writing at Flux.

He partially agreed with Locke's deduction of the knowledge from sensation & reflection. Condillac actively criticized those modern systems which were based upon abstract principles or upon unsound hypotheses. His polemic was directed against the innate ideas of the Cartesians, Malebranche's faculty-psychology & Leibniz's monadism.

Condillac considered mind to be an immaterial substance. Thus when it senses, nothing actually passes into it from the outside world or the body. Instead the action of external objects on the sense organs brings about changes in the body. He viewed these changes as the cause of the production of sensations in the mind. In Condillac's theory sensations were the modifications persons being. Therefore to understand them as images means to treat them as ideas rather than simply as sensations. Condillac asserted that sensations were as representative as any other thought experienced by human mind.

Condillac defined perception as the impression first occasioned in the mind by the action of objects on the senses. He thought that people are always conscious of perceptions, but that this consciousness comes in varying degrees. Attention was viewed as a high degree of consciousness. Normally attention is drawn to those perceptions that are most pleasurable or painful. Therefore experience of pleasure & pain is what first instructs people where to focus their attention.

He maintained that certain perceptions that person attends to can seem to drown out the others & produce the illusion that they alone exist, whereas those perceptions that one is less conscious of can be so faint that it is impossible to recall that one have had them the instant after the stimulus that produced them fades. Those perceptions that person attends to can also continue for some time after the stimulus that produced them has ceased. This produced an experience that Condillac called reminiscence. In his famous "Essay," Condillac distinguished between reminiscence, understood as the perception that one perceived something that one has perceived before, & memory. He did not see memory as the process of forming an image of something one has experienced before; instead, Condillac described it as the process of forming an idea just of signs that have been associated with a previously experienced object. Thus, he thought that the operation of forming an image of a previously experienced object was not memory but imagination. Imagination became possible once a perception had become familiar from a number of previous experiences, which give the mind a facility to repeat that perception at will. The operation of imagination was believed to be enhanced if the perception was simple, composed of simple parts that were organized in accord with some guiding principle that could be invoked in reconstructing it. Because links with other, customarily connected perceptions needed to be noticed, & attention was a function of need, which was in turn established by past experience of pleasure & pain, imagination is ultimately viewed as a function of past experience.

In Condillac's writings sensations were occasioned by the action of external objects. He thought that the objects that affect human sense organs must be extended. Condillac argued that while a person had a clear idea what it meant to attribute extension to an object, he didn't have a clear idea what it meant to say that objects were colored or scented, and that while there is evidence that proves that we do not always perceive the sizes or shapes of objects correctly, there is no evidence that proves that we are wrong to think that external objects have some form of extension. Condillac attempted to prove that experience leads one to form the idea that there are extended, external objects that bear the qualities of color, taste, & smell exhibited in one's sensations. He also stated that the question of whether material things exist was not one that we are in any position to answer. Condillac's theory of sensation also fit uneasily with his claim that the mind is immaterial, because he took sensations to be modifications of the mind's being. For example a being that we would describe as seeing yellow would at first experience itself as simply being yellow, & touch would instruct it to attribute this yellowness to other objects.

In his "Treatise" Condillac endorsed Berkeley's position that people learn to perceive depth. He also thought that people do not immediately appreciate the fact that colors are bounded & figured even in two dimensions, but need to learn that they have these features. The process of learning to perceive shape does not transform our color sensations & lead them to acquire properties they did not previously have. Condillac thus appears to have been committed to four mutually antagonistic propositions: colors being viewed as sensations, colors being extended, sensations being the modifications of the mind's being & the mind being unextended.

Julien Offray La Mettrie (1709-1751) was perhaps best known for combining Descartes' teachings with his own modified version of sensualism. He was born at Saint-Malo in Brittany to a wealthy merchant's family. He received his early education at the collages of Coutances & Caen. La Mettrie also went to College du Plessis in Paris & the Jansenist school of theology. In 1725 he enrolled at the D'Harcourt College to study philosophy & natural science. While at D'Harcourt, La Mettrie decided to turn to study of medicine. For five years, he studied at faculty of medicine in Paris. In 1733 La Mettrie went to Holland to study under the famous Dutch botanist & physician Herman Boerhaave. Few years later he started a medical practice in his home region of Saint-Malo, disseminating the works & theories of Boerhaave through the publication & translation of several works. In 1742 La Mettrie travelled to Paris where he obtained the appointment of surgeon to the Gardes Francaises regiment. One time during the attack of fever he made observations on himself with reference to the action of quickened blood circulation upon thought. This simple observation led him to a great conclusion that mental processes were to be accounted for as the effects of organic changes in the brain & nervous system. La Mettrie included & expanded this conclusion in his earliest philosophical works. His publications eventually became so popular that he chose to quit his position with the French Guards. La Mettrie's materialism was in many ways the product of his medical concerns, drawing on the work of 17th-century predecessors such as the Epicurean physician Guillaume Lamy.

La Mettrie was the founder of the unique theory of remorse, in which he expressed his view about the inauspicious effects of the feelings of guilt acquired at early age during the process of enculturation. This was the idea which brought him the enmity of virtually all thinkers of the French enlightenment. In 1746 La Mettrie fled to Leiden. There in 1747 he published anonymously his infamous work, "Man a Machine." By 1748 his works were burned even in Holland & he was forced to flee.

Eventually La Mettrie accepted Frederick the Great's offer of sanctuary in Prussia & lived there from February 1748. His famous "L'Homme plante" appeared in 1748. In it La Mettrie proposed (as did Condillac) that the degree of a creature's intelligence depends on the variety & number of needs experienced by that being. He not only adopted the engaging style of Enlightenment philosophers, but also applied a thoroughgoing materialism to human beings. Using evidence drawn from anatomy, physiology, & psychology, he demonstrated the effects of the body on the soul & the comparability between humans & animals. His La Mettrie's materialism did not distinguish between conscious, voluntary movement & unconscious, instinctive movement.

He often compared humans to lower creatures & placed all creatures in the context of the unfolding of matter & motion in an evolutionary process. La Mettrie examined the implications of materialism for moral values & questioned whether moral systems corresponded to human nature as corroborated by his physiological understanding of human beings. Vice & virtue, he concluded, were arbitrarily constructed by society to serve its interests, but those interests were often at odds with the physiological constitution of the individual. He hoped that, by recognizing the arbitrary nature of its moral notions, society would reward a greater array of human behaviors. La Mettrie was particularly critical of both stoicism & Christianity as moral systems.

One of the most influential thinkers during the Enlightenment in eighteenth century Europe was Jean Jacques Rousseau (1712-1778). He was born in Geneva. When Rousseau was 10 his father got into a legalbattle with a wealthy landowner on whose lands he had been caught trespassing. To avoid certain defeat he moved away to Nyon in the territory of Bern. At the age of 13 Rousseau was apprenticed to an engraver. In 1728 he moved to Annecy, where he met Louise de Warens, who played a crucial role in his conversion to Catholicism. At the age 30 Rousseau went to Paris to become a musician & a composer, but after two years spent serving a post at the French Embassy in Venice he returned. In 1745 he met Condillac & Diderot. Five years later, in 1750 he published an essay called "Discourse on the Arts and Sciences."

In 1757 Rousseau moved to lodgings near the country home of the Duke of Luxemburg at Montmorency, where some of his most significant works. In 1761 he published a novel, "Julie or the New Heloise." & in 1762, he published two major philosophical treatises: "The Social Contract" & "Emile." Because of their antireligious content both of these books were condemned. Rousseau was forced to flee France. He went to Switzerland where he wrote his autobiography. In1765 after encountering difficulties with Swiss authorities, he spent time in Berlin & Paris, & eventually moved to England at the invitation of David Hume. In 1767 he returned to the southeast of France incognito. Rousseau eventually returned to Paris in 1770 & wrote "Rousseau: Judge of Jean-Jacques" & the "Reveries of the Solitary Walker", which would turn out to be his final works. His "Confessions" were published several years after his death.

According to Rousseau the uncorrupted morals had the ability to prevail in the so called state of nature. He also denied the fact that morality was a construct of society; instead he considered it as "natural" in the sense of "innate", an outgrowth of man's instinctive disinclination to witness suffering. Rousseau's natural man was identical to a solitary animal & the "natural" goodness of humanity was thus, the goodness of an animal, which was neither good nor bad. He held that human civilization had always been artificial, creating inequality & envy.

Rousseau, just like Hobbes, was known to attack the classical notion of human beings as naturally social. The "Discourse on the Origin of Inequality" was comprised of four main parts: a dedication to the Republic of Geneva, a short preface, a first part, & a second part. In it Rousseau viewed society as an invention & explained the nature of human beings by stripping them of all of the qualities brought about by socialization. Thus, understanding human nature equals to understanding what humans are like in a genuine state of nature. He also denied that men were ever in the pure state of nature, citing revelation as a source which tells us that God directly endowed the first man with a capacity to understand. According to Rousseau some of the stages in the progression from nature to civil society were empirically observable in primitive tribes.

Rousseau argued that previous accounts have taken civilized human beings & simply removed laws, government & technology. Thus, they have failed to actually depict humans in the true state of nature. Rousseau held that purely natural human beings were different from the egoistic human kind proposed by Hobbs. He agreed that self-preservation was one principle of motivation for human actions, but unlike Hobbes, it was not the only principle. He thought that self-preservation, or more generally self-interest, was only one of two principles of the human soul.

Rousseau was trying to explain the complex series of historical events that moved humans from their original state to the state of present day civil society. He saw sees this development as occurring in a series of stages; from the pure state of nature, humans begin to organize into temporary groups for the purposes of specific tasks like hunting an animal, but the groups last only as long as the task takes to be completed, & then they dissolve as quickly as they came together. The next stage had more permanent social relationships including the traditional family, from which arises conjugal & paternal love. The following stage in the historical development took place when the arts of agriculture & metallurgy were discovered. Eventually there were distinct social classes & strict notions of property, creating conflict & ultimately a state of war.

At the time Rousseau was one of the few to attack the institution of private property. He held that the main goal of government should be to ensure freedom, equality & justice for all. Rousseau was against the statement that the will of the majority was always correct. His ideas about education have profoundly influenced modern educational theory. Although Rousseau gained fame as an educationist, his formal education ended at about the age of twelve, but despite his incomplete education he became one of the most dominant thinkers of the 18th century. Unlike Rousseau, Claude Adrien Helvetius (1715-1771) held that intellectual & moral qualities of a man are shaped by the unique circumstances of his life.

He was born in Paris into a family of distinguished physicians. Helvetius was taught privately until the age of 11, after which he enrolled in the Jesuits' Louis-le-grand school. Later he went to Caen to become a tax collector. Here he widened the scope of his interests; writing poetry, reading Hobbs, Locke & Voltaire.

In 1755 Helvetius wrote his famous "De l'esprit." In 1758 the book was offered for sale in Paris, but his fame was short lived, soon he was exiled for 2 years from Paris, & the sale of his book was forbidden. The Sorbonne condemned the book, while the priests persuaded the court that it was full of the most dangerous doctrines. The book was declared to be heretical & so atheistic that it was condemned by Church & State & was publicly burned. In 1764 Helvetius visited England & in 1765, Prussia. He wrote "De l'homme" & "Du Bonheur" in 1769. Two years later he died in Paris.

After the release of "De l'espirit" the religious authorities began to fear the spread of atheism and wanted to shut down this modern school thought as quickly as possible. This great publicity resulted in the book being translated into almost all the languages of Europe. Helvetius's theory was in many ways similar to Locke's presenting vices & virtues as the result of physical sensation. In it human beings were born with similar potential & impelled by self-interest.

Helvetius was a follower of the utilitarian school of philosophy which held that all man's faculties could be reduced to physical sensation, even memory, comparison, judgment. Helvetius's self-interest, founded on the love of pleasure & the fear of pain, was the only spring of judgment, action & affection. Thus self-sacrifice was prompted by the fact that the sensation of pleasure outweighs the accompanying pain.

According to Helvetius all men have an equal disposition for understanding. Just like Locke he viewed the human mind as a blank slate, but free not only from innate ideas but also from innate natural dispositions. In his theory physiological constitution was at most a peripheral factor in men's characters. All of the inequalities were independent of natural organization, & had their cause in the unequal desire for instruction, which in turn, emerged from passions. In his opinion such natural equality applied to all men in all nations, & thus the differences in national characteristics were not the result of innate differences between the people therein, but rather a byproduct of the system education.

The leader of French materialists Denis Diderot (1713-1784) held a different position. He was born at Langres, France. He was educated by the Jesuits. Diderot earned his Master of Arts degree in philosophy in 1732. He abandoned the idea of entering the clergy & decided instead to study law, but he changed his mind again & turned to writing. His father expected him to study medicine or law, but Diderot spent his time with books & women. When his financial support was ended, Diderot then worked for the attorney, as a tutor & a freelance writer. Diderot gained first notice in the 1740s as a translator of English books. In 1745 Diderot became the editor of the "Encyclopédie." This project absorbed most of his time. Eventually his editing work developed into an overview of world knowledge, which was intended to illustrate its inherent harmony & order. The "Encyclopédie" was published between 1751 & 1772 in 17 volumes of text & 11 volumes of engravings. While working on the "Encyclopédie" Diderot wrote most of his own important works as well, among them "Lettre sur les sourds et muets" (1751), "Pensées sur l'interprétation de la nature" (1753), & so on. Because of his radical thoughts several of Diderot's books were confiscated & came out posthumously. Diderot's "Supplement au Voyage de Bougainville", in which he indicted slavery & colonialism, was not published until 1796. In 1765 Diderot sold his library to Catherine II of Russia to increase her daughter's dowry. The Empress gave him money to improve the collections & for other similar services. 1774 Diderot made a long journey to St. Petersburg to thank Catherine personally & plan the creation of a Russian university. The hardships of the journey weakened his health, which was never robust. He died of gastro-intestinal problems in Paris on July 31, 1784.

Diderot was a materialist & a determinist He believed that individual character was principally the product of heredity, & man was generally susceptible to modification by environmental influences. He ascribed most of the evil he saw around him to the baleful influence of European & especially French society, but his attempts to develop a moral code based on natural principles were doomed to failure by the impossibility of formulating a definition of nature which could underpin social morality. According to Diderot only the virtuous man can know true happiness.

In his works Diderot developed his materialist philosophy and arrived at startling intuitive insights into biology and chemistry; in speculating on the origins of life without divine intervention, for instance, he foreshadowed the evolutionary theories of Charles Darwin & put forth a strikingly prophetic picture of the cellular structure of matter. His ideas, often propounded in the form of paradox, stemmed from a sense of life's ambiguities & a profound understanding of the complexities & contradictions inherent in human nature.

Diderot held a completely materialistic view of the universe, suggesting that all human behavior was determined by heredity. In addition he rejected the Idea of progress, because he thought that the aim of progressing through technology was doomed to fail. That was one of the reasons why he founded his philosophy on experiment & the study of probabilities. Diderot was also one of the pre-19th-century leaders in the movement away from mathematics & physics, as a source of certain knowledge, to biological probability and historical insight.

Another famous materialist of the late 18-th century was a physician Pierre Jean George Cabanis (1757-1808). He was an author of many improvements in public health & the founder of the French psycho-physiological materialism.

Cabanis was born at Cosnac, France to a wealthy family. His father was a lawyer and agronomist. When he was ten, Cabanis enrolled at the college of Brives, where he showed great aptitude for study. After being expelled from Brives (for constantly rebelling against teachers) he was taken to Paris by his father & left to carry on his studies at his own discretion. He spent two years in Poland & Germany. When he returned to Paris he decided to become a poet. His father convinced him to give up writing & consider a new career in medicine. In 1789 his "Observations on hospitals", won him an appointment as administrator of hospitals in Paris. Four years later Cabanis became professor of hygiene at the medical school of Paris. In 1799 he was the head of the department of legal medicine & the history of medicine.

Gradual decline of his health made it impossible for Cabanis to practice medicine. Because of this he became more interested in theory & problems of the medical science. Cabanis began writing his complete edition of in 1825. He eventually published five volumes. In his writings Psychology was directly linked to biology. In Cabanis's theory all of the intellectual processes were stemming from sensibility. Sensibility itself was viewed as a property of the nervous system.

Cabanis was a follower of the so called vitalistic school of biology, holding that life was something added to the organism. He stated that over & above the universally diffused sensibility there was some living & productive power known as Nature. He ascribed intelligence and will to this power. He sought a mechanistic explanation of the universe, nature & human behavior. According to Cabanis pleasure, self-interest & the pursuit of happiness along with self-preservation were the only motives of action. Cabanis refused to recognize notions not based on phenomena or sensations. He considered the understanding of the "mechanism of language" essential to the understanding of the "mechanism of the intellect."

In his work Cabanis described life as feeling & discussed the difference between sensitivity & irritability. He thought that the latter he was only a result of the former, which was the basic biological phenomenon. Cabanis was convinced that the action of the nervous system was only a specialized application of the laws of physical motion, which were in turn, the source of all phenomena. The nervous system was affected by internal changes, that is, by memory and imagination; thus within man exists "another internal man" in constant action. The generative organs were viewed as glandular & their secretions influenced the brain & the whole body. Essentially Cabanis was only interested in cause & effect on the level of phenomena. He was much influenced by La Mettrie & the so called man-machine school. He criticized the psychological method of Condillac & the sensationists, which was limited to external sensations. He preferred the physiological approach, which emphasized hereditary dispositions, the state of the organs, dreams & automatic impulses. Cabanis was interested in the moral and social improvement of humankind, which he considered possible through an understanding of physiology.

German Idealism

Immanuel Kant's (1724-1804) initial goal was to make philosophy truly scientific, but his jargon made his central writings nearly impossible for the uninitiated to understand. Perhaps his most original contribution to philosophy was his "Copernican Revolution," that, as he stated, it was the representation that made the object possible rather than the object that made the representation possible. This introduced the human mind as an active originator of experience rather than just a passive recipient of perception.

Immanuel Kant (1724-1804) was born in the East Prussian city of Konigsberg. He studied at the local university, & worked there as a tutor & professor for more than forty years, never travelling more than fifty miles from home. Kant's intellectual work easily justified his own claim to have affected a Copernican revolution in philosophy. Beginning with his Inaugural Dissertation (1770) on the difference between right- & left-handed spatial orientations, Kant patiently worked out the most comprehensive & influential philosophical program of the modern era.

Kant studied the philosophy of Leibniz & Wolff under Martin Knutzen, a rationalist who was also familiar with developments in British philosophy. He also introduced Kant to the new mathematical physics of Newton. Knutzen dissuaded Kant from the theory of pre-established harmony, which he regarded as "the pillow for the lazy mind". He also dissuaded the young scholar from idealism, which was negatively regarded by most philosophers in the 18th century. His father's death in 1746 interrupted his studies. Kant became a private tutor in the smaller towns surrounding Konigsberg, but continued his scholarly research. In 1749 he published his first philosophical work titled "Thoughts on the True Estimation of Living Forces." In 1755 Kant introduced his "General History of Nature & Theory of the Heavens" which argued that the system of heavenly bodies could have developed from an unformed nebula. Later he received his doctor's degree for the work On "Fire," & was appointed a lecturer at the university.

He end up teaching many different subjects like metaphysics, moral philosophy, natural theology, anthropology, as well as mathematics, physics,

& physical geography. After Kant had unsuccessfully applied in 1758 for professorship, he wrote an essay on optimism. In 1766 he worked as an assistant-librarian in the royal palace. He declined the offers of professor-ship at the universities of Erlangen & Jena, & eventually in 1770 Kant was appointed professor of logic & metaphysics at his native Konigsberg. His inaugural dissertation was "On the Forms and Principles of the Sensible and Intelligible World."

Kant was a dean of the faculties six times & rector of the university twice before retiring. During this period he published "Critique of Pure Reason," "Prolegomena to Any Future Metaphysics" (1783), "Critique of Practical Reason" (1788), & "Critique of Judgment" (1790). Kant never left his home town to see the world outside his study. He believed in his own rational thinking, & did not consider traveling necessary to solve the problems of philosophy.

Kant was convinced that the rational structure of the mind reflected the rational structure of the world. The paradoxes of Kant's efforts to recon-cile his conflicting approaches & requirements made it very difficult for most philosophers to take the overall system seriously.

In his theory science was distinct & separate from anything that would relate to morality or religion. The endless confusion & conflict that still results from people trying to figure out whether or how science & religion should fit together was avoided by Kant. In the world, everything affected everything else, but the traditional view was that God was free of any ex-ternal causal influences. His theory prevented psychological explanations for behavior, however illuminating, being used to excuse moral responsi-bility & accountability. One benefit of Kant's theory was that for the first time in the history of philosophy there is an explanation that can account for the simple phenomenon of sleep. Descartes apparently did not realize that when he made thought the essence of soul, this ruled out a state of non-thought for the mind, i.e. sleep or unconsciousness. Unconscious-ness, however, was as much of a theoretical challenge for the Empiricists as for the Rationalists. If the mind was the passive recipient of perception, & perception was conscious, the mind would be perpetually conscious. You can close your eyes to go to sleep, but hearing & sensations continue. Only with Kant's theory, of active synthesis, was consciousness an activity that may or may not take up certain sensations, or anything, into aware-ness.

Kant's exposition of the transcendental ideas began from the logical dis-tinction among categorical, hypothetical, and disjunctive syllogisms. The completion of metaphysical reasoning, according to Kant, required transcendental ideas of three sorts; 1.The Psychological Idea was the concept of the soul as a permanent substance which lived forever, 2.The Cosmological Idea was the concept of a complete determination of the nature of the world as it must be constituted in itself & 3.The Theological Idea was the concept of an absolutely perfect & most real being or god.

Kant's aim was to move beyond the traditional dichotomy between rationalism & empiricism. The rationalists had tried to show that we can understand the world by careful use of reason; this guarantees the indubitability of our knowledge but leaves serious questions about its practical content. The empiricists, on the other hand, had argued that all of our knowledge must be firmly grounded in experience; practical content is thus secured, but it turns out that we can be certain of very little. Kant thought that both approaches have failed because they were premised on the same mistaken assumption.

Progress in philosophy, according to Kant, required that we frame the epistemological problem in an entirely different way. The crucial question was not how we could bring ourselves to understand the world, but how the world came to be understood by us. Instead of trying, by reason or experience, to make our concepts match the nature of objects, Kant held, we must allow the structure of our concepts shape our experience of objects.

Later German Idealists believed that there were problems with Kant's system & sought to place it on firmer grounds. The three most prominent German Idealists were Fichte, Schelling & Hegel. Georg Wilhelm Friedrich Hegel (1770-1831) attempted, throughout his published writings as well as in his lectures, to elaborate a comprehensive & systematic ontology from a "logical" starting point. He was born in Stuttgart. At the age of three Hegel went to the "German School". When he entered the "Latin School" aged five, he already knew the first declension, having been taught it by his mother. In 1776 Hegel entered Stuttgart's Gymnasium. Hegel spent the years 1788-1793 as a theology student in nearby Tubingen. After receiving his theological certificate from the Tubingen Seminary, Hegel became a house tutor to an aristocratic family in Berne. During this period he composed the text which has become known as the "Life of Jesus" and a book-length manuscript entitled "The Positivity of the Christian Religion".

Around the turn of the century his interests turned to the issues in the "critical" philosophy of Kant. In the 1790s Jena had become a centre of both "Kantian" philosophy & the early Romantic Movement, & by the time of Hegel's arrival Schelling had already become an established figure.

In late 1801, Hegel published his first philosophical work, "The Difference between Fichte's and Schelling's System of Philosophy," & up until 1803 worked closely with Schelling, with whom he edited the "Critical Journal of Philosophy." In his "Difference" essay Hegel had argued that Schelling's approach succeeded where Fichte's failed in the project of systematizing & thereby completing Kant's transcendental idealism.

In 1807 Hegel published his first major work, the "Phenomenology of Spirit," which showed a divergence from his earlier, seemingly more Schellingian, approach. The occupation of Jena by Napoleon's troops as Hegel was completing the manuscript closed the university and Hegel left the town. Now without a university appointment he worked for a short time, apparently very successfully, as an editor of a newspaper in Bamberg, & then from 1808-1815 as the headmaster and philosophy teacher at a "gymnasium" in Nuremberg. In 1816 he managed to return to his university career by being appointed to a chair in philosophy at the University of Heidelberg. Then in 1818, he was offered and took up the chair of philosophy at the University of Berlin, the most prestigious position in the German philosophical world. In 1821 in Berlin Hegel published his major work in political philosophy, "Elements of the Philosophy of Right." During the following ten years up to his death in 1831 Hegel enjoyed celebrity at Berlin, & published subsequent versions of the "Encyclopedia."

Hegel became known for his criticism of the traditional epistemological distinction of objective from subjective. He offered his own dialectical account of the development of consciousness from individual sensation through social concern with ethics and politics to the pure consciousness of the World-Spirit in art, religion, & philosophy.

He offered a metaphysical & religious view of God. His theory had many similarities to the type of elaborate idealist metaphysics found in Leibniz. Hegel often invoked imagery consistent with the types of neo-Platonic conceptions of the universe. He held that the mind of God can become actual only via its particularization in the minds of "his" finite creatures. Thus, in our consciousness of God, we somehow serve to realize his *own* self-consciousness, and, thereby, his own perfection. Perhaps the most important consequence of Hegel's metaphysics concerned history & the idea of historical development or progress. Hegel had not only advocated a disastrous political conception of the state, but he had also tried to underpin such advocacy with dubious logical-metaphysical speculations.

In Hegel's theory the subjective Spirit was observed through truths about human nature. In every concrete instantiation, consciousness strived to reach perfect knowledge, & the path of its struggle could, of course, be described as the movement from thesis through antithesis to synthesis. The first level of consciousness was that of sensory awareness of objects. Despite the fact that sensory images invariably appear to us as concrete particulars, wholly unrelated to each other, we naturally universalize the apparent regularities of their appearance, imposing upon them the forms of space & time. According to Hegel these levels were transcended by their synthesis in universal consciousness, an abstract awareness of one's own place within the greater scheme of absolute spirit. The objects of one's experience & awareness were unified by the recognition that each was wholly contained in the fundamental reality of a common whole.

Hegelian objective Spirit involved the interaction among many selves that were the proper subject of ethics & social or political theory. He maintained that a correct understanding of these fields is to be derived not by generalizing from what we observe, but rather by tracing the dialectic through new triads.

His Ethics began with the concept of freedom understood as the right of each individual human being to act independently in pursuit of its own self-interest. Naturally the antithesis to this was the emergence of moral rules, which required the imposition of duty as a constraint upon the natural liberty. The synthesis of the two for Hegel was the ethical life, which emerged from a sincere recognition of the significance of one's own stake in the greater good of the others.

Hegel's logic was seemingly transcendental rather than formal. logic. Instead of treating the pure form of thought that had been abstracted from any possible content, transcendental logic treated thought that already possessed a certain type of content. Of course Hegel's transcendental logic was quite different from Kant's. Kant viewed transcendental logic as something that governed the thought of finite thinkers, whose cognition was constrained by the necessity of applying general discursive concepts to the singular contents given in sensory intuitions. Hegel, on the other hand, treated the finite thought of individual human discursive intellects as a type of "distributed" vehicle for the classically conceived infinite & intuitive thought of God.

Later in philosophy, Hegelian idealism underwent a revival in both Great Britain & the United States in the last decades of the nineteenth century. In Britain Hegel came to be one of the main targets of attack by the founders of the emerging "analytic" movement, Bertrand Russell & G. E. Moore. For Russell, the revolutionary innovations in logic starting in the last decades of the nineteenth century had destroyed Hegel's metaphysics by overturning the Aristotelian logic on which it was based. Similar things could be said of Hegel's reception from within the twentieth century phenomenological tradition which developed in continental Europe, but although marginalized within such core areas of mainstream academic philosophy, Hegel nevertheless continued to be a figure of interest within other philosophical movements such as existentialism & Marxism.

The philosophy of Ludwig Feuerbach (1804-1872) adopted a materialist approach to understanding the psyche. Unlike thinkers before him Feuerbach did not disconnect or oppose the man from nature, on contrary, he considered him to be a product & part of nature. He was born in Landshut, Bavaria. His father was a professor of jurisprudence. Feuerbach received his first education at the city gymnasium. In 1823 he entered the University of Heidelberg, to study at the Theological Faculty. Dissatisfied with the quality of teaching in Heidelberg, he moved to Berlin, where he attended lectures of Hegel. Later Feuerbach was appointed a lecturer at the Erlangen University, where he taught metaphysics, logic & history of philosophy. After the anonymous publication of scandalous "Thoughts of death & immortality" (1830), in which he denied the truth of ideas about the afterlife & a personal immortality, Feuerbach was dismissed from his post & could no longer continue his academic career. Despite all limitations he published number of important works such as: "The history of modern philosophy from Bacon to Spinoza" (1833), "On Leibniz (1837)," The Pierre Bayle (1838).

A new stage in the ideological development of Feuerbach came after 1839, when he wrote "Critique of Hegel's philosophy" (1839) & his most famous work - The Essence of Christianity (1841), which brought down the full weight of a materialistic & atheistic criticism to Christian beliefs & developed the so called new "religion of love." He also wrote "The Writer & the Man", "A number of comic-philosophical aphorisms," "Principles of the Philosophy of the Future" (1843), "The essence of religion" (1845) & etc. At the end of life Feuerbach had fallen into poverty & became interested in the ideology of Marxism & socialism, & for two years before his death, joined the Social Democratic Party. Ludwig Feuerbach died in Rahenberge near Nuremberg, on September 13, 1872.

Feuerbach held that the religion was a form of relation between human beings based on the affections. Feuerbach's theory did not simply accept mutual relations based on reciprocal inclination between human beings, such as sex love, friendship, compassion, self-sacrifice, etc., as what they were in themselves — without associating them with any particular religion which to him, too, belongs to the past; but instead he asserted that they will attain their full value only when consecrated by the name of religion. The most important factor to Feuerbach was not that these purely human relations existed, but that they shall be conceived of as the new religion. He viewed every bond between two people as a religion. Feuerbach argued that the periods of humanity were distinguished only by religious changes.

Ludwig Feuerbach introduced one of the first psychological approaches to religion. He maintained that the reality of God could be reduced to the human projection of a deity, a psychological comforter invented to overcome alienation from true fulfillment. Feuerbach was especially concerned with mankind & argued that religion was actually the study of man: "theology is anthropology."

In Feuerbach's theory there were three attributes of human nature; reason, will & love. These attributes were all projected onto image of God whereby reason became omniscience, will became omnipotence & love omni-benevolence. Feuerbach had a positive view of mankind & argued that a realization of these human attributes would lead to a progression towards utopia. He argued that as humans took control of their destinies they would come to realize their full potential removing the need for a psychological comforter.

Psychology of the 19-th Century

Reflex Studies

The anatomical studies of the nervous system created the necessary conditions for the future study of reflexes. The 19-th century was also the period in which neurophysiology professionalized & saw some of its most significant discoveries. Around the same time Charles Bell (1774–1843) & Francois Magendie (1783–1855) independently discovered the distinction between sensory & motor nerves in the spinal column.

Bell was born in Edinburgh, Scotland. He was a Scottish anatomist, physiologist, neurologist, artist & surgeon, who enjoyed a distinguished career in teaching & clinical practice in London between 1804 & 1836. In 1814, he was appointed to the surgical staff of the Middlesex Hospital. In 1824, he was elected Professor of Anatomy and Surgery at the Royal College of Surgeons of England. Later he was also elected Professor of Physiology at the University of London. In 1831, he was knighted on the accession of William IV. In 1836, he was elected to the Chair of Surgery in the University of Edinburgh, &remained there until his death in 1842. Bell was a prolific medical author, a brilliant medical researcher & a skilled artist. He discovered the distinct functions of the motor and sensory nerves, findings that were initially published in a pamphlet entitled "Ideas of a New Anatomy of the Brain." In 1821, Bell described the long thoracic nerve, which supplies the serratus anterior muscle, & which now bears his name. He also proved that lesions of the seventh cranial nerve produce facial paralysis (now termed Bell's palsy). He demonstrated that the fifth cranial nerve is of sensory importance to the face & controls the muscles of mastication, whereas the seventh cranial nerve principally controls the muscles of facial expression.

Bell held that sensory & motor functions might be served by different parts of the brain. He recognized the specificity of sensory nerves, identified the muscle sense & accepted the facts of reciprocal innervation. By dwelling on the delicate musculature of the fingers, and on the sensibility of the skin, he came to see the hand as the special organ of the sense of touch. In studying their comparative anatomy, he drew striking comparisons with the shoulder of the horse, elephant, and camel, and with corresponding organs of the mole, the bat, the anteater, and other species.

Bell maintained that a single nerve was in fact a bundle of nerves, each with its own function. These functions were determined by the segment of the brain to which the bundle was connected. He determined the functions of the various nerves simply by tracking their way from brain to extremities or organs.

Analogical conclusions were made by French physiologist Francois Magendie. He was born in Bordeaux, France. His father was a surgeon who was a devotee of Jean Jacques Rousseau. At the age of ten, Magendie, who had not yet learned to read or write, went to school for the first time. There, he combined his innate intelligence with his unorthodox upbringing. Magendie apprenticed to surgeon Baron Alexis de Boyer. In 1803 he passed the entrance examination for medical school & began traditional medical training. In 1808 e earned his M.D.

He was considered a pioneer of experimental physiology & best known for describing the foramen of Magendie. There was also a "Magendie sign," a downward & inward rotation of the eye due to a lesion in the cerebellum. Magendie was a faculty at the College of France, holding the Chair of Medicine from 1830 to 1855. Magendie conducted a number of experiments on the nervous system, in particular verifying the differentiation between sensory & motor nerves in the spinal cord. It became known as Bell-Magendie law. This led to an intense rivalry, with the British claiming that Bell published his discoveries first & that Magendie stole his experiments.

Magendie was a vitalist: he believed that the "life force" or "vital force" was essential both to health & recovery from illness. He opposed surgical & obstetric anesthesia because they weakened this hypothetical force, reducing the patient "to a corpse." According to Magendie pain was one of the prime movers of life.

Another great thinker of the 19-th century, Czech physiologist Jan Evangelist Purkinje (1787-1869) contributed to the future development of psychology by pioneering several important studies of vision. He also had valuable researches on the functioning of the brain & heart, pharmacology, embryology, & cells & tissue. In 1819 Purkinje described the visual phenomenon in which different-colored objects of equal brightness in certain circumstances appear to the eye to be unequally bright. This became known as Purkinje effect.

Purkinje was born in Libochovice, Bohemia (now in the Czech Republic), & studied at Prague. In 1823 he was appointed professor at Breslau (now Wroclaw in Poland) - perhaps through the influence of German poet

Wolfgang von Goethe, who had befriended him. In addition to his scientific work, Purkinje also translated the poetry of Goethe & Friedrich von Schiller. At Breslau, Purkinje founded the world's first official physiological institute. In 1850, he returned to Prague University. In 1832, he was the first to describe what are now known as Purkinje's images: a threefold image of a single object seen by one person reflected in the eye of another person. This effect is caused by the object being reflected by the surface of the cornea and by the anterior and posterior surfaces of the eye lens. Purkinje cells were large nerve cells with numerous dendrites found in the cortex of the cerebellum. Also in 1839, in describing the contents of animal embryos, Purkinje was the first to use the term "protoplasm" in the scientific sense.

The lack of positive knowledge & the negligence of scientific criteria gave rise to phrenology. The founder of this new movement was an Austrian doctor, physiologist, anatomist Franz Joseph Gall (1758-1828).

He suggested that the brain was divided into 27 separate organs. Each organ supposedly corresponded to a discrete human faculty, though Gall identified 19 of these faculties as being shared with other animal species. Gall's concepts on brain localization were revolutionary, and caused religious leaders and some scientists to take exception. The Roman Catholic Church considered his theory as contrary to religion.

Gall was born at Tiefenbrunn near Pforzheim, Baden, on the 9th of March 1758. After completing the usual literary course at Baden & Bruchsal, he began the study of medicine under J. Hermann at Strasburg. He moved to Vienna in 1781 & began to practice as a physician. At a comparatively early period he formed the generalization that in the human subject at least a powerful memory is invariably associated with prominent eyes; & further observation enabled him, as he thought, also to define the external characteristics indicative of special talents for painting, music & the mechanical arts. Around 1800, he developed "cranioscopy", a method to determine the personality & development of mental & moral faculties on the basis of the external shape of the skull. Cranioscopy was later renamed to phrenology by his follower Johann Spurzheim. Constant conflicts over his controversial theories made Gall leave his lecturer position in Austria. He sought a teaching position in Germany & eventually settled in France. In that country, he was also not fortunate, because Napoleon Bonaparte, the ruling emperor, & the scientific establishment, led by the Institute of France, pronounced his science as invalid. Despite all this, Gall was able to secure a comfortable existence on the basis of his specialty. Gall made many contributions to real science, such as his discovery that the gray matter of the brain contained cell bodies (neurons) & the white matter contained fibers (axons). His concept that brain function was localized was later proved to be mainly correct.

Gall's concepts were criticized by many different movements. Idealists were attacking him for destroying the immaterial postulate of the soul. French physiologist Marie Jean Pierre Flourens (1794-1867) was also critical of phrenology, especially questioning the experimental validity of it. He was born at Maureilhan, Herault. He studied medicine at Montpellier. He eventually moved to Paris, where he studied under the famous anatomist Georges Cuvier. In 1828 Flourens became a member of the "Académie des Sciences." Seven years later he was appointed a professor of comparative anatomy at the "Collège de France." In 1824 Flourens published his famous & highly influential "Experimental Researches on the Properties & Functions of the Nervous System in Vertebrates." In it described the main roles of different parts of the central nervous system. Flourens conducted a series of experiments in which he removed various parts of the brain & carefully observed the resulting changes. He concluded that the removal of the cerebral hemispheres of a pigeon destroyed the sense of perception & the removal of the cerebellum destroyed coordination. He also exposed the spinal cord of a dog from head to tail and found that while stimulation lower down would produce movement there came a point higher up where no muscular reaction could be elicited. Flouren's research clarified the mythological interpretation of the brain functions introduced by phrenology.

In the beginning of 19-th century the associative psychology was the only a psychological school, the subject of which - the consciousness - was recognized by all scientists. In the classical theories of associationism the content of consciousness was seen as a complex of sensations & ideas connected by the laws of association. In the middle of the 19-th century a new theory emerged that led to significant changes in the development of science. It was positivism, whose appearance resulted in a revision of the criteria of the scientific discipline. In order to remain independent & objective science, psychology had to revise its basic methodological principles & generate an objective & accurate method for the study of psychic life. An important factor that influenced the development of psychology in this period was the emergence of evolutionary theories of Darwin, which was crucial in turning psychology to natural science. Evolutionary theory allowed the review of the postulates that were hopelessly outdated mechanistic determinism. The new, biological determinant made it possible to correlate levels of consciousness & behavior, at the same time reviewing the subject of psychology.

In the beginning of 19-th century associative psychology had become a complete, canonical discipline evolving in accordance with the laws laid down by the previous generation of psychologists, like Hartley. Research psychology & new discoveries made during this period were aimed at improvement of associative psychology, without questioning its tenets, in particular the idea of the universality of the laws of association. One of the most prominent representatives of the associative movement in this period was a Scottish professor of philosophy Thomas Brown (1778-1820). Brown was the first to attempt to combine traditional Scottish school of thought with the new form of associationism. He was born at Kirkmabreck, Scotland. Brown received his early education at the University of Edinburgh. At the time he was only 14 years old. Brown became fascinated by Dugald Stewart's writings in 1793. One year later he decided to attend Stewart's lectures. After studying law for a time he took up medicine. In 1806 Brown became a medical practitioner. But despite his success, Brown preferred literature & philosophy. During an illness of Dugald Stewart in the session of 1808-1809, Brown acted as his substitute. Later he undertook much of Stewart's work. Brown was appointed as colleague to Stewart in 1810. This position he held for the rest of his life. Brown was against the notion that there were efficient causes in nature, or anywhere else, hidden from view. He devoted most of his time to the editing & publication of the numerous poems which he had written at various times during his life.

Brown was able to combine Hume's causal laws with complete absence of skepticism about both matter & God. He defended Hume's account of causation as nothing but invariable succession, mounting a powerful attack on the notion of power, particularly that of unexercised power. Brown's philosophical acumen was better displayed in criticism of rival theories. He agreed with Reid's reliance on consciousness as our only evidence for the mind's operations, as well as with Reid's use of first principles.

Brown viewed the mind as a simple substance. Its changes followed changes in the bodily organs of sense, & vice versa. The simplicity & distinctness of the mind enabled him to fend off materialism, according to which the bodily organs were mere aggregates of particles which our senses were too weak to distinguish. Brown also held that our knowledge of things was through their properties. Therefore the mind was considered as effect & cause of contemporary states of other substances. The affections of the mind caused by its own internal states Brown described in terms of ingeniously various laws of suggestion.

He also wrote a criticism of Darwin's "Zoonomia" & was one of the first contributors to the "Edinburgh Review," in which he introduced a criticism of the Kantian philosophy.

Later the development of associationism was marked by positivism & was aimed at the transformation of psychology into the objective (positive) science. Of course the central point in this process was to find an objective method of studying the psyche. One of the first attempts to rebuild associational psychology was done by Johann Friedrich Herbart (1774-1841).

The ideological climate of Germany at the time was quite different from Britain's. Philosophical traditions were of great importance in this country. Herbart was born at Oldenburg, Germany. He was home schooled by his mother until the age of 12, after which he was enrolled at the Gymnasium for six years. Here he showed great interest in philosophy, logic & especially Kant's writings. R he entered the University of Jena, where he studied philosophy. Three years later he left Jena to tutor the children of Herr von Steiger, who was the Governor of Interlaken. While tutoring in Switzerland, Herbart met and came to know Pestalozzi, the German educator involved with issues of reform in the schools. After resigning from his tutoring position, Herbart went on to study Greek & mathematics at Bremen. He eventually moved on to attend the University of Göttingen from (1801 to 1809), where he received his doctoral degree. He gave his first philosophical lectures at Göttingen around 1805, whence he removed in 1809 to occupy the chair formerly held by Kant at Königsberg. In 1833 he returned once more to Göttingen, & remained there as professor of philosophy till his death.

Herbart's system of philosophy was based on the analysis of experience. His system combined logic, metaphysics, & aesthetics as coordinate elements. Herbart opposed to all concepts of separate mental faculties, postulating instead that all mental phenomena resulted from interaction of elementary ideas. He held that educational methods & systems should be based on psychology and ethics, because psychology can provide necessary knowledge of the mind & ethics can be used as a basis for determining the social ends of education. He was also the first scientist to distinguish instructional process from subject matter. Herbart maintained that interest was being developed when already strong & vivid ideas were hospitable towards new ones, meaning past associations motivated apperception of current ones. He valued the study of the psychological processes of learning as a means of devising educational programs based on the aptitudes, abilities, & interests of students.

He advocated a system of Realism in metaphysics that was in complete opposition to the current idealistic movements. Herbart's ethics had many similarities to Kant's teaching, but instead of Kant's Categorical Imperative Herbart introduced five Moral Ideas; the Ideas of Inner Freedom, Perfection, Benevolence, Right, and Equity. His psychology was against the doctrine, of a soul endowed with certain native faculties or powers. Herbart tried to apply mathematics to the working of his presentations & to establish quantitative laws describing their mutual interactions.

The main foundations of Herbart's whole theory of education were his doctrines of apperception & interest. He viewed apperception as an act or process of assimilating, appropriating & identifying an object, impression or idea. Thus all progress in knowledge after the first percipient act was a process of apperception. He thought that the first sensation afforded no knowledge, but resulted in a presentation which persisted in existence gradually sinking down below the surface of consciousness.

Newton's influence was apparent in Herbart's beliefs about how forces mechanically interact with one another. Different ideas come into contact with each other and result in more complex ideas through the processes of blending, fusing, fading, & combining in a multitude of approaches. According to Herbart ideas were not precise imitations of the existing items in the world but that they were the direct consequence of the interactions of individuals' experiences. Herbart's theory, which contained new & relevant ideas, was one of the most popular & important psychological theories in the 19-th century. It played an important role in the further development of psychology & had a great influence on many well-known psychologists.

A new stage in the development of associative psychology was associated with the name of John Stuart Mill (1806-1873). He was a well known psychologist, an economist & public figure. Mill's tutor was his father, James Mill, who believed that the laws of psychology not only provided knowledge about the content of the spiritual life of man, but also suggested ways to improve its boundaries. He learned Greek at three, Latin a little later; by the age of 12, he was a competent logician & by 16 a well-trained economist. Mill became a Utilitarian and at the age of seventeen & formed a discussion group called the Utilitarian Society. Mill also began having articles published in the "Westminster Review." John Stuart Mill also wrote for other newspapers & journals including the "Morning Chronicle" & "Parliamentary History & Review."

In 1834 Mill founded the Radical journal, the "London Review" with William Molesworth. Two years later, Mill purchased the Westminster Review & merged the two journals. He refused to study at the University of

Oxford or the University of Cambridge, because he refused to take Anglican orders, instead he joined the imperialist East India Company. From 1830 to his death, he tried to persuade the British public of the necessity of a scientific approach to understanding social, political and economic change while not neglecting the insights of poets & other imaginative writers.

Mill was convinced that the psychic life of man was subject to the laws of association. He also suggested replacing "mental physics" with "mental chemistry". Such a change meant that, due to the connection of the primary psychic elements into a new product, the latter was able to acquire the qualities that were absent from its original elements. Mill believed that the same "chemical" changes occur in the psyche. Mill's doctrine of "mental (psychological) chemistry has played an important role in overcoming the weaknesses of the associative areas in psychology, especially in the development problems of creative thinking. Mill also revised the laws of association, introducing three major ones; 1) similarities; 2) adjacency; & 3) the intensity.

In addition Mill aimed at developing principles for the construction of scientific knowledge. Considering the association as derived from the laws of logic, scholars have argued that the logical operations dominate the communications experience within the individual mind. So the logic was the criterion of the correctness of human reasoning. According to Mill logic was the objective method which will help psychology to explore the contents of consciousness, especially occurrence of cognitive processes. This approach connected with the objective science of psychology & open in front of her path to further development as a natural & precise discipline. Another way of connecting psychology with natural science was with the help of biology, namely the theory of evolution. As mentioned above, evolutionary theory of Charles Darwin had a tremendous impact on psychological science. The opening of this theory meant expanding the object of psychology, the inclusion of new issues, to study the relationship of morphology & function, behavior & consciousness, etc. But most important was the fact that the theory of evolution introduced to psychology two new postulates; adaptation as the main determinant of mental development & the genesis of the psyche. The idea that one can identify the genetic stages in the development of the psyche, has led to the emergence of a new research method of genetic, which explored the patterns of general psychology, studying the gradual formation of a particular function.

Alexander Bain (1818-1903), one of the famous British Utilitarians, was an early proponent of scientific psychology. Together with James & John Stuart Mill, Bain was a major proponent of the British school of empiricism. He was born in Sutherland, Scotland. In 1836 Bain entered the Marischal College, which was one of Aberdeen's two universities. During his early years he showed a profound interest in mental philosophy, mathematics & physics. In 1841 Bain became a substitute professor of moral philosophy at Marischal. He taught one year (1845) at Anderson's University, Glasgow, but resigned to do free-lance work in London. There he joined a brilliant circle including George Grote & John Stuart Mill, with whom he already had close literary relationships. From 1860 to 1880 he held the chair of logic & English at the University of Aberdeen. After his retirement he was twice elected lord rector of the University. He made several valuable contributions to psychology. Remaining in the associationalist tradition of the Mills & sharing their distrust of metaphysics, he developed the current psychology in several directions. In discussing the will, he favored physiological over metaphysical explanations, pointing to reflexes as evidence that a form of will, independent of consciousness, inheres in a person's limbs. He sought to chart physiological correlates of mental states but refused to make any materialistic assumptions.

In his "Feelings & intellect" (1855), "Emotions & Will "(1859) Bain argued that the associative psychology must consider not only the associations that exist in the mind of the individual, but also those which exist in behavior. He also held that not only the brain, but the entire bodily system to a certain degree was associated with mental functions. Bain strongly defended the theory of psychophysical parallelism, origin of which was associated with the name of Leibniz.

While Interpreting the driving force of conduct, Bain came into conflict with the causal trend in physiology & psychology, where the main mechanism of behavior was considered a reflex. Instead of a reflex Bain introduced the concept of the spontaneous action, which later became one of the major categories of his psychology. He called spontaneous actions, for the occurrence of which the direct physical causes were not enough. Bain explained the emergence of skills with the help of the principle of spontaneous movements.

Bain paid greater attention to the factors that determine the transition from instinctive behavior to the behavior of strong-willed, led by the human mind. He argued that, just like nature selects the most productive species man also makes the transition from the unconscious, spontaneous behavior to an intelligent & strong-willed one. A person selects the most productive & efficient forms of reaction through trial & error. That is how the model of trial & error appeared in psychology. This model subsequently formed the basis of American psychology in an objective study of behavior.

The Nineteenth Century Positivism

There were five main principles in traditional positivism; 1. The logic of inquiry was the same across all social & natural sciences, 2. The goal of inquiry was to explain & predict 3. Scientific knowledge was testable, 4. Science did not equal common sense & 5.Theory & practice were inter-related.

Positivism as a movement was first founded by Auguste Comte (1798-1857) in the 1830s. He thought that scientific sociology alone could provide the basis for a new form of social integration. Comte's philosophical system of thought maintained that the goal of knowledge was simply to describe the phenomena experienced & not to question whether it existed or not. He was born in the southern French city of Montpellier. His father was a fervent Catholic & a discreet Royalist. Comte received his first education at the age of nine in the imperial "lycee" of his native town. Later he enrolled at the University of Montpellier & the "École Poly-technique" (the engineering school) in Paris. The latter was known for its adherence to the French ideals of republicanism & progress. Comte left École to continue his studies at the medical school of Montpellier.

After his return to Montpellier, Comte soon came to see unbridgeable differences with his Catholic & Monarchist family & moved again to Paris. In 1817 he became a student & secretary to Claude Henri de Rouvroy, Comte de Saint-Simon, who introduced Comte to intellectual elite & greatly influenced his thought thereon. It was during that time that Auguste Comte published his first essays in the various publications headed by Saint-Simon. In 1824, Comte left Saint-Simon, again because of unbridgeable differences. He published his famous "Plan of scientific studies necessary for the reorganization of society." In 1846 Comte, along with Mill developed a new "religion of humanity." He published four volumes of "Système de politique positive" (1851 - 1854). Comte last work was the first volume of "The Subjective Synthesis" published in 1856.

Comte attempted to create a naturalistic science of society, which would be able both to explain the past development of mankind & predict its future course. He also tried to formulate the conditions that account for social stability at any given historical moment. The study of social dynamics & social statics were the main goals in his system.

According to Comte the society of man should be studied in the same scientific manner as the world of nature. He held that Natural science had succeeded in establishing the lawfulness of natural phenomena, by discovering that the latter followed ordered sequences of development. He truly believed that the discovery of the basic laws will cure men of overweening ambition. But at the same time, men will also be enabled to act deliberately within given limits by curbing the operation of societal laws to their own purposes. Thus, once the new scientific dispensation comes into its own, men will no longer think in absolute terms, but in terms relative to a particular state of affairs in society. Comte argued that by recognizing the constraint that any social order imposes on action, men will at the same time be enabled freely to order their society within the bounds imposed by necessity. Instead of accepting canonical truths as everlastingly valid, he insisted on the continued progress of human understanding and the self-corrective character of the scientific enterprise. He thought that once men recognize the overriding authority of science in the guidance of human affairs, they will also abandon the dogma of unbounded liberty of conscience.

Comte's methods of inquiry were the same as in natural sciences: observation, experimentation & comparison. During his early years he was determined to discover through what fixed series of successive transformations the human race, starting from a state not superior to that of the great apes, gradually led to the point at which civilized Europe finds itself today. By applying the method of scientific comparison through time, Comte emerged with his central conception, "The Law of Human Progress." For Comte, each successive stage or sub-stage in the evolution of the human mind necessarily grew out of the preceding one. He maintained that the constitution of the new system cannot take place before the destruction of the old & before the potentialities of the old mental order have been exhausted.

Although Comte focused mainly on stages in the development & progressive emancipation of the human mind, he stressed that these stages correlated with parallel stages in the development of social organization & of the material conditions of human life. According to Comte, in organic periods, social stability & intellectual harmony prevailed & the various parts of the body social were in equilibrium, whereas in critical periods old certainties were upset, traditions were undermined, & the body social was in fundamental disequilibrium. Such critical periods were profoundly unsettling & perturbing to men thirsting for order. Yet they were the necessary prelude to the inauguration of a new organic state of affairs.

Comte's theory of the hierarchy of the sciences was closely connected with the Law of Three Stages. Just as mankind progressed only through determinant stages, each successive stage building on the accomplishments of its predecessors, so scientific knowledge passed through similar stages of development. Apparently different sciences progress at different rates. Comte postulated that any kind of knowledge reached its positive stage early in proportion to its generality, simplicity, & independence of other departments. This means that astronomy, the most general & simple of all natural sciences, was developed first. Later it was followed by physics, chemistry, biology, & finally, sociology. Each science in this series depended for its emergence on the prior developments of its predecessors. In order to supplement his theory of stages, Comte set out to investigate the foundations of social stability.

He convinced that the static study of sociology consisted in the investigation of the laws of action & reaction of the different parts of the social system. Upon dealing with the components of a social system, Comte emphatically refused to see individuals as elementary parts, claiming that the scientific spirit forbids us to regard society as composes of individuals. In the early ages of humanity the individual advantages of association were doubtful. To Comte it was obvious that the social state would never have existed if its rise had depended on a conviction of its individual utility.

Toward the end of his career Comte considered himself not only a social scientist but also, & primarily, a prophet & founder of a new religion that promised salvation for all the ailments of mankind. Although he possessed no observable evidence, he was convinced that the positivist stage was the last in human development. Comte also neglected to consider psychology in the formulation of his theories, leading to many unanswered questions regarding morality & ethics.

Along with Auguste Comte and John Stuart Mill Herbert Spencer (1820-1903) was one of the founders of positivism. He was born April 27th, 1820, at the height of British industrialism. He was educated at home in mathematics, natural science, history & English, among some other languages. Spencer obtained a job as a civil engineer on the railways at sixteen & wrote during his spare time. Later he became the sub-editor of "The Economist" in 1848, an important financial weekly at the time for the upper-middle class. Spencer published numerous articles in the radical press of his time. He advocated the abolishment of the so called Poor Laws, national education & a central church; he wanted the lifting of all restrictions on commerce & factory legislation. His book "Social Statics" was published in 1851 to great acclaim, but his quietly influential "Principles of Psychology" released in 1855 met with much criticism. Although one of the most influential figures in sociology & psychology, Spencer was overshadowed because of his somewhat controversial ideas. In 1883 Spencer was elected a corresponding member of philosophical section of the French academy of moral & political sciences. His reputation was at its peak in the 1870s & early 1880s, & he was nominated for the Nobel Prize for Literature in 1902.

For the first time since the days of Descartes, Spencer turned to the analysis of the subject of psychology. He reviewed the subject of psychology, defining it as the ratio of external to internal forms & the association between them. Thus, he expanded the area of mental to include not only the association between internal factors, i.e., the association in the field of consciousness, but consciousness & communication with the outside world. Also, Spencer wrote that there is an objective psychology, which studies the structure of the brain & the subjective psychology, dealing with the state of the soul. Exploring the different state of mind, he came to the conclusion that there were parallel stages in the development of internal & external mental acts. Thus, both internal & external became the subject of psychological research which, in turn, allowed generating objective research methods. In addition, Spencer stressed the specificity of psychological research, speaking about the uniqueness of psychology as the only science that considers the relationship of external & internal, while other disciplines are either in an external field (physics, chemistry) or internal (philosophy, physiology).

Spencer held that the psyche was a mechanism for adaptation to the environment. His approach implied that the psyche occurred naturally at a certain stage of evolution, when the living conditions were so complicated that the adaptation became impossible without adequate reflection. Of great importance was the fact that Spencer was studying the origin of the psyche, on the assumption that the human psyche was the highest stage of development, which appeared not once, but gradually, in the process complicating the lives & activities of living beings. He argued that the original form of mental life was the feeling developed from irritability, after which from the simplest sensations appeared many forms of mentality, reflecting the interconnected levels of the formation of consciousness & behavior. Spencer also held that the mental development must be viewed in terms of the principles of differentiation & integration, showing how from the individual mental qualities that were given to a child from birth, was formed the adult human psyche.

Spencer extended the laws of evolution not only on the psyche, but also in social life, having formulated an organic theory of society. He said that a person needs to adapt not only to nature, but also to the social environment, so his mind is developed along with society. He is one of the first psychologists that compared the psychology of the savage & modern man. He concluded that in modern man the development of thinking was stronger, while among primitive people was more developed the perception. Spencer's unconventional findings allowed scientists to develop comparative methods for the research of psyche. His theory won recognition among psychologists & had a big influence on the further development of psychology, primarily at strengthening its relationship with the natural sciences & the search for objective method.

Experimental Physiology

The discipline of experimental physiology dates back to 1830s. Johannes Muller (1801-1858) was the first to use the experimental method in physiology. He was also known for writing the notorious "Handbook of Physiology" which contained physiological researches of the period. Muller is of great importance to both physiology & psychology for his doctrine of the specific energies of nerves, according to which the stimulation of a given nerve always results in characteristic sensation because each sensory nerve has its own specific energy. This notion stimulated a great deal of research that sought to localize functions within nervous system & to delimit sensory receiving mechanisms on the periphery of the organism.

Johannes Muller was born in Koblenz, Germany. He entered the University of Bonn in 1819. By 1830 he was already a professor. In 1833 Muller went to Humboldt University of Berlin where he mastered anatomy & physiology till his death. He made contributions to numerous domains of physiology including understanding of voice, hearing & speech, as well as the chemical & physical properties of lymph & blood.

The early physiologists made important contributions to the study of the brain functions. Their work is especially important to psychology because they have discovered specialized areas of the brain & developed research methods that became widely used in later physiological psychology.

In nineteenth century there were two major experimental approaches to the study of the brain. The clinical method was developed by Paul Broca & the electrical stimulation method by Fritsch & Hitzig. In the beginning of his career Broca was mainly focused on the studies of histology of bone cartilage, as well as cancer pathology, aneurisms & infant mortality. He also made contributions to the understanding of the limbic system & rhinencephalon. Broca developed the clinical method while performing an autopsy on a man who had been unable to speak intelligibly for many years. The autopsy revealed a tumor in the third frontal convolution of the cerebral cortex, which Broca later labeled the speech center. Broca clinical method revolutionized the understanding of speech production. This method allows finding a damaged portion of the brain assumed to be responsible for behavioral condition that existed.

The other experimental method involved the exploration of the cerebral cortex with weak electric currents. Fritsch & Hitzig found that stimulation of certain cortical areas results in monitor responses. With the development of more sophisticated electronic equipment, the method of electrical stimulation has become the single most productive technique for studying the different functions of the brain. In addition considerable research was being conducted on the structure of the nervous system & the nature of neural activity.

In eighteenth century Galvani proposed that the nature of nerve impulse was electrical. During the nineteenth century the anatomical structure & the functions of the nervous system were the main focus of study. Soon it was discovered that the nerve fibers were actually composed of separate structures called neurons joined together by synapses. These findings were quite congruent with the mechanistic & materialistic image of man. The nervous system was believed to be composed of atomistic structures which, in turn, produced a more complex product.

In the 1840s a group of scientists formed the Berlin Physical Society. Many of them were former students of Johannes Muller. These scientists were committed to one overriding proposition: the belief that all phenomena could be accounted for in physical terms. Ultimately they were attempting to connect physiology with physics. The physiology of the nineteenth century was influenced by four major movements; materialism, empiricism, experimentation, & to a certain degree mechanism. The discoveries in early physiology indicate the kinds of research techniques that were supportive of a scientific approach to the psychological investigation of the mind. The direction of research in physiology influenced the newly emerging psychology. While philosophy was paving the way for an experimental attack on the mind, physiology was experimentally investigating the mechanisms underlying mental phenomena.

Herman von Helmholtz, Gustav Fechner, Ernst Weber & Wilhelm Wundt were the pioneers of new experimental approach.

Herman von Helmholtz (1821-1894) was a physician & psychiatrist who made several significant contributions in various fields. In physiology & psychology he is known for his theories of vision, ideas on the visual perception of space, color vision research & his researches on perception of sound. Helmholtz was born in Potsdam Germany. At the age of 17, he entered the Berlin medical institute. After army service he accepted a position as Associate Professor of Physiology at Konigsberg. Over the next 30 years he held academic appointments in physiology at Bonn & Heidelberg, & in physics at Berlin. Helmholtz was also a philosopher known for his ideas on the relation between the laws of perception & laws of nature, science of aesthetics & philosophy of science. Especially fascinating are Helmholtz's investigations of the speed of neural impulse, audition & vision. He provided the first empirical measurement of the rate of conduction by stimulating a motor nerve & the attached muscle from the leg of a frog. The experiment was done with different lengths of nerves, which allowed recording the delay between stimulation of the nerve near the muscle & the muscle's reaction. Later he experimented with the reaction time for sensory nerves with human subjects. Helmholtz studied the complete circuit from stimulation of a sense organ to the resulting motor response. The findings of the reaction time experiments were so inconclusive that he abandoned the research soon after. Eventually Helmholtz was able to prove that thought & movements follow one another at a measurable interval. However he was not interested in the physiological significance of this discovery, his main goal was to measure the speed of nerve impulse. Latter research was one of the first demonstrations that it was possible to experiment upon & measures a psycho-physiological process.

Helmholtz's researches on vision were popular as well. He extended a theory of color vision originally published by Thomas Young. No less important was his work on audition, including perception of combination tones & individual tones, theory of hearing & the nature of harmony & discord. Helmholtz considered psychology a separate discipline, allied to metaphysics. The psychology of senses, according to him, was an exception because it had links with physiology. Interestingly enough Helmholtz did not attempt to establish psychology as an independent science, yet his influence was so big that he was considered a contributor to the new science.

Ernst Weber (1795-1878), the founder of experimental psychology, was born in Wittenberg, Germany. He received his doctorate at Leipzig in 1815. In 1818 he was appointed an Associate Professor of comparative anatomy at the Leipzig University, where he was made a Fellow Professor of Anatomy in 1821. Weber discovered that the just noticeable difference of the change in stimuli magnitude was proportional to the stimuli magnitude rather than being an absolute value. Before Weber researches on sense organs were confined almost exclusively to the higher senses of vision & audition. Ernst Weber's work consisted mainly of exploring new fields, notably muscular & cutaneous sensations. He applied experimental methods of psychology to problems of a physiological nature. Weber's experiments on the sense of touch mark a fundamental shift in the status of subject matter of psychology. After this, the connection of the new science with philosophy was noticeably weakened. Weber saw psychology in connection with natural sciences using the experimental methods to study human mind. He is also known for his experimental determination of the accuracy of the two point discrimination of the skin- the distance necessary between two points before the subject reports two distinct sensations. Basically, in this experiment the subject is asked to report whether he feels one or two points touching the skin, without the use of vision. When the two points of stimulation are close, the subject reports a clear sensation of being touched at only one point. Gradually the distance between the two sources of stimulation is increased & the subject reports uncertainty as to whether he feels one or two sensations. In the end a distance is reached where the subject reports two distinct points if stimulation. Thus, a threshold is demonstrated at which the two points can be discriminated as such. This research marks the first experimental demonstration of the concept of threshold. Another important discovery of Weber's eventually led to the first quantitative law in psychology. He attempted to determine the smallest difference between the weights. In this experiment subject lifts two weights, a standard & a comparison weight, after which he reports whether one felt heavier than the other. The minor differences between the weights result in judgment of sameness, while large differences in judgment of display between the weights. The just noticeable difference between the weights was a constant ratio, 1:40, of the standard weight. Weber also investigated the contributions of muscular sensations in the discrimination of weights of differing magnitudes. He concluded that the subject could discriminate more accurately if the weights to be measured were lifted by the subject instead of simply being placed in his hands, because in lifting weights both tactual & muscular sensations are active.

Weber was able to prove that discrimination depends not on the absolute magnitude of the difference between two weights, but rather on the relative difference of to another. The noticeable difference between two stimuli can be then stated as a fraction that is constant for a given sense modality. Weber's visual discrimination experiments, in turn, proved that visual fraction was smaller than muscular sense fraction. From this he proposed that there exists a constant fraction for just noticeable differences for each of these senses. Latter meant that there is no one on one correspondence between the physical stimulus & the perception of it. Although his research revealed a unique way of investigating the relationship between the body & mind, Weber, just like Helmholtz, did not appreciate the significance of his work for psychology. The investigation of the stimulus & its resulting sensation indeed was a major breakthrough for both; physiology & psychology. Weber systematically varied the stimuli recording differential effects on the reported experience of the subject. Soon his experiments begun to stimulate a great deal of research & served to focus the attention of psychologists on the validity of experimental methods.

Gustav Theodor Fechner (1801-1887) was born in the village of Grob Sarchen, in Germany. He was educated at Sorau, Dresden & at the University of Leipzig. In 1834 he was appointed professor of physics, but five years later was forced to resign due to an eye disorder contracted while studying the phenomena of color & vision. Fechner was a talented, diverse scientist. He was a well known psychologist, psychophysicist, physicist & a philosopher. Fechner's disability made him to turn to philosophy directing the full force of his genius toward the question of the relationship between the mind & the body. He held that the mind & body are identical, because they are the two aspects of the same fundamental unity. The only difference between the two, according to Fechner, was the result of the way in which they are viewed. He was convinced that the law of the connection between the mind & body can be found in a statement of quantitative relation between mental sensation & material stimulus. Thus, the increase of the stimulus intensity does not produce increase in the intensity of the sensation. Rather a geometric series characterizes the stimulus, while an arithmetic series characterizes the sensation. In Fechner's theory the effects of stimulus are relative to the amount of sensation already existing. This means that the amount of sensation is depends on the amount of stimulation. In order to measure the change or increase in sensation one must measure the change or increase in stimulation. This is why Fechner thought it possible to quantitatively relate mental & material spheres.

In Fechner's theory there are two ways to measure sensation; first one must determine whether the stimulus is present or absent, after which it is possible to measure the stimulus intensity at which the subject reports the first appearance of sensation. What is being measured at this point is the absolute threshold of sensitivity; that is, that point below which no sensation is reported, & above which the subject experience a sensation. This measurement was very limited, because it allowed determining only one sensation value. In order to relate both intensities, one must be able to specify the full range of stimulus values & their resulting sensation values.

Later Fechner was using the differential threshold of sensitivity, which meant the least amount of change in a stimulus that will give rise to a change in sensation. He further held that for each sense modality there is a certain relative increase in the stimulus that always produces an observable change in the intensity of the sensation. Thus, the mind quality as well as the existing stimulus can be measured & relation between the two can be stated in the form of an equation: S= K log R. In this S corresponds to the magnitude of the sensation, K is a constant & r is the magnitude of the stimulus. The relationship is logarithmic since one series increases arithmetically & the other geometrically.

Fechner had an extensive program of research, which later was called psychophysics. As a result of this research he developed & systemized several fundamental methods of psychophysics. These methods; the method of limits, the method of constant stimuli & the method of average error, are still in use today. The average error method consists in having a subject to a variable stimulus until he perceives it to be equal to a constant standard stimulus. Over a number of trials the mean value of the differences between the standard stimulus & the subject's setting of the variable stimulus represents his error of observation. The method assumes that our sense organs are subject to variability so as to prevent the obtaining of a true measure. This means that a person obtains a large number of approximate measures, the mean of which represents the best approximation that can be made of the true value. Such technique can be useful in measuring the reaction time, visual & auditory discriminations, as well as the extent of illusions.

The method of constant stimuli was first introduced by Vierordt in 1852, but developed & finalized by Fechner. This technique involves two constant stimuli, the aim being to measure the difference between the stimuli that is required to produce a given proportion of correct judgments. For example, the subject first lifts the standard weight 100 grams & then lifts a comparison weight 88 grams, after which he must decide whether the second weight is heavier, lighter or equal to the first. This process is continued until a certain number of judgments have been made for each comparison. For the heavier weights subjects mostly report a judgment of heavier, while the lighter weights are almost always reported as lighter. From this data the stimulus difference is determined for that point at which the subject correctly reports heavier 75% of the time.

Fechner's method of limits at the time was known as the method of just noticeable differences. This method has been around for a while; Fechner developed it in connection with his work on vision & temperature sensations. The subject is presented with two stimuli which are later increased or decreased until the subject detects a difference.

Fechner, along with Wilhelm Wundt & Hermann von Helmholtz, is considered to be one of the founders of experimental psychology. Unlike his psychophysical concepts, Fechner's philosophical works were naïve, idealistic & animistic. He felt the thrill of life everywhere, in plants, stars, earth & total universe. Fechner saw natural laws as the modes of the unfolding of God's perfection. He had few valuable works in aesthetics. Fechner maintained that certain abstract forms & proportions are naturally pleasing to human senses & gave some new illustrations of the working of aesthetic association.

One of the most influential thinkers of the late 19-th century was Ernst Mach (1838-1916). He was an Austrian physicist & philosopher who established important principles of optics, mechanics, & wave dynamics. He was born in Chirlitz, in the Austrian empire (now part of the Czech Republic). According to some sources Mach was educated at home until the age of 14. He went briefly to gymnasium (high school) before entering the University of Vienna at the age of 17. He received his doctorate in physics in 1860 & taught mechanics & physics in Vienna until 1864, when he became professor of mathematics at the University of Graz. Later Mach became more interested in psychology & physiology of sensation. Toward the end of 1860 he discovered the physiological phenomenon that has come to be called Mach's bands, the tendency of the human eye to see bright or dark bands near the boundaries between areas of sharply differing illumination. In 1867 he joined the Charles University in Prague, where he conducted studies on kinesthetic sensation, the feeling associated with movement & acceleration. Between 1873 & 1893 he invented optical & photographic techniques for the measurement of sound waves & wave propagation. In 1887 he developed the principles of supersonics & the Mach number--the ratio of the velocity of an object to the velocity of sound. Mach returned to the University of Vienna as professor of inductive philosophy in 1895, but he suffered a stroke two years later & retired from active research in 1901. He continued to lecture & write in retirement, publishing "Knowledge & Error" in 1905 & an autobiography in 1910.

Mach held that all knowledge was derived from sensation, meaning that a given phenomena under scientific investigation can be understood only in terms of experiences. This concept led to the position that no statement in natural science was admissible unless it was empirically verifiable. According to Mach's physical principle inertia resulted from a relationship of the object with all the rest of the matter in the universe. Thus inertia was viewed as a function of the interaction between one body & other bodies in the universe, even at enormous distances.

Mach maintained that scientific laws were simply summaries of experimental events, constructed for the purpose of human comprehension of complex data. Thus he rejected the physicists' demand for demonstration or proof, which he called "misplaced rigor." According to Mach there could not be any a priori knowledge in mechanics; instead, the basis of all scientific knowledge was sense experience. He also thought that to describe things we analyze them into their separately sensible qualities, & that these elements were known to us through sensation. These simple sensations we can gain certainty, & thus, Mach argued, the scientific knowledge could be built up on a foundation of certainty through sensation. He believed theories to be provisional & based on analogies that were temporary substitutes for direct sensations. In Mach's view theories were valuable only as they led us to descriptions of observed phenomena.

Mach was very interested in the physiology & psychology of the senses. He insisted that, given two empirically equivalent conceptual schemes, theory choice was not arbitrary. Instead he suggested that it should be conditioned by considerations of simplicity, consistency, & depth. He also held that scientific laws were merely conceptual tools. In Mach's conception of science, theory could only go so far as to order knowledge, thus help us to effectively control & more importantly, predict our environment. His elimination of absolute space was simply part of a more general program in which he hoped to eliminate metaphysics. He stated that the world contained nothing but sensations & their connections. Mach's views influenced the important philosophical movement of logical positivism & had a serious impact on scientific practice.

Friedrich Nietzsche (1844-1900) was one of the most influential of modern German thinkers. Nietzsche was not a systematic philosopher but rather a moralist who passionately rejected Western bourgeois civilization. He regarded Christian civilization as decadent, & in place of its "slave morality" he looked to the superman, the creator of a new heroic morality that would consciously affirm life & the life values. That superman would represent the highest passion & creativity and would live at a level of experience beyond the conventional standards of good & evil. Nietzsche's thought had widespread influence but was of particular importance in Germany.

Friedrich Nietzsche was born in Röcken, Prussia. He descended from a long line of clergymen, including his father, giving him the theological background to challenge the familiar religious institutions. It was assumed Friedrich would be a minister. He received a scholarship to Schulpforta, an elite preparatory school with only 200 students, in October 1858. The scholarship was intended to fund Nietzsche's training for the clergy. In

1865 Nietzsche discovered Schopenhauer's "World as Will & Idea," which dramatically changed Nietzsche's view of the world. Schopenhauer's philosophy was rather dark for its time; it became a part of Nietzsche's worldview as it was well-suited to his nature. Nietzsche was conscripted into the military at the age of 23. While he had hoped to avoid the draft, he had no such luck. He was not destined to be in the military however, soon falling from a horse. He was released from service having not yet completed training. Nietzsche began his career as a classical philologist before turning to philosophy. Nietzsche studied Greek & Latin at Bonn & Leipzig & was appointed to the chair of classical philology at Basel in 1869. In his early years he was friendly with the composer Richard Wagner, although later he was to turn against him. Nervous disturbances & eye disorder forced Nietzsche to leave Basel in 1879. He moved from place to place in a vain effort to improve his health until 1889, when he became hopelessly insane. He lived his final years in the care of his mother & sister.

Nietzsche hypothesized moral systems developed from within a society. The societal systems, & their cultures, were examined in "Genealogy of Morals," published in 1887. In this book, Nietzsche discussed the Master Morality of aristocratic cultures, such as the Roman Empire, and the Slave Morality of Jewish communities. Nietzsche recognized that the two cultures were actually components of one greater society / culture, but the moral systems were markedly different. Nietzsche held that the slave class embraced democracy & the principle of equality in order to bring the naturally superior class down to their own level. In addition he viewed sin & evil as artificial constructs, created by the slaves & adopted by the leaders of this class. He also insisted that the slaves demeaned sex, human desire, & taught humility instead of respect for power & authority.

Nietzsche's relativism has had a powerful influence on two of modern French Deconstructionist philosophers, Jacques Derrida & Michel Foucault. Surprisingly enough, he had also been a powerful influence on certain theologians, like Paul Tillich. Also In "Beyond Good & Evil," Nietzsche demanded that psychology should be recognized as the queen of the sciences. Many of Nietzsche's insights were perhaps psychological, & many of his arguments invoked psychological premises. For example in Genealogy, he criticized the "English psychologists" for the "inherent psychological absurdity" of their theory of the origin of good & bad.

His famous statement "God is dead," occurring in several of Nietzsche's works, has become one of his best-known remarks & on the basis of it, most regarded Nietzsche as an atheist. In his opinion certain developments in the science of the time & the increasing secularization of European society had destroyed the Christian God, which in turn caused the loss of any universal perspective on things, as well as any coherent sense of objective truth. The death of God, according to Nietzsche, led to nihilism, which is the belief that nothing has any inherent importance & that life lacks any purpose.

Nietzsche's work was widely criticized for its absurd, unphilosophical use of aphorisms & irony. Serious consideration of the strictly philosophical aspects of his work did not appear until the advent of psychoanalysis & existentialism.

The French School of Psychology

The works of French scientists have helped to expand the scope of psychology to include not only unconscious, but also the collective psyche. The most important result of their research was the sense of a new factor affecting the formation of the psyche - the culture, historical development of society. This was an opportunity to present man not only as a result of biological, cultural & historical development, but had shown new aspects of the relationship of psychology with philosophy, history & sociology.

The psychological school in Nancy was led by Ambroise Liebeault (1823-1905). He used hypnosis in the treatment of various somatic & neurotic disorders, achieving significant therapeutic results. Liebeault was born in Favières, a small town in the Lorraine region of France. He enrolled at the University of Strasbourg, receiving his medical degree in 1850 at the age of 26. He then established a practice in the village of Pont-Saint-Vincent, near the town of Nancy. Liebeault's work was strongly influenced by the ideas of Scottish surgeon James Braid (1795-1860), as well as the ideas of Abbé Faria (1746-1819), Alexandre Jacques François Bertrand (1795-1831). His first book titled "Sleep and its analogous states considered from the perspective of the action of the mind upon the body" was published in 1866. He died on February 18, 1904 at the age of 80.

According to Liebeault suggestion can cause a hypnotic state (sleep state) in virtually any person. Linking the psychological characteristics of this state including the action of the imagination, Liebeault, & then his pupil Bernheim have developed methods of verbal suggestion. Their methods of post-hypnotic suggestion proved very effective, their clients unconsciously kept instill information for many years. These works attracted attention of Sigmund Freud during his visit to Nancy. Being engaged in the treatment of hysteria, the scientists of this school explained hysterical symptoms by suggestion from another person or by the subject himself (autosuggestion), assuming that such a suggestion & autosuggestion can occur unconsciously.

The head of the Paris school was a physician, neurologist & teacher Jean-Martin Charcot (1825-1893). He was born on in Paris, France. At first he studied medicine in Paris & after failing an examination in 1847, Charcot took a job at the Salpetriere hospital. Here Charcot made classical descriptions of multiple or disseminated sclerosis & in 1869 of amyotrophic lateral sclerosis, subsequently known as Charcot's disease, Lou Gehrig's disease, & ALS. In addition, Charcot was a professor at the University of Paris, where he remained for 33 years. Among Charcot's students were Alfred Binet, Pierre Janet, & Sigmund Freud. They were impressed with Charcot & went on to use hypnosis in their own way, but disagreed with their teacher that it was a neurological phenomenon. They considered the hypnotic state a psychological one.

Charcot's work encompassed other aspects of neurology as well. He was first to describe the degeneration of ligaments & joint surfaces due to lack of use or control, now called Charcot's joint. He did research to determine the parts of the brain responsible for specific nerve functions & discovered the importance of small arteries in cerebral hemorrhage. He died in 1893 in Morvan, France.

Pursuing questions of psychology of creative arts, Charcot was one of the first to observe the psychotherapeutic effects of the works of art. He closely studied various cases of hysteria & developed the theory of "traumatic hysteria," in which Charcot noted the similarity between the behavior of hysterics & people in a state of hypnosis. In contrast to the works Nancy school, he argued that people prone to hysteria are more exposed to hypnosis. Charcot began to use hypnosis in the treatment of hysteria. Since Charcot held that hysteria was a neuro-somatic illness, he viewed hypnosis as a pathological phenomena (just as hysteria) caused by the anatomical & physiological factors.

Based on many years of observation he identified the various stages of hypnosis - catalepsy, lethargy, & somnambulism. Charcot's work had enormous significance for the formation of psychological science.

The founder of the French school of psychology was an outstanding scientist, Theodule-Armand Ribot (1839-1916). He was born in Guingamp, France. He studied at the Lyceum de Saint-Brieuc

& later moved to Paris where. In 1875 he obtained his doctorate. He was professor of philosophy in schools in Vesoul & Laval. He then returned to Paris to engage in research in experimental psychology laboratories histology & physiology of some psychiatric hospitals. He was professor of experimental psychology at the Sorbonne since 1885. In 1888 he became professor of experimental psychology at the College de France.

He held that psychology must be liberated from "the yoke of metaphysics" & stressed the need for an empirical, biological approach to psychology & the limitations of an exclusive reliance on introspection. However, although he insisted on excluding metaphysics from the empirical sciences, he did not dismiss it altogether. Ribot's early writings were mainly expository & historical. In his "La psychologie anglaise contemporaine" Ribot surveyed English associationist psychology from David Hartley to Samuel Bailey. In "La psychologie allemande contemporaine" (1879), he introduced the work of Gustav Fechner, Wilhelm Wundt, Hermann Helmholtz, & others to the French public.

Later Ribot became interested in psychopathology. Despite a wealth of clinical, empirical material, the underlying motive of these of Ribot's works was philosophical. Ribot showed that the simplicity of such abstract words hides the complexity of the phenomenon named, a complexity revealed by the dissociation found in mental diseases. Ribot was among the first to study dissociations of personality, & his law of regression—that amnesia affects the most recent & least organized impressions and reactions first—was a lasting contribution to psychology.

Eventually Ribot's interest shifted to normal psychological phenomena, particularly to affective phenomena. The major work of this period, "La psychologie des sentiments" (1896), reflects Ribot's biological approach & his mild epiphenomenalism. He held that physiological drives underlie our elementary feelings of pleasure & pain, & more complex & evolved stages of these drives underlie more complex emotions. Ribot's last work, "La vie inconsciente et les mouvements" (1914), interpreted various manifestations of subconscious activity in terms of motor activity.

Another bright representative of the French school of psychology was Pierre Janet (1859-1947). Janet has developed a system of psychology & psychopathology, which he called "psychology of behavior." He received the philosophical education at the Teachers' Training Institute in Paris & taught seven years at the Lyceum in Le Havre. Janet eventually turned to the problems of medicine, in particular to the problem of hypnosis & suggestion, which was due to the influence of Charcot. From 1889 he worked as a head of the psychological laboratory Clinics at Salpetriere. In the same year he received a Ph.D. In 1892 he received a degree of Doctor of Medicine. From 1896 to 1934 Janet was a Professor of Psychology at the College de France, after which he transferred to Sorbonne.

Janet dealt with many challenges - developing methods of investigating such mental processes as perception, attention, memory, as well as, explored the structure of consciousness & personality, the relation of conscious & unconscious in the content of the psyche. He believed that mental activity in its primitive, elemental form was automatic, not based on freedom of will. Proving the secondary nature of will, he wrote about it a derivative of the objective process, which always represented a different person.

Studying the structure of consciousness, Janet stressed that all the higher manifestations of mind were based on the lower ones, where the action, emotion & intellect were fused. The higher mental functions had one important quality - the unity. This situation required the study of elementary forms of consciousness. Janet's Clinical observations showed that there was a so-called rudimentary consciousness that contained very isolated sensations, unable to act with each other. The initial sensation could lead to other images, but each image was isolated, not connecting with others. In the rudimentary consciousness of not only the sensations, but also emotions & associations of ideas could exist in their primary form. A characteristic feature of this consciousness was the fact that it was impersonal, i.e. not causing the idea of our "I."

On the basis of received submissions, Janet brought the laws that governed isolated phenomena of consciousness: 1) the feelings & images were accompanied by bodily movement, without which they could not exist, 2) all sensations evoked in the mind remained there until a new sensation emerged & 3) all feelings & emotions tend to evolve & end, always occurring in specific movements & actions.

According to Janet rudimentary consciousness was the lowest level in the structure of consciousness. The next steps in the hierarchy were the memory, character & personality. He held that memory when it is able to process certain sensations. In every human being the complex psychological phenomena, ideas, random movement, speech, & etc., are made up of images in a category, & the recollection of these complex elements depends on the reproduction of the elementary images. The unity of mental phenomena, observed & understood, gives rise to the concept of "I". Jane t maintained that "I" was synthesizing the various facts, stating them to the unity of the various mental phenomena, caused by external impressions or automatic play of associations, forming a new idea - the notion of identity. Thus, Janet came to the important position of his theory that the basis of identity formation, or "I" was memory. If the memory was changed, its modification led to a change in personality & the whole mental life. He also noted that without the interaction between people could not develop the psyche or formed personality.

Janet distinguished three levels of consciousness: 1. basic sense, 2. the memory, & 3. "I" or personality. He argued that personality was of metaphysical nature, unchanging & indivisible, unlike the idea of "I" which varied throughout life. Janet also introduced into the psychology an important concept, called the narrowing of the field of consciousness. Janet's field of consciousness was comprised of the large number of simple or relatively simple images, which could simultaneously exist in the same mind. The field of consciousness can vary it is not the same in all people & does not remain always the same in one & the same entity. The narrowing the field of consciousness was described as a mental weakness, which was characterized by reduction of the number of perceived phenomena. Janet also held that a limited field of consciousness was common among sick people & children. In children, this was manifested in intermittent, momentary anger or tears, & in patients - a distraction or concentration of mind on any one point, forgetting about the present & so narrowing the field of consciousness corresponds to the rudimentary psyche.

Investigation of the causes of narrowing of the field of consciousness has led Janet to the analysis a question of the relationship between the conscious & unconscious in the human psyche. At the same time he built his concept of psyche, different from the known theory of Freud. The study of patients with various mental illnesses found that mental disorders affect the stimulation of certain functions, which results in dissociation of either the newly formed or old function. During the process of dissociation the old function (which Janet attributed to the unconscious) remained almost untouched. The functions that exist in the field unconscious are separated from the personal consciousness. In other words the unconscious influence was viewed as an act, which has all the signs of mental act, except that it is never realized by a subject performing it.

In Janet's theory consciousness is connected with reality, & manifests itself in active work. This activity combines a number of phenomena in a new, different form. There are two ways to learn the phenomenon: the impersonal feeling & personal perception. The conscious feeling is a complex whole in which the combined psychic elements correspond with simple movements. The main factors determining a person's identity, according to Janet, are the two types of mental activity; creative & conservative. Creative activity synthesizes perception in judgments, general concepts, moral or scientific concepts. Conservative activity, on the other hand, is trying to save & repeat the information. Physical health & harmony of the spirit depend on a combination of creative & conservative aspects of mentality.

The founder of the French sociological school Emile Durkheim was born at Épinal, Lorraine, on April 15, 1858. Developing the positivist concept of

Comte, he sought to create an objective sociology as a science of society to address the specific spiritual reality. He entered the École Normale Supérieure in 1879. Durkheim became interested in a scientific approach to society very early on in his career. From 1882 to 1885 Durkheim taught philosophy in several provincial lyceums. A leave of absence in 1885-1886 allowed him to study under the psychologist Wilhelm Wundt in Germany. In 1887 he was named lecturer in education & sociology at the University of Bordeaux, a position raised to a professorship in 1896, the first professorship of sociology in France. In 1902 Durkheim was named to a professorship in sociology & education at the Sorbonne. There he remained for the rest of his career. Durkheim died in Paris on Nov. 15, 1917.

He was the first to introduce the term "sociologism" which was the irreducibility of the social reality of biological & psychological phenomena. According to Durkheim social phenomena must be linked with particular social environment, with a certain type of society, finding in it the characteristics of the causes of phenomena investigated. Durkheim stressed that there could be no society if there were only individuals. Over the individual is a spiritual power - the collective. The purpose of collective life, in his opinion, was the integration of individuals in the community, which accorded moral authority & therefore was able to perform an educational function. Individual needs the community, because in it he is not faced with his problems alone & has a support in moments of weakness. Therefore, as noted by Durkheim, a group of people can even sacrifice their interests for a common goal, & intellectual development is often associated with the desire to fulfill their social mission, i.e., the higher forms of human activity have a collective origin.

Analyzing the relationship between personality & social solidarity, Durkheim held that the individual tends to become more autonomous & at the same time more dependent on society. Based on his research, he came to the conclusion that the basis of a society is a mechanical & organic solidarity.

Durkheim maintained that collective life, as well as the psychic life of the individual, consists of performances. Both individual & social representations are comparable, since in both areas the same law applies. Society is a collection of associated individuals, & the system which they form, is modified depending on their location on the territory of the number & nature of communication, & social consciousness. Of great importance are social phenomena, i.e. the most characteristic features of collective life - Religious beliefs, rituals, rules of morality, legal requirements & etc. Durkheim's ideas about the development of collective consciousness have been used in the study of traditional cultures by a famous psychologist, philosopher & ethnographer Lucien Levy-Bruhl (1857-1939).

Levy-Bruhl was concerned primarily with the non-rational belief systems of primitive man. He was born in Paris. He first studied at the Lyceum Charlemagne, pursuing studies in music, philosophy, & natural science. Later he also taught philosophy at Poitiers & Amiens before he attended the University of Paris to pursue his doctorate in 1884. He taught in Paris until his appointment to the Sorbonne in 1896 as titular professor of the history of modern philosophy. In 1902 Levy-Bruhl wrote "Ethics & Moral Science," which marked the beginning of his anthropological interests.

In 1925 he co-founded the Institute of Ethnology at the Sorbonne. Levy-Bruhl wrote six books elaborating his concept of the nature of the primitive mind: "Mental Functions in Primitive Societies" (1910), "Primitive Mentality" (1922), "The Soul of the Primitive" (1928), "The Supernatural & the Nature of the Primitive Mind" (1931), "Primitive Mythology" (1935), & "The Mystic Experience & Primitive Symbolism" (1938). After his retirement Levy-Bruhl lectured at Harvard, Johns Hopkins, & the University of California. He died in Paris on March 13, 1939.

In the works "Primitive Thinking" & "The Soul of the Primitive" he used rich ethnographic material about the life of the peoples of Africa, Australia, Oceania, at different stages of social & cultural development. Levy-Bruhl argued that the various socio-historical structures correspond to certain types of thinking. Based on the latter, he formulated the theory of two types of thinking - primitive & logical. In the book "Mental Functions in Primitive Societies" he described the primitive thinking, illustrating it as a mystical content, pre-logical in its organization, thus, not sensitive to the contradictions & inscrutable for the experience. In contrast to the thinking of the representative of civilized society, it is not focused on the establishment of logical relations, instead it obeys the law of participation, in virtue of which objects are not united on the essential properties, but attributed them to the mystical qualities.

Levy-Bruhl stressed that "pre-logical" &"logical" thinking were not successive stages, but coexisting types of thinking. Pre-logical thinking, determining the content of collective representations of primitive man, did not extend to the sphere of personal experience & practical action. At the same time in a modern society dominated by logical thinking, are stored certain signs of pre-logical, such as religion, morality & rituals. Thus, in the process of historical development the relationship between primitive & logical thinking undergoes a major change.

The study of social contacts of people & their impact on the psyche of the individual involved was one of the main studies of Jean Gabriel Tarde (1843-1904). Tarde was born in Sarlat, to family of a military officer & judge. He attended a Jesuit school in Sarlat, obtaining a classical training, & read law in Toulouse & then Paris. From 1869 to 1894 he held several legal posts near Sarlat. Only after Tarde's mother died did he agree to leave Sarlat, & he accepted a position as director of criminal statistics at the Ministry of Justice in Paris. After 1894 he lectured in numerous peripheral institutions outside the university, and from 1900 until his death he held the chair of modern philosophy at the College de France.

He did not agree with the Durkheim's concept of sociology, especially with his thoughts on the mechanisms of formation of collective representations. The concepts of Tarde were formed under the influence of works of Liebeault & Charcot which proved the importance of suggestion & hypnosis in the life of the subject. Tarde introduced a concept according to which the basis of social relations of personality depends on three factors: imitation, invention & the opposition (resistance to innovation). He argued that among these factors imitation was more dominant as the basis for assigning individual plants, beliefs & feelings of others. Tarde also held that inspired (by outside) thoughts & emotions determine the nature of mental activity in a state of sleep & when awake. Tarde treated group behavior as hypnotism of many people, based on imitation. He emphasized that in society imitation has the same important role as heredity in biology.

Thus, the work of French scientists has helped to expand the scope of psychology to include not only unconscious, but also the collective psyche. The most important result of their research was the sense of a new factor affecting the formation of the psyche - the culture, historical development of society. This was an opportunity to present man as a result of not only biological, but cultural & historical development has shown new aspects of the relationship of psychology with philosophy, history, sociology.

Experimental Psychology

The experiment in psychology was the necessary, decisive factor in the transformation of psychological knowledge, because it separated the psychology from philosophy & turned it into an independent science. The Experimental Psychology used different kinds of psychological research & experimental methods. In late 19-th century scientists began the active study of elementary mental functions & human sensory systems. Initially, these were the first tentative steps which have brought the foundation for the building of Experimental Psychology, separating it from the other disciplines.

Wilhelm Wundt created the world's first psychological laboratory, which later was transformed into the Institute. From this institute came a generation of specialists in experimental psychology. In his first works Wundt put forward a plan for the development of physiological psychology as a special science, in which he used the method of laboratory experiment for the dismemberment of consciousness on the elements & for determining the regular connection between them. The focus of the early experimental psychology was centered on internal mental processes of a normal adult, which were analyzed using a specially organized self-observation (introspection). Eventually similar experiments were conducted on animals (C. Lloyd Morgan, E. Lee Thorndike). Experimental psychology began to investigate not only the general laws of mental processes, but also the individual changes in sensitivity, reaction time, memory, association.

For example Galton developed several methods of diagnostics capabilities, which began testing, statistical treatment of research results (in particular, the method of calculating the correlations between variables), the mass surveys. Cattell examined personality as a combination of a number of empirically (with testing) set and more or less autonomous psychological characteristics. Currently, methods of experimental psychology are widely applied in various fields of human activity. The progress of human knowledge is unthinkable without the techniques of experimental psychology, testing, mathematical & statistical processing of research results. Progress in experimental psychology is based on the use of methods of different sciences: physiology, biology, psychology & mathematics.

The methodology of experimental psychology is based on the following principles:

1. the principle of determinism with its essence to ensure that all mental phenomena were predetermined by the interaction of the organism with the environment. Experimental psychology assumed that human behavior & mental phenomena were due to any reason that was fundamentally explicable. (Whatever happened, it has its own reasons). No causal study would have been impossible.

2. The principle of objectivity. Experimental Psychology believed that the object of knowledge independent of the knowing subject, the object in principle knowable through action. Psychological methods can objectively know the reality. Methods of mathematical statistics can make knowledge objective.

3. The principle of unity of the physiological & mental. Hard gap between physiological & mental health does not exist. The nervous system provided the appearance & course of mental processes, but the reduction of psychological phenomena to physiological processes was impossible. On the one hand the mental & physiological constituted a unity, but it was not identity.

4. The principle of unity of consciousness & activity. Latter stated that it was impossible to separately study the behavior, consciousness & personality. All of them were mutually intertwined.

5. The principle of development, also known as the principle of historicism & the genetic principle. Development - the universal property of matter, the brain - also the result of a long evolutionary development. According to this principle the subject's psyche was the result of a long evolution in phylogeny & ontogeny.

6. Systemic-structural principle, according to which any mental phenomena should be considered as a holistic process. Principle stated that all mental phenomena should be considered as included in the hierarchy, in which the lower floors of senior managers, & higher includes the lower & lean them.

Theories of Personality

Personality can be defined in many different ways, but usually this term refers to our attempts to capture & summarize an individual's essence. Basically personality is the science of describing & understanding persons. Personality is comprised of characteristic patterns of thoughts, behaviors & feelings that make a person unique. Some of the fundamental characteristics of the personality include consistency, impact behaviors & actions, physiological & psychological aspects & multiple expressions. Consistency is an apparent characteristic, since there are strong orders & regularities determining person's behavior, causing a person to act in a similar or same ways in a variety of situations. Personality does not just influence how we move or respond in our environment, it also causes us to act in certain manner. Although personality is considered to be a psychological construct, it is also greatly influenced by biological processes & needs. Personality is characterized by multiple expressions, which means that it is displayed in more than just a behavior. It can also be seen in feelings, thoughts, social interactions & close relationships.

At birth, each person starts from scratch, with a unique genotype, built-in instincts & a capacity to learn various behaviors. Eventually biological, behavioral & psychodynamic processes unfold, interacting with the individual's genotype & together with social shaping process create the unique psychological characteristics of the individual. Thus personality further can be defined as the product of a long history during which it was advantageous for humans to adopt particular characteristic ways of thinking & behaving. Personality also characterizes the individual by virtue of latter's involvement in society as a whole. Thus personality is a specific quality which characterizes the individual from the viewpoint of his links with other individuals in the society to which he belongs.

If one bears in mind the unity but not identity of the personality & the individual, one can see the personality not just in one sphere or psychological dimension. The personality can be interpreted as a kind of property submerged in the sphere of subject's individual life. The personality stands out, above all by its individuality, in the ways it differs from other people. In the same dimension one finds social & cultural variants of the conception of personality which underline the social determination of the specific features of consciousness & behavior. This dimension also includes the conception of the personality as the subject of activeness. Such interpretations express the various ways of understanding the unique & the universal within the individual. Within his own unique & distinctive features individual stands out by virtue of his own non-identity with the universal. By doing so he manifests his personality through his non-merging with the universal. At the same time, the personality manifests itself positively in the idea of assimilation by the individual of elements of culture & of objective life of a society as a whole: through the assertion of its community with the social whole.

Another conception of the personality states that the sphere of interpersonal links represents the sphere of the personality's determination & existence. It is not the individual himself capable of activity, but the very processes in which at least two individuals are involved that are regarded as the bearers of the personality of each individual. This means that the personality as it is acquires a special existence separate from the corporeal existence of the individual. As the bearer of the personality, the individual vanishes from life but he continues, personalized in other people. It is an establishment of the destruction of the integrity of the psychological structure while preserving one of its parts. The personality can only be fully characterized by combining the investigation data of all dimensions of as the ideal representation of an individual mediated by social activity & manifested in other people, in the individual's interrelations with other people & in him as a representative of a society. Often the determining characteristic of the personality is considered to be his activeness, which is manifested in the interpersonal sphere in phenomena outside the limits of situational & role expectations. The personality alters itself in a process of changing others; therefore its contributions to others are alterations & transformations of its own unique characteristics. Metaphorically, personality can be defined as a source of powerful radiation which transforms people related to it in conditions of activity based mediation.

If the personality & the individual are not identical then it is possible to have an individual that have not developed his personality. Naturally the individual without personality is just as exceptional a phenomenon as the so called "quasi-personality" without an individual, but the consideration of this kind of hypothetical situation as a mental experiment is instructive for understanding the problem of the unity & non-identity of the individual & the personality.

The discussions of personality & its psychological characteristics became exceptionally topical in the 1960s & 1970s. The so called accumulative approach which transformed the personality into a sphere containing traits of temperament & character along with predominant needs & interests was being reconsidered. Such an approach regarded personality as a collection of traits, properties, characteristics & features of a person. The idea of a personality as a collection of traits was quite unhelpful if only because it effaced the line dividing the concept "individual" from the concept "personality," broke up the personality into separate juxtaposed parts, & because it deprived the concept personality of its content, without which no single psychological conception can be formed.

Individual's body with its advantages & defects has a powerful influence on a course of his psychic processes & features, but it doesn't mean that the majority f his personality should be given away to biology as a particular substructure. One can only predict a person's behavior if it is based on the stable structure of his personality. But in addition to the elucidation of the stability of personality structures, it is important to realize their relative nature. Accordingly, the psychological problem of the structure of the personality seems to be more social than individual.

The traditional schools of psychology have played a major role in revealing the numerous psychological phenomena of personality, which taken together, ensure the individual uniqueness of the personality. These psychological phenomena are essentially correlative, meaning that a specific social environment is presupposed, in relation to whom the personality manifests conformity, aggressiveness & anxiousness. But, whereas the features of personality are seen in these studies as flexible & changeable, the social environment is regarded as invariable, amorphous & even empty. Such a traditional & at the same time mechanistic interpretation of the social surroundings in the correlation "personality-environment," which has generated countless studies of the dependence of "changes in attitudes" of the personality on "changes in the environment," interprets the environment either as an object which can be influenced by an active individual or as a force of group pressure on the individual. The idea of the active nature of interaction between the individual & its social environment was interwoven neither into the theoretical construction of the psychology of the personality, nor into the experimental psychological methods of studying the individual in the group. However, the approach to social surroundings as well as to environment has given rise to theoretical ideas of the personality in general, regardless of the system of socially determined interrelations in which it exists.

Interest in the processes of interaction between people emerged in the early stages of social development. The first observations of social behavior were made in antiquity in the works of Epicurus, Democritus, Plato & Aristotle, & later during the Enlightenment by Montesquieu, Holbach, Helvetius, Diderot & others. Although their system of knowledge was incomplete, their observations awaken the need for an understanding the laws of an individual's development in the society & thus prepared the way for the first social psychological conceptions. Eventually the positivism of August Comte served as the philosophical basis for the elaboration of social psychological theories. The first significant efforts to create a social psychological theory were made by Gabriel Tarde, Gustave Le Bon, William McDougall & Emile Durkheim. In explaining the laws of the interaction of the individual & society, & the functioning of the most varied human associations, the pioneers of social psychology disclaimed the decisive role of class, social & economic factors & tried to find universal laws which would explain social phenomena from the position of psychology alone. Gabriel Tarde attempted to explain the sources of solidarity & cohesion among people in the categories of so called imitation. Le Bon is known for his attempts to define the law of so called spiritual unity. In turn, Durkheim was concerned with the studies of collective representation. Overall, it is safe to state that they incorrectly subtitled the laws of psychology for the laws of history, reducing all social phenomena to psychological phenomena.

The writings of Charles Cooley & Georg Simmel greatly promoted the development of social psychology, because they were the first to regard the individual not abstractly, linking his traits & peculiar features to the processes of interaction within & among groups. They presented individual traits & features as unique projections of the individual's interrelation with social groups. In their theory the self-conception is the reflection of what the individual believes others think about him. Therefore, how a person evaluates himself corresponds to what he believes to be the opinion of the people with whom he comes into contact. Cooley held that self-conception is not a constant value, but a function of relations with other people. Also Simmel & Cooley maintained that the individual should not be studied outside of his social context & environment. Cooley was the first to introduce the term "primary group" into psychology, showing the decisive role of family & informal associations in the formation of the individual. While substantiating the social nature of an individual's psychic life, Cooley at the same time idealistically interpreted society as the sum total of psychic relations. He overlooked the fact that a group is not something autonomous & exclusive but always remains a part of society or a class. As a result, the focusing of attention on purely psychological relations concealed the real picture of primary group relations.

In the 1920 social psychology became a major trend in the development of psychological science in Western countries. The wide scope of applied studies was mainly stimulated by leading industrial enterprises & military forces. Many institutes & laboratories carried out research into the so called human factor. Later Walter Moede & Floyd Allport conducted studies showing the influence that primary groups have on their members. The objective was to discover in what instances the individual's attitude to the group was positive & in what instances it was negative. It turned out that the mere presence of observers was enough to create a group atmosphere promoting an increase in productivity of the whole group & its members. Moede presents an example when, under the influence of primary group & figures of authority, the individual threshold of sensitivity to electric current were noticeably decreased in certain individuals.

AboutStructuralism

Wilhelm Wundt's finding of the new experimental science of psychology marked the beginning of the systemic position or school of thought in psychology, structuralism. The influence of British empiricism & German experimental psychology were quite evident in formation of structuralism. This new movement absorbed the experimental methods & basic approach of the older natural sciences. It adapted the scientific methods of investigation for its own use & proceeded to study its subject matter in the same way the natural sciences were studying theirs. Thus, the spirit of the times helped to shape both the subject matter & the methods of investigation of the new psychological movement.

The main goal of the early structuralists was to discover the nature of elementary conscious experiences, by analyzing consciousness into separate parts. In Wundt's opinion the subject matter of psychology was the immediate experience as opposed to mediate experience. Wilhelm Wundt (1832-1920) was born in the town of Neckarau, outside of Mannheim. Wundt studied at the Gymnasium at Bruchsal and Heidelberg, after which he entered the University of Tubingen. After one year he transferred to the University of Heidelberg, where he majored in medicine. By his third year he published his first work. Nevertheless, doctoring was not Wundt's vocation and he turned instead to physiology, which he studied for a semester under Johannes Muller. Wundt took his doctorate in medicine at Heidelberg. Two years later, the physicist, physiologist, & psychologist, Hermann von Helmholtz received the call to Heidelberg as a professor of physiology. It was a decisive moment for Wundt's career, because the two worked in the same laboratory until 1871.When Helmholtz moved to Berlin, Wundt was passed over as Helmholtz's replacement; three years later he took the chair in "inductive philosophy" at the University of Zurich. He stayed at Zurich for only one year before receiving an appointment to a first-class chair of philosophy at Leipzig in 1875. Wundt became famous at Leipzig. It was here, in 1879, that the university formally recognized his little room of equipment as a bona fide laboratory the world's first devoted to psychology.

In order to understand Wundt's philosophical importance one must know something of his intellectual context. The nineteenth-century German psychology labored under the looming shadow of Kant & his arguments that a science of psychology was in principle impossible. In founding the experimental science of psychology, Wundt, simply triangulated "a media via" between the available options: he rejected Fechner's mysticism while maintaining his experimental approach; at the same time, Wundt went beyond the purely physical interpretation of physiological experiments of Helmholtz, arguing that at least in humans experimentation could reveal law-like regularities of psychological reality.

Wundt considered the experimental psychology to be the unmediated study of consciousness, supported by the experimental protocols of the natural sciences. His definition involved two contestable assumptions: first, that "consciousness" was susceptible to experiment; second, that psychology, had for its object consciousness. Wundt defined consciousness as "inner experience," claiming that it is only the immediately real phenomena constituting this experience. Wundt's project was not only a psychology that rejected soul but also a science without a substrate. He presented himself as a radical empiricist. The subject of psychology was itself determined wholly & exclusively by its predicates, since these predicates derived solely from direct, internal observation. The main domain of inquiry was that of individual psychology. Wundt declared that individual psychology must become a science via the experimental manipulation of inner phenomena.

Wundt's investigations were mainly focused on sensation and perception. For Wundt sensations & somatic sensory apparatus were important for his project of physiological psychology. He viewed sensations as the contact points between the physical and the psychological. The psychologist, according to Wundt, was supposed to control the external, physiological side (experimentally), in order to generate diverse internal representations that only can appear to the introspective observer. In Wundtian theory the representations that constitute the contents of consciousness all have their elemental basis in sensations. Thus, sensations were never given to us as elemental, however; we never apperceive them purely, but always already connected in the representation of a synthesized perception. His treatment of quality and intensity were especially important for getting a clearer notion of his concept of psychological experimentation. It is a fact of inner experience, says Wundt that every sensation possesses a certain intensity with respect to which it may be compared to other sensations. So the outer sensory stimuli may be measured by physical methods. Wundt saw two possible tasks for psychophysical measurement of sense-stimuli: the determination of limit-values between which stimulus-changes are accompanied by changes in sensation; & the investigation of the lawful relations between stimulus-change and change in sensation.

In psychology consciousness is divided into three major act-categories: representation, willing, and feeling. In Wundt's theory representations were viewed as representational acts (never the "objects with constant properties" propounded by adherents of a so-called theory of substantiality). This identity of representation and representational act typifies what was called Wundt's monistic perspectivism.

Despite the fact that all consciousness originates in sensations, latter are never given to consciousness in a pure state as individual sensory atoms. Sensations are always perceived as already compounded into representations, that is, into images of an object or of a process in the external world. Representations, according to Wundt, may be either perceptions or intuitions. The same representation can be called a perception if considered as the presentation of objective reality and an intuition if considered in terms of the accompanying conscious. If the representation's object is not real but merely thought, then it is a so-called reproduced representation.

In structuralism the formative process by which sensations are connected into representations either through temporal sequencing or spatial ordering constitutes a main aspect of the activity called consciousness. Wundt claims that all representations are formed through so called psychological synthesis of sensations. Supposedly this synthesis can accompany every representational act.

Wundt viewed consciousness as a function of the scope of attention, which may be either broader or narrower. Apperception, in turn, may either actively select or focus upon a perceived representation, or it may passively find certain representations suddenly thrusting themselves into the center of attention. Since there is no distinct boundary between the perceived and the apperceived, Wundt's analogy may be misleading to the extent that it gives the impression of two separable forms of attention able in principle to subsist together. For Wundt, the distinguishing feature of the apperceptive focus is that it always forms a unitary representation, so that a narrower focal point results in a correspondingly higher intensity of attention. Therefore the degree of apperception is not to be measured according to the strength of the external impression but solely according to the subjective activity through which consciousness turns to a particular sense-stimulus.

For Wundt the possibility of a physiological psychology as opposed to a purely physiological inquiry into sensation depends on the possibility of self-observation. Self-observation, in turn, is of scientific use if & only if the sequence of "inner" phenomena of consciousness is assumed to fall under an independent principle of psychic causality. If the inner phenomena could be shown to fall under the physical causality of the natural sciences, then there would be no need for a special psychological method, such as self-observation. In fact, however, a system of psychic causality can be determined, Wundt argues, one that at no point is reducible to physical causality.

Wundt was also known for dividing the sciences into two large families, the "formal" and the "real." The former included mathematics; the latter study the natural and spiritual aspects of reality, & correspondingly are divided into the natural and the human sciences. The human sciences in turn were divided into two genera, one of which dealt with spiritual processes, the other with spiritual products. The former just was the science of psychology; the latter included the general study of these products as such (e.g., philology, political science, law, religion, etc.), as well as the parallel historical study of these products as they have in fact been created. Since the process preceded the product, psychology as "the doctrine of spiritual processes as such" was the foundation of all the other human sciences. Philosophy, in turn, took psychology's results and again abstracted from them the normative rules governing the organization of the human. In this way psychology was a science mediating between the sciences and philosophy.

Wundt's view of logic was quite unusual, yet fully in line with his rigorously anti-metaphysical monistic perspectivism. He had no logical "third realm," but merely a single process called "thinking." Wundt said that it was an immediately given fact of thinking that there were logical laws that stood over against all our other thoughts and representations. Their psychological immediacy does not, Wundt thinks, compromise their normativity, since what is given in consciousness precisely is their normative character. Once this character is taken for granted, the science of logic develops its systems of correct deductions without further worry about the source of that normativity.

Wundt postulated that the three features of logical thinking that set it apart from all other types of representational connection were its spontaneity, evidence and universal validity. His notion of the spontaneity of logical thinking was the most psychologistic of the three. Thinking was experienced immediately as an inner activity. That is why we must regard it as an act of will and accordingly regard the logical laws of thought as laws of the will. In other words, logical thinking was accompanied essentially by a feeling of the thinking subject's freedom in thinking. But while logical thinking may be accompanied by an especially strong self-awareness of the mind's own activity, this feeling is not unique to logical thinking, since active apperception more generally is also accompanied by the sense of subjective activity. Thus, logical evidence and universal validity are characteristics possessed by logical thinking to a higher degree than by any other psychic function. By "evidence," Wundt meant the character of compelling necessity accompanying a logical judgment. Thought may exhibit immediate certainty, obvious without any mediating thought-acts; or a thought may be mediately certain, grounded in prior thought-acts. Therefore immediate and mediate evidence have their source and foundation in intuition; immediate evidence immediately, mediate; mediately. According to Wundt intuition was not identical with evidence, for evidence only came to be at the moment when logical thinking related the contents of intuition & presupposed the relations of such intuitive contents as objectively given. Wundt thus charted a middle course between making logical evidence a transcendent or transcendental function of thinking & considered it an empirical trait of sensible objects.

Wundt was undoubtedly committed to developing a new brand of logical psychologism. But while he rejected any interpretation of the origin of logical principles that would impugn their normative character of necessity, he also rejected the opposite extreme, what he calls "Logizismus"—the complete divorce of logical thinking from thinking as it actually occurs in minds. For Wundt, the logicist makes a metaphysical leap as suspect as it is unnecessary in conjuring up a pure, absolute, transcendental, but in any case separate source of logical normativity. As opposed to solving the puzzle of logical normativity, he exacerbates it by adding the puzzles of the ontological status of a third realm, or of a transcendental ego. Wundt finds a simpler solution in his perspectivism. The logical may be considered purely from a logical point of view, meaning in terms of its normative character, or genetically from a psychological point of view. But there are no logical laws that are not also describable psychologically. Being describable in this sense is not the same as being explicable, and it is this separate task of explanation that falls to logic and psychology.

Despite his numerous contributions Wundt's conception of psychology was always controversial, at least in Germany. The timely struggle over the status and philosophical meaning of consciousness resulted, on the one hand, in the exclusion of Wundtian empiricism from philosophy departments, striving to maintain their speculative purity, and, on the other, the institutional establishment of experimental psychology. This was not the outcome Wundt had desired. He had wished to reform philosophy not as a synthetic science, but with a direct, indispensable, juridical relation vis-à-vis both the natural and human sciences.

The classical Wundtian brand of the new movement in psychology was brought to United States by Wundt's most devoted follower Edward Bradford Titchener, & underwent its fullest transformation at his hands. The knowledge of Wundt's psychology provides a reasonably accurate picture of Titchener's system though the two positions are not identical. Titchener differed on some points with Wundt nonetheless the new structuralism is unmistakably Wundtian in methods.

Edward Bradford Titchener (1867-1927) was born in Chichester, Sussex. His family intended Titchener for the Anglican clergy, but his interests were not in religion. In 1885 he entered Brasenose College, Oxford, on a classics scholarship but soon turned to a study of biology & then comparative psychology. Titchener remained interested in comparative psychology, but there was not enough structure or rigor in the subject matter to satisfy him fully.

Several years earlier Wilhelm Wundt had founded psychology as a systematic & experimental science of the human mind. Finally Titchener found the kind of study he had been seeking, and this analytic study of human experience occupied him for the rest of his career.

After receiving his doctorate in 1892, Titchener accepted a position in the recently founded laboratory of psychology at Cornell University. Later he rose to full professor and head of the department of psychology when psychology became independent from philosophy. Soon he published"Outline of Psychology" (1897) & his monumental "Experimental Psychology" (1901-1905). He was an inspiring speaker, and his lectures became legend among generations of Cornell students. Titchener emphasized psychology as a science, in contrast to technology, desiring to understand the facts of experience with no particular notion of application. His new, structural school studied the world of experience in terms of the experiencing individual and explained experience in terms of the nervous system. At this time the model for structuralism was chemistry, the task being to analyze the complex experiences of everyday life into their elemental components and then to attempt to understand the nature of the compounding. Titchener's main tool was of course introspection, the systematic description of experience. Titchener's "A Textbook of Psychology," written in 1910 became the bible of the school.

As I mentioned earlier the main tool that Titchener used to try & determine the different components of consciousness was introspection. Unlike Wundt, Titchener had very strict guidelines for the reporting of an introspective analysis. For example, the subject would be presented with an object, such as a book. The subject would then report the characteristics of that book (color, length, etc.). The subject would be instructed not to report the name of the object (book) because that did not describe the raw data of what the subject was experiencing. Titchener referred to this as stimulus error.

It is obvious that Titchener's ideas on how the mind worked were heavily influenced by Wundt's theory of voluntarism & his ideas of Association & Apperception. Titchener attempted to classify the structures of the mind, not unlike the way a chemist analyzes chemicals into their component parts. Titchener believed that if the basic components of the mind could be defined and categorized that the structure of mental processes and higher thinking could be determined. What each element of the mind is, how those elements interact with each other and why they interact in the ways that they do will was the basis of reasoning that Titchener used in trying to find structure to the mind.

In Titchener's theory consciousness is defined as the sum of person's experiences accumulated during his lifetime. Mind & consciousness are seen as the same, except that consciousness involves mental processes occurring at the moment rather than the total accumulation of processes. Titchener maintains that psychology should study the generalized human mind, not individual minds, & differences against them. Titchener's psychology thus is a pure science that has no applied or utilitarian concerns. He also opposed child psychology, animal psychology, & any area of the science that did not fit in with his introspective experimental psychology of the content of consciousness.

Psychology, as a science greatly depends on observation of conscious experience or introspection. The new structuralistic form of introspection was even more highly developed & formalized than Wundt's. He realized that people learn to describe experience in terms of the stimulus, & that in everyday life this is beneficial & necessary. The influence of the mechanistic spirit is evident in the image structuralism developed of the human subjects who supplied its data. Titchener believed that observation in psychology must be not only introspective in nature but also experimental.

Titchener's three aims of psychology are quite similar to those of Wundt. The psychologist must attempt 1 to reduce conscious process to their simplest, basic components; 2 to determine how these elements are combined; 3 to bring the elements into connection with their psychological conditions. Thus, the goals of psychology coincide with those of the natural sciences. Titchener held that there are three elementary states of consciousness: sensations, images & affective states. He finds the sensations to be the core of perceptions, but images accrue to the core to lend meaning to the complex of sensations, which means that past experience makes present experience meaningful.

In Titchener's theory verbal as well as concrete images play an important role in conveying meaning. Images were described as the elements of ideas found in the process that reflects experiences not actually present at the moment, such as a memory of past experience. It is not totally clear from Titchener's writings that he considered sensations & images as belonging in mutually exclusive categories. In reality he even emphasized the similarity between the two while nevertheless arguing that they could be distinguished. Affections were considered the elements of emotion & believed to be found in experiences, such as love & hate.

Titchener presented a vast majority of elements of sensations, made up of even more sensation qualities, the majority of which were visual & auditory. Each element was believed to be conscious & distinct from all others, yet at the same time each could be blended & combined with others to form perceptions & ideas. The elements can be classified just as chemical elements, although they are basic & irreducible. To the previous, Wundtian attributes of quality & intensity Titchener added duration & clearness, since he considered these four attributes basic characteristics of all sensations that are present to some degree in all experience.

The key characteristic that distinguishes each element from the other is quality, while intensity is described as the strength or weakness, brightness or loudness of a sensation. Duration is presented as a flow of a sensation over time & clearness as the role of attention in conscious experience. It is a fact that sensations & images possess all of the four above mentioned attributes while affection has only three- it lacks clearness. Titchener held that it was not possible to focus attention directly on the quality of pleasantness, because when such thing is attempted the affective quality disappears.

The active criticism of introspection before Titchener & Wundt sharpened & modified the method of structuralism to bring it in line with the requirements of experimentalism. Titchener seems to have had a difficult time defining introspection with any degree of rigor & attempted to do so by relating it to the particular experimental conditions. He also held that the experimental conditions of the experiment must be closely controlled so that the conscious contents could be correctly determined, then two observers should have the same experience & their results should serve to corroborate one another. There was also an opinion that introspection was, in reality retrospection, because some period of time must elapse between the experience itself & the reporting of it. Since forgetting is particularly rapid after an experience, it seems likely that some of the experience would be lost. The structuralists' answer to this argument was to specify that the observers work with very short time intervals. They also postulated the existence of a primary mental image that was alleged to maintain the experience for the observer until it could be reported. The method of structuralism was not the only target of criticism this movement was accused of artificiality & sterility, because of its attempt to analyze conscious process into elements. It was argued that the whole of an experience cannot be recovered by any synthesis or compounding of the elemental parts. Accordingly experience does not come to man in sensory or affective elements, it comes in unified wholes.

Psychology was growing in a number of areas & the structuralists referred to exclude these newer areas if they were not congruent with their definition & method of psychology. Titchener's conception of psychology was too narrow to contain the growing data being accumulated by an increasing number of psychologists.

Despite his top position as an organizer in the early days of psychology, Wundt's monopoly on the new science was eventually lost. Many early psychologists disagreed with Wundt on his theory, but almost all of them were convinced that the introspection was the only efficient method that can be used in psychology. Some of these psychologists came to influence structuralism by their opposition to it rather than by any direct contribution to this movement. Almost all of the Wundt's opponents had different points of view, but all of them were engaged in a common enterprise of developing the new psychology. Many of these psychologists were German. While German psychologists were busy developing their theories, Charles Darwin introduced his theory of evolution. Around the same time Sir Francis Galton began his study on the psychology of individual differences. After its founding, the new science became divided into many differing & opposing directions. Because of these developments Wundt's structuralism became only one of several distinct varieties.

Hermann Ebbinghaus (1850-1909) was born in Barmen, a German town which later was incorporated into the city of Wuppertal. He studied at the University of Bonn, where he was first drawn to philosophy. His education was interrupted in 1870 by Franco-Prussian War, in which he served with the Prussian army. After war he returned to the University of Bonn, where he completed his dissertation on Eduard von Hartmann's "Philosophy of the Unconscious." Ebbinghaus received his doctorate in 1873. He was the first psychologist to experimentally investigate memory & learning. Ebbinghaus was also known for the discovery of forgetting curves & the spacing effect. His researches drastically changed the way in which association & learning were being dealt with. Before Ebbinghaus the British empiricists were studying associations by dealing with only those associations already formed. This means that the investigators were working backwards, attempting to determine how associations had been formed. Ebbinghaus' methods made it possible to control the conditions under which the associations were being formed, thus to make the study of learning more objective. In 1893 Ebbinghaus published his famous "Theory of Color Vision" in which he argued that the perception of color can only be accomplished with the aid of higher mental processes. He had discovered that two white hues produced by spinning either red or green or blue & yellow color-tops indeed appeared the same at certain levels of brightness, but appeared different when the illumination was reduced. Ebbinghaus' so called double-pyramid was intended to demonstrate that at least something was unconnected to both light stimulus & physiological reaction. With this discovery an era in which colors were simple came to an end.

His investigation of learning & forgetting was the first venture into the psychological problem area. For the basic measure of language Ebbinghaus adopted a technique from British associationism, which had gradually been emphasizing the principle of frequency of associations as a condition of recall. He held that the difficulty of learning material can be measured by simply counting the number of repetitions needed to learn the material to a criterion of one perfect reproduction. Ebbinghaus repeated the same material over & over so as to be assured of the accuracy of his results. He also used similar materials to avoid variable errors from trial to trial. Then he could take the average measure. Ebbinghaus invented a nonsense syllable for the material to be learned. He recognized an inherent difficulty in using the poetry or prose. These already formed associations & can facilitate the learning of the material & since they exist at the time of the experimentation, cannot be meaningfully controlled. Ebbinghaus conducted number of experiments to determine the influence of various conditions on both learning & retention. One of these studies dealt with the difference between his speed in memorizing lists of nonsense syllables & in memorizing meaningful materials. He concluded that meaningless material is nine times as hard to learn as meaningful material. Ebbinghaus was the first to investigate the effect of the length of the material to be learned on the on the number of repetitions necessary for a perfect reproduction. He found that longer material required more repetitions & consequently more time to be learned. These results were of course predictable enough in general way, the more we have to learn, the longer it will take us.

Ebbinghaus also studied the effect of overlearning, repeated learning & the influence of the passage of time between learning & recall. Later his research on the influence of passage of time produced the famous Ebbinghaus curve of forgetting. This curve shows that material is forgotten very rapidly in the first few hours after learning.

Although he did not found a school or a formal system, Ebbinghaus is of great importance not only to the study of learning & memory but also to experimental psychology as a whole. It is because of Ebbinghaus that the concept of association changed from mere speculation to its investigation with the aid of the scientific method.

George Elias Muller (1850-1934) was born in Grimma, Germany. He received his doctorate in 1873, under supervision of Rudolf Hermann Lotze in Gottingen. Though Muller was a philosopher & a physiologist by training, he also had a strong interest in psychology. Muller's work was so powerful that Titchener delayed for two years the volume of his "Experimental Psychology" so that he could incorporate material from Muller's new book.

Muller conducted several researches in color vision. He was very critical of Fechner's psychophysics. Muller was one the first to work in the field of experimental study of memory & learning (originally founded by Ebbinghaus). His professional research verified & extended many of Ebbinghaus' early findings. As we already know, Ebbinghaus' approach was strictly objective; meaning, he had not recorded any introspections about his mental processes while engaging in learning tasks. Muller thought that Ebbinghaus' reports made learning process appear too mechanical. He was convinced that mind is more actively involved in learning, & so, while he used the objective methods of Ebbinghaus, Muller added introspective report. His results showed that the learning of his subjects was proceeding mechanically, that the subjects were quite actively involved in learning. Muller later concluded that association by contiguity alone cannot adequately account for learning because the subjects seem to be actively searching for relations among the stimuli to be learned. He suggested that there is a set of mental phenomena such as readiness, hesitation, & doubt that actively influence the learning. In addition, Muller, along with Friedrich Schumann developed the memory drum, a revolving drum that makes possible the uniform presentation of material to be learned.

Muller was a great methodologist of psychological experimentation. He was recognized by his contemporaries as the master experimenter & methodologist in three areas of experimental psychology: the study of memory, visual perception & psychophysics. Muller was the first in the field to discover that the learning & recall involved active processes like grouping, rhythms & basic conscious organizational strategies for the verbal tasks. He also developed a concept of forgetting according to which the new learning interferes with the old one. Despite the lack of translated material Muller's work is of utmost importance to the development of experimental psychology. After Fechner, Muller's work in psychophysics stands out as the most significant in the history of experimental psychology.

Franz Brentano (1838-1917) was born in Marienberg am Rhein, Germany. He studied philosophy, mathematics, poetry & theology in Munich, Berlin & Wurzburg. At high school he became acquainted with scholasticism. At university he studied Aristotle, Comte & Mill, all of whom had a great influence on his work. Brentano received his Ph.D. in 1862, with his thesis "On the Several Senses of Being in Aristotle." After graduation Brentano joined the Catholic Church & continued his academic career at the University of Wurzburg. Despite the fact that he was a priest, Brentano eventually became a full professor in 1873.

Brentano's main principle was that philosophy should be done with methods that are as rigorous and exact as the methods of the natural sciences. This position was clearly mirrored in his empirical approach to psychology. Brentano's use of the word "empirical" deviated substantially from what has become its standard meaning in psychology today. He held that all our knowledge should be based on direct experience. He did not hold, however, that this experience needs to be made from a third-person point of view, and thus opposes what has become a standard of empirical science nowadays. Brentano rather argued a form of introspectionism: doing psychology from an empirical standpoint meant for him to describe what one directly experiences in inner perception, from a first-person point of view.

Brentano's approach was harshly criticized with the rise of scientific psychology in the tradition of logical positivism, especially by the behaviorists. This should not obscure the fact that Brentano did play a huge role in the process of psychology becoming an independent science. He distinguished between genetic and empirical, a distinction that is most explicitly drawn in his "Descriptive Psychology."

Brentano attempted to lay the basis for a scientific psychology, which he defined as "the science of mental phenomena." In order to give flesh to this definition of the discipline, he provided a more detailed characterization of mental phenomena. He introduced six criteria to distinguish mental from physical phenomena, the most important of which were: 1.

mental phenomena are the exclusive object of inner perception, 2. they always appear as a unity, & finally 3. They are always intentionally directed towards an object.

According to Brentano all mental phenomena have in common that they are only perceived in inner consciousness, while in the case of physical phenomena only external perception is possible. The former of these two forms of perception provided an unmistakable evidence for what is true. Because the German word for perception (Wahrnehmung), literally translated, means "taking-true", Brentano argued, that it is the only kind of perception in a strict sense. He maintained that perception must not be mixed up with inner observation, meaning it must not be conceived as a full-fledged act that accompanies another mental act towards which it is directed.

Brentano opposed the idea that there could be unconscious mental acts: since *every* mental act is incidentally directed towards itself as a secondary object, we are automatically aware of every occurring mental act. He stated, however, that people can have mental acts of various degrees of intensity. In addition, he held that the degree of intensity with which the object is presented was equal to the degree of intensity in which the secondary object, i.e., the act itself, was presented. Thus, if we have a mental act of a very low intensity, our secondary consciousness of this act also will have a very low intensity Brentano further concluded that sometimes people are inclined to say that they had an unconscious mental phenomenon when actually they only had a conscious mental phenomenon of very low intensity.

In Brentano's theory consciousness always formed a unity. While people can perceive a number of physical phenomena at one and the same time, they can only perceive one mental phenomenon at a specific point in time. Brentano's views on the unity of consciousness entailed that inner observation was strictly impossible, i.e., that we cannot have a second act which is directed towards another mental act which it accompanies. One can remember another mental act one had earlier, or expect future mental acts, but due to the unity of consciousness one cannot have two mental acts, one of which being directed towards the other.

Brentano proved that we can be directed towards one and the same object in different ways and he accordingly distinguished three kinds of mental phenomena: presentations, judgments, and phenomena of love and hate. Presentations were the most basic kind of acts; we have a presentation each time when we are directed towards an object, be it that we are imagining, seeing, remembering, or expecting it, etc. Brentano held that two presentations can differ only in the object, towards which they are directed. Later he modified his position, though, and argued that they can also differ in various modes, such as temporal modes. The two other categories, judgments and phenomena of love and hate, were based on presentations. In a judgment we accept or deny the existence of the presented object. Thus, a judgment is a presentation plus a qualitative mode of acceptance or denial. The third category (which Brentano names "phenomena of love and hate,) includes emotions, feelings, desires and acts of will. In these acts we have positive or negative feelings towards an object.

Brentano attributed psychology a central role in the sciences; he considered especially logics, ethics, & aesthetics as practical disciplines that depended on psychology as their theoretical foundation. His conception of these three disciplines was closely related to his distinction between the three kinds of mental phenomenon: presentations, judgments, and phenomena of love and hate. Logic was the practical discipline that was concerned with judgments, said Brentano, meaning that with the class of mental phenomena in which we take a positive or a negative stance towards the object by affirming or denying it. Thus, judgments can be correct or incorrect; they have a truth-value. According to Brentano, a judgment was true when it is evident, that is, when one perceived that one judges with evidence.

Truth for Brentano was not a subjective notion: if one person affirms an object and another person denies the same object, only one of them judges correctly.

As we know aesthetics is based on the most basic class of mental phenomena: on presentations. According to Brentano, every presentation is in itself of value; this holds even for those that become the basis of a correct, negative judgment or a correct negative emotion. While judgments & emotions consisted in taking either a positive or a negative stance, the value of a presentation was always positive, but coming in degrees: some presentations were of higher value than others. Not every presentation was of particular aesthetic value. In order to be so it had to become the object of an emotion in which one correctly takes a positive stance towards it. In short, an object was beautiful if a presentation that was directed at it aroused a correct, positive emotion, or a form of pleasure; it was ugly, on the other hand, if a presentation that was directed at it aroused a correct, negative emotion or a form of displeasure. Latter shows that Brentano's philosophy has strong psychological tendencies. Whether or not one is to conclude that he does adopt a form of psychologism depends on the exact definition of the latter term: Brentano vehemently rejected the charge of psychologism, which he took to stand for a subjectivist and anthropocentric position. Meanwhile he defended the claim that psychology was the theoretical science on which practical disciplines of logic& ethics were based.

Apparently Brentano's interest in the history of philosophy was not only reflected by his extensive work on Aristotle, but also by his historiographical considerations. He argued the metaphilosophical thesis that progress in philosophy can be explained according to principles of cultural psychology. In philosophy progress took place in circles: each philosophical period, Brentano held, could be subdivided in four phases. The first was a creative phase of renewal and ascending development; the other three were phases of decline, dominated by a turn towards practical interests, by skepticism, and finally by mysticism. This scheme was successful in giving his philosophical preferences an intellectual justification, because it allowed him to explain his fascination for Aristotle, the Scholastics, & Descartes as well as his dislike of Kant and the German idealists.

Carl Stumpf (1848-1936) was born Wiesentheid, Germany. He came onto contact with science at a very early age. As student at the Wurzburg he was captivated by Brentano & began to study philosophy & science. Since Brentano had not been habilitated to supervise dissertations, he recommended that Stumpf study with Hermann Lotze in Göttingen. Stumpf attended Lotze's lectures on psychology, history of philosophy since Kant, philosophy of nature and practical philosophy. He graduated in 1868 with a dissertation on Plato & then returned to Wurzburg in order to study with Brentano. In 1870 Stumpf entered the ecclesiastical seminary in Wurzburg. He eventually returned to Göttingen to prepare his habilitation on mathematical axioms under the supervision of Lotze & successfully defended it in October 1870. From 1870 to 1873 he lectured at the University of Göttingen, also in 1873 he published an important treatise on the origin of space perception, and dedicated it to Lotze. From 1873 to 1879 he was appointed to his first professorship at the University of Wurzburg.

Just like Brentano & Lotze, Stumpf was fascinated by the history of philosophy. Naturally this interest was not strictly historiographical; Stumpf's point of departure was Brentano's theory of the four phases in the history of philosophy, and he worked out his own philosophy of history, which formed the basis of his diagnosis on the course of philosophy in the nineteenth century, which was inseparable from the way he conceived his own practice of philosophy. In Brentano's theory, each of the three main periods in the history of philosophy was characterized by four stages or moments. The first stage corresponded to the ascending development of philosophy and was characterized by a practice of philosophy guided by purely theoretical interests. Its key figures were Aristotle for Antiquity, Aquinas for the Middle Ages and Descartes for the modern period. The three other stages coincided with the decline of philosophy, the last stage being philosophy's extreme state of degeneracy. For Stumpf and for the majority of Brentano's students, the dogmas and the invention of artificial means of achieving knowledge based on principles devoid of any intuition was characteristic of this particular moment in the history of philosophy. Plotinus, Nicolas of Cusa, Kant and the German idealists belonged to this fourth stage, in their respective epochs. Brentano's thinking on the history of philosophy partly explains Stumpf's repeated criticisms of Kantianism throughout his career.

Stumpf discarded the metaphysical postulate of an empty space & the conception of sensations as unstructured and shapeless material serving as support for the activity of understanding. He only agreed with Kant that there is no representation of matter without form, no quality without extension, since it is the form that allows the ordering of the sensitive multiplicity. He did not, however, admit that it was possible to imagine the perception of space or form without a sensory quality or a positive content that serves as its foundation and is a necessary condition to the space order.

Descriptive psychology was one of the main focuses of Stumpf's program in philosophy. His treatises in this domain ranged from animal & developmental psychology to acoustic psychology and Gestalt psychology. Over the years, Stumpf developed several important concepts such as analysis, attention, relations, & the well-known concept of fusion, which was the basis of his theory of music.

Descriptive psychology's task was the classification of acts or psychical functions based on the distinction between two classes: intellectual & emotional functions. Thus, all functions falling under either of these two classes had relationships ranging from the simplest to the most complex, so that functions of the second class presupposed & were based on lower level functions of the first class. This class of intellectual functions subsumed all acts ranging from sense perception to judgment. Sense perception in this classification had a particular status as a channel. It gave direct access to first order phenomena and, as such, it was the function of consciousness. Basically, it served as the foundation of all functions in that it provided them their sensory materials. Between perception and judgment, there was a series of intermediate acts: the act of presentation, which had as content second order phenomena, the act of abstraction, and what he called the acts of synthesis.

Stumpf's works in the field of emotions gave rise to a debate with Brentano & to many discussions, in particular with Titchener. At issue was whether the nature of pleasure provided by an object such as a work of art for instance is intentional, as in Brentano's theory, in which it is closely related to the class of emotions, or phenomenal as in Husserl's & the sensualist theories of James and Mach. Stumpf claimed that there was a big difference between sense-feelings & emotions which are intentional states directed towards states of affairs. So between emotional & intellectual functions, there was the same relation of foundation as that between judgment & perception, since judgment, or more precisely states of affairs, were presupposed by emotional functions which, although more complex than these, were structured in the same way. In addition to emotions, this class of feelings subsumed the acts of desire & will, upon which the field of ethics was based. Between emotions & will, there was a hierarchy comparable to that of the class of intellectual states, with the difference being, however, that the phenomenal basis of the class of emotional acts was nothing other than sense-feelings. Accordingly, emotions belonged to the subclass of passive feelings, while desire & will belonged to the subclass of active feelings. Feelings were considered to be passive in that that they had something existent as object, while active feelings were related to a duty. Values were the specific content of the class of active feelings while the contents of an emotion were states of affairs.

Stumpf constantly criticized both the Kantians, who tried to liberate the theory of knowledge from psychology, and psychologists who claim in general to reduce the theory of knowledge & philosophy to psychology. According to Stumpf the neo-Kantian argument against psychologism was that psychology could never lead to the knowledge of so called general & necessary truths, & that we could even ignore it altogether since, as Kant argued in the first *Critique*, the sources of knowledge lie in *a priori* forms of intuition & thought. This pure form of "antipsychologism" can therefore be described as metaphysical in the same sense as the postulate of an empty space. Stumpf recognized the value of the Kantian's objections directed against psychologism, but he argued that it was wrong to deny any contribution made by psychology to the theory of knowledge. He held that excluding psychology altogether in the theory of knowledge amounts to refusing the important & indispensable resources which we need to account for the origin of those categories and synthetic judgments for which Kantianism had no explanation.

Although psychology was essential to a theory of knowledge, its field of study differed from the latter. Stumpf considered psychology to be the science of psychical functions; for example acts of judgment whose contents were states of affairs. It is well known that descriptive psychology differs from genetic or physiological psychology, which studies the physiological, processes underlying psychical acts. But the kind of psychologism that Stumpf criticized did not take this distinction into account when it was assigned to a theory of knowledge the task of accounting for the physiological processes and causal connections underlying mental acts. Stumpf argued that the task of descriptive psychology differed from that of the theory of knowledge in that it studied the origin of concepts, while the theory of knowledge's main task was questioning the origin and justification of knowledge, not the physiological causes, but the contents of acts and their relations to thought. Stumpf's position on justification was similar to Brentano's. It was based on the evidence of inner perception.

Stumpf maintained that issues pertaining to the origin of knowledge were closely related to the research fields of the three neutral sciences partly overlapping the theory of knowledge. Because of the latter statement the debate on psychologism took a somewhat different meaning, since recognizing the merits of the principle of separation between psychology, understood as the foundation of human or social sciences, and the theory of knowledge, based on the three neutral sciences, the objection against Kant and his theory of knowledge was not only to have neglected psychology in the narrow sense of the term, but also to have underestimated the use of phenomenology & relations theory to solve epistemological problems. On the other hand, considering Husserl's criticism against Mach's psychologism, he stated that the error of this kind of psychologism was to overestimate the domain of phenomenal experience, to which Mach reduced the objects and laws of the natural sciences.

Stumpf was very critical of Gestalt psychology of the Berlin school. This criticism was motivated by the principles of descriptive psychology & focused on the perception of forms and some philosophical presuppositions. The first assumption that Stumpf challenged was a form of sensualistic naturalism. The second was the metaphysical question of the psychophysical relations & the attempt by Köhler to introduce the concept of form into the field of physics. Stumpf was convinced that the theory of isomorphism that postulated an identity between the structural laws of the mental & physical worlds, presupposed the theory of parallelism, which Stumpf rejected. As to the perception of Gestalts, Stumpf argued that the Berlin school went too far in its criticism of classical psychology, especially in assimilating the founding contents, or parts within the whole of the Gestalt. A Gestalt, according to Stumpf conceived as a complex of structural relations, and this presupposed, among other things, the perception of relations, the possibility of phenomenal content that was unnoticed, and the distinction between phenomena and mental functions. The members of this school rejected these three presuppositions linked to what W. Köhler called the constancy hypothesis.

Oswald Kulpe (1862-1915) was a disciple & follower of Wundt. He was one of the prominent structuralists of the late 19th and early 20th century. He was born at Kandau, Courland. In 1879 Kulpe graduated from the Gymnasium at Libau, where he taught for the next two years. He was strongly influenced by his mentor Wundt, but later disagreed with him on the complexity of human consciousness.

Kulpe was a student of history at the University of Leipzig when he encountered Wundt and decided to change his major to work with Wundt. After graduation he became Wundt's assistant. After leaving Leipzig for the University of Wurzburg, he began to practice what he called systematic experimental introspection. His subjects were asked to complete complex tasks & then provide a retrospective account of their cognitive processes during the task. Kulpe's main finding was known as "imageless thought."He argued that thoughts can occur without a particular sensory or image content. Kulpe left Wurzburg in 1909 & after three years at the University of Bonn, he moved to the University of Munich.

Kulpe's philosophical position was closely related to his work in psychology. Later in his career he came to regard the positivistic attempts of Ernst Mach & Richard Avenarius to reduce mental processes to sensations as incapable of accounting for the findings of introspective experiments. In one of his experiments Kulpe presented cards with nonsense syllables of varying colors and arrangements to subjects who were asked to report either the color, pattern, or number of items seen. Each person abstracted the features he had been instructed to report, remaining unconscious of the other features of the cards. This helped Kulpe to conclude that the process of abstraction depends not only on the material presented to sensation but also on the subject's apprehension. This further proved that sensations—as well as physical phenomena—must be distinguished from their apprehension. Thus he questioned the equation of "being" with "being perceived," even at the level of sensation.

Eventually Kulpe abandoned the sensationalist psychology of contents in favor of a psychology recognizing both contents and acts of mind. Abstraction was a mental act or function that could not be directly observed, but its occurrence was undeniable, even though it was discoverable only retrospectively. He recognized both, thought contents & thought processes. The latter included the impalpable acts of thinking, meaning, and judging, which were not merely relations among contents but activities of the ego that transform the actualities of consciousness into realities.

Kulpe was always very critical of naive realism and idealism. Against the former, he argued that thought, although it does not produce the object of knowledge, is nevertheless genuinely spontaneous & creative in contributing to the realization of the object. His argument against idealism held that the facts of conscious experience require the existence of independent objects.

In aesthetics, Kulpe attempted to support Gustav Fechner's results concerning the golden section. Just like Wundt, he maintained that the aesthetic pleasure produced by ideally proportioned objects results from mental economy. Thus, when the ratio of a whole to its larger part is the same as that of the larger to the smaller part, the perception involves the least effort combined with the greatest possible diversity.

In addition Kulpe contributed to the development of experimental aesthetics by such methods as asking people to record their reactions to glimpses of slides showing works of art. His findings showed no sympathetic empathy on the part of his subjects, thus opposing the contention of Theodor Lipps that such empathy is the basic condition of all aesthetic enjoyment. Kulpe discovered that form, orderliness, symmetry, & harmony were related to attractiveness. He recognized the limited validity of his findings, admitting that aesthetically inexperienced people might respond differently than his subjects. Such reluctance to claim more for a theory than was warranted by experimental findings was characteristic of Kulpe's work in psychology.

About Wurzburg school

In the beginning of the 20th century there were many laboratories of experimental psychology operating in various universities. The members of the Wurzburg school were Karl Marbe, Adolf Meyer, Henry Watt, Narziss Ach, Karl Buhler, & Otto Selz, as well as August Messer.

Marbe (1869-1953) was known for being the author of the valuable experimental work generated by the school. Marbe was also the first to conclude that judgment was a logical concept & to present the term called conscious attitude. At the end he criticized the school for the acceptance of the procedure of introspective analysis.

August Messer (1867-1937) at first worked in the University of Hesse, but eventually joined the Wurzburg school where he conducted the "experimental psychological experiments into thought," in which he was illustrating the distinction between the acts of consciousness & content of consciousness.

Henry Watt (1879-1925) published a paper called "Experimental materials for a theory of thought" in which he introduced two concepts-one, of the task as being the determinant of the process of thought, & the second, of set as being that which unknown to the subject, directed the process.

Karl Buhler (1879-1963) created a new orientation in the experimental practice in the school. His new method was to set the subject a complex problem: he then had to describe what went on in his consciousness during the process of solving the problem.

Narziss Ach (1871-1946) confirmed by experiment Kulpe's theory that the subject was "pretuned" to perform a given task. Such pretuning was named by Ach as a determining tendency. Ach also found another term, "that existing only in consciousness" which denoted the non-sensory content of consciousness.

Otto Selz (1881-1944) was in charge of providing an experimental analysis of how the process was dependent of upon the structure of the task to be solved. Selz came up with the concept of "anticipatory schema" which filled out the data previously acquired on the role played by the role or set.

At first there did not appear to be anything remarkable in the experimental studies of the Wurzburg laboratory. The significant changes had begun with the slight alteration of the instructions given to the subject. The subject now was asked not just to say, for example, which one of the objects was heavier, or to produce one word in reaction to another, but to recount exactly what processes took place in his consciousness before he reached his conclusion on weights or said a word as requested. In Wurzburg laboratory the experimental subject was presented with a complex stimulus or a logical problem & after processing it for a time retrospectively reported to the experimenter all that had passed through his consciousness during the interval. In the process the members of Wurzburg laboratory claimed to have discovered a number of new elements of consciousness including consciousness sets, awareness & thoughts. The change in the requirement shifted the emphasis from the effects of the subject's behavior to operations performed by the subject. For the first time the subjects were asked to make the object of their self-observation not the result but the process; to describe what events took place in their consciousness in course of the solution of their problem.

No matter how meticulously the subjects observed themselves, they could distinguish only indeterminate states. Such states were in no way reminiscent of sensory elements. The whole picture of the consciousness was brought into doubt. The closest observation of self failed to find any sensory elements in the consciousness of a subject engaged upon solution of a mental problem. The similar conclusion was reached in experiments performed outside of Kulpe's laboratory. So it appeared that there were non-sensory elements in consciousness. A key role in a study played the psychic state preceding reception of a stimulus, & because such a state was found before certain types of reaction it became known as "set towards." The many versions of the experiment indicating that in the preparatory period, when the subject was being instructed a set was produced- an orientation towards solution of the problem. Prior to the receiving of the stimulus this set was supposedly preregulating the course of the process, without entering the subject's awareness. As for any function for sensory images in the process, they were either unnoticed by the subject, or if arising were nit of vital meaning for accomplishment of the task. Another important achievement of the Wurzburg school was that the study of thought process began to acquire a psychological dimension. Before, the laws of logic were presented as the laws of thought, carried into effect in the individual consciousness according to the rules of formation of associations. Although the associative principle was considered to be universal, no specifically psychological aspect of the thinking process was distinguished. Eventually it became clear that this aspect had its own properties & regularities, differing both from those of logic & from those of association. Such a unique structure of the thought-process was explained by stating that in this case associations were subordinated to determining tendencies, the course of which lay in the very task presented to the subject.

The followers of the Wurzburg school attempted to bring new & valid variables into psychology. For example, set which appears when the task is taken in, or a goal which arose from determining tendencies. There were also processes which were viewed as a succession of search operations & affective intensity which was described as a sum of non-sensory components in the composition of consciousness. They presented a new schematic outline instead of the traditional one where the determinant of the process was the external stimulus. Perhaps the most valid point in the Wurzburg approach was the way in which they categorized the psychic function as an act which had its own determination, dynamics & structure.

About Functionalism

With the introduction of Functionalism psychology became more concerned with the investigation of the functions of psyche (as opposed to structure), which would have disclosed it psychological features of the relationship of a living organism with the environment. The pioneers of this new direction in psychology came to the conclusion that it was necessary to study the dynamics of mental processes & factors contributing to their orientation towards a specific goal. The historical development of functionalism was largely influenced by a number of intellectuals with a variety of backgrounds & interests. Functionalism is concerned with as it functions or as it is used in the adaptation of the organism to its environment. The followers of functionalism focus on the very practical question of what the mind & mental processes accomplish. In functionalism the mind is studied from the point of view of the mind as a conglomerate of activities which lead to eminently practical consequences in the real world. Unlike structuralism, functionalism was a deliberate movement of protest directed against "unilateral" psychological movements. The psychology of structure was seen too restrictive & narrow, unable to answer the key questions of psychology. Despite their opposition to many psychological movements, functionalists used some of the older school findings, like introspection & experimental study of consciousness. Functionalists modified the existing orthodoxy in psychology without feeling the need to totally replace it.

One of the key scientists to play a major role in the development of functionalism, along with Charles Darwin, was Sir Francis Galton (1822-1911). He was born at Sparkbrook, England. Galton was Charles Darwin's half cousin. Galton was a child genius. He was reading by the age of 2, at age 5 he knew some Latin Greek & by the age of six he had moved on to adult books. At 16 he was a student at the Birmingham King Edwards School. A year later the he enrolled at the Birmingham General Hospital &King's College, London Medical School. He followed up his medical education with mathematical studies at Trinity College (University of Cambridge).

Galton has made important contributions in many fields of science, including meteorology (the anti-cyclone and the first popular weather maps), statistics (regression and correlation), biology (the nature and mechanism of heredity), criminology (fingerprints) & psychology (synaesthesia).

Galton spent many years exploring variation in human populations & its implications. He eventually introduced a research program which embraced many aspects of human variation, from mental characteristics to height, from facial images to fingerprint patterns. This required inventing new measures of traits, devising large-scale collection of data using those measures the discovery of new statistical techniques. Galton was eager to prove the hereditary nature of human abilities, so proposed to count the number of the relatives of various degrees of eminent men. He thought that if the qualities were hereditary there must be more eminent men among the relatives than among the general population. He demonstrated that the numbers of eminent relatives dropped off when going from the first degree to the second degree relatives. Galton viewed this decline as evidence of the inheritance of abilities.

Galton conducted several twin studies. His method was to see if twins who were similar at birth diverged in dissimilar environments, & whether twins dissimilar at birth converged when reared in similar environments. He used the method of questionnaires to collect various sorts of data, which were tabulated and described in a paper called "The History of Twins." Galton's first significant work to influence psychology was "Hereditary genius." The purpose of this book was mainly to demonstrate that individual greatness or genius follows family lines with a frequency of occurrence too great to be explained on the basis of environmental influences. Mainly the biographical studies reported in Galton's work were investigations of the ancestries of famous people. Galton believed that if men & women of considerable talents were selected & mated, a highly gifted race of people would be the eventual result.

Galton's interest in measurement & statistics never seemed fully satisfied, until he had found some means of quantifying the data & statistically analyzing them. His work in statistics resulted in one of science's most important measures, the correlation. Contemporary techniques for determining validity & reliability of tests & the factor analytic methods are direct outgrowths of Galton's discovery of correlation. He devised the graphic means to represent the basic properties of the correlation coefficient & even developed a formula for its calculation. Galton used his method of variations in physical measurement, demonstrating a correlation between body height & head length.

The notion of correlation continues to be fundamentally important in the social & behavioral sciences. Francis Galton was the founder of certain specific tests. He started by assuming that intelligence could be measured in terms of personal level of sensory capacity. Galton thought that sensory ability is correlated with intelligence. The main goal of Galton's testing program was to determine the range of human capacities for a large number of abilities & attributes.

Galton's work on association is also remarkable. He turned his focus on two problems: the study of the wide range of associations & the study of the time it takes to produce associations.

Galton's study of mental imagery marks the beginning of the era of psychological questionnaires. His work began a long line of research on imagery, focusing on demonstration of hereditary similarities. He even attempted to put himself into the state of mind of the insane, discovering that it takes hours for this state of mind to wear off & that it was too easy to reestablish. Galton even investigates the relationship between theology & evolution, concluding religious beliefs are valid just because large numbers of people believe in them. He also believed that there is little difference to be found between those who profess a belief in one of the many brands of religion & those who do not, in terms of their dealings with their fellow man or in their own emotional lives. Galton spent nearly a decade engaged in activities of a psychological nature strongly influencing the direction in which psychology was soon to go.

Toward the end of nineteenth century, the influence of German experimental psychology was very strong in the United States. Many American psychologists went to Leipzig to study under Wilhelm Wundt, later developing their own laboratories on the Wundtian model. But some scientists preferred to use Galton's model of research.

William James (1842-1910) was the leading precursor of functional psychology & pioneer of the new scientific psychology in America. The new psychology had an experimental, scientific direction, although James himself was emphatically not an experimentalist. William James was born in New-York city to a family of wealthy theologian. He suffered from physical ailments, during his adulthood, including those of the eyes, back, stomach, and skin.

James received medical education at the Harvard Medical School. In 1869 he earned his M.D. Three years later he accepts offer from the President of Harvard to teach undergraduate course in comparative physiology. In 1874 James established the first American laboratory of psychology. In 1880 he was an assistant professor of Philosophy & a psychology teacher at Harvard. In 1882 James travels to Europe to meet Carl Stumpf, Ernst Mach & Wilhelm Wundt.

Although James studied medicine, physiology & biology, he was more drawn to the scientific study of the human mind. Even after his retirement in 1907, James continued to write & lecture. Hi health was gradually declining. It worsened in 1909 while he worked on a philosophy text (unfinished but posthumously published as "Some Problems in Philosophy"). James went to Europe in the spring of 1910 to take experimental treatments which proved unsuccessful. He died in 1910 at his home in New Hampshire.

In his psychological studies, James introduced a set of concepts that formed the basis of different approaches in modern psychology, from behaviorism to humanistic psychology. James studied many different areas; from the brain development & cognitive processes & emotions to personality psychology & psychedelic research.

Rejecting the strictly rationalist approach to knowledge, James did not agree with the fact that any science should strictly logically explain all the observed facts. He also argued that the task of philosophy was to describe & systematize the observed facts, revealing their importance for practical activity. He held that in real life people often deal with problems for the resolution of which there are no sufficient theoretical grounds. Therefore, the truth should not be viewed from the standpoint of theory, but from the standpoint of practice & its realization in life.

In William James pragmatic & slightly peculiar theory of truth the true beliefs were those that proved useful to the believer. James's theory contained elements of correspondence theory of truth & some coherence theory of truth. According to James, truth was verifiable to the extent that thoughts & statements corresponded with actual things & events. James also thought that the value of any truth was greatly dependent upon its use to the person who held it.

Even when James was eagerly working in psychology, he remained very much himself, refusing to be absorbed by any single system or ideology. Therefore James was neither a follower nor a founder. He was certainly aware of everything that happened in psychology & very much a part of it, but he was able to select from among the various positions only those parts that were congenial with his view of psychology. William James did not found functional psychology, but he wrote & thought most clearly & effectively in the functional atmosphere permeating American psychology & influencing the functional movement.

The concept of functionalism in explicit in James's psychology, in which he presented what eventually became the main tenet of American functionalism: the study of the living person as he adapts to his environment, as opposed to the discovery of elements of experience. James held that psychology is the science of mental life, both of its phenomena & of their conditions. In terms of subject matter the key words are "phenomena" & "conditions."Phenomena indicate that the subject matter is to be found an immediate experience. Conditions refer to the importance of the body, particularly the brain. James maintained that physical substructures of consciousness form an important part of psychology. He recognized the importance of considering consciousness in its natural setting-the physical human being. James was against the narrowness of the structuralist position. In his opinion experiences are simply what they are, not groups or amalgamations of element like structuralists claim. He attacks the structuralistic view of psychology by declaring individual simple sensations do not exist in conscious experience. In functionalism consciousness is seen as a continuous flow, therefore any attempt to subdivide it into distinct elements can only distort it. Consciousness is constantly undergoing changes & a person can never have same thoughts twice. Human consciousness is cumulative in nature & mind: sensibly continuous. One of the main characteristics is selectivity, which allows a person to choose from among the many stimuli.

In James' theory pure experience is a continuous flow of life, which provides the material for person's further reflection. But then our reflection, i.e. consciousness is not a static object, it is a continuous movement, the flow of thought. In this case the truth or falsity of thought does not lie in itself, but in relation to other parts of our experience with a real practical benefit of this idea. James came to the idea of stream of consciousness, that is, the continuity of human consciousness, despite the external discrete, partially caused by unconscious mental processes. Continuity of thought explains the possibility of identity, despite the constant breaks in consciousness. At the same time James emphasized not only continuity, but also the dynamism, constant volatility of consciousness, stating that the awareness of even common things constantly changes.

In James's opinion the purpose of consciousness is to better adapt man to his environment by enabling him to choose. He also makes a distinction between conscious choice & habit, the latter being involuntary. Psychology usually deals with a highly personal consciousness that is why introspection in functionalism is seen as a main tool. Functionalists were convinced that it is possible to study various states of consciousness by an examination of one's own mind. Since consciousness is not capable of analysis, according to James, his form of introspection could not be of the rigid type practiced by Wundt & Titchener. James, being aware of the difficulties & limitations of introspection, accepts it as an inferior form of observation. In order to aid the introspective & experimental methods, James urged the use of comparative method in psychology.

Psychological views of James are closely intertwined with his philosophical theory of pragmatism, so he paid much attention to applied psychology, arguing that its importance is not less than the theoretical value. Especially important, for James, was the connection between psychology & pedagogy. He was convinced that psychology played a more important role in the formation & development of moral & ethical habits. He even published a special book for teachers "Conversations with teachers about psychology" (1899), which demonstrated the enormous opportunities of education & self-education, as well as, the importance of forming correct habits in children.

Of great importance was James's description of feelings & emotions caused by different structures & parts of the personality, especially the description of self-evaluation (self-satisfaction & dissatisfaction with self), the role of which was first suggested by him. Considering the impact of self-esteem on human behavior, James derived a formula of self-esteem, which was a fraction, the numerator of which was the success, & the denominator - the claim. This formula was the basis of a hierarchy of personalities, aspirations, rights to self-improvement & success, diseases & neuroses, assessment of self & experienced emotions.

James' theory of emotions pointed to the link between emotions & physiological changes. His theory of emotions completely contradicted the existing theories of the time. It had previously been formulated that the experience of emotion precedes its physical or somatic expression. James opposed above mentioned formulation & stated that the arousal of the physical precedes the appearance of the emotion. James's concepts of the nature of emotion are partially confirmed by modern research in the field of psychopharmacology & psycho-correction. His theory of emotion was the only specific theory to become famous.

James had done a lot for the development of psychology as an independent science. He is considered one of the most prominent American scientists, who had an enormous impact not only on psychology but also philosophy & pedagogy.

Another bright representative of functionalism, Raymond Bernard Cattell (1905-1998) was born in England, in a town near Birmingham. While he was studying Chemistry at the London University he was quite aware of the ferment of social & political ideas that broke out after World War

I. Cattell's excellent grades in high school allowed him to attend London University. He was studying chemistry. After war Cattell switched to psychology. He earned his PhD at King's College (1924-1929) & masters in education at the London University College (1932). While working on his Ph.D., Cattell accepted a position teaching in the Department of Education at Exeter University. In 1937 Cattell moved to United States. He was invited by Thorndike to work at the Columbia University. Then, when the G. Stanley Hall professorship in Psychology became available at Clark University in 1938, Cattell was recommended by Thorndike and was appointed to the position

In 1941 Cattell was invited by Gordon Allport to join the Harvard University. At Harvard he planned & began some of the research in personality that would become the foundation for much of his later work. During World War II Cattell worked with the U.S. government researching & developing tests for selecting officers in the armed forces. After the war Cattell moved to the University of Illinois, where founded the Laboratory of Personality Assessment & Group Behavior.

Cattell organized an international symposium to increase communication among psychological researchers who were using multivariate statistics to study human behavior, which resulted in the foundation of the Society of Multivariate Experimental Psychology. He retired in 1973.

After the retirement Cattell continued his career as a part-time professor & advisor at the University of Hawaii. He also served as adjunct faculty of the Hawaii School of Professional Psychology, which became the American School of Professional Psychology. During the last two decades of his life in Hawaii, Cattell continued to publish a variety of scientific articles, as well as books on motivation, the scientific use of factor analysis, two volumes of personality and learning theory, the inheritance of personality and ability & structured learning theory.

He influenced psychology most through his work on individual differences & mental tests. Cattell defines personality as that which permits a prediction of what a person will do in a given situation. Later Cattell formulated his definition as follows R=f (s.p) which reads, R, the nature & magnitude of a response, is a function of both environmental situations in which the individual finds himself & his personality. He was convinced that this is a working definition more denotative than connotative. Since personality connotes all of the behavior of the individual, precise description & measurement which are the first stages of the scientific study of personality must begin with a relatively restricted definition. When adequate descriptions have been carried out, the more restricted units of behavior must be integrated into the larger whole which is the true picture of the functioning personality as it exists in its natural environment. Cattell formulates traits as relatively permanent features of personality. Traits are inferred from the individual's behavior & are of two fundamental kinds, surface traits & source traits. Surface traits are revealed by correlating "trait-elements" which in turn, are essentially behavior samples. For instance, tests or ratings of independence, alertness & energy level tend to form a cluster revealing the existence of surface trait of "Energy, Boldness, & Spiritedness."

By using such correlation techniques Cattell found that the hundred of traits used to describe & measure personality could be reduced to between fifty & sixty "nuclear clusters." Therefore, if two trait tests correlate positively to a relatively high degree they are describing & measuring essentially the same behavior. According to Cattell traits are bipolar opposites. Such convention is typical of personality systems which depend upon statistical methods of description & measurement. The underlying assumption is that traits are normally distributed in a continuous manner with few individuals showing extreme degrees of the trait under consideration & with most people falling in the middle or median range.

Source traits are revealed by factor analysis, & represent deeper, more significant aspects of personality. While surface traits are merely descriptive units, the source traits upon which they depend are, in part, explanatory representing underlying causes of the observed correlations among surface traits.

In repeated factoral studies of surface trait correlation clusters, Cattell has found evidence for the existence of as many as twenty source traits. In regard to the descriptive phase of Cattell's system, traits may be categorized as dynamic, ability, or temperamental. This threefold category refers to the manner in which trait is expressed. Dynamic traits are concerned with goal-directed behavior; ability traits, with how well the individual works toward a goal; & temperamental traits, with emotional reactivity, speed, or energy with which he responds.

From the psychological point of view human personality may be considered as an integration of traits. The individual's behavior as he interacts with his environment reflects a relatively large number of surface traits. In any given culture, according to Cattell such traits are common to most individuals & can therefore be measured by objective tests & ratings. Surface traits are dependent upon underlying source traits which, in turn, may be identified by factor analytic studies of surface trait correlation clusters. Such studies have thus far revealed a limited number of such traits, some of which are related to basic constitutional factors & others to environmental influences. Traits may also be described in terms of how they are expressed- as abilities, as dynamic, or goal-directed traits, or as reactive-temperamental traits.

In Cattell's theory the development of the human personality is viewed as the unfolding of maturational processes & their modification through learning & experience. Maturation thus, contributes the basic perceptual & motor abilities, while learning is responsible for the organization of the self.

During the childhood, according to Cattell, personality undergoes its most significant developmental phases. The years from one to five are critical for the development of both normal & abnormal traits. Either type of trait remains remarkably constant from the five until puberty. About the ages from seven to eight the child begins to be weaned from parental influence. Around the age of ten or eleven secondary groups (like school), begin to exert as much influence on the developing personality as does the home.

Some children at this age begin to experience cleavage between home & peer-group approved forms of behavior. Adolescence is a period which makes great demands on the child. At one & the same time he is confronted with the many biological & intellectual changes typical of the period. Cattell maintains that person strives to win parental approval in the face of his growing independence, attempting to satisfy four different sets of demands which arise from the following sources: the parents, adolescent peers, adult culture pattern & the superego.

Next period, maturity, is characterized by a gradual & steady decline of the biologically based mental processes, during which the average individual substitutes familial interests for social interests. With the onset of old age, new adjustments are demanded as a result both loss of occupation & the decreased social evaluation put upon the aged in the culture.

Cattell summarizes his theory of personality development under seventeen principles of personality formation. The laws & principles are concerned with learning, the effects of deprivation, frustration & blockage, the formation of sentiments, the development of the self, & the individual in the social context. In the laws of learning, Cattell accepts both contiguity & a modified law of effect. His treatment of goal- directed behavior, & frustration closely follows the functionalistic point of view; however there are also strong overtones of Gestalt psychology & field theory noticeable throughout his elaboration of the principles. The principles underlying the formation of sentiments consist in the application of the laws of learning, whereas the principles underlying the formation of the self lean heavily on Freudian concept.

Since the individual personality is embedded in the larger social context, prediction of individual behavior is contingent upon the psychologist's knowledge of the individual's relationship to the social context.

The influence of Chicago school

In 1984, John Dewey (1859-1952) & James Angell (1869-1949) came to the newly organized University of Chicago. The combined influence of the two men was largely responsible for the University's becoming a leading center of functionalism.

John Dewey's short paper, "The Reflex Arc Concept in Psychology," published in 1896 was the point of departure for the new movement. In it Dewey attacked the psychological molecularism, elementism, & reductionism of the reflex arc with its distinction between stimulus & response. He was born in Burlington, Vermont. Dewey graduated from the University of Vermont in 1879, & received his PhD from Johns Hopkins University in 1884. He started his career at the University of Michigan, teaching there from 1884 to 1888 & 1889-1894. In 1894 he became the chairman of the department of philosophy, psychology, & pedagogy at the University of Chicago. In 1899, John Dewey was elected president of the American Psychological Association, & in 1905 he became president of the American Philosophical Association. Dewey taught at Columbia University from 1905 until he retired in 1929.

Dewey's was an epistemologist. In Dewey's view traditional epistemologies had drawn too stark a distinction between thought & the world of fact to which thought purportedly referred: thought was believed to exist apart from the world, epistemically as the object of immediate awareness, ontologically as the unique aspect of the self. The commitment of modern rationalism to a doctrine of innate ideas, ideas constituted from birth in the very nature of the mind itself, had affected this dichotomy; but the modern empiricists, beginning with Locke, had done the same just as markedly by their commitment to an introspective methodology & a representational theory of ideas.

According to Dewey, nature was a continuously flowing stream, which It used thought as an instrument to pass from an inferior situation, full of ambiguities and disharmonies, to a new, superior situation. Although this new situation could contain elements implied in the former, it was better because of its complexity & new meaning. Thus, Dewey's "instrumentalism" was set to prove that cognition consists in forging ideal tools or instruments with which to cope with a given situation.

Dewey viewed philosophy as the criticism of those socially important beliefs which were part of the socio-cultural life of human communities. His criticism involved a close examination of the way in which ideas functioned within a wider context. It was in this way that a theory of knowledge, psychology, aesthetics, & metaphysics became necessary. Dewey was against transcendental philosophers, because they ignored the kind of empirical situations to which their themes pertain. Even the most transcendental philosophers often use empirical subject matter. Dewey never made philosophy subservient to the vested interests of any class or nation. He insisted that philosophy, in contrast to all other human activities, must be allowed to remain outside the public domain in order to maintain sound relations with these other human activities. Dewey was also against any isolation of cognitive experience and its subject matter from other modes of experience.

He further denied that the characteristic object of knowledge had a privileged position of correspondence with an allegedly ultimate reality. Dewey was convinced that action was involved in knowledge & that knowledge was not subordinate to action or practice.

He maintains that the behavior involved in a reflex response cannot be meaningfully reduced to its basic sensory-motor elements & that behavior tends to lose its meaning when such an artificial reduction & analysis takes place. All that is left is the abstraction that supposedly exists in the minds of the psychologists performing the dissection. Dewey held that behavior should not be treated as an artificial scientific construct, but rather in terms of its significance to the organism in adapting to the environment.

He was influenced by the theory of evolution & his philosophy was based on the notion of social change. Dewey was against static state of things, favoring the progress gained through the struggle of man's intellect with reality. In this struggle according to Dewey, both consciousness & activity function for the organism, with consciousness bringing about the appropriate activity that enables the organism to survive & progress. A function is a total coordination of an organism toward achieving an end. Thus, functional psychology is the study of the organism in motion. It is important to note that Dewey's philosophical works brought him more fame than his psychological studies. He was especially concerned with welfare of man & his physical, social, & moral adjustment. Psychological processes, such as thinking & learning are very important in person's life, since thinking in Dewey's view is a tool used by man to meet the obstacles of life. He also held that the human effort to survive results in knowledge, which is a weapon in the fight for survival, & an important factor in the process of adjustment.

Another representative of new functionalism was James Rowland Angell (1869-1949), who molded the functionalist movement into a working school &, in the process, made the psychology department in Chicago the most important. Angell was born in Burlington, Vermont. His father was a president of the universities of Vermont & Michigan & his grandfather was president of Brown University. Academic studies were not taken seriously by the young Angell until he read John Dewey's text on psychology during his sophomore year at the University of Michigan. Angell did his undergraduate work at the University of Michigan, where he studied under John Dewey. He graduated from the University of Michigan with his Bachelor's Degree in 1890 & in 1892 he received his Masters from Harvard University. After a brief study abroad, he taught at the University of Minnesota. In 1905 Angell became a president & head of the psychology department in the University of Chicago. Later, he served as president of Yale University from 1921 until he retired in 1937. In 1937, he became educational counselor of the National Broadcasting Company.

Angell's functional psychology was strongly identified with Darwinian evolution theory. For example, his theory of habit formation represented an adaptation to individual experience of Darwin's doctrines of natural selection, according to which, early stages of habit formation were characterized by excessive reactions from which useless movements were gradually eliminated & successful movements selected. Thus, consciousness was required most in early stages in which behavioral coordination was least organized.

Angell held that functional psychology had been a significant part of psychology from the earliest times, claiming that it was structural psychology that had set itself apart from the older & more truly pervasive functional form of psychology. Further he brought together the three conceptions of functionalism that he considered the major themes of the movement. According to Angell functional psychology is the psychology of mental operations in contrast to the psychology of mental elements, like structuralism. The Wundtian & Titchenerian elementism was still quite strong & Angell promoted functionalism in direct & open opposition to it. The purpose of functionalism was to determine how a mental process operates, what it accomplishes, & under what conditions it appears. In Angell's view mental function, unlike a given moment of consciousness studied by the structuralists, is not a momentary perishable thing. Rather it persists & endures in the same manner as do biological functions. Angell's functionalism is the psychology of the fundamental utilities of consciousness, which is viewed in utilitarian spirit. Functionalism is designed to study mental processes not as isolated & independent events, but as an active ongoing part of the larger geological activity & indeed, as part of the larger movement of organic evolution. Structures & functions of the organism exist as they are because by adapting the organism to the conditions of its environment they have enabled it to survive. Angell held that since consciousness has survived, it too must perform an essential service that organism could not otherwise accomplish. The main purpose of consciousness was to understand the changes that occurred in the new, increasingly complex environment. Functionalism had to discover precisely what this service was, for consciousness as well as for more specific mental processes.

Since functionalism includes the entire system of somatic & mental functions, it leaves open the study of unconscious & habitual behavior. According to Angell functionalism is designed to form a relationship with the mental & physical spheres. Angell's theory supposedly finds no distinction between the mind & the body, considering them not as two different entities but as belonging to the same order, & assuming an easy transfer from one to the other. He also insisted that functionalism did not really constitute a school & should not be identified exclusively with the psychology of the Chicago school.

Another representative of the Chicago school Harvey Carr (1873-1954), emerged when functionalism was no longer opposing structuralistic trend. He was born on an Indiana farm. Carr began his undergraduate work at DePauw University & continued at the University of Colorado where he studied psychology, earning his BS in 1901 & MS in 1902. Later he went on to the University of Chicago to study experimental psychology with John Dewey, James Rowland Angell & John B. Watson. He earned his Ph.D. in 1905. Carr's doctoral dissertation was on a visual illusion of motion during eye closure. In 1905 Carr taught at the high school in Texas and one year later at the State Normal School in Michigan. He also worked at the Pratt Institute in Brooklyn until 1908 when he was invited to replace Watson at Chicago. Carr stayed at Chicago until his retirement in 1938.

Carr was a director of the animal laboratory at Chicago. He was working on Watson's study of the senses used by albino rats for getting through mazes. Carr invented an improved maze which became widely adopted for experiments of this sort. He had admired Watson's animal work and encouraged his students to choose thesis topics in comparative psychology.

Carr's psychology was an expression of the finished form of functionalism, since he defined subject matter of psychology as mental activity. By activity he meant processes such as memory, feeling, imagination, will, judgment & perception. Carr maintained that the function of mental activity is to acquire, organize & evaluate experiences, using them in the determination of action. He termed the specific form of action in which mental activities appear, "adjustive" behavior.

In discussion of the methods of studying mental activity, Carr acknowledged the validity of both introspective & objective observation. He held that experimental method is the more highly desirable but admitted that adequate experimental investigation of the mind is extremely difficult. Carr also felt that the study of cultural products, such as literature or social & political institutions can provide information on the kind of mental activities that produced them.

The new school of psychology produced at least the beginning of a shift away from the exclusive study of the subjective matter to include the study of the overt behavior. Functionalism helped to prepare the way for American psychology to go to the opposite extreme from the structuralists; that is, to focus only on the study of behavior, dropping the study of the mind altogether. The functionalists thus provided a shaky bridge between structuralism & behaviorism.

Carr considered attention to be a process that ensures selectivity of perception. This is accomplished partly by suppression of some stimuli & in part by the synthesis of other stimuli. By synthesis Carr meant the whole complex of cooperative adjustments in the sense organs & in the body in general. The organization of incoming sensory data depends upon past experience. According to Carr the principle tends to puzzle, when first experienced. Regardless of how attentive the observer may be, until he has had sufficient experience with the stimuli in question, they remain disorganized & meaningless. When a person is shown the hidden figure in the puzzle or when he learns the language, the organizing effect of experience is so strong, that the individual can no longer stop seeing the hidden figure.

Carr held that meaning is also dependent on the arousal of previous experiences, while associations from past experience must not be in the form of complete integrations of experience in order for meaning to occur. In many cases a partial or indirect reactivation of associations is sufficient to arouse meaning. Exactly how complete a reactivation of previous experience takes place for any given perception depends upon how well-practiced the association in question are.

The nature of the whole perceptual complex is independent upon additional factors such as the environmental situation, the individual's purposes & activities at the moment of perception, & the sensory modality involved.

In Carr's opinion perception is a form of mental activity in which the meaning of present situations, objects, & events is determined, in part, by learning however meaning is also related to a present or contemplated act of adjustment. The initial stage in perception is the attentive phase, characterized by receptor & bodily adjustments which make for selectivity of perception. Past experience, according to Carr provides organization & interpretation for the incoming stimuli, thus perception is a highly functional & useful process in adaptation.

Carr defined mental activities as those processes concerned with the acquisition, fixation, retention, organization & evaluation of experiences, & their subsequent utilization in the guidance of conduct. He begins by defining learning as the "acquisition of a mode of response in a problem situation." Problems in turn are a result of a lack of adjustment brought about in one of several ways. First, the environment may be lacking in some needed substance or the individual may be confronted by obstructions which must be circumvented if a goal is to be reached. Second, an organism may lack the required skill to respond to a situation.

Carr also considers a variety of factors which govern the success or failure of adaptive learning, such as the animal's capacity for learning, the strength of his motivation, the nature of the problem situation & the repertoire of previously learned modes of adapting which the animal has available & is bringing to a given problem situation. Clearly the well-adapted organism with high capacity for learning that has had experience in solving similar problems is more likely to succeed in a given situation than the organism lacking such qualifications.

Carr then considers the complicated problem of how the correct responses in adjustmental learning are fixated while the incorrect responses are eliminated. He begins by stating the Law of Effect as a descriptive statement of what takes place.

Carr concludes his discussion of learning as adaptive behavior by considering the problems of transfer, association, & habit, & by relating these processes to his overall scheme of adjustmental learning. In working with transfer, he points out that all learning involves the utilization of previous experience. Carr also points out the practical utility of transfer & argues that as the organism is confronted with new situations it both utilizes

& modifies habitual modes of behavior. Carr relates his theory of adaptive learning to associationism by arguing that whenever two aspects of experience are associated they are organized in the form of S-R relationship, which means, once associated, the presence of one will arouse the other.

Further Carr relates the concept of habit to his psychology of learning by emphasizing the "automatic" nature of habitual behavior. The well established complex of associations is easily aroused & is relatively difficult to disturb by the introduction of outside stimuli. On the other hand, habit strength is dependent upon number of repetitions of an act, the degree to which competing activities have been eliminated & the constancy of the environmental conditions under which it is performed.

In Carr's theory emotions are treated as the background of mental life. He defines them as organic readjustments which occur automatically in the face of appropriate behavioral situations. Thus according to Carr, the emotion of anger arises when the organism is confronted with a serious obstacle to freedom of movement. In this case the organic readjustment involves a mobilization of energy to aid the individual in his efforts to overcome the obstacle. Carr also maintains that the various emotions can be readily identified & defined only in terms of behavioral situations in which they occur. He held that the reaction in emotional states is highly similar to that found in any kind of vigorous exercise or activity. The key feature of emotional state arises from the fact that they occur in cases where there is a lack of adequate motor outlets.

Overall Carr treats emotions as psychophysical events which are organic readjustments occurring in certain behavioral situations. The name given to the emotions depends upon the situation in which it occurs. Whereas emotions are organic readjustments, not all emotions are biologically useful. Carr was especially interested in perception & learning. Emotions were treated somewhat incidentally as part of the so called background of mental life.

Along with the Chicago school of functional movement was supported by Columbia School, headed by Robert Woodworth (1869-1962). He was born in Belchertown, Massachusetts. Woodworth received a Bachelor's degree in philosophy from Amherst College in 1891, after which he taught undergraduate level courses in science & mathematics. In 1895, he enrolled at Harvard University, receiving a Master's degree in philosophy in 1897. Woodworth eventually turned to psychology, completing his doctoral degree at Columbia University. Woodworth earned his Ph.D. in 1899, with a dissertation on "The Accuracy of Voluntary Movement."

After receiving his Ph.D., Woodworth accepted a one year instructorship in physiology at Columbia. His friend & fellow student from Harvard, Thorndike had also moved to Columbia & they collaborated on a series of articles regarding the transfer of training. In 1902 Woodworth completed a postdoctoral fellowship at the University of Liverpool. Later, in 1903, he landed a full-time instructorship in psychology at Columbia. James McKeen Cattell, who at the time was the head of the Psychological Department at Columbia, delegated to Woodworth various administrative responsibilities, as well as supervisory duties. In 1909, he was given a full professorship. In 1914, Woodworth was elected president of the American Psychological Association. In 1918, he published his Dynamic Psychology, in which he advocated use of a combination of behavioral, physiological, & introspective methods in psychological inquiry.

During World War I, Woodworth was commissioned to prepare a test for emotional stability that might be used in the evaluation of recruits. The result was Woodworth's Personal Data Sheet which was produced too late to be thoroughly tested on recruits. It was, however, subsequently revised & used by others in the field of personality measurement.

From 1918 to 1927, Woodworth served as the head of the Psychological Department at Columbia University. He published several important books in 1930s, including his "Experimental Psychology" (1938), which became a standard handbook in laboratory work. Woodworth retired from teaching in 1942. He died in New York City, on July 4, 1962.

Woodworth was the founder of the so called "dynamic psychology". The main provisions of this approach to psychology, he set out in the papers "Dynamic Psychology" (1918) & "Dynamics of behavior" (1958). Studies in the field physiology partially reflected in his psychological views. His first research was devoted to the problem of "transfer" in learning. By analyzing the stimulus-response connection, he stressed the importance of active intervention of the organism in the system of interaction, which changed the traditional formula, making it a stimulus-organism-response. In his view, in order to understand behavior it was essential to study the intermediate variable, which could completely change the initial relationship between stimulus & response.

Studying the development of behavior, Woodworth highlighted the important role of motivation in this process. He saw the purpose of dynamic psychology in the study of motivation. Work on the analysis of behavioral mechanisms that led him to believe that there are two stages in the process of activity - the preparatory (installation) & the final reaction, which achieves the target.

Woodworth also stressed the existence of a dynamic, flexible relationship between motivation & mechanism. Motivation was designed to activate the mechanism causing it to start. But when the need is satisfied, the application of the mechanism itself becomes a motivating force. Thus, what was originally a mean becomes a target.

As a general viewpoint, functionalism was so successful that it became a part of the mainstream of psychology. Its early vigorous opposition to structuralism was of immense value to psychology at a time when the new science was beginning to develop. The long lasting consequences of the shift in emphasis from structure to function were also important. One result was that rapidly increasing research on animal behavior became a vitally important part of psychology. Animal research was in accord with a functional psychology, but was irrelevant to functional psychology, for which introspection was the indispensable tool.

In addition to studies of animals, the functionalists' broadened definition of psychology was able to incorporate studies of children, the mentally retarded, & the insane. It also allowed psychologists to supplement the method of introspection with other ways of securing data such as psychological research, mental tests & objective descriptions of behavior. All of these methods, which were anathema to the structuralists, became respectable sources of information to psychology.

About Behaviorism

There are three types of behaviorism, methodological, analytical & radical. Methodological behaviorism is a theory about the scientific conduct of psychology. It holds that psychology should not concern itself with the behavior of organisms, or with constructing internal information processing accounts of behavior. Methodological behaviorists are convinced that mental states, such as animal's desires add nothing to what psychology can & should understand about the sources of behavior.

Psychological behaviorism is a research program within psychology that attempts to explain human & animal behavior in terms of external physical stimuli, responses, learning histories & reinforcements. The most famous representatives of psychological behaviorism are Ivan Pavlov (1849-1936), Edward Thorndike (1874-1949), John Watson (1878-1958) & Burrhus F. Skinner (1904-1990).

Analytical behaviorism also known as logical is a theory within philosophy about the meaning of mental terms & concepts. In it the very idea of a mental state is the idea of a behavioral disposition or family of behavioral tendencies. Analytical behaviorism traces its historical roots to the philosophical movement known as logical positivism. Logical positivism proposes that the meaning of statements used in science be understood in terms of experimental conditions or observations that verify their truth. Such positivist doctrine is known as verificationism. In psychology verificationism underpins the analytical behaviorism, especially, the claim that mental concepts refer to behavioral tendencies & so must be translated into behavioral terms. Analytical behaviorism helps to avoid substance dualism, which is a doctrine that mental states take place in a special, non-physical mental substance, so called immaterial mind.

Psychological behaviorisms historical roots consist in the classical associationism of the British empiricists, like John Locke & David Hume. In classical associationism, intelligent behavior is the product of associative learning. As a result of pairings between perceptual experiences or stimulations on the one hand, & ideas on the other, person acquires knowledge of his environment.

The main goal of psychological behaviorism is to specify types of association, understand how environmental events control behavior, discover & elucidate causal regularities or laws of functional relations which govern the formation of associations.

In his historical foundations, methodological behaviorism shares with analytical behaviorism the influence of positivism. Though logically distinct, methodological, psychological & analytical behaviorisms often are found in one behaviorism. It follows analytical strictures in paraphrasing mental terms behaviorally, when they cannot be eliminated from explanatory discourse.

Radical behaviorism is concerned with the behavior of organisms therefore it is a form of methodological behaviorism. It treats behavior as a reflection of frequency effects among stimuli, which means that it is a form of psychological behaviorism.

In the second decade of the twentieth century, less than forty years after Wundt formally launched psychology, the science had undergone drastic revisions. While structuralism was still a vital & strong position attracting its share of loyal adherents, the new movement of functionalism had seriously eroded the earlier positions of primacy in the field. In 1913, a revolution erupted, directed against both of these positions. This was truly a revolt, a total war against the establishment, intent on shattering both points of view. There was nothing gradual about this transition. It was sudden & dramatic.

The new movement was called behaviorism & its leader was the 35 year old psychologist John Broadus Watson. John B. Watson (1878-1958) was born near Greenville, South Carolina. At the age of 16, he entered Furman University, from which he graduated five years later with a basic introduction to psychology. Watson worked as a principal of a small private school after which he obtained admission to the University of Chicago (1900). At the time Chicago was the center of a new American psychology. From 1903 to 1908, Watson remained at Chicago as an assistant & then an instructor in experimental psychology. He received his Ph. D in 1903 at the age of twenty-five, in which he did his dissertation on the relation between behavior in the white rat and the growth of its nervous system. He then stayed at the University of Chicago as an assistant and as a teacher at the university. After only one year, he married one of his students, Mary Amelia Ickes. Perhaps, due to the experience of witnessing his father's affairs as a child, John too began dating other women on the campus, while his wife Mary was home with the children. These promiscuous behaviors became a hot topic of conversation for students and faculty at the University of Chicago. To avoid further problems with the faculty in Chicago,

Watson made the decision to leave the University of Chicago and further his career at Johns Hopkins University in Baltimore, Maryland. He set up his own laboratory where he ran a variety of psychological experiments in the direction of animal behavior. Watson published his first famous article, "Psychology as a Behaviorist Views It," in Psychological Review, in which he explained his beliefs that psychology was a science of human behavior, yet very similar to animal behavior. His second major accomplishment was his publication of "Behavior: an Introduction to Comparative Psychology." In it, he explained his belief in the importance of using animal subjects to study reflexes activated by heredity. Watson also published over thirty-five papers, books, and reports.

In 1915 he was elected president of the American Psychological Association. In 1919 Watson published his "Psychology from the Standpoint of a Behaviorist." Watson was dismissed from the university because of his relationship with a student but still continued to do research and write.

1925 he published "Behaviorism," & then in 1928 he published "Psychological Care of Infant and Child." In addition, he published a revision of "Behaviorism" in 1930.

Watson was also well known for his "Little Albert" experiment. He attempted to condition a severe emotional response in Little Albert, a nine-month-old child & later concluded that white, furry objects, such as a rat, a rabbit, & cotton, did not produce any negative reaction in the baby. However, pairing together a neutral stimulus (white, furry animals) with an unconditioned stimulus (loud noise) that elicited an unconditioned response (fear), Watson was able to create a new stimulus-response link: When the baby saw white, furry objects, this conditioned stimulus produced a conditioned response of fear. This study was generally introduced as a seminal work that provided evidence that even complex behaviors, such as emotions, could be learned through manipulation of the environment. The main tenets of Watson's behaviorism were simple, direct, & bold. He called for a totally objective psychology- a science of behavior, which deals only with observable behavioral acts that could be objectively described in terms such as stimulus & response. He wanted to apply to human beings the experimental procedures & principles of animal psychology, a field in which he had been active. Watson's positive interests shed light on what he wanted to discard. If behavioristic psychology was to be an objective science then all mentalistic concepts & terms had to be rejected. Such words as "consciousness"& "mind" were therefore meaningless & the technique of introspection, which assumed the existence of conscious processes, was irrelevant.

Watson's insistence on the need for increased objectivity in psychology was by no means new by 1913. The movement has a long history, beginning with Descartes, whose attempts at mechanistic explanations of the body & mind were among the first steps in the direction of greater objectivity.

By the beginning of the 20-th century, objectivism, mechanism & materialism had grown strong. Their influence was so pervasive that they led inexorably to a new kind of psychology; one without consciousness or mind; one that focused on only what could be seen & heard & touched.

Watson held that behaviorism is a direct outgrowth of studies in animal behavior during the first decade of the 20-th century. The most important single antecedent to the development of Watson's program was animal psychology which grew out of evolutionary theory. It led to attempts to demonstrate the presence of mind lower organisms & the continuity between the human & animal minds. By the beginning of the 20-th century, the study of animal behavior within a biological framework had become widespread. During this same time, experimental animal psychology-most notably the work of Thorndike developed rapidly.

Edward Lee Thorndike (1874-1949) played a key role in the development of animal psychology. He was the first to introduce true experimental investigation of animals. He was born in Williamsburg, Massachusetts. Thorndike was a son of a Methodist minister.

Thorndike became interested in the field of psychology after reading William James's famous "Principles of Psychology." He graduated from Weslyan University at Harvard. His research interest was mainly with children, but his initial study of "mind reading" led to their unavailability for future study. Later he developed projects that examined learning in animals to satisfy requirements for his courses and degree. He continued his animal research with Cattell in Columbia University. He used chicks, cats & dogs in his experiments. In 1898, he was awarded the doctorate for his thesis, "Animal Intelligence: An Experimental Study of the Associative Processes in Animals", in which he concluded that an experimental approach is the only way to understand learning and established the so called Law of Effect, which he pioneered.

After graduation Thorndike returned to his initial interest, Educational Psychology. In 1899 he became an instructor in psychology at Teachers College at Columbia University, where he remained for the rest of his career, studying human learning, education, & above all, mental testing.

Eventually Thorndike's studies with animal behavior led him to declare his Law of Effect. According to this law 1) Responses to a situation that are followed by satisfaction are strengthened; & 2) Responses that are followed by discomfort are weakened. Thorndike's Law of Exercise continued this line of thought; 1) Stimulus-response connections that are repeated are strengthened, & 2) Stimulus -response connections that are not used are weakened. Thorndike characterized the two most basic intelligences as Trial-and-Error and Stimulus-Response Association. In 1903 Thorndike & his students used objective measurements of intelligence on human subjects. During the 1920's he developed a test of intelligence that consisted of completion, arithmetic, vocabulary, and directions test (CAVD). It was designed to measure intellectual level on an absolute scale. The logic underlying the test predicted elements of test design that eventually became the foundation of modern intelligence tests. Thorndike recognized three classes of intellectual functioning. He held that standard intelligence tests measured only "abstract intelligence". Also important were "mechanical intelligence - the ability to visualize relationships among objects and understand how the physical world worked", and social intelligence - the ability to function successfully in interpersonal situations".

Thorndike was the founder of new psychological connectionism. He was convinced that through experience neural bonds or connections were formed between perceived stimuli and emitted responses; therefore, intellect facilitated the formation of the neural bonds. Thus, people of higher intellect could form more bonds and form them more easily than people of lower ability. The ability to form bonds was rooted in genetic potential through the genes' influence on the structure of the brain. In this theory the content of intellect was a function of experience.

Edward Lee Thorndike published about 500 books and articles throughout his 55 year career.Thorndike developed an objective & mechanistic theory of learning, focusing only on overt behavior, with minimal reference to consciousness or mental processes. He held that psychology only must study behavior, not mental elements or conscious experience in any form. With this statement he reinforced the already growing trend toward greater objectivity that the functionalists were bringing to psychology, & interpreted learning not in terms of highly subjective ideas, but rather in terms of concrete connections between stimuli & responses.

Thorndike created an experimental approach to associationism, which he called connectionism & which included several important departures from the more classical tradition. This associationistic position was a direct descendant of the older philosophical associationism with one significant difference. Instead of talking about associations or connections between ideas, Thorndike talked about connections between situations & responses. His study of learning also differed from classical associationism in that his subjects were animals rather than humans; this method had become acceptable as an aftermath of the Darwinian notion of continuity of species. In Thorndike's opinion to study behavior, it must be broken down or reduced to its simplest elements: stimulus response units, which are elements of behavior, the building blocks out of which more complex behaviors are compounded.

The influence of another behaviorist, Ivan Pavlov (1849-1936) was felt broadly in many areas of psychology. His work in the area of association or learning helped bring about the shift of associationism from its traditional applications to subjective ideas, to completely objective & quantifiable glandular secretions & muscular movements.

Pavlov was born on September at Ryazan, Russia. His father was a village priest. He was educated first at the church school in Ryazan and then at the theological seminary there. Pavlov was inspired by the progressive ideas of Pisarev (Russian literary critic) and I. M. Sechenov, the father of Russian physiology. Eventually Pavlov abandoned his religious career & decided to devote his life to science. In 1870 he enrolled in the physics & mathematics faculty to take the course in natural science. Soon Pavlov became passionately absorbed with physiology, which in fact was to remain of such fundamental importance to him throughout his life. It was during this first course that he produced, in collaboration with another student, Afanasyev, his first learned treatise, a work on the physiology of the pancreatic nerves.

Pavlov completed his course with an outstanding record and received the degree of Candidate of Natural Sciences in 1875. However, impelled by his overwhelming interest in physiology, he decided to continue his studies and proceeded to the Academy of Medical Surgery to take the third course there. After a competitive examination, Pavlov won a fellowship at the Academy, and this together with his position as Director of the Physiological Laboratory at the clinic of the famous Russian clinician, S. P. Botkin, enabled him to continue his research work. In 1883 he presented his doctor's thesis on the subject of «The centrifugal nerves of the heart». In this work he developed his idea of nervism, using as example the intensifying nerve of the heart which he had discovered. He also introduced the basic principles of the trophic function of the nervous system. Pavlov proved that the existence of basic patterns in the reflex regulation of the activity of the circulatory organs.

In 1890 Pavlov organized & directed the Department of Physiology at the Institute of Experimental Medicine. Under his direction, which continued over a period of 45 years to the end of his life, this Institute became one of the most important centers of physiological research. The same year Pavlov was appointed Professor of Pharmacology at the Military Medical Academy & five years later he was appointed to the Chair of Physiology, which he held till 1925.

He developed the surgical method of the «chronic» experiment with extensive use of fistulas, which enabled the functions of various organs to be observed continuously under relatively normal conditions. This discovery opened a new era in the development of physiology. With his method of research, Pavlov opened the way for new advances in theoretical & practical medicine. With extreme clarity he showed that the nervous system played the dominant part in regulating the digestive process.

Eventually Pavlov's research of the physiology of digestion led him to create a science of conditioned reflexes. A series of experiments caused him to reject the subjective interpretation of «psychic» salivary secretion &, on the basis of Sechenov's hypothesis that psychic activity was of a reflex nature, to conclude that even here a reflex was involved.

This discovery of the function of conditioned reflexes made it possible to investigate by experimental means of the most complex interrelations between an organism and its external environment.

In 1903 (at the 14th International Medical Congress in Madrid) Pavlov read a paper on «The Experimental Psychology and Psychopathology of Animals». In this paper the definition of conditioned and other reflexes was given and it was shown that a conditioned reflex should be regarded as an elementary psychological phenomenon, which at the same time is a physiological one. Thus, conditioned reflex was a clue to the mechanism of the most highly developed forms of reaction in animals & humans to their environment.

Pavlov was a leader of a great school of physiologists, which produced many distinguished students. He left the richest scientific legacy - a brilliant group of scientists, who would continue developing the ideas of their master.

Pavlov mainly focused on three research problems. The first problem was concerned with the function of the heart & the second with the primary digestive glands. His third research area, the one for which he is best known, & for which he occupies such a vital role in the history of psychology, was the study of the higher nervous centers in the brain. One aspect of Pavlov's work dealt with the function of saliva, which would be involuntary secreted when food was placed in the dog's mouth. He also noted that sometimes saliva would be secreted before the food was given to the animal; there was an anticipatory saliva flow. The reflex of secretion with its unlearned response of salivation had somehow become attached to stimuli that had previously been associated with feeding. Such reflexes were aroused in the animal by stimuli other than the original one, which was food, & Pavlov realized that this happened because these other stimuli had so often been associated with the ingestion of food. The asociationists called this phenomenon "association by frequency of occurrence."

Pavlov eventually discovered that any stimulus could produce conditioned salivary response so long as it was capable of attracting the animal's attention without activating fight or anger. With Pavlov more objective measures & terminology were introduced into the study of association & learning. He also showed that higher mental processes could be effectively studied in psychological terms & with the use of animal subjects. Thus, he influenced psychology's shift to greater objectivity in subject matter & methodology. The effects if these shift are seen in the development of behaviorism, in which the conditioned reflex forms a central part. This concept provided the science of psychology with a basic element of behavior a workable unit to which the highly complex behavior of man could be reduced & experimented with under laboratory conditions. Pavlov's work influenced John B. Watson to assemble a new behavioristic school of thought. Watson, like Wundt, set out quite deliberately to found a new school of thought. He held that only the objective methods of investigation are admissible in the behavioristic laboratory. These methods were observation, conditioned reflex method, the verbal report method & testing method. Accordingly the method of observation was the necessary basis for the other methods. Objective tests were already in use but Watson proposed that test results be treated as samples of behavior, & not as measures of mental qualities. In Watson's opinion tests did not measure intelligence or personality rather it measured the responses the subject made to the stimulus situation of the test, & nothing more. The most important research of behaviorism- the conditioned reflex method-was not adopted until 1915.Overall Watson's conceptual behaviorism has proved to be of greater importance for psychology than his methodological behaviorism. Despite the reduction of behavior to stimulus-response units, Watson argued that behaviorism deals with overall behavior of the whole organism. He seemed to have thought of a response in terms of accomplishing some result in the environment, rather than as an assemblage of muscular elements. These individual acts can be reduced to lower level motor or glandular responses. Responses are classified in two ways: learned or unlearned, & explicit or implicit. Watson considered it important for behaviorism to distinguish between innate responses & those that are learned, & to discover for the latter the laws of learning. Explicit responses are overt & directly observable. Implicit responses such as nerve impulses, take place inside the organism. Though such moments are not overt, they are nonetheless items of behavior. The movements or responses occurring within the organism are theoretically observable through the use of instrumentation. The exciting stimuli, like the responses, may be complex. A stimulus may be something relatively simple (a light wave striking a retina), but it can also be a physical object in the environment, or total situations. Just as the constellation of responses involved in an act can be reduced to particular responses, so the stimulus situation can be resolved into its component specific stimuli.

Behaviorism deals with the behavior of the whole organism in relation to its environment. Specific laws of behavior can be worked out through the analysis of the total stimulus & response segments. Behavior, to Watson was concerned with the total organism & could not be restricted to the nervous system alone. Watson focused on larger units of behavior that is the whole response of the organism to a given situation.

In both subject matter & methodology, the new psychology of John B. Watson was an attempt to construct a science that was completely free of mentalistic notions & subjective methods.

Watson developed his psychology in accordance with his fundamental theses therefore all areas of behavior, feelings, emotions & so on were treated in objective stimulus response terms. For example,Watson's position on the role of instinct in behavior changed from an acceptance of instincts to a denial of their existence in humans. Since, according to Watson there are no instincts, the adult is strictly a product of childhood conditioning. His views on learning demonstrated a noticeable change in direction of the incorporation of conditioning as a basic part of the Watson's system.

According to Watson emotions are no more than bodily responses to specific stimuli. His bold pronouncements won him a large following not only among psychologists, but among the lay public as well. Watson's conditioning experiments convinced him emotional disturbances in adults cannot be traced back to sex alone. These disturbances can be traced to conditioned & transferred responses established in infancy & youth.

Watson's primary lasting contradiction was his advocacy of a completely objective science of behavior. He exerted an enormous influence in rendering psychology more objective, in both methods & terminology. Eventually behaviorism as a separate school has been replaced by newer forms of psychological objectivism that built upon it. The acceptance of Watsonian behaviorism was function of the clarity & force of the man himself. Although his positions of specific topics have stimulated a great deal of research, Watson's original formulations on these topics are no longer of use.

In the beginning of the 1920 new behavioristic systems appeared on the scene. Almost immediately, this movement began to branch out into distinct subsystems, creating much controversy that has continued up to the present day. The dominant behavioristic movement in American psychology was strengthened by the development of the principle known as operationism. Operationism is more of a general principle than a formal school. The main goal of operationism is to rid science of those problems that are not actually observable, or demonstrable. Thus operationism holds that the validity of a given scientific finding is dependent on the validity of the operations used in arriving at that finding. Further the operationist viewpoint was developed by Percy W. Bridgman, who proposed that physical concepts must be defined in more precise terms & that all concepts lacking physical referents must be discarded.

According to Bridgman propositions that cannot be put to experimental test have no value. He brings an example of a pseudo-problem such as the existence & nature of the soul. Hence if something cannot be measured or observed it has no use for science. It follows that the concept of an individual & private consciousness is a pseudo-problem in psychology, for neither its existence, nor its characteristics can be determined or investigated through objective methods. Such an approach is not really new; it is little more than a formal statement of methods that had already been used in psychology, when the meaning of words & concepts were defined in terms of their physical referents.

Operationism failed to win universal recognition in psychology. Controversy continues about the relative unity or futility of limiting psychologies subject matter to only that which has empirical reference.

The support for the main provisions of behaviorism & most importantly, its desire for objective investigation of mentality included certain differences that have arisen in dealing with specific scientific problems. The results of the experiments conducted by K. Lashley (1890-1958) & W. Hunter (1886-1954) were raising doubts about the validity of certain principles of Watson. Lashley held that complex behavior corresponded with complex brain connection. In his experiments the animal first fashioned some skill after which the various parts of the cortex were removed in order to determine whether these parts are responsible for the formation of the skills. Lashley discovered that after the destruction of a particular zone of the cerebral cortex of the animal its functions assumed another area of the brain. Based on the results of his experiments Lashley proposed the concept of "equipotential" or equal value of parts of the brain, which give the ability to retain part of the cortex to compensate for the loss.

W. Hunter was best known for his study of delayed reactions. In these experiments, monkeys were given, for example, the ability to see which of the two boxes was put banana. Then, between it & the boxes was placed a screen, & after a few seconds the monkey was given the opportunity to make a choice. The animal was able to successfully find the correct box. That decision proved that the animals possessed not only the immediate but also the delayed reaction to the stimulus. Hunter's Experiments have shown the role of installation, which was prior to the outwardly observable reaction & expressed the orientation of the organism to a specific stimulus. Ignoring this installation mediating the relationship between stimulus & response rendered the possibility of psychology to explain many phenomena of behavior.

One of the early adherents of behaviorism was Edward Chase Tolman (1886-1959), the founder of so called purposive behaviorism. He studied under the Gestalt psychologists, such as Kurt Koffka & while being trained in the Wundt-Titchener tradition, Tolman became acquainted with Watsonian behaviorism.

He was born at Newtown, Massachusetts Tolman received education at the Massachusetts Institute of Technology. He awarded a doctorate degree in 1915. For many years Tolman worked at the University of California at Berkeley. Here he developed his theory of learning. Tolman stressed the importance of latent learning, reward expectancy & the formation of animal learning hypotheses. He attempted to use behavioral methods to gain an understanding of the mental processes of humans & animals. Tolman was determined to demonstrate that animals could learn facts about the world that they could subsequently use in a flexible manner, rather than simply learning automatic responses that were triggered off by environmental stimuli. Because of his convictions Tolman was considered to be an "S-S" (stimulus-stimulus), non-reinforcement theorist. He held that animals could learn the connections between stimuli & did not need any biologically significant event to make learning occur.

Tolman's system of purposive behaviorism is often viewed as a blend of two contradictory terms: purpose & behavior. Attributing purpose to an organism seems to imply consciousness. Indeed, such a mentalistic concept can have no place in a behavioristic system. Tolman rejected introspection of structuralism, showing no interest in assumed internal experiences that were not accessible to objective observation. The references to conscious processes Tolman phrased in terms of cautious inferences from observed behavior.

Tolman was far from being a Watsonian behaviorist, for the differed in many respects, mainly Tolman was not interested in studying behavior at the molecular level & unlike Watson he was not concerned with elemental units of behavior. His focus was molar behavior, which meant the total response actions of the whole organism.

Perhaps Tolman's biggest contribution to psychology is his concept of the intervening variable. He believed that the initiating causes of behavior & the final resulting behavior itself must be capable of being objectively observed & correctly defined. Tolman's initiating causes of behavior consist of five independent variables: the environmental stimuli (S), physiological drive (P), heredity (H), previous training (T) & age (A). In the case of animal subjects, the experimenter can easily control these variables, but he would have less control with human subjects. Behavior then is a function of these independent variables.

$$B = fx (S, P, H, T, A)$$

The concept of the intervening variable has been useful to many psychologists, though it has been often criticized as well. Intervening variables appear to be of value in developing an acceptable theory of behavior so long as they are empirically related to both experimental & behavior variables. According to Tolman behavior (animal & human) is capable of modification through experience. He discarded with Thorndike's law of effect, claiming that reward or reinforcement has little, if any role in learning. Tolman preferred a cognitive theory of learning in which the continued performance of a task builds up sign Gestalts, which are learned relationships between cues in the environment & the organism's expectations.

Tolman was a great figure in psychology, especially in the area of learning. He has been criticized for his inability to develop a fully integrated theoretical system.

Another famous behaviorist Edwin Ray Guthrie (1886-1959) strongly believed that science must deal with objectively observable conditions &

events. He opposed the practice of attempting to relate behavioral events to what he considered the invisible brain & nervous system.

He was born in Lincoln, Nebraska. He graduated & received a master's degree from the University of Nebraska, specializing in philosophy, mathematics & psychology. In 1912 Guthrie received his doctorate (University of Pennsylvania). His training & background reflected his analytical frame of reference in many of his writings. In 1914 Guthrie accepted an instructorship in philosophy at the University of Washington. Eventually he transferred to the department of psychology, where he remained until his retirement in 1956. During his rise to full professor in 1928, he developed his learning theory in association with Stevenson Smith, who was then department chairman of psychology at Washington. Guthrie was elected president of the American Psychological Association. During World War II he was a lieutenant in the U.S. Army, serving as a consultant to the overseas branch of the general staff of the War Department. He was made dean of the graduate school at the University of Washington in 1943.

Guthrie thought that the principle of learning was all or nothing in the first trial, meaning that the association between the stimulus & response does not change or improve with practice. He further held that perfection was attainable on the first try & that practice did not make perfect, it only appeared to improve with repetition. Guthrie was sure that his theory of learning applied in all instances & that there was only one type of learning. He held that movement-produced stimuli were a sensation produced by the movements themselves in maintaining sequential responding. He viewed stimuli and movements as a combination. Guthrie saw difference between movements and acts.

Guthrie cooperated with George P. Horton. They used puzzle boxes to demonstrate their learning theory. They put cats in the puzzle boxes & watched their escape behaviors. A tube was released to the front door of the puzzle box to allow the cats to escape. The purpose of the experiment was to demonstrate one-trial learning. Guthrie believed this could be shown by a stereotyping of behavior. According to their theory when the cat escaped from the box it should be able to remember the last thing it did to be able to perform the escape again. Guthrie and Horton reported that in each trial the cats made one association, a trial/escape.

Guthrie advocated a psychology of observable behavior consisting of muscular movements and responses elicited by environmental stimuli. Thus, his theory of associations was asserting relatively few principles to account for learning. In addition, Guthrie did not accept Thorndike's reinforcement principle based on the "law of effect," instead, he considered

Thorndike's secondary notion of associative shifting as the true basis of learning process.

According to Guthrie's law of contiguity a combination of stimuli which had accompanied a movement, on its recurrence, was followed by that movement. Guthrie's learning was mainly based on a stimulus-response association, in which movements were small stimulus-response combinations. He argued that these movements were components of an act. In Guthrie's theory learned behavior was comprised of series of movements. He held that each movement produced stimuli & the stimuli then became conditioned. Various motions served as a stimulus to many sense organs in muscles, tendons & joints. Stimuli which were acting at the time of a response turned into conditioners of that response. Movement-produced stimuli had become conditioners of the succession of movements. Such movements formed a series often referred to as a habit. Guthrie was against the law of frequency & the dependence of learning on reinforcement. He was more attracted to one-trial learning, which learning stated that a stimulus pattern gained its full associative strength on the occasion of its first pairing with a response.

In Guthrie's theory associative inhibition occurred when one habit prevented another due to some stronger stimuli. His contiguity theory stated that forgetting was a form of retroactive or associative inhibition. Guthrie was convinced that forgetting was due to interference because the stimuli became associated with new responses. He also believed that one can use sidetracking to change previous conditioning. This complex process involved discovering the initial cues for the habit & associating other behavior with those cues. Sidetracking caused the internal associations to break up. It was easier to sidetrack than to break a habit. Other methods used to break habits included threshold, fatigue, & the incompatible response method. Fatigue was a change in behavior-altered chemical states in the muscle & blood stream. It had the effect of decreasing the conditioned response. The stimulus, in turn, conditioned the other responses thus inhibiting the response. Finally the threshold method involved presenting cues at such low levels that the response did not occur.

Guthrie's used his contiguity law to prove that a combination of stimuli that has accompanied a movement will on its recurrence be followed by that movement.

Guthrie differed from the rest of the Watsonian behaviorists. His most important influence of psychology is his formulation of an extremely simple learning theory. Guthrie was known as forceful proponent of a theory of learning which has based on one principle; contiguity. He rejected

Thorndike's laws of effect & frequency as well as Pavlov's reinforcement, instead relying on so called "simultaneous conditioning," which he recognized as the basic law in psychology. Guthrie relates learning modification to contiguity of stimulus & response. Accordingly, if a stimulus just once elicits a response, then the S-R association is established. Guthrie's system has no mention of internal drive states, or receptions of the stimulus-response pairings. His several books contain evidence of an anecdotal nature & comparatively little in the way of experimental evidence. It seems that Guthrie preferred writing & argumentation to experimentation. There is however, empirical support for his theory, particularly his own research involving stereotype in the behavior of the cat in a puzzle box.

Many criticize Guthrie, claiming that simplicity with which he presents his theory of personality is a result of a failure to deal explicitly with certain major problems in learning.

Nevertheless, Guthrie was able to successfully maintain his theoretical position & stature as a leading learning theorist.

Clark Leonard Hull (1884-1952), a devoted behaviorist & a well respected psychologist was known for his consistent devotion to the problems inherent in scientific method & for applying the language of mathematics to psychological theory. Hull also devoted ten years to the study of hypnosis & suggestibility.

Clark L. Hull was born in Akron, New York. He went to study at the Alma College, but his education was interrupted by bouts of typhoid fever and poliomyelitis. The sudden disease gave Hull sometime to consider possible vocational choices; he decided upon psychology. He received his bachelor's degree at the University of Michigan, after which Hull went to the University of Wisconsin. He received his doctorate in 1918. Staying on at Wisconsin to teach, Hull was at first torn between two schools of psychological thought which prevailed at the time: early behaviorism & Gestalt psychology. He was not long in deciding in favor of the former. One of his first experiments was an analytical study of the effects of tobacco on behavioral efficiency. Hull's lifelong emphasis was on the development of objective methods for psychological studies designed to determine the underlying principles of behavior.

He published "Hypnosis & Suggestibility," while employed as a research professor at Yale University. This is where he developed his major contribution, an elaborate theory of behavior based on Pavlov's laws of conditioning. In a way Pavlov influenced Hull to become interested in the problem of conditioned reflexes and learning. In 1943 Hull published,

Principles of Behavior, which presented a number of constructs in a detailed Theory of Behavior.

Hull believed that the environment provides the stimuli & the organism responds, all of which is observable. Yet there is a component that is not observable, the change that the organism needs to make in order to survive within the environment. Thus, when survival is at risk, the organism is in a state of need (when the biological requirements for survival are not being met) so the organism behaves in a fashion to compensate for that need. Being an objective behaviorist, Hull viewed human behavior as mechanical, automatic and cyclical, which could be reduced to the terms of physics. He thought in terms of mathematics convinced that behavior should be expressed according to these terms. At the time three specific methods were used by researchers; observation, systematic controlled observation & experimental testing of the hypothesis. Hull added a new method; the "Hypothetico Deductive" method. This new method involved deriving postulates from which experimentally testable conclusions could be deduced & tested.

Hull believed the drive to be non-specific, which meant that the drive does not direct behavior rather it functions to energize it. Also the reduction of the drive was viewed as the reinforcement.

The strength of the drive was determined upon the length of the deprivation, or the intensity of the resulting behavior. He held that organisms were motivated by other forces; so called secondary reinforcements, which meant that previously neutral stimuli could assume drive characteristics because they were capable of eliciting responses that were similar to those aroused by the original need state. He held that human behavior involves a continuing interaction between the organism & the environment, noting that the objective stimuli provided by the environment along with the behavioral responses provided by the organism are facts. Such interactions occur within a much larger context that cannot be totally defined in observable stimulus-response terms. The wider context is the biological adaptation of the organism to its unique environment. According to Hull, need is a situation in which the biological requirements for survival are not being met. When in a state of need, the organism acts in a manner designed to reduce that need. The behavior, therefore serves to reinstate the optimal biological conditions necessary for survival.

Hull thought that the link between the S-R relationships could be anything that might affect how an organism responds; learning, fatigue, motivation, etc. His formula was

$$sEr = (sHr \times D \times K \times V) - (sIr + Ir) +/- sOr$$

He labeled this relationship as "E", a reaction potential, or as sEr. Habit strength, sHr, was determined by the number of reinforces. Drive strength, D, was measured by the hours of deprivation of a need. K was the incentive value of a stimulus & V is a measure of the connectiveness. Inhibitory strength, sIr, was the number of none reinforces. Reactive inhibition, Ir, was when the organism had to work hard for a reward and became fatigued. The last variable in his formula was sOr, which accounted for random error. Hull believed that this formula generate more accurate empirical data, which would eliminate all ineffective introspective methods.

Overall Hull's system is a unilateral, radical behaviorism in which he attempted to reduce every concept he used to physical terms. He was totally committed to objective psychology, nearly negating mentalistic notions like purpose & consciousness. Hull's system very definitely couched in mechanistic terms. He viewed human behavior as automatic & cyclical, capable of reduction to the terminology of physics. Hull's approach to psychology is characterized by quantification. He believed that the laws of behavior must be stated in the precise language of mathematics. In terms of specific research methodology Hull provides four methods useful to science: simple observation, systematic controlled observation, experimental testing & hypothesis & hypothetico-deductive method.

Hull's system primarily was concerned with motivation. Eventually he became less concerned with learning & more concerned with other factors capable of influencing behavior. In his system, Hull attempts to integrate Thorndike's law of effect with Pavlov's conditioning. He held that learning could not be explained by the principles of recency & frequency, & that major focus of learning should be the principle of reinforcement. Hull's law of primary reinforcement states that if a stimulus-response relationship is followed by a reduction in need, then on subsequent occasions, the probability is high that the same stimulus will evoke the same response. Hull maintained that the S-R connection is strengthened by the number of reinforcements, calling the strength of the S-R connection habit strength. The so called habit strength refers to the persistence of the conditioning & is a function of reinforcement. Accordingly learning cannot take place in the absence of reinforcement that is necessary to bring about a reduction of the drive. Because of this emphasis on reinforcement, Hull's system is called a need reduction theory. His system is presented in terms of highly specific & detailed postulates & corollaries all of which are phrased in difficult verbal & mathematical form. As a leading exponent of neo-behaviorism, Hull is subject to the same kind of criticism aimed at others who followed behaviorism. Hull's system lacks generalizing ability, in his attempts to define variables with total precision in quantitative terms he operated too specifically, functioning at times on a narrow miniature system basis. His system is so thoroughly & minutely developed in quantitative terms that incomplete or inaccurate formulations are very easy to spot.

Burrhus Frederick Skinner (1904-1990), was one of the most influential figures in psychology. In many ways Skinner's position represents a renewal of the older Watsonian behaviorism. He was born in the small Pennsylvania town of Susquehanna. Skinner received his BA in English from Hamilton College in upstate New York. He got his masters in psychology (1930) & his doctorate (1931) in Harvard.

In 1936 Skinner moved to Minneapolis to teach at the University of Minnesota. In 1945, he became the chairman of the psychology department at Indiana University. In 1948, he was invited to come to Harvard, where he remained for the rest of his life. Here Skinner conducted many researches, guiding hundreds of doctoral candidates as well as writing many books.

In his book "About Behaviorism," he took pains to point out that Watson, in his zeal to establish psychology as a science, made an exaggerated commitment to the study of introspective life. Skinner held that psychologists must provide adequate explanations of private events, insisting that the events studied must be capable of being reliably & objectively recorded. Verbal reports can provide acceptable data for Skinner if scientific criteria are met. But because other people have difficulty teaching us the appropriate labels for private experiences, we must be cautious in accepting such reports at face value. Thus, Skinner did not accept Watson's simplistic stimulus-response formulation. He maintained that such an approach was obsolete & claimed to recognize the complexity of human behavior.

Skinner considered the study of personality legitimate, but only if established scientific criteria are met. He would not accept the idea of a personality or self that guides behavior. Skinner believed that the study of personality involves a systematic examination of the idiosyncratic learning history & unique genetic background of the individual. The study of the personality further involves the discovery of the unique set of relationships between the behavior of an organism & its reinforcing or punishing consequences.

In Skinner's system behavior takes place in situations & produces outcomes. Operant behavior includes numerous activities. The establishment of an association between behavior & its consequences is called operant conditioning. Through operant conditioning, the occurrence of behavior is made more or less probable.

The stimuli preceding the behavior are important because they provide the occasion under which reinforcement is likely to occur if the behavior is performed. Thus, people learn how to discriminate. In the presence of a certain stimuli, or some situation person's behavior is likely to be reinforced. Sometimes behavior is likely to be punished in certain situations, whereas the same behavior under different circumstances is unlikely to be punished. When person's responses are differentially controlled by antecedent stimuli or situations, they are considered to be under stimulus control. According to Skinner the majority of human behavior is controlled by stimuli.

A response that is repeatedly reinforced in a particular situation is likely to be repeated in that situation. Situations on the other hand, consist of complex sets of stimuli that often share common properties. Skinner held that the control exerted by a given stimulus is shared by other similar stimuli. Stimulus generalization occurs if a behavior that is reinforced in one situation also increases in other situations, even though it is not reinforced in those situations. Generalization is opposite to discrimination. When a person discriminates between two situations it means that his response failed to generalize from one situation to the other. When person's response does generalize across two situations, it means that he has failed to discriminate the two situations & make the same response in both situations. These two phenomena have important implications for person's psychological health & well-being.

Behavior is controlled not only by antecedent stimuli, but also by its consequences. Positive refers to an increase in the frequency of a behavior when that behavior is followed by positive reinforcements. There are two types of positive reinforcements: primary which are automatically & naturally reinforced & secondary which acquire their reinforcing properties through association with primary reinforcers or with other conditioned reinforcing factors. Examples of secondary reinforcers are attention, good grades & praise. Negative reinforcers are aversive stimuli, or punishers- for example loud noises, bright lights or physical assault. The removal of an aversive stimulus following a response increases the probability of that behavior occurring in the future under the same or similar circumstances. Negative reinforcement refers to the removal of an aversive stimulus following a response, thereby increasing the rate of occurrence of that response. The principle of reinforcement is that a behavior will increase in frequency when it is followed either by the presentation of a positive reinforcer or by the removal of a punisher.

The principle of punishment refers to a decrease in the frequency of a response when that response is followed immediately by certain consequences. Punishers can be applied to behavior to make its occurrence less probable. This procedure is called positive punishment. Primary punishers are stimuli that are inherently avers. Secondary punishers acquire their aversive properties by being paired with primary punishers or other conditioned punishers, like criticism.

Overall Skinner saw punishment as the most common technique of control in modern life. He thought that punishment temporarily suppresses behavior, not forgetting to note its negative effects. To explain changes in personality over time, Skinner looked to unique environmental schedules of reinforcement rather than the emergence of maturational stages. Although he acknowledged some predictive value in Freud's theory, Skinner generally opposed him. He held that Freud's approach does not allow control or manipulation of events, a procedure he considered crucial for a science of behavior. In Skinner's view, there is no qualitative difference between so called normal & abnormal individual, since the same set of reinforcement principles accounts for the behavior of all individuals. According to him, we should focus more on the environmental determinants of behavior than on inner determinants. He would eliminate all references to a mental apparatus such as Freud employed. Such theorizing he found to be imprecise, ambiguous & leading to pseudo explanations of behavior.

Skinner introduced the concept of "shaping" as a way to deal with to deal with complex sorts of behaviors. Shaping, also known as the method of successive approximations was designed to reinforce a behavior only vaguely similar to the one desired. Once that is established, we must look out for variations that are a little closer to what we want, & so on, until we have the animal performing a behavior that would never show up in ordinary life. Skinner and his students have been quite successful in teaching simple animals to do some extraordinary things.

Skinner also believed that Freud contributed much to our understanding of behavior & that many of his ideas translate into terms amenable to scientific inquiry. In Freud's theory ego defense mechanisms were presented in terms of people's attempts to avoid punishment. In Skinner's theory punishment makes the stimuli associated with punished behavior aversive. As a result, any behavior that reduces stimulation becomes positively reinforcing.

Primarily Skinner was interested in the experimental analysis of behavior. He was determined to identify those environmental variables that control behavior. As the functional analysis of behavior is a complicated matter that involves the interplay of a multitude of variables, Skinner focused on specific behaviors & those environmental events considered to be controlling influences. He believed that his approach could be implemented best by analyzing the behavior of nonhuman species, since their environments are relatively easy to control & many of their behaviors are simple & quantifiable.

Perhaps Skinner was the only major figure in the history of behaviorism to offer a socio-political worldview based on his commitment to behaviorism. His social worldview contains both his aversion to free will as well as his reasons for claiming that a person's history of environmental interactions controls his behavior.

Joseph Wolpe (1915-1997) was best known for developing theories & experiments in systematic desensitization & assertiveness training. He was in Johannesburg, South Africa. At first he attended local college. Later he earned his M.D. from the University of Witwatersrand. During the Second World War he worked in the army as a medical officer. Here he invented the concept now known as desensitization. Systematic desensitization is a type of behavioral therapy used in the field of psychology designed to help effectively overcome fears, phobias, & other anxiety disorders. To begin the process of systematic desensitization, one must first be taught relaxation skills in order to control fear and anxiety responses to specific phobias. Once the individual has been taught these skills, he or she must use them to react towards and overcome situations in an established hierarchy of fears. Wolpe held that much of human behavior (both good & bad) was learned therefore it could be unlearned as well. Following the war Wolpe worked at the University of Witwatersrand, after which he moved to the United States, where he taught at the University of Virginia. In 1965, he became a professor of psychiatry at Temple University Medical School in Philadelphia. Wolpe was also a director of the behavior therapy unit at the nearby Eastern Pennsylvania Psychiatric Institute. In addition he served as the second president of the Association for the Advancement of Behavior Therapy, from which he received a lifetime achievement award. Wolpe's last job was at the Pepperdine University, where he lectured until a month before his death.

He conducted experiments with cats which were given mild electric shocks accompanied by specific sounds & visual stimuli. Once the animal learned to equate the unpleasant shock with these images or sounds, the images & sounds created a feeling of fear. By gradually exposing the cats to these same sights & sounds-with food being given instead of shocks-the cats gradually "unlearned" their fear.

From his experiments Wolpe concluded that sometimes the problem may not be fear of the object per se, but a negative association coming from another source. His research also led to assertiveness training. As with desensitization, it required a gradual move into new behaviors. A person who had trouble asserting himself was very much like a phobic in that he feared confrontation & conflict. Necessary in such cases assertiveness training gave them the framework to build their confidence, relax in formerly stressful situations, & conquer their fear.

Wolpe was the first behaviorist to combine two seemingly disparate disciplines. Many psychologists and psychiatrists felt that methods based in applied science lacked the humanistic touch they felt was so important when dealing with people. What Wolpe did was show that effective, compassionate therapy could be combined with empirical methods in a way that used both to their best advantage.

The American scientist George Mead (1863-1931), who worked at the University of Chicago, tried to take into account the peculiarity of the conditioning of human behavior in its concept, called social behaviorism. He was born in South Hadley, Massachusetts to a middle class protestant family. At the age of 16 Mead enrolled at Oberlin College. He graduated in 1883 with an AB degree & began teaching grade school, after which he worked as a surveyor for the Wisconsin Central Rail Road Company.

In autumn 1887, Mead decided to enter the Harvard University to study philosophy & psychology. After receiving his Master's degree in philosophy Mead moved to Leipzig to study with Wilhelm Wundt. After studying in Germany, Mead transferred to the in 1891. Here he met Charles H. Cooley & John Dewey. Three years later Mead moved, along with Dewey, to the University of Chicago, where he taught until his death.

Research stages of entering the child into the world of adults led Mead to the idea that the child's personality was formed during its interaction with others. Thus, child's personality was like the union once personal roles, which he himself took. Of great importance in the formation, and in the knowledge of these roles has a game in which children first learn to assume different roles & abide by certain rules.

Mead's theory was also referred to as the theory of expectations, since, in his view, children lose their roles depending on the expectations of adults. Children in many ways play the same role based on their expectations & on past experiences. The notion of "generalized other" was introduced by Mead to explain why children do obey the rules of the game, but cannot meet them in real life. In addition Mead distinguished between the theme games & games with rules. He held that games with certain themes taught children to accept & play various roles, modify them during the game. He found this to be a positive experience since before these games the children knew only one role - a child in family. Now they were learning to be a mom, & a laborer, & a cook, & so on. Games with rules were designed to help children to develop the arbitrariness of reference, to master those standards that were accepted in society.

In Mead's social behaviorism mind was not a substance located in some transcendent realm. He did not view it merely a series of events that takes place within the human physiological structure. Mind, according to Mead, arose within the social process of communication & could not be understood apart from that process. The communicational process involved two phases: 1. "conversation of gestures" & 2. Language or the "conversation of significant gestures." These phases presupposed a social context within which two or more individuals were in interaction with one another.

Mead's conversation of gestures was an unconscious communication. It was, however, out of the conversation of gestures that language, or conscious communication, emerged. Mead's theory of communication was evolutionary. In it communication developed from more or less primitive toward more or less advanced forms of social interaction. Mead described language as a communication through significant symbols. A significant symbol was a gesture (usually vocal) that called out in the individual making the gesture the same (that is, functionally identical) response that was called out in others to whom the gesture was directed.

Eventually behaviorism has lost its strength & influence. Its laboratory routines are neglected by psychologists convinced that its methods are irrelevant to studying how animals & people behave in their natural & social environment. Also its traditional relative indifference towards neuroscience is rejected by neuroscientists sure that direct study of the brain is the only way to understand the causes of behavior.

The main reason for behaviorisms decline in influence is its commitment to the thesis that behavior can be explained without reference to non-behavioral mental activity. It is obvious that the occurrence & character of behavior does not depend upon person's reinforcement history, although that is a factor, but on the fact that the environment or learning history is represented & how it is represented.

One important feature of traditional behaviorism is that it tried to free psychology from having to theorize about how animals & people represent their environment. It seemed that behavior/environment connections are a lot clearer & more manageable experimentally than internal representations. Unfortunately, for behaviorism it is hard to imagine a more restrictive rule for psychology than one which prohibits hypotheses about representational storage & processing.

About Freudianism

In the beginning of the 20-th century psychoanalysis had made its impact felt in every department of human thought. Its influence was especially marked within the arts, medicine & social sciences. The violent reaction born of conservatism & prudery during the first two decades of the 20-th century had given way for enthusiastic acceptance in some quarters, & in others to at leastlimited recognition of the value of the Freudian insights. Certain developments within the rapidly growing sciences of anthropology, sociology & medicine began to exert a reciprocal influence on psychoanalysis.

Psychoanalysis was developed as a narrow, but distinct theoretical field in answer to the demands of growing medical practice. I n the beginning it was just a specific method for treatment of neurosis, used instead of hypnosis. Eventually it became the foundation for a new movement in psychology. Currently it constitutes a whole social philosophy, whose adherents claimed universality of their theory. They also maintain that their methods can be applied for the resolution of not merely medical & psychological problems, but social problems as well. Since it first came into being psychoanalysis has advanced considerably, particularly as regards the growing importance of its socio- philosophical implications. Normally the expression social philosophy is used to describe the emergence & gradual development of efforts on the part of psychoanalysis within their field is, apply their methodology to the study & exposition of essential significance of social phenomena. When considering the evolution of ideas pertaining to social philosophy within the field of psychoanalysis, it is as well to distinguish between 2 stages in the history of psychoanalysis: the bio-psychological stage during which Freud's sociological conception really came into being & the anthropological-psychological stage during which Erich Fromm's social philosophy took shape.

Sigmund Freud (1856-1939) was born in a small town of Freiberg, Moravia. A brilliant child, always at the head of his class, he went to medical school, one of the few viable options for a bright Jewish boy in Vienna those days. He became involved in research under the direction of a physiology professor Ernst Brucke. Brucke believed in reductionism: "No other forces than the common physical-chemical ones are active within the organism." Freud would spend many years trying to "reduce" personality to neurology, a cause he later gave up on.

Freud was concentrating on neurophysiology, even inventing a special cell-staining technique. Brucke helped him to get a grant to study, first with the great psychiatrist Charcot in Paris, then with his rival Bernheim in Nancy. Both these gentlemen were investigating the use of hypnosis with hysterics. After spending a short time as a resident in neurology and director of a children's ward in Berlin, he came back to Vienna, married his fiancée of many years Martha Bernays, and set up a practice in neuropsychiatry.

Freud's lectures & books brought him fame and ostracism from the mainstream of the medical community. Eventually he drew around him a number of very bright sympathizers who became the core of the psychoanalytic movement. Some separated from him on friendly terms; others did not, and went on to found competing schools of psychology. Freud moved to England just before World War II when Vienna became an increasing dangerous place for Jewish people, especially ones as famous as him. Not long afterward, he died of the cancer of the mouth and jaw that he had suffered from for the last 20 years.

During the elaboration of the theory of causes of neurosis & the corresponding techniques of treatment Freud widened his research beyond solely medical issues, because in his analysis of the cause of disorders, Freud has concentrated from the outset on the role & significance of moral & social factor, although he had not examined the extent of their influence outside the family

In his study of the causes of hysteria symptoms Freud drew the conclusion that pathological phenomena appears as a result of the shift from the field of consciousness to the subconscious of those emotions, urges & reactions which are undesirable to the conscious human ego. Such studies led Freud to view the social conditions of human existence as the main obstacles to person's mental health. At one point he was forced to reduce the problem of etiology of neurosis to the conflict between man's natural instincts & society.

Freud maintained that man's aggressive & sexual impulses, inherent in his very nature always conflict with social necessity & contradict the moral demands & values of any society. According to Freud the main cause for the emergence & progression of nervous diseases are the bridling of sexual instincts by social morals & excessive suppression. Such article was to herald the emergence of a sociological trend within the scope of Freud's theory of psychoanalysis. Freud's theory is of the bio-psychological character, centered on instincts. With reference to the theory of immutable innate biological instincts & also to the hypothesis of the eternal conflict between life & death in every organism Freud attempted to find the source of mans mental activity. In his theory the psyche was biological by nature & did not in any way depend upon the external world. Convinced that man's instinctual make-up determined his behavior Freud denied categorically that man's environment might influence his mental structure. Contemporary theoretical & empirical psychological research demonstrates that the metaphysical theory of instincts on which psychoanalysis is based, is mystification pure & simple. While it is with reference to the theory of instincts that Freud attempted to disclose the causes of man's mental activity, it was to the theory of repression that he turned in order to explain the dynamics of human behavior. Freud held that man is obliged by the harsh demands of self-preservation to suppress his instincts & direct his energies along socially acceptable channels.

Freud refers to this capacity of man's to redirect his sexual impulses under pressure of social demands sublimation. In his theory the sublimation is determined by the capacity of this or that individual in question which in its turn depends on the strength of his sexual instinct. Freud maintained that criminals & neurotics are made when the demands of civilization are inexcess of the individual's capacity of sublimation. According to Freud in society there are three paths open to man prey to strong instincts demanding satisfaction when man's inner impulses are not held in check at all he becomes neurotic, & finally if they are sublimated in socially use full activity he is able to live in a given society without any friction.

In order to rule out the first two possibilities which introduce inevitable discord to social life, two types of therapeutic measures are in Freud's mind essential: firstly, society must somehow be compelled to reduce the demands it makes on the individual, thus relaxing the unduly rigorous repression of instincts, & secondly, the power of man's consciousness in the struggle with his instincts must be enhanced & his capacity for sublimation increased by means of improved rational control. According to Freud the search for individual's optimal adaptation to social demands is the only acceptable solution for the conflict between man's biological nature & society. The qualitative diversity of human behavior could be reduced to aspects of the process of instinct repression, to the various types of conflicts between man's biological nature & his social environment.

The conflicts at work on an unconscious level between social & biological pressures which Freud described do not reflect complex, so much as real correlations between external & internal factors determining man's mental activity; they do not reveal the true motive forces behind his behavior. In his work an immutable system of external social conditions is seen in conflict with a static system of man's inner world in the form of immutable instincts. In away the interaction between the internal & external is also depicted as a static. The conflict between human nature & society is seen not as a dialectical whole & interpenetration of opposites but merely as a confrontation of two separate sides that were not dependent on each other. Freud did not consider that the external social conditions of man's existence determined his mental activity; he considered that they merely impeded the manifestation of that activity, holding back the realization of man's instinctive urges. This socio-psychological interpretation of the relationship between human nature & society confronted Freud with a dilemma which he found himself unable to resolve: on the one hand he sees the bridling & rejection of instincts as one of the essential conditions for the very existence of the society, indeed civilization as a whole, & on the other the un impeded & total satisfaction of instincts is presented as an essential condition for man's mental health.

Freud saw society as the product of three independent variables: 1. Necessity stemming from nature; 2. A dualistic pair of instincts: love & death; 3. various institutions & ideals which constitute the social environment or society. The advance of civilization is shaped by the interaction of these three variables. In his opinion society is a profoundly tragic phenomenon, since it is unstable & unreliable, given that synthesis & reconciliation of these three components not only will never be effected but is in principle quite impossible. Despite the fact that society seeks to make use of man's instinctive impulses so as to preserve & consolidate social life, all it can do is establish a dubious balance that is always exposed to the danger of man's unbridled instincts. Quite frequently Freud calls attention to the inner contradictions intrinsic to society, stressing the impossibility of surmounting them.

Social life is often presented by Freud as an everlasting struggle between instincts & morality, between the individual's biological needs & the demands made upon him by the group or society to which he belongs.

Society according to Freud does not answer any real need stemming from human nature. Such theory leads him on to the paradoxical conclusion that man is not created for social living but at the same time needs society. Freud's ideal is a society in which no pressures would be brought to bear on the individual & he would be assured free scope for the satisfaction of his instincts. Yet since this ideal is unfeasible, because instincts by their very nature are antagonistic to society, Freud asserts that violence & coercion are therefore the logical foundation for any society that actually exists. Each individual is viewed by Freud as a potential enemy of society not only because he bears within himself destructive desires, but also because the overwhelming majority of men are in his opinion lazy, unreasonable, & maladapted to community living. Society, accordingly, asserts by constantly overcoming the masses' resistance & inertness & its task consists not only in suppressing destructive urges, but also in compelling men to reconcile themselves to those restrictions & sacrifices which society demands of them while offering them in exchange all manner of compensations. The latter comprise so called "physical inventory of a civilization" embracing morals, religion, art & politics. Freud reduces society's influence on man to little more than a greater or lesser degree of suppression of his instincts. Society guarantees specific control over man's instincts in order to render possible the existence of human social relations. It emerges as a result of the need to bridle unruly sexual & aggressive desires in man, to restrain & purify his instinctive impulses.

Freud's theory of the human condition & human nature bears a close resemblance to conceptions by Machiavelli; any principle of good is alien to the human essence & therefore evil, destructive tendencies predominate in the world. In Freud's theory man has never had & still does not have any humane feelings, impulses, & only fear of violence restrains him & holds in check his anti-social nature. Freud's view of prospects for the development of civilization is equally pessimistic. He holds that as civilization develops, the need to bridle instincts becomes more & more acute & that history cannot help but eventually degenerate into universal neurosis. In his conviction that man has no hope whatsoever of changing the existing state of affairs Freud recommends that he should submit to the inevitable. Life should be courageously accepted such as man finds it, is the conclusion offered. Thus the world in which we live in is the best of worlds only in so far as it is the only possible world. The future is an illusion, which means that all fundamental ideals & faith in human progress are also illusory. The only aim in life according to Freud is the process of existence itself, namely the eternal struggle for survival. This pessimism of Freud's is a natural consequence of his psychoanalytical theory of the origin & development of civilization.

Freud extrapolates conclusions drawn from analyses of behavior of individual patients to social or ethnic groups. Brushing to the one side the qualitative difference between the normal & the pathological, he maintains that the healthy individual differs from the neurotic in so far as the former is subject to a socially useful form of neurosis. In his view neurotic phenomena are not of a coincidental character, but rather of a universal character intrinsic to all men without exception at all times. The conclusion drawn by Freud from analyses of individual behavior is used by him to characterize social phenomena, to interpret laws of historical development. This universalization of pathologic phenomena, makes history, as interpreted by Freud, appear as no more than a progressive neurosis of the whole mankind. Freud approaches the history of social development from the angle of his psychoanalytical theory. The idea of the universal neurosis affecting all mankind provides a kind of psychoanalytical analogue for the naïve religious doctrine of original sin.

The philosophical foundation on which Freud's psychoanalytical theory was based, & in particular his sociology, was drawn from the idealist principles of the philosophy of Plato, Kant, Nietzsche & Bergson. Although Freud did not regard himself as an adherent of any philosophical doctrine, nevertheless his attention was attracted by those philosophical systems which expressed open irrationalism.

The vital role in man's diverse mental activity is ascribed to unconscious, biologically determined instincts. Reason is only present as an attendant element. Idealism & metaphysics constitute the philosophical foundation on which the cumbersome edifice of psychoanalytical constructions is built up. In the context of social history Freud's thought reflected the mood of terror & despair that came over the bourgeois strata at the end of 19-th century. As Freud started referring more & more to his psychoanalytical theory & its clinical applications in his study of social problems, this theory began to play a part of a specific method for explaining various phenomena of social life. Freud was convinced that without prejudice to the essence of psychoanalysis it could be used with the same success in connection with mythology, language folklore, national character & the study of religion, as for the treatment of neurosis. Freud's sociological ideas are not simply a side-product of his psychoanalytical theory, but the logical outcome of the essential development of that theory, is indispensable ingredient. The socio-political which follow on from Freud's social philosophy are reactionary in character; they have been used on numerous occasions, & indeed still are being used by certain ideologists to demonstrate the permanence & probity of social injustice, conflict, crime, war, & to demonstrate the impossibility of establishing just human relations. His reduction of all men's social life to unconscious processes, to inner conflict of a sexual character was to prove increasingly inadequate as science developed. It is precisely in Freud's sociological ideas that the weaknesses inherent in the initial methodological principles of his theory come to the foremost strikingly of all, & it is from these principles that radical criticism of all aspects of orthodox Freudian thought started out.

Freud's Theory of Personality

In Freud's theory mental life is divided into three parts: the conscious, the preconscious, & the unconscious. The conscious refers to those ideas & sensations of which we are aware. It operates It operates on the surface of personality & plays a relatively minor role in personality development & functioning. It is a known fact that psychologically healthy people demonstrate greater awareness than unhealthy ones, but Freud was convinced that even relatively mature people are controlled, to a much greater degree than they would care to admit, by unconscious needs & conflicts.

Freud defines preconscious as experiences that are unconscious, but with a potential to become conscious with little effort. When it comes to unconscious, Freud finds it to be deepest level of personality, because it consists of those experiences & memories of which the man is not aware. The mental states often remain out of awareness because making them conscious could create tremendous pain & anxiety. The unconscious includes strong emotional reactions of anger or rage towards certain authority figures, or painful feelings of shame & humiliation growing out of competitive experiences. Therefore repressed memories cannot simply disappear once they have been thrust from awareness; they continue to operate outside awareness, & seek expression in various defensive, disguised & distorted ways, that why unconscious ideas, memories & experiences interfere with conscious & rational behavior.

Instinctual drives are initiated when bodily needs motivate people to seek gratification, so that bodily processes can return to their prior state of equilibrium or homeostasis. Painful feelings are associated with instinctual stimulation, while pleasurable feelings are associated with a decrease in this stimulation.

Instincts pose four basic characteristics: 1. A source in some bodily deficit; 2. an aim gratification of the need; 3. an impetus that propels the person to act; 4. an object through which the instinct achieves its aim. The majority of objects in the external world provide gratification of man's biological needs. Instincts move from object to object in their attempt to gain maximum gratification. Instincts sometimes can turn inward on the individual, as when a person's aggressiveness toward others turns toward self & result in acts of self-mutilation.

Freud held that each person has instinctive urges that seek to preserve life. Each man is motivated to satisfy his hunger, thirst, & sexual needs. Without food & water we cannot survive; the typical consequence of efforts to achieve sexual satisfaction is procreation, which helps perpetuate the species. The energy associated with these instincts Freud called libido. At first he maintained that libido is only associated with sexual instincts, but later, revising his position, he viewed libido as psychic & pleasurable feelings associated with gratification of the life instincts. In addition to the life instincts Freud had an interesting view regarding death instincts. He thought that the goal of all life is death & that people strive to return to an inorganic state of balance that proceeded life, in which instincts operate, however, to ensure that death is delayed as long as possible, so that human beings can obtain many other satisfactions before they die.

A major derivative of the death instincts is aggression, whereby individuals try to destroy others or themselves. Freud believed these aggressive impulses to be very strong; accordingly, his view of human nature was very negative. He thought that society would not survive for long if its members were allowed to express all their impulses. Stronger people would take advantage of weaker ones, by using their superior power. Instability in society could easily result from allowing people to mate indiscriminately whenever the urge arose. Thus even though people may wish to act out their sexual & aggressive impulses, society does not permit them to do so.

To understand the dynamics of the individual's conflicts, Freud postulated constructs that allowed describing the ways in which these conflicts originated & influence the behavior. To this end he proposed three systems of the mind-id, ego, & superego- that compete for the limited amount of psychic energy available, energy that has its starting point in the instinctual needs of the individual.

Freud constructed the id to be the original aspect of personality, rooted in the biology of the individual & to consist of unconscious sexual & aggressive instincts. These instincts might operate jointly in different situations to affect our behavior.

Freud likened the id to a "seething cauldron" that contains powerful & primitive urges & desires. He was convinced that these urges insistently seek expression in external reality. The id is unconcerned with the niceties & conventions of society & operates according to the pleasure principle. The aim of these impulses is an immediate & complete discharge & satisfaction. The pleasure principle maintains that people always strive to maximize pleasure & minimize pain.

Mature conduct demands that we control our impulses in a wide variety of situations. According to Freud, this control becomes possible when the ego is differentiated from the id. The ego, in his view, is the organized aspect of id, formed to provide realistic direction for the person's impulses. It comes into existence because the needs of the person require appropriate transactions with the environment if they are to be satisfied. The ego, therefore, develops partially to carry out the aims of the id. At the same time, it functions to keep the impulses of the id in check until a suitable object is found.

Superego is used to describe the individual's internalization of special values. Such values are instilled in the person primarily by parents, who teach which behaviors are appropriate or in appropriate in given situations. The superego thus represents a set of learned ideals.

Freud eventually came to the conclusion that superego has two major components, conscience & ego-ideal. Conscience is acquired through the use of punishment by the parents, while the ego-ideal is learned through the use of rewards. The basic functions of the superego are to inhibit the urges of the id, to persuade the ego & to substitute moralistic goals for realistic ones.

Human ego often tries to exert control over both an id that is concerned only with gratification of its instinctual urges & a superego that constantly seeks perfection. Meanwhile permanent control over the id & superego can never be established. There are times when ego is able to bring these two agencies under some control, helping the individual to function effectively. To this end, the ego seeks to find realistic outlets for the person's id impulses. Control over the superego may be established when the ego convinces the person to give up perfectionism & to substitute more realistically attainable goals in these areas.

Freud compares the ego with a battlefield where the armies of the id & superego constantly clash. It is known that much of the ego operates in consciousness, yet some of its processes are unconscious & serve to protect the person against anxiety. The individual needs protection from anxiety because it is a highly unpleasant state that signals a danger to the ego. The danger may be that the person's instinctual impulses are out of control & are threatening to overwhelm him or her. Also, the danger may arise because the individual fears punishment from his or her conscience for thinking about doing something that the superego considers wrong. In the face of dangers, the person's ego unconsciously attempts to regain control by activating defensive processes.

Such defense mechanisms serve a useful purpose in that they protect the person against pain. Also, they are normal & universally used reactions to pain. Often our disbelief allows us to cope with the shock & to assimilate it in a more gradual & less painful manner. However, Freud held that defense mechanisms can be potentially pathogenic when they are used indiscriminately, compulsively, & in ways that continually contradict the reality of the situation.

The main defenses are repression, suppression, denial, displacement, sublimation, regression, projection, reaction formation, rationalization, intellectualization, undoing & compromise formation.

Repression is an attempt by the ego to keep undesirable id impulses from reaching consciousness. In the process of analyzing dreams, Freud concluded that certain thoughts are blocked from consciousness, because they are too painful to acknowledge. All of the attempts to make patients aware of these experiences meet with resistance. The battle between the ego & the id involves an opposition between energy forces. The driving forces he called cathexes; the restraining forces anticathexes. Certain unconscious wishes are energized & strive for expression in consciousness, but are met by other ideas energized by other restraining forces located in the ego. When the ego forces dominate the wishes become repressed & forced back into unconscious. On the other hand when the id forces dominate, the person acts out his or her socially unacceptable impulses.

Freud considered repression the most fundamental of all defense mechanisms. As he said "the theory of repression is the pillar upon which the edifice of psychoanalysis rests". Repression occurs mostly on an unconscious level & involves preventing unpleasant experiences that are repulsive to the ego from reaching consciousness. Repressed memories are not under conscious control of the person.

Another mechanism, suppression, involves the individual's active & conscious attempt to stop anxiety causing thoughts by simply not thinking about them. If a boy finds himself thinking sexual thoughts about his nanny, he may actively suppress them because of his moral training. Such thoughts are later stored in the preconscious & reactivated.

Another common mechanism, denial, refers to a person's refusal to perceive an unpleasant event in external reality. Many parents often indirectly teach or encourage their children to use the mechanism of denial, using constant reassurance.

Displacement is an unconscious attempt to obtain gratification for id impulses by shifting them to substitute objects, if objects that would directly satisfy the impulses are not available.

Sublimation is a type of displacement in which the unacceptable id impulses themselves are transformed, rather than the object at which they aim. The unacceptable impulses are displaced by socially acceptable ones. A person with a strong need for aggression channels his energies into activities that are socially acceptable. For example, becoming an outstanding scientist, or first-rate novelist. By so doing, he demonstrates his superiority & domination of others, but in a way that contributes to society. In like manner poets & painters may satisfy some of their sexual needs through their art. Freud believed that creative sublimations of human instincts are necessary if civilized society is to survive. He also believed that such creativity is available only to the few people with special gifts & talents.

Regression is characterized by a movement from mature behavior to immature. When the ego is threatened, the person reverts to an earlier, more infantile form of behavior as a means of coping with a stress. For example, a man who is having marital problems leaves the home he shares with his wife & moves into his parents house.

When the person protects the ego by attributing to his or her own unwanted characteristics to others, we can infer that projection is occurring. For example, a boy who hates his father may be convinced that his father hates him.

The conversion of an undesirable impulse into its opposite is called reaction formation. Freud considered it a lower form of sublimation. A woman who hates her husband & yet is exceedingly kind to him is an example. In other words she is killing him with kindness.

Rationalization is the justification of behavior through the use of plausible, but inaccurate excuses. For example, a young athlete, dropped from the team because of lack of ability, concludes that he didn't really want to be on the team, because it is a losing team.

Intellectualization is a process that allows individuals to protect themselves against excessive pain. It involves dissociation between ones thoughts & feelings. For example, a woman conjures up an elaborate rationale to explain to explain the death of her young husband. By citing reasons & focusing on the logic of her argument, she avoids the tremendous pain associated with such a traumatic experience.

Sometimes a person who thinks or acts on an undesirable impulse makes amends by performing some action that nullifies the undesirable one, a defense mechanism known as undoing. Such actions are typically irrational & can be seen in various superstitious rituals & some religious ceremonies. By performing the undoing act, the person is convinced that the wrong has been rectified.

Compromise formation involves the use of contradictory behaviors to gain some satisfaction for an undesirable impulse. For example, when two women hate each other they exchange complements like "what a nice outfit".

Psychosexual Development

The structural components of personality were widely used by Freud in the scheme of psychosexual development. The theory is based on the inevitable unfolding of a series of stages in which particular behaviors occur. Normal development supposes the coursing of libidinal or sexual energy through a variety of earlier stages to a final genital. Immediately preceding the genital stage is the latency period, in which sexual energy is considered to be dormant. When an abnormal development occurs during early childhood, the person undergoes traumatic experiences. Such experiences prevent the flow of significant amount of libidinal energy through the various stages, resulting in fixation & making the person more vulnerable to crisis later in life. Freud differentiates five significant stages; oral, anal, phallic, latency & genital.

According to Freud in oral stage the infant is all id, unable to distinguish between the self & the environment. An infant is controlled by biological impulses & is basically selfish. The focus of pleasurable sensations or "sexual" impulses during the first stage is the mouth. Pleasurable sensations occur as the infant takes in food & water. The parents' behavior is important in determining whether or not the infant will experience personal difficulties later in life. These difficulties occur as a result of parental over indulgence of the infants needs during the first year.

In anal stage, which occurs during the second & third years, pleasurable sensations are focused on the anal cavity. The main pleasures for the child involve retention or expulsion of feces. During this stage ego processes are being differentiated from the id & the child begins to assert his or her limited independence. This independence does not involve rational decision making, in which the child weighs the conflicting evidence & comes to reasonable conclusions. In a way, it is a negative independence in which the child rejects out of hand whatever is being offered by the parents.

Freud held that primary contest revolves around toilet training. In most cultures cleanliness is a virtue, & parents typically place heavy stress on regulating defecation & urination. Children often resist these demands.

During the fourth & fifth years, sexual tension is focused on the genital area. At this phallic stage, Freud believed that both boys & girls derive pleasure from self-manipulation. Boys develop a longing for sexual contact with a mother. In the most general sense, they seek affection & love from the mother. At the same time child is increasingly aware that there is asexual relationship between his parents & that the father is his rival. But the father is bigger & stronger physically, & the boy fears he will be punished for his desires. Child fears that his penis will be cut off. In this way, his sexual desire is diverted into more socially acceptable channels. These feelings & process by which they are resolved Freud named the Oedipus complex, a term borrowed from Sophocle's tragedy Oedipus Rex, in which the Greek king Oedipus, unwittingly kills his father & commits incest with his mother. The superego is an outgrowth of the resolution of this complex, as the child takes on the values of his parents & their attitudes toward society.

Freud postulated a latency stage from the sixth year to puberty, during which sexual development is assumed to be at a standstill. He believed that the person's characteristic ways of behaving are established during the first five years of life & that radical personality change is extremely difficult. At this point in their development, children turn to the world of school & peers & begin to learn the social & technical skills that will allow them eventually to take their place as responsible & effective citizens in their society.

With the advent of puberty, sexual tension increases dramatically. The reproductive organs have matured, & both sexes are now capable of procreation. Previously, the aims of the sexual instincts have been predominantly autoerotic, but now goal is to mate with an appropriate sex object. At this genital stage, an adequate heterosexual adjustment depends on the amount of libidinal energy available to the person. If there have been no severe traumatic experiences in early childhood, with corresponding libido fixations, an adequate adjustment is possible. When adulthood is reached, the person typically marries & settles into family life.

For Freud, the normal person is the one who makes satisfactory adjustments in two major areas- love & work.

People who are fixated at the oral stage have problems later in life that are related directly to receiving or taking things from the external world. So called oral receptive character is a result of overindulgence in infancy. The individual is habituated to receiving support & encouragement from other people & thus is excessively dependent on others for gratification. Such people tend to be too trusting, too accepting, & they admire strength & leadership in others but make little attempt to fend for them. They also tend to be rather incompetent & most of their gratification is derived from what others do for them & not from what they themselves accomplish- & to be overly optimistic. This type of person inevitably experiences conflicts with others because not everyone is supportive like mother.

Fixation may also occur when parents severely frustrate the needs of their infants. In this case, the person learns to exploit others & may develop sadistic attitudes.

Anal eroticism stems from difficulties during toilet training, when children are locked in a bottle over power & control with their parents. If the parents are highly punitive & demanding, children may defiantly decide to keep their prized possessions from the parents. The anal character, according to Freud, is delineated by a particular constellation of traits: parsimony, obstinacy, & orderliness. Parsimony in anal characters means that they are stingy, greedy, & hoarding; whereas obstinacy suggests that they are stubborn, defiant, & resistant to control by others. Orderliness means that they are overly conscientious, neat, clean & proper.

The difficulties experienced by the phallic character stem from inadequate resolution of the Oedipus complex

In males it is a reaction to severe castration anxiety; they behave in a reckless, resolute, & self-assured manner. Overestimation of the penis is reflected in excessive vanity & exhibitionism. Such males have to prove that they are real men. One way of doing this is by repeated conquests of women. For women the primary motive is penis envy. They constantly strive for superiority over men by criticizing, ridiculing, & humiliating them. Such females are considered to be castrating females.

Freud viewed the genital character as the ideal type. Such people are sexually mature & capable of orgasm. Their libidinal energies are no longer dammed up because they have found appropriate love objects. In Freud's view, the key to happiness is the ability to love & be loved. Sexual love is one aspect of intimacy that provides us with happiness. Although establishing intimacy is central to happiness, Freud reminds us that, love also makes us vulnerable to rejection by the loved one.

Genital characters are capable of sublimating their id impulses by expressing them in the form of productive & creative work. The creative activities that bring happiness differ for each individual.

World War One had a profound impact on Freud's thinking & research. Distressed by the mass killing & suffering, he eventually came to attribute these experiences to a universal death instinct. Despite his pessimism about the future of humankind, however, Freud continued to elaborate his ideas in a long series of books.

Freud's Theory of Life & Death Drives

Freud had an interesting view regarding death instincts. He thought that the goal of all life is death & that people strive to return to an inorganic state of balance that proceeded life, in which instincts operate, however, to ensure that death is delayed as long as possible, so that human beings can obtain many other satisfactions before they die.

A major derivative of the death instincts is aggression, whereby individuals try to destroy others or themselves. Freud believed these aggressive impulses to be very strong; accordingly, his view of human nature was very negative. He thought that society would not survive for long if its members were allowed to express all their impulses. Stronger people would take advantage of weaker ones, by using their superior power. Instability in society could easily result from allowing people to mate indiscriminately whenever the urge arose. Thus even though people may wish to act out their sexual & aggressive impulses, society does not permit them to do so.

Freud came up with the death drive only in his later years. He approached the paradox between the life drives and the death drives by defining pleasure and unpleasure. According to Freud, unpleasure referred to stimulus that the body receives, while pleasure was a result of a decrease in stimuli. If pleasure increases as stimuli decreases, then the ultimate experience of pleasure for Freud would be zero stimuli. Because of this Freud acknowledged the tendency for the unconscious to repeat unpleasurable experiences in order to desensitize the body. Supposedly the compulsion to repeat unpleasurable experiences explained why traumatic nightmares occur in dreams, as nightmares seem to contradict Freud's earlier conception of dreams purely as a site of pleasure & fantasy. On the one hand, the life drives promote survival by avoiding extreme unpleasure and any threat to life& on the other, the death drive functions simultaneously toward extreme pleasure, which ends in death.

Freud's ideas were similar to the philosophies of Friedrich Nietzsche& Arthur Schopenhauer. Schopenhauer's pessimistic philosophy describes a renunciation of the will to live that corresponds on many levels with Freud's Death Drive. Similarly, the life drive clearly parallels much of Nietzsche's concept of the Dionysian.

It is safe to say that Freud did not consider himself a philosopher, although he greatly admired Franz Brentano & Theodor Lipps. According to Freud Philosophy is not opposed to science, it behaves itself as if it were a science, and to a certain extent it makes use of the same methods; but it parts company with science, in that it clings to the illusion that it can produce a complete and coherent picture of the universe, though in fact that picture must needs fall to pieces with every new advance in our knowledge.

After Freud

Among Freud's early followers the most prominent were Alfred Adler & Carl Jung both of whom broke with Freud & literally forged new schools of psychoanalysis.

Alfred Adler (1870-1937) was in Penzing, Austria. He did not walk until age four because of rickets; at age five Adler developed pneumonia and was diagnosed as unlikely to survive. He did recover, but was so profoundly shaken by the experience that he resolved to become a doctor himself someday in order to help the suffering caused by such illness. This accomplishment began to look out of reach later when he was struggling in school and failing at math. Adler then became determined to excel and to show the teacher just how wrong he was. He was soon at the top of his class in mathematics. Such experiences helped to shape Adler's theories of personality development, in particular his belief that the most basic human drive is the striving from an initial state of inadequacy. In 1895 Adler successfully earned his medical degree, graduating from the University of Vienna. In the course of his work as a physician he made study of the interplay between what he termed "organ deficiency" and an individual's personality and self-image.

At first Adler considered a career in ophthalmology but eventually he switched to general practice. The turning point in Adler's career happened when Sigmund Freud himself, invited him to join an informal discussion group that included Rudolf Reitler and Wilhelm Stekel (in 1902). This group marked the beginning of the psychoanalytic movement. Eight years later a long-serving member of the group, Adler became President of the Vienna Psychoanalytic Society. He remained a member of the Society until 1911 when he and a group of supporters formally disengaged. This departure suited both Freud and Adler since they had grown to dislike each other. During his association with Freud, Adler frequently maintained his own ideas which often diverged from Freud's.

After his break from the psychoanalytic movement in 1912 Adler founded the Society of Individual Psychology. Adler's team included some orthodox Nietzschean adherents. After founding an independent school of psychotherapy & a unique Personality Theory he traveled and lectured for a period of 25 years promoting his socially oriented approach. During World War One Adler served as a doctor with the Austrian Army. After war his influence increased greatly. In the 1930s, he opened up a number of child guidance clinics & from 1921 onwards, he was a lecturer in Europe and the United States.

Adler was one of the first psychotherapists to use the analytic couch instead of two chairs. His new methods were not limited to treatment after-the-fact but were extended to the realm of prevention by preempting future problems in the child. Prevention strategies include encouraging and promoting social interest, belonging, and a cultural shift within families. Naturally Adler's popularity in part was related to the comparative optimism and comprehensibility of his ideas & methods. Unlike Freud, he often wrote for the lay public. Adler's approach was pragmatic & goal oriented. He held that the main life tasks were occupation, society and love.

It is obvious that Adler was influenced by the ideas of the philosopher Hans Vaihinger & the literature of Dostoyevsky. Adler was also influenced by Immanuel Kant, Friedrich Nietzsche & Rudolf Virchow. Adler's School Individual Psychology was both, a social & community psychology. Adler was known for his concept of prevention. He emphasized the training of parents, teachers, & social workers & so on in democratic approaches that allowed a child to exercise their power through reasoned decision making. Adler was a socialist & to a certain degree Marxist. His goal was to construct a social movement united under the principles of community feeling & social interest.

Adler was a big supporter of feminism in psychology. He held that feelings of superiority and inferiority were often gendered and expressed symptomatically in characteristic masculine and feminine styles, & that these styles could form the basis of psychic compensation.

In 1930 most of Adler's Austrian clinics were closed due to his Jewish heritage. Adler was forced to leave Austria. He became a professor at the Long Island College of Medicine. Adler died from a heart attack in Scotland during a lecture tour in 1937. Adler' ideas and approaches remain strong and viable more than 70 years after Adler's death.

Adler emphasized the foundational importance of childhood in developing personality. Accordingly the best way to inoculate against personality disorders was to train a child to be and feel an equal part of the family. Thus, Adler was against corporal punishment and cautioned parents to refrain from pampering and neglect. In addition, he held that, the responsibility to the optimal development of the child is not limited solely to the Mother or Father but to teachers and society as well. When children do not feel equal, and are abused through pampering or neglect, they are likely to develop inferiority or superiority complexes and various accompanying compensation mechanisms. These mechanisms exact a social toll by seeding higher divorce rates, the breakdown of the family, criminal tendencies, & subjective suffering in the various guises of psychopathology.

Unlike Freud Adler saw the infant not as sexual creature but as one that is helpless & needs total care from the more powerful adults. This dependence on adults produces feelings of inferiority & creates a striving to gain power & independence. The will to power is the driving force for Adler & male sexuality is a symptom of striving to overcome female domination. He also maintains that women feel inferior because of their underprivileged status in society. Adler viewed sexual problems as forms in which neurosis appears. He rejected the biological instincts of Freud & substituted the social relationships within the family, especially the child's position in the birth order of siblings. Adler largely deemphasized the unconscious & the belief in future possibilities, often unrealistic, toward which individuals strive. Basically he accentuates the future in contrast to Freud's accent on the past. Adler called his approach individual psychology. His therapy dealt with overt problems & did so in a short period of time, in contrast with the multi- year duration of Freud's psychoanalytic therapy.

Unlike Freud, Adler was a follower of the more socially oriented psychoanalysis. His recognition of women's cultural disadvantages became a theme for a number of movements.

Adler did agree with Freud on some major issues relating to the parenting of children & long term effects of improper child rearing. He acknowledged two parenting styles that he argued will cause almost certain problems in adulthood. The first was pampering, referring to a parent overprotecting a child, & sheltering him from negative realities of life. As the child grows older he will be maladapted to deal with these realities, may doubt his abilities or decision making skills. Thus, the best approach is to protect children from the evils of the world, but not shelter them from it. Such an approach will allow them to feel negative aspects of the world while still feeling the safety or parental influence. Adler believed that order in which a child is born inherently affects his personality. First born children who later have younger siblings suffer the most. These children are given excessive attention by their parents until the little brother or sister arrives, making them inferior. The birth order theory maintains that first born children often have greatest number of problems as they get older. Middle born children may experience fewer problems, since they are not as pampered as their older siblings. Adler held that middle children have a high need for superiority & are often able to seek it out such as through healthy competition. The youngest children may experience personality problems later in life, because they grow up knowing that they have the least amount of power in the family. They constantly feel the superiority & strength of their older siblings often feeling inferior to others.

Adler also emphasized the importance of equality in preventing the various forms of pathology & espoused the development of social interest & democratic family structures for raising children. His emphasis on power dynamics is rooted in the philosophy of Nietzsche. Adler was among the first in psychology to argue in favor of feminism making the case that power dynamics between men & women are crucial to understand human psychology. He held that personality can be explained teleologically, separate stands dominated by the guiding purpose of the individual's unconscious self ideal to convert feelings of inferiority & superiority. The desires of the self ideal were countered by social & ethical demands. When the corrective factors are disregarded & the individual overcompensated, the inferiority complex begins to develop.

According to Adler psychology is psychodynamic in nature & unlike Freud's metapsychology that emphasizes instinctual demands, his psychology is guided by goals. Just like Freud's instincts Adler's pseudo-goals were mainly unconscious. Adler's goals had a teleological function. The metaphysical side of Adler's theory does not complicate the notion of teleology, since concepts such as eternity match the religious aspects that are held in tandem. The constructivist Adlerian threads like modernist & postmodernist seek to raise insight of the force of unconscious fictions- which carry all of the inevitability of fate- as long as one does not understand them. Accordingly teleology itself is fictive yet experienced as real. This part of Adler's theory is similar to the principles developed in Rational Emotive Behavior Therapy & Cognitive Therapy. Adlerians often excavate the past of client/patient in order to alter their future & increase integration into community in the so called "here-and-now."The "here-and-now" aspects are especially relevant to those Adlerians who emphasize existentialism & humanism in their approaches.

Adler also developed a very interesting scheme of personality types. These types are to be taken as provisional since he did not, in essence believe in personality types. The problem with typology is to lose sight of the individual's uniqueness & to gaze reductively, acts that Adler opposed. According to Adler the so called "leaning" types are those who selfishly take without giving back, they also tend to be antisocial & have low activity levels. The "avoiding" types are those who hate being defeated. They may be successful, but have not taken any risks getting there. They also have a low social contact in fear of defeat. The "dominant" types strive for power & are willing to manipulate situations & people. People of this type are also prone to anti-social behavior. The "socially useful" types are those who are very outgoing & very active. They have a lot of social contact & strive to make changes for the good.

Carl Jung (1875-1961) was an influential thinker & a founder of analytical psychology called Jungian psychology. He was born July in the small Swiss village of Kessewil. Jung was surrounded by a fairly well educated extended family. He went to boarding school in Basel, Switzerland, where he found himself the object of a lot of harassment. He began to use sickness as an excuse, developing an embarrassing tendency to faint under pressure. Jung had no plans to study psychiatry, because it was held in contempt in those days. But as he started studying his psychiatric textbook, he became very excited when he read that psychoses are personality diseases. He realized this was the field that interested him the most. It combined both biological and spiritual facts and this was what he was searching for.

In 1895, Jung studied medicine at the University of Basel. In 1900, he worked in the psychiatric hospital in Zurich. His dissertation, published in 1903, was titled "On the Psychology and Pathology of So-Called Occult Phenomena." In 1906, Jung published "Studies in Word Association" & later sent a copy of this book to Freud, after which a close friendship between them followed for some six years.

World War I was a painful period of self-examination for Jung. It was, however, also the beginning of one of the most interesting theories of personality the world has ever seen.

Jung traveled widely, visiting tribal people in Africa, America, and India. He retired in 1946, and began to retreat from public attention after his wife died in 1955. He died on June 6, 1961, in Zurich.

In Jung's theory the psyche was divided into three parts. The first was the ego, which he identified with the conscious mind. Related to it was the personal unconscious, which included anything which was not presently conscious. The personal unconscious was similar to most people's understanding of the unconscious in that it included both memories that were easily brought to mind and those that had been suppressed for some reason. Jung added the part of the psyche that made his theory differ from all others: the Collective Unconscious. It was considered the reservoir of human experiences. Supposedly it influenced all of human experiences and behaviors, especially the emotional ones.

Jung held that there were some experiences that showed the effects of the collective unconscious more clearly than others, for example, the experiences of love at first sight & the immediate recognition of certain symbols and the meanings of certain myths. These experiences were interpreted as the sudden conjunction of the outer reality and the inner. Other examples were the creative experiences shared by artists and musicians all over the world & in all times.

Jung's views were often ambivalent & inconsistent. He was fascinated by Nietzsche and lectured on Nietzsche's "Zarathustra" but distrusted the aestheticism colored his judgment of literary works. However, he had a special interest in trivial literature. From H. Rider Haggard's novel "She" Jung found an embodiment of the anima. He was especially interested in the mythic and archaic elements in literature. Like Nietzsche, Schopenhauer, and Hesse, Jung was convinced of the value of Oriental wisdom. He later visited Egypt and India. To Jung, the religious symbols of Buddhism & Hinduism& the teachings of Zen Buddhism all expressed differentiated experiences on the way to man's inner world Jung also searched for traditions in Western culture which compensated for its one-sided extroverted development toward rationalism and technology. He found these traditions in Gnosticism, Christian mysticism, and, above all, Alchemy. For Jung, the alchemical texts were astonishing symbolic expressions for the human experience of the processes in the unconscious. Some of his major works were deep & lucid psychological interpretations of alchemical writings.

Unlike Freud, Jung held that it is not just the past that is responsible for neurotic conditions but also the present & one's goals for the future. Jung viewed ego as fully conscious. It represses memories into the personal unconscious. Hidden more deeply is a collective unconscious that contains so called archetypes. Such instincts, according to Jung are inherited by all humans, regardless of their race. They result from the experiences of our ancestors & predispose us to perceive & to think in particular ways. These archetypes also contain symbols, & Jung claimed to have discovered the archetypes by examining the symbols of art & myth across cultures & periods of time. Jung's archetypes include 1 persona, the mask that we present to other people, 2 anima, the feminine side of men, & the animus, the masculine side of women; 3 the shadow, an animal instinct that goes back to our pre-human form & involves immoral impulses; & 4 the self, which integrates all of the others into a unified being. Thus, the self appears only in middle age & often uses religion & mystical experiences for its integrating role.

Jung divided people into introverts & extroverts & these terms became widely used as Adler's complex of inferiority. Introverts & extroverts could be paired in any combination of the four functions; intuiting, sensing, feeling & thinking. Any two of these may predominate & suppress the other two & be paired with introversion & extroversion. The results in typologies such as thinking-intuiting introvert, perhaps a creative scientist who likes to work alone. Jung maintained that these primordial urges could be directed toward the divine or toward the self actualization, but if not adequately handled by the ego they could produce neurosis or psychosis. He largely rejected scientific evidence & turned to mythology & art for his inspiration. Neurosis is viewed as the suffering of the soul that has not found meaning embedded in it. Jung encouraged his patients to use their willpower & to seek the divine.

Harry S. Sullivan (1892-1989) was born in Norwich, New-York. He studied at the Smyrna Union School after which he enrolled in Cornell University. Sullivan received his medical degree in1917 at the Chicago College of Medicine& Surgery. Sullivan's research methods were based on direct and verifiable observation. He developed a theory of psychiatry based on interpersonal relationships, a theory where cultural forces are largely responsible diseases. In his words, one must pay attention to the "interactional", not the "intrapsychic". This type of search for satisfaction via personal involvement with others prompted Sullivan to characterize loneliness as the most painful of human experiences. He also extended the Freudian psychoanalysis to the treatment of patients with schizophrenia.

Sullivan was the founder of the so called interpersonal psychoanalysis, which was a unique school of psychoanalytic theory & treatment that stressed the exploration of the nuances of patients' patterns of interacting with others. He was also the first to use the term "problems in living" to describe the difficulties with self and others experienced by those mental illnesses. Sullivan was the founder of an interesting configuration of the personality traits, developed in childhood & reinforced by positive affirmation and security operations developed in childhood to avoid anxiety & threats to self-esteem. He called it the Self System. Sullivan further defined the Self System as a steering mechanism toward a series I-You interlocking behaviors, meaning, what an individual does is meant to elicit a particular reaction. Sullivan called these behaviors parataxic integrations. He maintained that such action-reaction combinations can become rigid and dominate an adult's thinking pattern, limiting its actions and reactions toward the world as the adult sees it. The resulting inaccuracies in judgment Sullivan termed parataxic distortion. Sullivan also introduced the concept of "prototaxic communication" as a more primitive, needy, infantile form of psychic interchange. The mature type of emotional interaction was called "syntactic communication."

Sullivan thought that Freud's system was essentially valid but that it needed to consider cultural factors. He conceived of personality as involving a psychic tension or so called dynamism that somewhat parallels Freud's libido. This overt energy transfer involves some part of the body. One source of this tension arises from biological requirements such as hunger, thirst, & even sex. Relieving these tensions brings satisfaction, & fulfilling them completely produces exaltation. This seems to be Freud's pleasure principle. The second source of tension is threats, either actual or imagined. Such threats create anxiety which interferes with interpersonal relations, confounds thinking, & upsets the sequence of satisfying needs. Reduction of anxiety creates certain feelings of security. Anxiety usually arises from insecurities created when the child was nursing.

Sullivan is also known for converting Freud's psychosexual stages of development to seven social stages & his unique viewpoints on schizophrenia.

Erik Erikson (1902-1994) was born in Frankfurt, Germany. After graduating high school, he was determined to become an artist. When he was 25, his friend Peter Blos, a fellow artist &, later, psychoanalyst suggested he apply for a teaching position at an experimental school for American students run by Dorothy Burlingham, a friend of Anna Freud. Besides teaching art, he gathered a certificate in Montessori education and one from the Vienna Psychoanalytic Society. Following Erikson's graduation from the Vienna Psychoanalytic Institute in 1933, the Nazis had just come to power in Germany. He emigrated with his wife, first to Denmark & then to the United States. Erikson's transition paid off, he became the first child psychoanalyst in Boston, holding positions at the Judge Baker Guidance Center, Massachusetts General Hospital & at Harvard's Medical School.

In 1950, he wrote "Childhood and Society", which contained summaries of his studies among the Native Americans, analyses of Maxim Gorky, Adolph Hitler, a discussion of the "American personality," & the basic outline of his version of Freudian theory. In the 1960s, Erikson was a professor of human development at Harvard. He remained at the university until his retirement in

Erikson was a Freudian ego-psychologist, that is, he accepted Freud's ideas as basically correct, including the more debatable ideas such as the oedipal complex. He also accepted the ideas about the ego that were added by other Freudian loyalists such as Heinz Hartmann & Anna Freud. It appears that Erikson was much more society and culture-oriented than most Freudians.

Unlike others Erik Erikson remained closest to Freud's original system, although he gave much greater emphasis to social factors. In his theory ego & self develop over an entire life span. He also held that adult experiences can help heal childhood wounds. Erikson attempted to modify Freud's psychosexual stages. He recognized total of eight stages comprising the life cycle. Each one of these stages includes a conflict or a psychological struggle that enters into the development of personality. The dialectical outcome can be either positive or negative, but the person must resolve the crisis in order to remain healthy. For instance, in the first "oral-sensory" stage, if the nursing procedure is satisfactory the infant responds with trust; & the first social situation is off to a good start. If the mother frequently ignores the infant's hunger, the infants feels threatened & develops mistrust. Erikson is well known for his formulation of the adolescence "identity crisis." In this crisis the individual becomes confused, is truant or leaves school, & resorts to drugs, alcohol, dereliction, vandalism, & sometimes crime. In Erikson's theory the adolescence identity crisis is viewed as the most important crisis in life. Its satisfactory resolution requires the support of parents & others, & is essential for successful marital & sexual relations. In young adulthood the conflict is intimacy versus isolation, & in adulthood it is despair versus integrity. Erikson retained many of the fundamentals of Freud's stages of psychosexual development but gave them a more social orientation.

Another theoretician, psychologist Heinz Hartmann (1894-1970) was known for his successful attempts in reformulation of traditional psychoanalysis. He was born in Vienna, Austria. After completing secondary school he entered the University of Vienna where he received his medical degree in 1920. His interest was in Freudian theories.

He undertook his first analysis with Sandor Rado. The death of Karl Abraham prevented Hartmann from following the didactic treatment he had envisioned following him. In 1927 he published "Les fondements de la psychanalyse," which he followed with a number of studies on psychoses, neuroses & twins.

Hartmann worked with Freud in Vienna denying a position at the Johns Hopkins Institute. In 1937he presented a study on the psychology of "Me" a topic on which he would later expand when writing his work translated into French. Eventually, this work will mark the development of the theoretical movement known as Ego-psychology.

He left Vienna in 1938 to escape the Nazi Regime. Hartmann arrived in New York in 1941 where he quickly became one of the foremost thinkers of the new Psychoanalytic Society. In 1945 he founded an annual publication "The psychoanalytic Study of the Child." Hartmann became the president of the "International Psychological Association" in 1950.

He eliminated many inconsistencies & made it more systematic & integrated. Hartmann also removed the dialectical polarities of id demands versus ego defense, fixation versus anti-fixation, life instinct versus death instinct, pleasure principle versus reality principle, & others. His most celebrated accomplishment was giving the ego more autonomy & complex functions than it received in Freud's conceptualization, in which it was the outgrowth of the id. Thus, the patient could use his or her autonomous ego functions to take a more active role in assessment & interpretation of thoughts, memories, dreams & transference. Before Hartmann analysts assumed that any disagreement with the analyst's interpretation was due to resistance & negative transfer. Hartmann is also known for attributing to the ego an aggressive role as important as that of libido, & removed its instinct of self-preservation. Hartmann's work led a movement within psychoanalysis that conceived of the ego as more prominent than orthodox theory had held it to be. Under his formulations the superego too gained independence; & id, ego, & superego became equally important in their respective roles in a newly defined tripartite psychic structure. Hartmann opened up alternative approaches to psychoanalysis without necessitating the rejection of Freud's clinical methods. This modification was an important step in the evolution of psychoanalytic theory along with the social & cultural emphasis that theorists from Adler to Sullivan provided.

Melanie Klein (1882-1960) was born Vienna, Austria in an orthodox Jewish family. Klein was introduced to Freudianism when she & her family moved to Budapest in 1910. There she encountered Freud's work for the first time in his book "On Dreams". After that, psychoanalysis became her lifelong interest& passion. In 1917 she had a chance to meet Freud at a meeting between the Austrian and Hungarian Societies. And, by 1919, she got to read "The Development of a Child", her first paper, to the Hungarian Society. Following this appearance, she was asked to become a member of the Budapest Society. Melanie was introduced to Karl Abraham in 1921. She was impressed with him and he encouraged her practice of child analysis. This prompted her to move to Berlin in open a psychoanalytical practice with both adults and children.

Klein developed the technique of play therapy. As a substitute for Freud's free association, of which very young children are incapable, Klein developed the technique of play therapy to uncover children's unconscious motivations. She held that children, through the use of play and drawings, projected their feelings in therapeutic sessions. She was determined to prove that the way children played with toys revealed earlier infantile fantasies and anxieties & that their unconscious lives could be understood by analysts through their non-verbal behavior. She demonstrated how these anxieties affected a child's developing ego, superego, and sexuality to bring about emotional disorders. Through these methods she attempted to relieve children of disabling guilt by having them direct toward the therapist the aggressive and oedipal feelings they could not express to their parents. This was in major disagreement with Anna Freud, who felt that children could not be analyzed that way.

Klein also researched the use of projective identification. In projective identification it was not the impulse only, but parts of the self and bodily products that were in fantasy projected into the object. When pain came, she said, one would put the pain on someone else. The aims of projective identification could be manifold: getting rid of an unwanted part of oneself, a greedy possession & scooping out of the object, control of the object, and so on. One of the results was identification of the object with the projected part of the self. She also contributed to the idea of object relations. Freud introduced the idea of object choice, which referred to a child's earliest relationships with his caretakers. Such people were objects of his needs and desires. The relationship with them became internalized mental representations. Later Melanie Klein introduced the term part objects (for example the mother's breast) which played an important role in early development and later in psychic disturbances, such as excessive preoccupation with certain body parts or aspects of a person as opposed to the whole person.

In Klein's theory artistic creativity and bodily pleasures were arenas in which the central human struggle between love, hate, and compensation was played out. She viewed men and women as deeply concerned about the balance between their own ability to love and hate. Further, Klein viewed sexual intercourse as a highly dramatic arena in which both one's impact on the other and the quality of one's own essence were exposed and on the line. Thus, the ability to arouse and satisfy the other represented one's own compensation capacities; to give enjoyment and pleasure suggested that one's love was stronger than one's hate. The ability to be aroused and satisfied by the other suggested that one was alive.

Klein moved to England in 1927. She was working with the British Psychoanalytic. She continued her practice and expanded on areas of psychoanalysis such as the death instinct and the Oedipus complex. She and her children remained there until her death on September 22, 1960.

The Kleinian theory founded by Melanie Klein deals with both instincts & object relations. Supposedly life & death drive the child's mental activity, but these instincts are attached to objects, meaning the parents. Usually the infant is able to relate immediately to both external objects & those of internal fantasy since a primitive ego is present at birth. Klein maintained that by six to twelve months child's world is fraught with intense conflict in which its innate hate, envy, aggressiveness, death wish & desire vie with its love for its mother. The infant develops the so called "schizoid position," since it perceives the breast as good & bad. The mother's body is the foundation of the profound love & satisfaction, but at the same time it can invoke envy & despair that the helpless infant can only endure. Sometimes the infant feels hostility & a desire to injure the mother by biting. The ego splits into good & bad parts & takes with it the death instinct that was present at birth. The part of ego makes the breast an ideal object, a life object. Thus, finding gratification at the breast leads to persecution & the threat of annihilation on the one hand, & comfort, love, & nourishment on the other. The fear that the death instinct will prevail over the ideal object creates the "paranoid-schizoid position." The splitting of the ego is schizoid, & the anxiety is paranoid. Position indicates that the condition is not a temporary stage of development but continues throughout life. The split of both object & ego into good & bad parts allows the infant to project destructive impulses out to the bad objects.

By the time the infant begins to distinguish people as a whole, it recognizes a connection between father & mother, & this produces the Oedipal complex. It fantasizes its parents in intercourse, wants those same gratifications for itself & feels deprived. In fantasy the infant attacks & incorporates the parents as part of its inner world. By incorporating breasts as part objects & persons as whole objects, the infant projects its destructive impulses & then faces the threats of both internal guilt & projected external deprivation of what it has destroyed. The infant despairs over loss of good object that it has destroyed, & this gives rise to the "depressive position." Klein was one of the pioneers in child analysis. She engaged children in psychoanalytic sessions in which play overcame the child's limited language skills & became the equivalent of adult free association. She interpreted what she saw in play as the unconscious manifestation of innate conflicts & used this material to construct her theory. In her theory all play indicated transference &, as with adults, she reported that transference neurosis occurred between the analyst & the child. The procedures of the adult analysis were applicable to the child, including interpretation of the sexual meaning of play, oedipal conflicts, desires to kill the parents, & other assertions from the theory.

The British Army psychiatrist Wilfred Bion (1897-1979) became known by adding the paranoid-schizoid & depressive positions to Freud's Oedipus complex.

He was born in India. Bion first came to England at the age of eight to receive his schooling. During the First World War he served in France as a tank commander. Bion studied medicine at University College, London, before a growing interest in psychoanalysis led him to undergo training analyses with John Rickman and, later, Melanie Klein. Later he turned to the study of group processes. He became a director of the London Clinic of Psycho-Analysis in 1956. In 1962 Bion took over British Psycho-Analytical Society. From 1968 he worked in Los Angeles, returning to England two months before his death in 1979.

According to Bion every group, is divided into the work group & the basic assumption group. The work group is that aspect of group functioning which has to do with the primary task of the group - what the group has formed to accomplish. The basic assumption group describes the tacit underlying assumptions on which the behavior of the group is based. Bion further identified three basic assumptions: dependency, fight-flight & pairing. Bion was convinced that interpretation by the therapist of this aspect of group dynamics would result in insight regarding effective group work. In dependency, argued Bion, the essential aim of the group is to attain security through and have its members protected by one individual. The group members behave passively, and act as though the leader, by contrast, is omnipotent. The leader may be idealized into a kind of god who can take care of his or her children, and some especially ambitious leaders may be susceptible to this role. In the basic assumption of fight- flight the group behaves as though it has met to preserve itself at all costs. In fight, the group may be characterized by aggressiveness and hostility; in flight, the group may tell stories, arrive late or any other activities that serve to avoid addressing the task at hand. The leader for this sort of group is one who can mobilize the group for attack. Finally the pairing, according to Bion, exists on the assumption that the group has met for the purpose of reproduction. Meaning two people, regardless the sex of either, carry out the work of the group through their continued, productive interaction. The remaining group members listen eagerly and attentively with a sense anticipation & relief.

Although Melanie Klein had refined & extended psychoanalysis, Bion was the one who defined schizoid-paranoid position as feelings of disintegration & meaninglessness. He also advanced a concept in which knowing truth & evading knowing were as instrumental in integration & disintegration. He assigned a mother a role of knowing the emotions of her child, thereby contributing to its thoughts about its own emotions & being able to tolerate those thoughts.

Bion's has made numerous valuable contributions to psychoanalytic theory, for example the recognition of the role of the mother in personality development & the studies of the cognitive element in emotional development.

Donald Winnicott (1896-1971) was born in Plymouth, Devon. The family was prosperous and ostensibly happy, but behind the veneer, Winnicott saw himself as oppressed by his mother, who tended toward depression, as well as by his two sisters and his nanny. The early experiences of his childhood became the basis of his interest in working with troubled young people. In 1914 Winnicott enrolled his in Jesus College (Cambridge), but with the onset of World War One his studies were interrupted. During the war he was a medical trainee at the temporary hospital in Cambridge. Three years later he joined the Royal Navy as a medical officer. In 1918 Winnicott entered St Bartholomew's Hospital Medical College in London, studying medicine. During the Second World War, Winnicott served as consultant psychiatrist to the evacuee program.

Winnicott's treatment of psychically disturbed children and their mothers gave him the experience on which he built his most influential concepts. He had a major impact on object relations theory, particularly in his 1951 essay "Transitional Objects and Transitional Phenomena." His research was mainly focused on familiar, inanimate objects that children use to stave off anxiety during times of stress. Winnicott began used his experience with children to develop his innovative ideas. He has made great contributions to psychoanalytic theory, particularly in the tradition of object-relations theory. Borrowing from Klein & his own work with children Winnicott began setting forth his own version of object relation theory. He held that the mother's protection of the infant allows the infant to put together the concept of mother & to feel itself a person through the mother's caring of its body. Usually object relations begin through receiving the mother's breast precisely when the infant desires it & without signaling its desire, thereby giving the infant the illusion that it has created the breast. Most mothers, according to Winnicott, not only know the infant's needs before it signals but also know when it can wait & that it will signal it's needs when they arise. In this manner the infant learns that it is not a unity with the mother but separate from her. When the developing child feels threatened, it splits into a true self that goes into hiding & a false self that complies with the parents' demands to divert attention away from the true self & thereby protect it. Winnicott believed the individual could relieve these events of his or her infancy & with the help of analyst correct the errors of the relations with the mother. He stated that analyst can best provide healing by compensating for shortcomings of the parental treatment. Such treatment consists of a new holding environment in which the client can feel safe while relieving the conflicts of the object relations in which transference with the analyst plays a key role.

Strongly influenced by Klein, Winnicott accepted much of her thinking, particularly with regard to the internal world & its objects & fantasy. However, he differed from Klein on the effect of environmental position & emphasized the importance of early real relationships. He also wrote about the effects of mothers unconscious states, including her unconscious hatred of her baby. Together with Klein, Winnicott extended his influence to social work, education & developmental psychology.

Heinz Kohut, (1913-1981) an Austrian born American psychoanalyst is well known for his so called self-psychology, which is a school of thought, designed to transform the practice of analytic & dynamic treatment approaches. Kohut was born on 3 May, 1913 to Jewish family. He received his MD in neurology at the University of Vienna. Like many others, Kohut fled Nazi Regime & settled in Chicago. He was a prominent member of the Chicago Institute of Psychoanalysis.

Self psychology is a theoretical school of designed to provide the necessary theoretical basis for most of the therapeutic benefits of contemporary psychoanalysis. It rejects the primary importance of innate Freudian sexual drives in the organization of the human psyche. Kohut's self psychology was the first major psychoanalytic movement in the United States to recognize the critical role of empathy in explaining human development and psychoanalytic change. This movement transformed the practice of psychoanalysis and psychotherapy by deepening the therapist's empathic attunement to the patient and describing fundamental human needs for healthy development. According to this theory healthy narcissism is the appearance of a strong, vital, cohesive self striving with ambition and ideals toward the full realization of a person's skills. On the other hand ordinary narcissism is the appearance of a weak, vulnerable self, which strives to maintain self-cohesion & bolster self-esteem. Freud's method of free association within the empathic ambience of the consulting room eventually develops into the analyses of so called selfobject transferences. Any disruption in this ambience is viewed as empathic failures of the analyst & must result in a restoration of the empathic ambience in order for the analysis to proceed. Continuous repetitions of this disruption-restoration process allow a person's sense of self to change & develop in fundamental ways.

The uniqueness of Kohut's psychology is in its understanding & explaining of the development of the self. He was critical of all classical psychoanalytic theory & saw his work as more accurately describing the role of narcissism in normal adult psychology. Kohut reinterpreted many of the phenomena originally examined by Freud. For example he criticized Freud's libido theory, which held that individuals are driven by sexual & aggressive instincts to gratify their urges. According to Kohut people do not look for relationships with other people primarily to gratify these instinctual needs. The satisfaction of aggressive & sexual needs is secondary to person's basic needs for human relatedness. As we know Freud maintained that the repression & frustration of aggressive & sexual instincts causes pathological behavior. Kohut also held that threat & damage to the self produce aberrant sexual & aggressive behavior. Kohut was convinced that Freud's preoccupation with instinctual needs in personality development caused him to obscure the needs that all individuals have for contact & affiliation with others. According to Kohut the id, ego, & superego are all facets & agencies of an underlying self; their actions are controlled & directed by the self when it is functioning in a healthy way. Also coherent functioning of the self structure leads to feelings of well being & also secondarily to an increase in the strength of the ego. In Kohut's theory neonate has no self. Parents care for their children comforting & consoling them when they are distressed, thus creating a strong bond. Such pleasant interaction n between the parents & children contributes to the development of a core or so called nuclear self within the first two or three years of life. Naturally the mothers are the key self-objects, because they constantly minister the infant's needs. According to Kohut infants exist in a state of primary narcissism, which is a state of perfect self-love where all of the child's needs are fulfilled by the mother. The infant exists in a state of primary narcissism which is a state of perfect self-love, where all of the child's needs are fulfilled by the mother. Eventually the equilibrium of this primary narcissism is disturbed by the unavoidable delays of the mother's care. Sometimes caregivers, mostly mothers cannot respond immediately to infant's demands, causing them to remove this so called equilibrium. If the mother is not responsive, a traumatic state ensues, causing the infant to restore the original state of perfection by establishing a grandiose self, which in turn is comprised of the child's unconscious belief that he or she is perfect.

Kohut maintained that children have a need to be mirrored, that is a yearning to be admired & to have an impact on others. The mirroring & empathizing makes it possible for the child to internalize others' approval & admiration. The healthy development of the child depends on the mothers effort to support realistic change in the child's grandiose self by setting limits on expressions of his or strongly unrealistic needs & by helping the child accept realistic limits of his or her actual abilities & talents, which according to Kohut can be done with the help of optimal frustration. It means that the mother handles the immature needs of her child by adopting a loving attitude as she makes clear the unrealistic nature of the child's strivings. As a result of these enforced frustrations, the child undergoes transmuting internalization, which means that he or she can disengage some of the primitive narcissistic libido from the grandiose self & invest it in an emerging new psychic structure. Optimal frustrations in parental responsiveness facilitate maturation because, because when self-object support is phase-appropriate & gradually limited, the child learns to do without assistance what had previously been done for him or her by the parents. Usually grandiose wishes become clearly inappropriate once the child is two or three years old.

Kohut did not completely abandon Freud's theory of psychosexual development he maintained that the child develops oral & anal fixations during early period. He explained these as the result of the child's defensive efforts to cope with so called damaged nuclear self. Kohut also believed that in oral stage child demands an emotionally supportive food-giving self-object to attend his or her needs. If the mother is incompetent the child's self-esteem becomes damaged resulting in pleasure seeking oral stimulation. He also believed that the personality is still subject to considerable change after age five, since superego is fragile & subject to change not only during the latency period but in adolescence as well.

Roy Schafer (born 1922) is an American psychologist & psychoanalyst who became known by emphasizing a psychoanalytic concept of narrative. He was trained at the Menninger Foundation and Austen Riggs Center, and he was a staff psychologist for Yale's health service (1961–1976) & professor of Psychiatry at Cornell University, Medical College (1976–1979). In 1979 he established a private practice in New York. His developed a unique method of psychological testing. Schafer is an author of many works including Aspects of Internalization (1968), A New Language for Psychoanalysis (1976), The Analytic Attitude (1983), Retelling a Life (1992) & Bad Feelings (2003).

He presents traditional psychoanalytical concepts not as scientific principles but as interpretative storylines. For Schafer the value of an interpretation lies not in its objectivity or correctness, but in its potential for opening up new forms of experience & allowing the patient to claim a deeper sense of its own activity. He also held that psychoanalysis has taken the language of physical science while dispensing with reasons, choices & intentions- which are really fundamental to psychoanalysis. Activity became a function; reasoning became a force & so on. In addition psychoanalysis adopted a deterministic position, &, as a consequence, never referred to choosing. This language borrowed from physics & evolutionary biology precludes the emphasis on subjectivity which should be central. Because of this language, Freud had to anthropomorphize his constructs in order to change physical mechanisms & structures into meanings. He spoke of the ego, for example, as an independent entity that made choices & created meanings. It was a mind within a mind. Schafer finds the same shortcomings in Kohut's theory: self is an independent thing that makes demands, an ego thing. The self of the neo-Freudians also has the same refined status & anthropomorphic function in its reference to experimental acts. In some of its urges, such as self actualization the self is set up not only as the existential referent of the behavior but as all at once the drive force & the end point of the journey of existence. Schafer finds it ironic that the self has become "it." This anthropomorphizing, according to Schafer, has the major disadvantage of taking meaningful action & responsibility away from the actions of the human being. Thus psychoanalysis must remove psychodynamics from its theory & give the action back to people.

Schafer maintains that such Freudian terms as id, fixation, sublimation & unconscious are anthropomorphic & mechanistic, finding it necessary to come up with new language system for psychoanalysis. Such language always speaks of concrete actions of the individual, thus it preserves Freud's important insights, at the same time redirects the system in such a way as to better accommodate present understandings of the role of development & culture. Schafer approaches this goal by describing all events with verbs & adverbs, which means that he not only expurgates such nouns as ego but such adjectival modifiers as "rigid defense" & "intense emotion." He also insists that such terms as psychodynamics, impulses, drives & forces need to be expunged. While modifying Freud with action language, Schafer attempts to retain such discoveries as infantile & unconscious modes of acting, the role of wishing & the history of responding to body stimuli. It is safe to say that what is important to Schafer's version of psychoanalysis is how reasons for actions appear to the individual. Schafer also states that action itself is the subject of psychoanalysis & not something additional that makes the action occur.

Eventually Schafer has turned to viewing psychoanalysis as dealing less with the past & more with the present. It becomes a narrative procedure that replaces the traditional interpretation about hidden motives. As the patient tells & retells stories around such psychoanalytic terms as erogenous zones & the conceptualization of feelings & ideas the neurotic characteristics are transformed in the revised narratives. In Schafer's theory language is a means of constructing events & since even facts to Schafer are only what the analyst's theory construes them to be, psychoanalysis has to deal with constructing the present instead of reconstructing the past.

Donald Spence takes a position similar to Schafer's which is viewing narrations as fables about the past in which fact & fantasy are intertwined. He graduated from the Lincoln School in 1943, Harvard University in 1947, and Columbia University in 1955, with a Ph.D. in clinical psychology. He served in the U.S. Army from 1944 to 1946 in Europe.

From 1954 to 1974, Spence conducted research and taught at the Research Center for Mental Health of New York University. In 1974, he became professor of psychiatry at the Robert Wood Johnson Medical School at the University of Medicine and Dentistry of New Jersey.

The author of more than 100 articles and book reviews, he published Narrative Truth and Historical Truth, widely considered a classic text in the field, in 1982. Two other books followed, as well as several translations into other languages. His many honors and awards included, most recently, the Lifetime Achievement Award for the Theoretical and Philosophical Division of the American Psychological Association in 2004. Following his retirement in 1996 he became involved in many Princeton activities.

Memories of childhood incest may be nothing more than unverifiable tales. This he calls narrative truth rather than historical truth. Since there is no knowable truth, the only guidelines are those of aesthetics & pragmatics. The important thing for the clinician is to make a story as artistically coherent as possible, so that the client can benefit from it. Accordingly improvement in the client's condition occurs by helping him or her to find new truths rather than by dealing with historical facts. Spence maintains that all of psychoanalytic theory arises from theoretical argument rather than from multiple observations & inductive generalizations. In his work Spence reviews such shortcomings as selective reporting of cases to illustrate a contention, deference to authority rather than utilization of independent objective evidence & so on. He also notes the dependence on the analyst's memory of just what was said instead of the use of transcripts or recordings & unquestioning acceptance of author's statement of events & his or her interpretation of them. Spence seems to have no quarrel with case materials as data, only with their unsystematic & biased usage. Omission of detail, he indicates, is the main source of uncritical acceptance of a conclusion. As a remedy he advocates making verbatim recordings of complete series of sessions & using computers to analyze them. By this means it should be possible to find coherences & causal relationships that the analyst would overlook, test hypotheses, avoid biases, & provoke a data base open to public inspection.

The drastic revisions in Freud's theory began with his first followers & continue to this day. Hartman's revisions in sixties were the only attempt to rework the entire system, attempting to bring order & consistency while retaining its fundamental metapsychology. Since then the diversity of viewpoints has become ever greater, with present trends toward dialogue & intersubjectivity.

Anna Freud (1895 –1982) was born in Vienna; she was the youngest child of Sigmund Freud. She loyally followed the path of her father & contributed to the new born field of psychoanalysis. Anna Freud & Melanie Klein were the founders of psychoanalytic child psychology. Her interests were quite practical & most of her energies were devoted to the analysis of children and adolescents. Sigmund Freud, after all, had focused entirely on adult patients. Although he wrote a great deal about development, it was from the perspectives of these adults.

The relationship of the child to the therapist is different form adult, because child's parents are still a part of his or her life, a part the therapist cannot and should not try to usurp. But neither can the therapist pretend to be just another child rather than an authority figure. Anna Freud found that the best way to deal with this problem was the way that came most naturally: be a caring adult. A major problem with analyzing children is that their symbolic abilities are not as advanced as those of adults; they have trouble relating their emotional difficulties verbally. Since children's problems are more immediate, Anna viewed them in terms of the child's movement along a developmental time-line. Thus, children keeping pace with most of their peers in terms of eating behaviors, plays styles, relationships with others & so on, could be considered healthy. When one aspect or another of a child's development seriously lagged behind the rest, the clinician could assume that there was a problem.

Anna Freud was more interested in the dynamics of the psyche than in its structure, and was particularly fascinated by the place of the ego in all this. Anna was probably best known for her book "Ego & the Mechanisms of Defense." In it she describes how the defenses work, including some special attention to adolescents' use of defenses. This focus on the ego began a movement in psychoanalytic circles called "ego psychology." It takes Freud's earlier work as a crucial foundation, but extends it into the more practical world of the ego, because this way, Freudian theory can be applied, not only to psychopathology, but to social and developmental issues as well.

About Neo-Freudianism

Erich Fromm (1900-1980) was born at Frankfurt am Main. He started his academic studies in 1918 at the University of Frankfurt with two semesters of jurisprudence. In 1919 Fromm studied at the University of Heidelberg where he switched to sociology. He received his Ph.D. in sociology from Heidelberg in 1922. During the mid 1920s, he was trained to become a psychoanalyst. He began his own clinical practice in 1927. In 1930 Fromm joined the Frankfurt Institute of Social Research & completed his psycho-analytical training. Because of the pressures of Nazi Regime Fromm, (he was Jewish) was forced to leave Germany. He moved Geneva & then, in 1934, to New York. Here Fromm helped to form the New York branch of the Washington School of Psychiatry. In 1946 co-founded the "William Alanson White Institute of Psychiatry", Psychoanalysis, and Psychology. He was on the faculty of Bennington College from 1941-1950. Toward the end of his career, he moved to Mexico City to teach. He had done considerable research into the relationship between economic class and personality types there. He died in 1980 in Switzerland.

The contradictions between various tenets of Freudian theory & the find-ings of experimental psychology, anthropology & sociology gave rise to the neo-Freudian trend in psychoanalysis in the thirties, which was char-acterized by a special emphasis on problems of social philosophy. It was with the emergence of the cultural psychoanalysis that the second stage in its orientation towards social philosophy began. This stage was marked by an abrupt switch from bio-psychological interpretation of human be-havior to an interpretation based on sociology & anthropological psychol-ogy.

The neo-Freudians reject Freud's theory of aggressive & sexual instincts, take a new look at the correlation between conscious & the unconscious & the structure of man's mind & also make a critical reevaluation of other tenets of classical psychoanalysis. The neo-Freudian trend was represent-ed by a large number of analysts, anthropologists, & sociologists. Particu-larly prominent among them were Erich Fromm, Karen Horney & Abram Kardiner.

According to Fromm the classic Freudian theory was not valid enough to explain the question of the interaction between the individual & society. The reappraisal of classic Freudianism creates the impression that the neo-Freudians are actually breaking with the metaphysical approach to human behavior & providing an accurate picture of the relationship between man & the social conditions of his existence. Nevertheless, the closer examination reveals that they are far removed from a true understanding of the real interaction between man & his social environment & from a truly scientific analysis of the role played by society in man' development.

While leaving untouched Freud's fundamental thesis concerning the all-significant role of "unconscious" in man's life, the neo-Freudians simply reiterate that manifestation of unconscious is dependent upon the specific essence & qualitative peculiarities of a given society. Most of the theoretical arguments put forward by the neo-Freudians on the subject of the relationship between man & society, although couched in modern sociological terminology, are still confined to the framework of the subjective idealist, metaphysical conceptions typical of classical Freudianism. While rejecting the biological approach which characterizes Freud's psychological theory, the neo-Freudians do not leave to one side his views on the role of instincts as such. They replace Freud's biological instincts that determine human behavior with man's 'substantalized' psychological needs, which are referred to by different names by the various neo-Freudians. Although they criticize & attempt to improve Freud's theory, neo-Freudians do not abandon the basic principles of his psychoanalytical theory, & in fact present us with a modernized version of the same. Neo-Freudians admit that while criticizing classical Freudian theory, they set out not so much to disclose & emphasize what is wrong with psychoanalytical theory as through eliminating the debatable elements, to enable psychoanalyses do develop to the heights of its potentialities. That is why their criticism of Freudian theory is not a refutation of its methodological foundation.

Erich Fromm himself, for example, holding that the development of any scientific theory demands as a general principle the constructive reinterpretation of basic visions maintains that Freud's greatest discoveries, that of the Oedipal complex & death instinct, were hobbled by his philosophical premises & that, freed from them & translated into a new frame of reference, Freud's findings become ever more potent & meaningful. The neo-Freudians in their reappraisal of classical psychoanalysis reject only such details as do not affect the essence of the theory. While criticizing its unduly biological & pansexual features they leave intact the fundamental principles of psychoanalytical theory, such as the concept of repression, the concept of resistance & transference, the pre-eminence of the unconscious in the determination of man's behavior & so on.

The paths leading the various neo-Freudians to the culture oriented form of psychoanalysis differed; while it was mainly experience of practical psychoanalysis on which Horney based her reinterpretation of classical Freudianism, Fromm started out from his sociological findings. Karen Horney's readiness to make a critical reevaluation of psychoanalytical theories had its origins in dissatisfaction with therapeutic results. As psychoanalysis developed & came to be practiced in an increasingly wide scale, analysts raised doubts as to its therapeutic effectiveness on numerous occasions & this matter was soon to be the subject of heated theoretical controversy. Yet until neo-Freudianism took shape as a well defined trend, it was commonly accepted that the reason for this lay in its imperfections as a method of treatment, & all the efforts of the analysts were confined in the min to more detailed elaboration of various psychoanalytical procedures, to the subtle nuances of the psychoanalytical method of treatment. The practical experience gleamed from the study of American patients suffering from neurotic disorders demonstrated that their emotional traumas were the result not of sexual perturbations in their childhood, but rather of factors connected with the social aspect of human existence. Karen Horney encountered symptoms quite different from those in Freud's patients at the end of the 19-th century. All this led Horney to have serious doubts not in the therapeutic procedure as much, but in the approach to the treatment. The standard psychoanalytical preoccupation with singling out certain suppressed sexual desires did not yield results of any significance. Horney could not fail to notice that the radical change in the type of patient she was dealing with could be explained to a large extent by the complication of man's social existence since Freud's day. The unique exacerbation of social contradictions in U.S. in the thirties & forties, the depression & the general instability of life could not fail to leave their mark on the inner lives of the men of that time. The patient in such social context was no longer a patient in the ordinary sense of that word, because he turned to the analyst not as a patient, but as an individual in need of advice, in order to learn how he might cope more successfully with complex social pressures. Face to face with such patients, the psychoanalyst often turned social philosopher, since to treat his patient he would go beyond the confines of the purely clinical aspects of the case & attempt to see it in a specific social context. The new psychological problems that confronted the person made completely new demands on the analyst & thus gave rise to a radical change in the treatment to be administered. This in its turn demanded the reappraisal of certain tenets of classical Freudianism.

Her radical experience convinced Horney that the diversity & peculiarities of man's mental activity could not be explained in terms of his biological nature, & that such an approach to a large extent obstructed our understanding of the real forces which determined man's principles & actions.

Eventually it became obvious that it would be impossible to go on talking in terms of the structure & motives of the individual's behavior without taking into consideration social factors. Horney called for a sociological orientation in psychoanalysis, being convinced that culture should be accorded the central place in the theory of the development of the individual, that culture was decisive, all important factor in the formation of the individual's psychological character. Unlike Horney, Fromm comes forward first & foremost as a social psychologist, a social philosopher. He came to neo-Freudianism anxious to understand the laws of the individual man, & the laws of society. Although convinced that Freud was a founder of a truly scientific psychology, Fromm nevertheless took a negative view of his social philosophy. The reduction of all man's social life to bio- instinctual conflict situations within the mind struck him as highly improbable. Major historical events such as the First World War constituted the social platform in which Fromm's socio-political ideas took shape. Anxious to grasp the causes behind the emergence, development & consequences of these phenomena Fromm turned to the writings of Karl Marx. His own observation & consideration of socio-historical phenomena & his study of Marx's convinced Fromm that Freud had only a naïve notion of what goes on in society.

The social philosophy orientation of neo-Freudianism can be approached from either a narrow or a broader point of view. In a narrow sense the sociological aspect of neo-Freudianism consists in no more than a fact all its adherents regard the origin of mental disorders & man's mental development in general as being dependent on the influence of man's social environment. Although statements of this kind have a declaratory air about them, & do not pinpoint the true link which exists between man & society, nevertheless the neo-Freudians can be seen in this respect to have made a step forward as compared to Freud, who reduced all physical phenomena to man's bio-psychological nature.

The sociological approach of the neo-Freudians in a broader sense is expressed in the fact that in their research a general socio-philosophical theory takes shape, a theory which attempts from the psychological angle to explain the motive forces & advance of social development.

Erich Fromm lays emphasis on the social orientation of the neo-Freudianism in the broad sense of the word. The theory of the neo-Freudian social philosophy belongs to Fromm. The preoccupation with social philosophy which emerged in the field of classical psychoanalysis & was based on Freud's bio-psychology is not only developed in Fromm's philosophy, but in a way finds its culmination in his works. Fromm's theory, which provides a fullest & most vivid reflection of the social philosophy school in neo-Freudianism consolidated once & for all the reputation of psychoanalysis as a philosophical method claiming to provide explanations for the essence of social phenomena. In his philosophical theory Fromm examines first & foremost the laws & principles of action peculiar to the subjective human factor in the socio-historical process. Fromm endeavors to single out the role which psychological factors play as active forces in the social process & to solve related but wider problem of the interaction psychological, economic & ideological factors, & their role in social development. The problem constitutes the core of his social theory. The basic principle for its resolution which determined the direction of Fromm's theoretical search was his conviction that in order to comprehend the dynamics of the social process we must understand the dynamics of the psychological processes operating within the individual, just as to understand the individual we must see him in the context of the culture that molds him. The need to resolve the problem of the socio-psychological interaction between individual & society compelled Fromm to refer certain other psychological & socio-philosophical theories. It was at this point that he turned his attention to Freud & Marx. Taking as his bases Freud's psychological theory & Marx's philosophy, Fromm tried to arrive at synthesis which followed from the understanding & the criticism of both thinkers. He laments the fact that such a fundamental work of Marx's as "Capital" while containing an enormous amount of pithy psychological descriptions & other psychological concepts was nevertheless not based on any specific, integrated psychological theory. Fromm explains this omission not by Marx's lack of interest in psychology which he could have applied to the problems of man.

Justification for the linking together Marx's sociology & Freud's psychological theory was, according to Fromm, to be found in the fact that the problem of the individual was central to both theoretical systems. The difference lay merely in the motive forces behind the behavior of the individual as depicted by the two thinkers, these being of a socio-historical nature in Marx's system & of a purely biological order in Freud's theory. This led Fromm to conclude that the theories elaborated by Marx & Freud could supplement each other.

The social theory which Fromm created, presenting as it does the logical result of his injection of a maximum possible dose of sociology into psychoanalysis, while keeping to the framework of general Freudian theoretical propositions, brought into striking relief the utter groundlessness of attempts to find a third path outside materialism & idealism. The improvement of the Freudianism has not only failed to obviate the shortcoming & weaknesses of classical psychoanalysis, but has served to silhouette them even more clearly. No neo-Freudian sociological argument, with which Fromm attempts to preserve & uphold the grain of truth discovered by Freud, could help to conceal the blatant errors & fallaciousness of the idealist & metaphysical methodology intrinsic to Freud's theory. While on the other hand for the construction of his theory Fromm adopted the ideological & methodological principles of the classical psychoanalysis- a fact impossible to disguise even by resorting to new concepts for the presentation of the old content of psychoanalytical postulates- his approach to Marx's sociology is blatantly inadequate. From the very outset, in his attempts to synthesize Marxism & Freudianism Fromm adopts a biased approach in his assessment of Marx's philosophical theory. What Fromm synthesizes with Freud's theory is not pure Marxism, but a neo-Freudian version of it.

Fromm tends to interpret Marx's theory through the prism of his own views that is from the angle of the anthropological psychology. Fromm starts out from a false premise to the effect that Marx's philosophy is neither idealism nor materialism but a synthesis: humanism & naturalism. His own theory of human's psychoanalysis he refers to as a "dialectical humanism" & he considers that from the ideological point of view it represents something neutral. Thus Fromm achieves this synthesis of Freudian & Marxist theory by first of all turning Marx into an existentialist thinker of a neo-Freudian slant & thus presenting Marxism in a distorted light. Fromm's work demonstrates time & time again the obvious & indisputable truth that any attempt to combine Marxism with principles contradictory to it or to link it to philosophical theories whose very essence & methodological principles are diametrically opposed to it, is impossible without distorting & misinterpreting the content of Marxist theory. In his attempt to develop Marxism & Freudianism through synthesis of the two Fromm achieves the opposite. On the one hand, despite his outwardly positive attitude towards Marxism, he distorts its essence developing it in a Freudian style, while in a practice not accepting its fundamental revolutionary conclusions. On the other hand, when attempting to develop Freud's theory & bring it up to date with a help of Marxist philosophy, Fromm once gain reveals the fundamental incompatibility of the methodological foundation of these theories & thereby to all intents & purposes brings nearer the crisis of psychoanalysis. Fromm's attempt to integrate mutually exclusive principles of Freud's idealist & metaphysical theory &

264

Marx's dialectical & materialist theory, to combine the essentially anti-historic psychoanalytical theory with Marx's theory of history, introduces nothing constructive to social theory & is inconsistent from a scientific point of view. This attempt leads to the emergence within the theory elaborated by Fromm of an inner contradiction between acceptance of the role of the external social environment in the development of the individual & continued belief in unconscious dynamics within the individual's mind as the basic motive force behind that development.

Fromm's reference to Marxism & his endeavor, with Marxism as his instrument, to modernize Freudianism & to save it from demise testifies on the one hand to the growing influence of Marxist ideas & on the other to the profound crisis which Freudianism as a theory was passing through. It is difficult to imagine that Fromm in his theoretical work is deliberately distorting Marxist tenets, yet the dialectics of the ideological struggle are such that regardless of a scientist's motives his activity is determined by the stand adopted by the camp to which he belongs. Fromm's biggest mistake lies in the fact that after selecting Freud's psychological theory & Marx's social theory as a point of departure for his own philosophy & setting out to bring the two together, he has failed to appreciate that this is a fundamentally impossible task, since the theoretical systems created by Marx & Freud are based on diametrically opposed methodologies. After giving due acknowledgement to significance of social theory as means of resolving various problems, & searching for a social theory, which would combine within itself sociological & psychological principles he found himself faced by a dilemma: whether to evolve his own socio-psychological theory on a basis of Freudian psychology & its subjectively idealist & metaphysical methodology, or alternatively on a basis of Marxist sociology.

The Freudian ideological & methodological slant peculiar to Fromm's work was largely instrumental in determining his response to Marx's historical materialism & his interpretation of the same. Fromm's attempt to synthesize Freud's theory & Marxism was indeed nothing new. It served merely to resurrect the idea of "Freudo-Marxism" which had been popular in the twenties & thirties in many countries of Western Europe.

Anthropological psychologism & Neo-Freudian views

Psychological needs are not simply intrinsic to man from birth, but they take shape in the process of his active life directed towards modification of the historical conditions in which he exists. For man the concrete historical world around him represents both the foundation of his essence, & also the limit of his possibilities. The development of man in the course of history is a creative, active & constructive process. Man, as he changes reality, extends the limits of his possibilities, as he realizes his possibilities; he broadens his horizons of his current existence. Only in purposeful activity which transforms the surrounding world & humanizes it does man change & mould anew his essence. This self-perfecting process, this development of man's essential nature is unending, just as is the development of the real world itself. It is precisely while engaged in this creative, socially practical activity that man emerges as both a recondition of history, & its result. In order to understand the essence of interaction between man & society it is vital to analyze mans practical, purposeful activity, in which the inner link between man & society & their independence are manifested, for this activity is at one & the same time both a means for the historical change of human nature & a means for the affirmation & renewal of social life.

Throughout history the problem of man & essence has been a focus of various sciences. There are many different definitions for the essence of man; however it is possible to single out two main approaches to the question that have become traditional in social philosophy & which are opposed to each other- namely substantialist &relativist approaches. In the history of philosophy the problem as to the correlation between the substantial & relative in man has been interpreted both in an idealist & a materialist spirit. When the substantialist approach is used the man is regarded as mere biological substance, as a fixed & unchanging conglomeration of specific psychological needs & desires. When man's essence is interpreted in this way, his behavior & activity, the existence of various public institutions can be deducted directly from the psychological properties of human nature. The essence of the socio-historical process can then be reduced to the biologically determined behavior if individuals.

Social theories that pivoted on the essence of man were of a conservative mould, for their adherents strove to explain shortcomings of social practices. Such theories were commonly used by the ideologists of the upper classes to justify the arbitrary rule, lawlessness & inhumanity dominating culture. The relativist view of the essence of the man is no more than a simple projection of the social milieu in which he exists. The concept of the unchanging permanence of human nature is rejected when this approach is used. Also the content & evolution of human nature is presented as directly & entirely dependent on a constantly changing social environment. The socio-philosophical theories which gave expression to the relativist approach for the definition of human nature played a progressive role in the past since they explained the evil in man as a result of the existence of unfortunate social conditions, & called for a change in the latter. These theories were especially popular at the time of bourgeois revolutions of the 17-th & 18-th centuries. Their weakness however lay in the fact that they made man fatally dependent on society, turning into a blind puppet of the social forces which confront him.

After making the problem of man central to his socio-philosophical theory, Fromm could not avoid the classical antinomy of bourgeois society-either society moulds man, or man shapes society. The social thought reveals that whenever the problem of man & the dynamics of the historical process were made central to a theory, the theoretician in question was obliged to resolve that dilemma. How the problem was resolved determined in the final analysis the nature of the socio-philosophical theory elaborated by the social scientist in question. Neo-Freudians understood the essential inadequacy of the substantialist & relativist interpretations of human nature. For example, Fromm, in his efforts to define the essence of man tried to find a different approach to the problem which might enable him to avoid the dualism & one-sidedness of these two methods. Fromm's theory provides the point of departure for his social philosophy & it is precisely this which lends it its strictly anthropological character & predetermines the solutions reached for the problem of the interaction of man & society, & that of historical development. This very starting point provided the source of Fromm's numerous not only theoretical mistakes, but also socio-political errors & illusions, which were subsequently to manifest themselves in his social program, in the picture he painted of an ideal society of the future. The possibility of avoiding such extremes as bio-substantialism on the one hand, & social relativism on the other Fromm saw to lie in the definition of man's nature as a contradiction inherent in human existence. This approach to the problem of the individual Fromm held to be neither biological nor sociological. Fromm was convinced that he was transcending such dichotomy by the assumption that the main passions & drives in man result from the total existence of man or in other words that they derive from the human situation. Refusing to acknowledge biological processes inherent in man's constitution as the source of specifically human needs, Fromm, unlike Freud maintained that the most beautiful as well as the most ugly inclinations of man are not part of a fixed & biologically given human nature, but result from the social process which creates man. Unlike Freud, according to whom the antagonism between the individual, possessed of a specific quantity of biologically determined needs, & society, whose role is limited to thwarting, suppressing, or sublimating these needs, was irreconcilable,

Fromm held that society performs not only a negative, repressive function, but also a creative one. Fromm's acceptance of society's creative role in the development of man leads up to a proclamation of the idea that society should not intervene in the spontaneous process of the self-revelation of the inner potential with which the individual is endowed, no more no less. While believing that society exerts some influence on the development of the individual, Fromm at the same time is skeptical of those psychologists & sociologists who think of man as a blank sheet of paper on which each culture writes its text. The relativists, in his view, while denying the existence of any universal in human nature but acknowledging in word the oneness of the human race; actually leave hardly any content & substance to this concept of humanity. In answer to the relativists & substantialists Fromm in an attempt to provide his own interpretation of the substantial in man, resorts to analysis of the anthropological conditions of human existence. In his opinion, only the human situation in which each individual finds himself from the moment of birth expresses the common factor, that which is intrinsic to all man of all historical epochs, which makes them resemble each other in their essential nature & enables them to express through themselves the essence of the human race. Fromm begins his exposition of the problem of human nature with an analysis of the human condition his own philosophy & anthropogenesis. As he sees it, the genetic precondition for the appearance of man was the decline in animals' geological adaptability to their environment which took place at the specific stage of the natural world's evolution. The inadequate biological apparatus for instinctive adaptation to the world proved, the more man's brain & capacity for thought & conscious powers of orientation developed.

The emergence of a man endowed with reason & self-awareness disrupts his natural, primitive links with the natural world, destroying the harmonious accord between early men & nature & gives rise to the existentialist contradiction which Fromm's opinion constitutes the heart of the problem of human existence. On the one hand man is a part of nature & subject to its physical & biological laws, while on the other thanks to his reason he raises himself above the limits imposed on him by nature confronting it as a self-aware agent. This means that while a part of nature the individual at the same time in conflict with it. Man cannot return to the condition of pre-human harmony with nature, & therefore in Fromm's view he should seek unity with by developing & perfecting his rational, truly human capacities. This very need to resolve the problem of human existence, with other individuals is as Fromm sees it the source of all human feelings, emotional reactions & worries. All man's inner psychological potentialities are, according to Fromm, determined by his endeavor to find a new harmonious correlation between him & nature to replace the original relationship which he had lost, peculiar to the pre-human, namely purely animal existence. Fromm sees man as the only living creature for which its own existence presents a problem & he is convinced that he must come to terms with it, for only that can make a man out of him. According to Fromm the separation of man from nature is not only the primary stimulus, the motive force behind the development of man & history, but also the principle which as it were predetermines for all intents & purposes the ultimate goal & inner significance of that development. The universal & unique problem of human existence which has faced all men at all times & in which are concentrated all historically concrete problems stems from the natural conditions of human evolution. Fromm was convinced that Freud was mistaken in singling out man's biological constitution as the source of all human motivation & believed that all passions & strivings of man are attempts to find an answer to his existence & that the understanding of man's psyche must be based on the analysis of man's needs stemming from the conditions of his existence. The close analysis of the concept on which Fromm bases his theory of the essence of man, makes it clear that from the psychological point of view his theory is based on instincts as much as that of Freud's. His theory only differs from his predecessor's only in so far as it is based on the anthropological rather than the biological aspect.

While in Freud's theory innate biological instincts are anti-social in character, in Fromm's unchanging needs, intrinsic to human nature & extra-historical in origin, manifest themselves in the form of positive urges. Anxious to refute Freud's bio- substantialist interpretation of the essence of man, Fromm goes to the other extreme, a kind of anthropological panpsychism. He depicts human nature as a physical substance made up of man's existential extra-temporal needs. His conception of man's essence proves in the final analysis to be purely theoretical, ideal construction bereft of any kind of socio-historical significance. Fromm sees human nature as shaped by imperative drive to restore a unity between him & the rest of nature. For him it constitutes a highly specific system of needs incorporating the need for relationships with other people, the need for self-preservation, for devotion, for frames of orientation & the need to make sense of his own being. These fundamental needs of man which determine all his mental activity are presented by Fromm as needs of a markedly abstract, asocial & purely anthropological character & this of course makes itself felt in Fromm's choice of solutions for different social & psychological problems. In the process of both person's ontogenetic & philogenetic development the satisfaction of his natural needs prede-termined by the anthropological human situation is effected in Fromm's view in two completely different ways. One of these methods the devel-opment & advance of man & the other obstructs that advance. Each of the methods for satisfying man's needs provides a specific answer to the problem of man' existence, the one a progressive answer & the other a regressive one.

In Fromm's view each individual in his attempts to resolve the problem of man's existence can either return to an archaic, pathogenic solution, or he can progress toward & improve his human quality. If man tries to de-stroy that which makes him man at the same time tortures him-his reason & self-awareness-in his anxiety to regain his lost oneness with nature & to free himself from the fear of uncertainty, he sets foot on the regressive path for the resolution of the problem of human existence. I f man seeks new harmony with the world by means of full & comprehensive develop-ment of the human capacities he was born with, then he selects a pro-gressive means for resolving existential problem. The progressive resolu-tion of the existential problem is in the interests of man's mental health & development & also according to Fromm in keeping with the needs of human nature. A regressive decision leads to mental disturbance & anguish. In neo-Freudian view, both the mentally normal person & the neurotic are prompted to act by an insuperable need to find an answer to the question of human existence & move beyond the state of uncertainty into which they have been plunged by the very fact of separation from na-ture. Because of this man's behavior can never be explained as the result of the repression or sublimation of the individual's instincts. The need for relationships with other people can be satisfied by the means of domina-tion & subordination, which leads to the loss of individual's freedom. On the other hand the need for self-perfection can be satisfied either in the creative process or in destructivism.

The need for devotion can be satisfied regressively through preservation of original links with nature which guarantee man that peace & confidence in existence, which he lost through birth, or progressively, i. e. through breaking these natural ties typical of an animal existence & a full development of his human essence, resulting from the establishment of new solidarity with other people & a harmonious sense of oneness with the world. The need for man to make sense of his own being can be satisfied either through revival of his original links with nature or through full creative development of all human capacities. In the latter case man becomes aware of his unique individuality, acquiring inner strength & confidence.

The need for frames of orientation & devotion can be satisfied by irrational or rational means. The diverse systems of orientation & devotion which have been devised by man in his efforts to solve the problem of human existence constitute various religious & ideological systems. Fromm finds that only rational means for satisfying this need provide a feasible basis for man's full & comprehensive unfolding of his life forces. Each individual regardless of when he was born always finds himself confronted by the choice between a progressive answer to the problem of human existence, which would facilitate the satisfaction of his natural needs, a regressive one which leads to the stifling of those needs. In every individual there is an innate potential for development, for growth, since from birth he is equipped with the ability to walk, talk, think & love. Inner potentialities of human nature are always actualized spontaneously, when the proper conditions are present. According to Fromm within every individual, on account of his ambivalent socio-biological nature, two principles are simultaneously at work from the very day of his birth- the "animal" & the "human"- each of which is the product of the existential contradiction between man & nature, result of the human situation.

The ethical approach to the assessment of human nature elaborated by Fromm makes it possible to conclude that he rejects both the idea that man is by nature an evil creature & the opposite idea that man essentially good. The essence of man cannot be in any way categorized as either wholly good or evil. Fromm disagrees with Freud's idea that good & evil are simultaneously present in man & constantly warring against each other. A realistic view sees both possibilities as real potentialities.

Fromm proposes that human nature is completely neutral in ethical sense- "neither good nor evil." How men will emerge in the concrete historical condition of a given reality will depend on the external conditions in which he finds himself, since in man there are simultaneously inherent two potentialities that are neutral in regard to each other. The primary potentiality is actualized if normal social conditions are to hand, while the secondary potentiality embodies all that is opposed to the productive orientation & is actualized in case of abnormal conditions which impede the actualization of the primary potentiality.

Fromm views as the end product of the self-actualization of a physical substance anthropological by nature. At the same time he makes this development dependent on society, to which he allocates no more than auxiliary role in the actualization of man's substantialized psychological nature. Unlike substantialist & relativist who, starting out from recognition of the actual fact of the interaction between man & society, stressed in a partial way the importance of one of the sides of that interaction, making it absolute, Fromm attempts to single out the dynamics of that interaction allocating a specific role to each of the two sides. The relations between man & society he depicts as some kind of dynamic parallelism. When considering the problem of man & society he starts out from recognition of the complete autonomy of the two phenomena. This prevents him from correctly analyzing the real nature of their interaction. Fromm believes that human nature has its laws & goals of evolution & development which are completely different from those of society's socio-economic organization. Their existence & inner development are not independent, but having coexisted in time throughout history they are permanently involved in a definite relationship with each other. Thus any given social order does not create these fundamental strivings, but it determines which of the limited number of potential passions will become a manifest of dominant. Society only develops or deforms that which is already potentially inherent in man's very nature. It is something outside the needs stemming from human nature & constitutes an entity existing side by side with man's essence contradicting it at the same time. The existence of the needs inherent in human nature as some kind of potentialities does not in any way depend on this or that concrete historical society, whose role consists in either bringing nearer the realization of those potentialities, or not, as the case may be.

Fromm's approach reduces the dynamics of the historical process to the psychological conflict between the needs of human nature & the possibility of their satisfaction within a concrete social structure. History in his opinion bears witness merely to the degree to which those needs are satisfied & to the nature of the influence of a given social structure on these needs.

In Fromm's theory society, with its economic & socio-cultural institutions stands counter to human nature as something self- sufficient, & it exists in its own right, as a separate entity. His construction of an abstract psychological model for human nature reveals the inconsistency of his methodological approach not only to the problem of the substantial & relative in man, but also to the correlation between the social & biological. The neo-Freudian theory of anthropogenesis presents the process of the origin of man a something purely negative in the course of which instinctive biological adaptation of a specific species of animal only attains its minimum; man's needs are defined with the help of an analogy with animal instincts.

Man's creative & active relationship to nature, which proved to the basic motive force behind his evolution & development, is not brought to light; indeed hardly touch upon in the neo-Freudian theory of anthropogenesis. Not in single one of his numerous works does Fromm analyze the formation of man's biological inclinations which made him capable of social activity. While stressing early man's adaptability to nature & his loss of those advances which animals posses, Fromm assesses man in terms of an animal existence. He contrasts the reason which man developed with the instincts he has lost, & thus ignores the historical character of the evolution of human consciousness as a more developed & universal capacity than any mere instinct.

The specific nature of a man as a rational being consists not in biological inadaptability, but on the contrary man's special adaptability in reaction to nature, for precisely thanks to his reason man is able to establish a new oneness with nature at a higher level.

The neo-Freudian approach to the question of human nature in which social human is to be found side by side with a biological being leads on to the conclusion that only by chance were the biological & social elements in the evolution process brought together, as a result of which the existential situation brought forth man. Fromm does not attempt to trace the origin of the social element & depicts its qualitative nature or what distinguishes it from the biological element; he contents himself with simply drawing a distinction between the two & establishing a kind of parallelism between them.

The development of the social element is a lengthy process which is still going on now; meanwhile the animal element is completely dependent on nature, & its development entirely determined by the laws of biological existence. The evolution of man, who set himself apart from nature & is possessed of consciousness, is by now determined by the laws of social development. The more diverse & complex man's activity becomes, the further he leaves his old nature behind him & the more significant is his dependence on social reality which he himself creates, on his humanized nature. The social factor in man, shaped in its evolution by his humanized nature, which constitutes a historical product, the result of the activity of a whole number of generations is something higher than the biological factor which in its evolution is determined by the necessity of external nature. Such social factor is a qualitatively different designation of a new, more complex form of material existence. Fromm's establishment of the parallelism which he draws between the social & biological principles in man does not have anything in common with the actual state of affairs. His conception of the individual suffers from an innate contradiction. While acknowledging in word true role of man's social environment in his development, Fromm attributes decisive importance in the determination of various forms of social activity to an inner innate system of man's essential needs. Such conception of human nature is a naturalistic one, for it presents man in the form of some fixed psychological structure, which determines in advance all his intentions, strivings & actions.

One of the unique features of Erich Fromm's neo-Freudian theory resulting from its instinctivism, consists in the fact that the relationship between the individual & his social environment is viewed one-sidedly, meaning only from the angle of adaptive, defensive reactions. When metaphysical approach is adopted for an examination of the relationship between the individual & the conditions of his existence, problems of the psychology of the individual are reduced to the problem of the individual's adaptation to his social environment. When this approach is used the question as to the true source of man's real socio-transforming is left open.

In his central assessment of Freud's views on the nature if individual Fromm attempts to make use of certain tenets of Marxism. In his works on human nature Fromm often refers to Marx & when he takes over one or the other of his ideas adopts it to suit his abstract psychological constructions. Everything which he cannot alter to fit his own logical scheme is ignored. In Fromm's opinion Marx, being an opponent of biosubstantialist & social-relativist definitions of man's essential nature, never arrived at the full development of his own theory concerning the nature of man, transcending both the unhistorical & relativist positions.

The legacy of classical Freudianism prevented Fromm from reaching an objective assessment of Marx's social theory; his psychologist's interpretation of it in anthropological sense serves to distort its very essence. In his false interpretation of Marx's statements with regard to human nature, Fromm is so convinced of the infallibility of his own views that in defiance of the facts he goes out of his way to demonstrate that Marx was more or less the forerunner of the neo-Freudians.

The development of man occurs hand in hand with changes in society itself, accordingly there is no such thing as human nature in general. There can be only historically determined human nature which is modified in each new epoch as history itself develops. Man, as he modifies his environment, in doing so modifies himself as well, realizing those of his opportunities which reflect the objective trends to be discerned in that environment. The needs of a concrete historical individual serve to express the demands of evolving social reality, which eventually become the individual's life forces. As a result the realization of man's needs always coincides with change in his social environment.

Neo-Freudians consider that an understanding of man's mind must be based on an analysis of man's needs stemming from the conditions of human existence. This would also be an acceptable point if Fromm implied by conditions of human existence concrete historical reality, as opposed to the anthropological situation. Then these needs would assume not an abstract generalized character but the concrete needs of real individuals. It is quite incomprehensible the existential situation, which in neo-Freudian theory represents the original, anthropological conditions of human existence, brought forth human needs as are only feasible in a socially developed situation. The historical situation, in which alone it is possible for man's real needs to crystallize, is substituted in Fromm's theory by the anthropological, existential situation, which once gave birth to all man's possibilities & needs. In Fromm's view the individual's concrete historical needs are none other than a system f needs stemming from man's abstract-psychological nature, a system modified in specific historical conditions of existence. Yet man's needs being social by their very nature, grow & find fulfillment in accordance with the changes in economic relations, which they serve to express. Man's essence cannot precede his existence. Neo-Freudians skirt the obvious fact that precisely historical conditions of human existence constitute the only possible & real existential situation for man.

It is nearly impossible to give a correct evaluation of the neo-Freudian conception of the essence of man & the psychological dynamics of the historical process without defining Fromm's view of the unconscious, or its role in men's socio-historical activity. Neo-Freudians also attempt to strip away the veil of mystery surrounding the unconscious, a subject which for many decades has been a constant preoccupation of authors contributing to scientific journals on psychology & psychoanalysis. Fromm criticizes those psychoanalysts & psychologists who see the unconscious as something with which the individual is biologically equipped. According to Fromm, Freud's approach to personality as the receptacle for un-

conscious biological & instinctive desires at odds with society that prohibits their emergence into conscious plane played an enormous role in the
spread & acceptance of this idea.

In psychoanalysis as a specific system of ideas it is possible to single
out certain fundamental premises: first, the idea that man, whether he
likes it or not is obliged in his everyday life to suppress his awareness
of many feelings & emotions; second, the idea that a conflict arises between the implication of unconscious & consciousness, a conflict which
nearly always results in neurosis; & third, the certainty that this conflict
will disappear as soon as the unconscious is brought to the threshold of
man's consciousness. While leaving untouched the basic assumptions of
classical psychoanalysis concerning the unconscious & the mechanism
of repression, Fromm sets out to reinterpret & analyze both these in a
neo-Freudian light. Unlike Freud, who regarded the unconscious as an
extra-historical, anti-social phenomenon biological by nature, Fromm
maintains that the unconscious, like consciousness, is also a social phenomenon, determined by the social filter.

In his theory he focuses his attention on the social unconscious, namely
those areas of repression which are not individual but common to most
members of a society. Only by going out of its way to prevent its members from apprehending the so called social unconscious with the help
of socially conditioned filter can society ensure its stable functioning,
given that society has to grapple with specific inner contradictions. Neo-
Freudians maintain that experience cannot enter awareness unless it can
penetrate this filter. Only that which penetrates the filter can enter the
sphere of consciousness.

Karen Horney's Theory

Karen Horney (1885-1952) was born in Hamburg, Germany. In 1013 she received an M.D. at the University of Berlin after which she undertook psychoanalytic training at the Berlin Psychoanalytic Institute. By 1919 she was a faculty member & a practicing psychoanalyst. Horney was mainly interested in modifying & extending Freud's work. She wrote many articles touching upon feminine personality & demonstrating quite a few disagreements with Freud's concepts. In 1934 she moved to United States to work as an associate director of the Chicago Institute for Psychoanalysis. In 1934 she had begun a private practice, at the same time teaching at the New-York Psychoanalytic Institute. Eventually her growing disagreements with Freudian concepts caused her to resign her post. Horney founded the American Institute of Psychoanalysis & remained its leader until her death.

It is safe to say that Horney considered herself a disciple of Freud's although she had many points of disagreement. At times her parts of her theory are so strongly at variance with Freud's that it is difficult to consider her ideas as falling within Freudian framework. Horney argued that some of Freud's basic assumptions were influenced by the spirit of the time. She did not agree with the notion that personality development depends on unchangeable instinctive forces, denying the preeminent position of sexual factors. She was also challenging the validity of the Oedipus theory, Freudian structure of personality & libido. Horney agreed with Freud on the existence of emotional & nonrational motives, unconscious motivation & the belief in absolute determinism.

The main concept of Horney's theory is basic anxiety which results from many different expressions of parental attitudes & behavior toward the child. Anything that disturbs the secure relations between the child & his parents (like lack of protection or dominance) is capable of producing anxiety. Instead of Freud's life & death instincts as major motivating forces, Horney considered the helpless infant to be seeking security in a world that is hostile & threatening. She held that the decisive driving power for man is the need for safety, security & freedom from fear.

Horney, like Freud, believed that the personality develops in early childhood, but whereas Freud detailed psychosexual stages of development, Horney focused on the way the growing child is treated by his parents. She denied the validity of oral stage or Oedipus complex, claiming that the possible development of such stages & tendencies result from parental behaviors. Instead of Freudian universalization, Horney relied on dependency on socio-environmental factors, claiming that developmental conflicts ascribed to instinctual forces could be attributed to social forces. An environmentally produced anxiety forces a child to develop a number of behavioral strategies in attempt to deal with hid feelings of insecurity. Thus, according to Horney, children structure their personality in response to the demands of their specific environment. Often behavioral strategies become a fixed part of the personality & eventually they turn into so called neurotic needs. Horney had three categories for these needs: 1.Movement toward people, as in the need for love; 2.Movement away from people, as in the need for independence; & 3.Movement against people, as in the need for power.

In Horney's theory movement towards people means acceptance of helplessness & an attempt to win affection. The movement away from people means staying apart from others, avoiding any situation of dependence. Movement against the people involves the acceptance of hostility & aggression against others. According to Horney, none of the above mentioned ways are realistic enough to deal with anxiety. When a person establishes his ways of dealing with anxiety, his behavior ceases to be flexible enough to allow alternative modes of expression.

Horney also invoked the concept of neurotic's idealized self-image, which provides him with a false picture of his personality. Accordingly, the self image is a misleading mask that prevents the neurotic from understanding & accepting his true self. Horney believed that neurotic's main conflicts are neither innate nor inevitable, but arise out of undesirable social situations in childhood. Such situations, thus, are preventable if child's home life is full of understanding, warmth, security & love.

Unlike majority of neo-Freudians Horney was overly optimistic about the possibility of avoiding neurotic conflicts. Her contribution to psychological theory is especially great since she was the only neo-Freudian to introduce a model of personality that focuses mainly on social factors. Although Horney's optimistic theory was more appealing than Freud's pessimism, it lacks clarity, internal consistency & a level of formal development. As history proves it is easier to either accept or reject a theory than to attempt to reshape it.

Gestalt psychology

While major movements such as structuralism, functionalism & opposing both, behaviorism were forming & advancing in the United States, another movement was beginning in Germany. It was another protest against structuralism, further testimony to the importance of that initial school of thought as an inspiration & impetus for opposing points of view & as an effective base from which psychologists attack on structuralism in Europe was simultaneous with the American movement. I n the beginning both movements opposed Wundt's structuralism, but later they came to oppose each other. There were serious differences between Gestaltists & behaviorists: The former accepted the value of consciousness but disallowed attempt to analyze consciousness into elements, whereas behaviorism refused to do anything at all with consciousness, even acknowledge it.

Wundtians held that perception of objects consists in the accumulation of elements into groups or collections. The Gestalt psychologists maintained that when sensory elements are brought together, something new is formed. The Gestaltists feel there is more to perception than meets the eye. Perception goes beyond the basic physical data provided to the sense organs.

The basis of Gestalt position can be found in the work of the German philosopher Immanuel Kant (1724-1804). Although less extensive than his contribution to philosophy, his contribution to psychology is important. Kant influenced psychology through his stress on the unity of a perceptual act. He held that when we perceive objects, we encounter mental states that might seem to be composed of bits & pieces. However these elements are meaningfully organized in a priori fashion & not through the mechanical process of association. Perception is not a passive combination, but an active organization of these elements into a unitary experience. The raw material of perception is thus given form & organization by the mind. According to Kant some of the forms imposed on experience by the mind are innate, such as space & time. Wundt, in his role as a target for criticism, was a precursor of Gestalt psychology. He also was a more direct influence, however, in that his principle of creative synthesis recognized that new characteristics might emerge when elements are combined into wholes.

The work of the physicist Ernst Mach provided more direct influence on the Gestalt revolution. Mach spoke of sensations of space-form & time form, considering spatial patterns & temporal patterns as sensations. He argued that one's visual & aural perception of an object does not change, even though the perceiver may change his spatial orientation with regard to the object. Mach's work was expanded by Christian von Ehrenfels (1859-1932), who is often considered the most important antecedent of the Gestalt movement, although Gestalt psychologists denied this. Von Ehrenfels suggested that there are qualities of experience that cannot be explained in terms of combination of the traditional kinds of sensations.

While Mach & von Ehrenfels certainly thought along the lines that came to be known as Gestalt psychology than deviated little from the older elementistic position of the structuralists. Rather than opposing the very notion of elementism as the Gestalt psychologists later did, they simply added a new element. Thus, while they attacked the same position as the Gestalt psychologists, they offered quite a different solution.

In United States the antecedent of Gestalt psychology was William James. He regarded elements of consciousness as purely artificial abstractions & noted that we see objects, not bundles of sensations.

Another significant influence was the phenomenological movement in German philosophy & psychology. Phenomenology refers to a free & unbiased description of immediate experience exactly as it occurs. It involves the ordinary experience of common rather than experience as reported by a trained introspector with a special systematic orientation.

It is necessary to note that the formal movement known as Gestalt psychology grew out of a research study conducted by the German psychologist Max Wertheimer. He was the oldest of the three original Gestalt psychologists & the intellectual, the leader of the movement.

German psychologist Max Wertheimer (1880-1943) was born in Prague. At the University in Prague he first studied law and then philosophy. Later he continued his studies in Berlin and then in Wurzburg, where he received the doctorate in 1904. During the following years his work included research on the psychology of testimony, deriving no doubt from his early interest in law and his interest in the nature of truth. He also carried on research in music. In 1910 Wertheimer performed his now famous experiments on apparent movement, that movement which we see when, under certain conditions, two stationary objects are presented in succession at different places. This marked the beginning of Gestalt Psychology- a major revolution in psychological thinking.

The phenomena which Wertheimer was investigating could not be explained by the then-prevailing psychology. Psychology was, in 1910, characteristically analytical: in naïve imitation of the natural sciences, it attempted to reduce every complex phenomenon to simpler ones, the elements which were supposed to make up the whole. It was becoming obvious that this analytical procedure could not account for many well-known psychological facts. The various difficulties of the older psychology went far beyond its failure to explain special laboratory findings. All of the findings that were once vital & essential seemed to be lost in the traditional approach. The trouble, according to Wertheimer, was not in the scientific method itself but rather in an atomistic assumption generally made about that method.

The viewing of complex wholes as "and-sums, " to be reduced to accidentally and arbitrarily associated elements, Wertheimer described as an approach "from below, " whereas many situations need to be approached "from above." What happens in the whole cannot be understood from a knowledge of its components considered piecemeal; rather the behavior of the parts themselves depends on their place in the structured whole.

Wertheimer became a lecturer in Frankfurt in 1912. Later he went to Berlin and in 1929 returned to Frankfurt as professor. All this time he was developing his ideas and influencing students who themselves became distinguished psychologists. Although he preferred the spoken to the written word as a vehicle for communication, he wrote some notable articles applying the new approach "from above" to the organization of the perceptual field and to the nature of thinking. The focus of Wertheimer's theory was the idea of grouping. He held that characteristics of stimuli cause a person to structure or interpret a visual field or problem in a certain way. The primary factors that determine grouping were: 1 proximity - elements tend to be grouped together according to their nearness, 2 similarity - items similar in some respect tend to be grouped together, 3 closure - items are grouped together if they tend to complete some entity, and 4 simplicity - items will be organized into simple figures according to symmetry, regularity, and smoothness. These factors were called the laws of organization and were explained in the context of perception and problem-solving.

Wertheimer's main concern was problem-solving. He provides a Gestalt interpretation of problem-solving episodes of famous scientists (e.g., Galileo, Einstein) as well as children presented with mathematical problems. The essence of successful problem-solving behavior according to Wertheimer is being able to see the overall structure of the problem. If a certain region in the field becomes crucial, it does not become isolated as well. A new structural view of the situation was developed, involving changes in functional meaning & the grouping of the items. Directed by what is required by the structure of a situation for a crucial region, one is led to a reasonable prediction, which like the other parts of the structure, calls for verification, direct or indirect. In this process two directions are involved: getting a whole consistent picture, and seeing what the structure of the whole requires for the parts.

Wertheimer's findings often seem trivial & straightforward since the tests with tachistoscope had been known for many years. Despite all of the objections Wertheimer believed that the phenomenon verified in his laboratory was in its own way, as elementary as a sensation, yet it obviously differed from a sensation or even a succession of sensations. He called such phenomenon phi. According to Wertheimer apparent movement does not need explaining, it simply exists as perceived & could not be reduced to anything simpler.

Max Wertheimer did not write a great deal, at least not as much as Koffka & Kohler, but a paper on creative thinking was published in 1920 he wrote an influential article on perceptual grouping. Wertheimer's principles & Gestalt principles were in direct opposition to most of the academic tradition of psychology in Germany. At that time behaviorism was less of an immediate revolution because functionalism had already brought about some change in American psychology. The pronouncements of the Gestaltists were too bold for the German structuralism. Consider the main points of Gestalt psychology in the light of Wundt's brand of psychology: 1 complex mental experience can have an existence of its own, 2 the primary data of perception are not elements but significantly structured forms, 3 it is acceptable when introspecting to use simple & descriptive words. The pioneers of the Gestalt movement knew that they were taking on a powerful tradition, attacking the very foundation of psychology of their time. Gestaltists were demanding a complete revision of the old theories. After the study of apparent movement they seized upon other perceptual phenomena to support the Gestalt position. Gestaltists held that perception itself shows a character of totality, a form, a Gestalt, which in the very attempt at analysis is destroyed. Gestalt psychology gets back to naïve perception, to immediate experience untouched by learning. It sets no assemblages of elements, just unified wholes. The concept of Gestalt can be applied far beyond the limits of sensory experience. The term "Gestalt" has caused some difficulty since it doesn't clearly indicate what the movement stands for & it doesn't have an exact English counterpart. Several equivalents like form, shape & configuration are in common use

& in modern usage Gestalt has become a part of the English language. According to Kohler "Gestalt" is used in two ways in German. One usage involves the denoting of form or shape as a property of objects & the second usage denotes an entity that is concrete & has as one of its attributes a specific shape or form. In this sense, the word would refer to triangles, whereas in first usage it refers to a notion of triangularity.

The word is used in reference to objects rather than to the characteristic forms of these objects. In these sense, Gestalt refers to any segregated whole.

According to Wertheimer there are wholes the behavior of which is not determined by that of their individual elements, but where the part-processes are themselves determined by the intrinsic nature of the whole. It is the goal of Gestalt theory to determine the nature of such wholes. Gestalt theory deals with concrete research; it is not only an outcome but a device: not only a theory about results but a means toward further discoveries. Wertheimer held that problems in science cannot be solved by listing possibilities for systematization, classification & arrangement. Often the explanation of Gestalt theory is difficult due to its complex terms; such as intrinsic determination, whole or part. All of them have been the topic of many discussions where each disputant has understood them differently.

One of the best known propositions offered by Gestaltists was Wertheimer's principles of perceptual organization, in which he took the position that a person perceives objects in the same immediate manner in which he perceives apparent motion that is as unified wholes.

Unlike the general principles of psychology, Wertheimer's principles stated that in perception organization occurs instantly whenever different shapes & patterns are felt. Parts of the perceptual field connect to each other & unite to form structures that are distinct from the background. The basic perceptual organization is spontaneous & inevitable whenever an organism looks about its environment. In Gestalt theory the primary brain process in visual perception is not viewed as collection of small separate activities, it is a dynamic system. The visual part of the brain does not respond in terms of separate elements of visual input, with these elements being connected by a principle of association. The brain is a dynamic system in which all those elements active at a given time interact. Elements that are dissimilar do not combine.

The factors of perceptual organization do not depend on the higher mental processes of the individual, or on his past experience, but are present in the stimuli themselves. It seems that Gestaltists & Wertheimer in particular tended to concentrate on the more direct & primitive peripheral factors of perceptual organization, rather than on experience or the role of learning.

Perception has always been the main focus of interest to the Gestalt psychologists, & they took the position that learning plays only a small role in perceptual processes. For example Wertheimer's theory of creative thinking suggests that such process should be done in terms of wholes. He believed that the detailed aspects of the problem should be considered only in relation to the structure of the total situation, & that problem solving should proceed from the whole problem downward to the parts. Wertheimer believed that if a teacher arranged problems so that elements of classroom exercises were organized into meaningful wholes, than insight would occur. He also held that once a principle of a problem's solution had been grasped, it readily transferred to other situations. Wertheimer widely criticized the associationistic theory of learning, stating that the repetition is not productive enough. He believed that repetition is useful to a point, but that its habitual use can produce habits of strictly mechanical behavior, resulting in robot like performance rather than productive thinking. After formulating perceptions as organized wholes, Gestaltists turned their attention to the problem of the cortical mechanism involved in perception & attempted to develop a theory of the neurological correlates of perceived Gestalten. Brief mention was made earlier of the Gestalt view of the cortex as a dynamic system in which the elements active at a given time interact. Such view was in sharp contrast to the so called "machine" conception of the nervous system, which likens nervous processes to a telephone switchboard that mechanically connects the sensory elements received via associationistic principles, according to which brain functions are passive & unable of active organization of the reactive sensory elements.

Wertheimer was convinced that cortical activity is a configurative whole process, & since apparent & actual motion are experienced identically, the cortical processes for actual & apparent motion must be similar. In order to account for the phi phenomenon, there must be a correspondence between the psychological experience & the underlying brain experience.

The principle of so called "isomorphism" states that experienced order in space is always structurally identical with a functional order in the distribution of underlying brain processes. According to the principle of isomorphism there is no one-on-one correspondence between the stimulus

& the perception. It is the form of the perceptual experience that corresponds to the form of the stimulus. Therefore, Gestalt is considered as true representation of the real world. A percept is not a real copy of the stimulus, just as a map is not a literal copy of the terrain it represents.

Another early Gestaltist, Kurt Goldstein (1878-1965) was a German-Jewish physician & psychiatrist. He was born at Katowitz, Upper Silesia (now part of Poland). Goldstein was educated at Breslau & Heidelberg. He received his medical degree from the University of Breslau in 1903. Goldstein's doctoral dissertation was on the structure of the posterior columns of the spinal cord. His interest in aphasia was kindled by Carl Wernicke, whom Goldstein assisted for a short time during his medical training.

Later Goldstein taught at the Universities of Frankfurt, Berlin, Columbia, Harvard and Brandeis and practiced neurological and psychiatric medicine in hospitals in Europe and the United States.

He assembled a clinic at Lazarett Hospital, Frankfurt Germany, & served as the director from 1916 to 1933. During World War I, Goldstein was Director of the Military Hospital for Brain-Injured Solders. This experience led to him writing a book on the after-effects of brain injuries. After the war Goldstein became Director of the Moabit Hospital in Berlin. Around same time he became Professor of Neurology & Psychiatry at the University of Berlin, but was forced to leave because of anti-Semitism. In 1933 he moved to the University of Amsterdam, where he wrote his famous book called "The Organism." After a year in Holland, Goldstein went to U.S. Here he worked at the Psychiatric Institute in New York City & established relations with Columbia University. He also worked at Montefiore Hospital as Attending Neurologist. He developed a laboratory of neurophysiology there and was chief until 1940. From 1940 to 1945, Goldstein served as Clinical Professor of Neurology at Tufts Medical School in Boston. Thereafter he returned to NYC and engaged in private practice.

Goldstein had a holistic theory of the human organism, one that challenged reductivist approaches and approaches that dealt with "localized" symptoms. He influenced Merleau-Ponty, Canguilhem, Cassirer, Binswanger and field of Gestalt psychology (from book cover of "The Organism" and Gregory's Oxford Companion of the mind, 1987).

During his clinical practice years Goldstein came to the conclusion that symptoms did not explain the disease, but were simply a manifestation of the entire organism. He was convinced that the organism behaved as a whole, not as a collection of parts. Goldstein refused to separate the mind & the, & chose to study them as a part of interconnected system.

He further held that the laws governing the parts of the organism also govern the whole organism. Goldstein presented three dynamic concepts that influenced human development: equalization; in which the organism attempts to balance itself to an average or centered state after a period of exertion, self-actualization; which was the purpose the human organism, & mastering the environment; which was the means of fulfilling its potential.

Perhaps his main contribution was that of organismic approach to aphasia. Goldstein thought that the disturbance of the language module was the cause of aphasia. Thus he reclassified aphasic phenomena using the following main criteria. First was the disturbance of peripheral language mechanisms or of the instrumentalities of speech equaled pure motor & sensory aphasia. In this inner speech & the periphery were intact but interrupted from each other. Second was the disturbance of the central language system or inner speech equaled central aphasia. And finally third was the disturbance of non-linguistic cognitive abilities.

Kurt Koffka & Wolfgang Kohler served to promote Wertheimer's more prominent position, though each was highly influential in his own right. Wertheimer's research problem involved the perception of apparent movement that is the perception of motion when no actual physical movement has taken place.

Kurt Koffka (1886-1941) was born in Berlin. He received his Ph.D. there in 1909 as a student of Carl Stumpf. Koffka spent one year at the University of Edinburgh in Scotland where he developed his strong fluency in English, a skill that later served him well in his efforts to spread Gestalt psychology beyond German borders. Koffka was working at the University of Frankfurt when Max Wertheimer arrived in 1910 and invited Koffka to participate as a subject in his research. In 1912 Koffka left Frankfurt to take a position at the University of Giessen where he remained until 1924. Koffka then traveled to the United States, where he was a visiting professor at the Cornell University from 1924 to 1925, and two years later at the University of Wisconsin. In 1927, he accepted a position at the Smith College in Northampton, Massachusetts, where he remained until his death in 1941. Koffka's approach directly opposed the mechanistic psychology of the nineteenth century. Instead of focusing on the components of reality and reducing perception to its parts, Koffka suggested that humans perceive whole configurations. Things around us—for example, a car or a house—are seen as whole objects, not as a set of lines, colors, and other elements of which they are made.

Koffka held that our mind naturally organizes individual sensations and experiences into meaningful wholes. He proposed his hypothesis of infant perception, saying that infants at first cannot distinguish individual objects, but perceive everything holistically. As they grow older, infants learn to discriminate and respond to individual objects. Thus, instead of building up meaning from separately perceived elements, Koffka suggested that we first perceive an impression of the whole environment. In the beginning of his career Koffka studied movement phenomena & psychological aspects of rhythm. His early researches combined elements of physiology and experimental psychology. Koffka published his "Principles of Gestalt Psychology" in 1935.In it he attempted to sum up all his research on perception and present the basic ideas of the Gestalt school.

Koffka was against the notion in psychology that took for granted that veridical perception need not be explained. Until then it had been thought that the perceptions of certain elements that comprise objects are fixed. In mathematics, a line that is five centimeters long will always be longer than a four centimeter line. Psychologists assumed that such a line would also always look longer. Koffka, on the other hand, demonstrated that when certain elements are combined with other elements, our perception of those elements changes. Examples of this are the Ponzo & Muller-Lyer illusions. That is why Koffka believed that psychologists need to always look at the things holistically, in the context of where those things are located, because the purpose of science is not to simply collect facts, but to incorporate facts into a theoretical whole. Theoretical systems must be designed to incorporate all the facts and create a rational system. Since all the facts are interdependent, a successful theoretical system will not deny or neglect even the smallest fact, says Koffka. He further criticized scientists who created theoretical systems based on facts that fit into their system, while denying facts that did not fit.

Wolfgang Kohler (1887-1967) was born in Reval, Estonia. Kohler studied at the Tubingen, Bonn & Berlin. He focused mainly on the link between physics and psychology. He ended up studying with two leading scholars in those fields, Max Planck & Carl Stumpf. In fact Kohler completed his Ph.D. with Stumpf as his professor. In 1910 he became an assistant at the Frankfurt Psychological Institute in where he worked under Max Wertheimer along with Kurt Koffka. In Frankfurt, Kohler and Koffka functioned as subjects for Wertheimer's studies of apparent movement. Together they worked on the founding of a new holistic attitude toward psychology called Gestalt theory. In 1913 Kohler moved Tenerife in the where he became the director of the Prussian Academy of Sciences. Here he wrote a book on problem solving called "The Mentality of Apes."For many years Kohler observed the manner in which chimpanzees solve problems, such as that of retrieving bananas when positioned out of reach. He noted that they stacked wooden crates to use as makeshift ladders, in order to get the food. Later Kohler concluded that the chimps had not arrived at these methods through trial-and-error, but rather that they had experienced an insight in which, having realized the answer, they then proceeded to carry it out. Kohler returned to Germany in 1920. The same year was appointed acting director and then professor and director of the Psychological Institute at the University of Berlin.

In 1934-35 Kohler was lecturer at Harvard and in 1935 a visiting professor at the University of Chicago. That same year he was forced to leave Germany after speaking out against the Nazi regime. He began teaching at Swarthmore College in Pennsylvania and became an American citizen in 1946.One year later Kohler was elected to the National Academy of Sciences & president of the American Psychological Association in 1959. He was given the American Psychological Association's Distinguished Scientific Contribution Award in 1956, the Howard Crosby Warren Medal. In 1955 he became a research professor at Dartmouth College in New Hampshire.

Kohler's main contribution to Gestalt psychology has made a lasting impact. As we already know Gestalt psychology was a rebellion against Wundt and Titchener's structuralism theories of perception where experiences were reduced to individual parts, and against behaviorism's reduction of experiences to simple stimulus-response reflexes. With roots in Husserl's phenomenology and Kant's philosophy, Gestalt psychology viewed the perceptual process as the joining of perceptual elements together to form a holistic interpretation of a stimulus, a synergistic collaboration where the parts were far less important than the whole. There was considerable excitement in the prospects of leaving behind the other German psychologies (structuralism, functionalism, and psychoanalysis) for something new. Kohler felt that there was something lacking in the field of psychology; that something was needed that was more applicable than structuralism and functionalism. He was the right person at the right time to help to bring this to life.

One of the main Gestalt ideas was perceptual constancy; the inclusiveness and perpetuation of objects parts in a perceptual experience. Another Gestalt idea dealt with the perceptual organization principles of proximity, continuity, similarity, closure, simplicity, and figure/ground. Proximity suggested that objects seen close together will be perceived as being part of a single object. Similarity suggested that objects that have the same appearance will be perceived as a single object. Continuity suggested that perceived patterns will be continued. Closure suggested that an automatic process will complete gaps in an object to perceive a solid object.

Many of Gestalt perceptual ideas have influenced the areas of cognitive, social, and clinical psychology. While these ideas can now be found in the counseling approaches of Gestalt Therapy, they have only a conceptual relation to Kohler's original work. His perceptual ideas have contributed to the understanding of learning, memory, and the nature of associations.

As a part of his animal studies Kohler experimented with chickens, but to a lesser extent than with the apes. He trained chickens to peck at a gray board when shown with a black board, after which observed them peck at a white board when shown with a gray board. He thought that they were able to see the relationship between the stimuli, instead of simply learning a single task. Kohler called this process "transposition." Transposition can be seen in humans when one transfers the knowledge from one situation to another. Eventually his experiments were criticized as less than rigorous and poorly controlled. Nonetheless, the information he generated proved useful in understanding animal and human learning. Kohler wrote extensively on his research, much of which was published through the journal that he co-founded. He was a pioneer in understanding thought processes and the errors within, such as with judgments and associations. His numerous contributions won him recognition from several psychological associations.

The New Generation of Gestalt Movement

Gestalt movement became a strongly united, coherent school in 1930. It was especially developed in Germany & United States. Gestalt principles & doctrines were being used in child psychology, sociology, applied psychology, education & anthropology. By the 1940 with the appearance in American journals of Gestalt doctrines & the Gestalt oriented research, Gestalt psychology became a vital part of American psychology. In Germany Gestalt psychology was greatly suffering from the departure of its leaders & the effects of Nazi regime, eventually, Gestalt psychology was reduced to a minor position in the German academic system.

Gestalt psychology has shown renewed vitality since the 1950 as a part of a vigorous resurgence of interest psychology in West Germany.

One of the tendencies of 19-th century science was to think in terms of field relationships & to move away from an elementistic & atomistic framework. The concept of the field theory generated within psychology as an analogy to the concept of fields of force in physics. In psychology the term "field theory" was referring to the work of Kurt Lewin (1890-1947).He was born in Mogilno, Poland (then Prussia) to a middle-class Jewish family. When he was only15 Lewin moved to Berlin to attend the Gymnasium. In1909 he enrolled at the University of Frieberg to study medicine before transferring to the University of Munich to study biology. He received a doctoral degree at the University of Berlin.

During his studies Lewin became acquainted with Gestalt psychology. In 1914 he volunteered for the German army and was later injured in combat. These experiences played a major role in the development of his Field Theory. In 1921 Kurt Lewin began lecturing on philosophy and psychology at the Psychological Institute of the University of Berlin. In 1930 Stanford University invited him to be a visiting professor. Lewin eventually emigrated to the U.S. and took a teaching position at the University of Iowa, where he worked until 1944.

Today Lewin is well known for his terms life space & field theory, but he was perhaps even better known for practical use of his theories in studying group dynamics, solving social problems related to prejudice, and group therapy. Lewin attempted to describe the group life, at the same time investigating the unique conditions and forces which bring change or resist change in groups. In the field approach, Lewin believed that for change to take place, the total situation has to be taken into account. When only part of the situation is considered, a misrepresented picture is likely to develop. In field theory, a "field" is defined as the totality of coexisting facts which are conceived of as mutually interdependent.

Lewin was convinced that Individuals behave according to the way in which tensions between perceptions of the self and of the environment were worked through. He held that Individuals participate in a series of life spaces like family, work, school and church which were constructed under the influence of various force vectors. Lewin thought that behavior was determined by totality of individual's situation. Thus, behavior was a function of the field that existed at the time the behavior occurred.

His field theory stated that human behavior was the function of both the person & the environment: expressed in symbolic terms, $B = f (P, E)$. According to Lewin behavior was related both to personal characteristics and to the social situation in which person finds himself. This theory may seem simple now, but most early psychologist did not believe in behaviorism. Many psychologists at the time believed in the psychoanalytic theory that held human motives to be blind pushes from within. Lewin thought of motives as goal-directed forces. He held that behavior was purposeful. Field theory eventually led to the development of actual field research on human behavior. Lewin manipulated complex situational variables in natural settings. His approach has guided experiments in the field of social cognition, social motivation, and group processes. The concept of group dynamics resulted out of Lewin's work with field theory. Lewin was especially interested in the uniformity found in many group interactions and looked extensively at how field theory came into play in group settings.

His fascination with group dynamics can also be seen in his research involving democracy and groups. Lewin, along with Ronald Lippitt, looked at the effects of democratic, autocratic, and laissez-faire methods of leadership on group structure and the behavior of group members. Results showed that groups with efficient change that occurred in democratic ways lead to superior group results. Superior results were found with the basis that as all individuals can participate and become an identifiable part of the group. On the other hand groups that contained more authoritarian structures were found to be more rigid & lead to dysfunctional decision making. Finally, groups that contained laissez-faire styles were found to be very inefficient and unproductive.

Another area of interest for Lewin was the so called "Action Research." Action research was a term that emphasized research that was directly purposed at understanding and generating practical applications & solutions to real world problems. Lewin broke down this process into a cyclical pattern, which involved identifying a general idea and examining the facts of the situation. This then led into planning for the first step of action to take. After the first step the cycle of evaluating, planning & fact finding continued leading to an overall plan and additional steps of action. This process continued throughout the action research process. Apparently Lewin was more interested in practical applications than in conducting pure scientific research. Action research involved studies in real life situations that encountered a wide variety of social problems. Lewin's studies were conducted in factories or housing projects, & led to community studies & further research on minority groups.

Lewin was also known for developing a model of change. He described it as a three-stage process. The first stage called "unfreezing" involved overcoming inertia and dismantling the existing "mind set". In this stage the defense mechanisms had to be bypassed. In the second stage the change occurs. This was typically a period of confusion & transition. A person becomes aware that the old ways are being challenged but does not have a clear picture as to what we are replacing them with yet. The third and final stage was called "freezing". The new mindset was crystallizing and one's comfort level was returning to previous levels.

Lewin's position in relation to Gestalt psychology is not clear. He is often regarded as the developer of the separate but related system. In the beginning he was working independently, but later Lewin became closely associated with Kohler & Wertheimer. In his work Lewin went beyond the traditional framework of Gestalt position. Lewin's work was mainly focused on needs, personality & social factors. Unlike Gestaltists who stressed psychological constructs to explain behavior, Lewin considered psychology more as a social science. Kurt Lewin's system is an elaboration of the Gestalt movement. Since his position fits the Gestalt system more readily than any other.

Throughout his 30 years of professional activity, Lewin devoted himself consistently to the broadly defined area of human motivation. His research emphasized the study of human behavior in its total physical & social context. He analyzed the basic structure of science, which he believed had evolved through three stages: speculative, descriptive & constructive. Accordingly early Greek science represents the first stage which was given to large scale speculative theorizing that attempted to encompass all natural phenomena. The second, descriptive stage involves the accumulation of the greatest possible number of facts, which were described precisely & objectively. The final, constructive stage was the one within which Lewin developed his system. The goal of Lewin's system was the discovery of laws that would permit the prediction of individual phenomena. In this system events are lawful & orderly even if they occur in only one case. Taking this constructive stage as his model, Lewin argued that laws of behavior need not be based on statistical averages in order to have value. His psychology thus focuses on the individual, not the mean responses of groups of individuals. He maintained that the specific individual & the total situation in which he performs must be understood in order to predict behavior. Field theory led Lewin to consider that the psychological activities of a person occur in a kind of psychological field or life space. The life space comprises all of the events that may possibly influence a person a person it may show varying degrees of differentiation as a function of the amount & kind of experiences the individual has accumulated. Because it lacks experiences, the infant has few, if any, differentiated regions in its life space. The educated adult shows complex life space as a function of his past experiences.

Lewin attempted to use a mathematical model to represent his theoretical concept of psychological processes. He chose topology, a form of geology to show all the possible goals of an individual & routes leading to it. Topology deals with transformations in space by representing spatial relationships in non-quantitative fashion. It is a conception of space that deals with the order of relationships, but not with their direction or distance. Lewin developed a new type of qualitative geometry called bodological space, in which he used vectors to represent directions of movement toward a goal. To complete the schematic representation of his system, Lewin introduced the notion of valences to refer to the positive or negative value of objects in the life space. For example, objects that are attractive to the individual have positive valence while objects that threaten him have negative valence.

Lewin maintained that there is the equilibrium between the person & his environment. When such equilibrium is not balanced, a tension arises that leads to locomotion in the attempt to restore equilibrium. Lewin's model of human behavior involves the continual appearance of tensions, locomotions & reliefs. This sequence of tension-locomotion-equilibrium is akin to need-activity-relief. Whenever the need is felt, a state of tension exists, & the organism acts in order to release the tension by restoring the equilibrium. Lewin's theoretical system generated a great deal of important & influential research. A series of studies were conducted involving

Lewin's assumption of a tension system. Tension in this case was similar to motivation or need. In one of the tests subjects were given a series of tasks & were allowed to complete some of them, but were interrupted prior to their completion of others. The predictions derived from such system are that: 1 a tension system develops in a subject when he is given a task to perform, 2 if the task is completed, the tension is reduced, 3 if the task is not completed, the persistence of the tension results in greater likelihood of recall of the task.

In the beginning of his career, Lewin was mainly concerned with theoretical problems & issues, but later he became very interested in social psychology & his outstanding efforts in this field alone are sufficient to justify his position in the history of psychology.

One of the most important features of Lewin's social psychology is called "group dynamics." It is the application of concepts dealing with the individual & group behavior. Just as the individual & his environment form a psychological field, the group & its environment form asocial field. Social behaviors are seen as occurring in, & resulting from simultaneously existing social entities, such as subgroup members, barriers & channels of communication. According to Lewin group behavior is a function of the total field situation existing at a given time.

Lewin's social-psychological research was concerned with behavior in various kinds of social climates. He also stressed the importance of social action research which involved the study of relevant social problems with a view to introducing change. Lewin was very concerned with racial conflicts & conducted studies in the community on the effects of integrated housing on prejudice, on equalizing opportunity for employment & on the development & prevention of prejudice in children. An important contribution to social psychology is his founding of the society for the psychological study of social issues, which fosters research oriented toward the solution of social problems.

Lewin's experimental programs & research findings turned out to be more useful than his theoretical views. His views & concerns are being extended & elaborated very actively in psychology today.

Gestalt psychology has been criticized on many different levels including the basis of its physiological assumptions regarding isomorphism. Its opponents maintained that the isomorphic principle of map in the brain relating to what one received was a unique speculative explanation with a quite questionable proof. Such speculation was especially damaging to the validity & acceptability of the experimental results.

The complexity of the Gestalt theory was often used by its opponents to point out its metaphysical nature. It has been also postulated that Gestalt movement isn't new at all & that its principles have been discovered & used long time ago. Critics have said that Gestalt psychologists were conducting poorly controlled, non-statistical experiments, since they were dependent upon introspection, a method that was difficult to replicate. Gestalt opponents have charged them to provide subject's unnecessary cues in experimental situation that have affected their problem solution ability, making the result biased one. In addition to that Gestalt psychology has failed to define organization: its key term. The term "organization" was never properly distinguished from non organization.

Overall Gestalt psychology was too dependent upon theory at the same time lacking the sufficient evidences to support the theory. In many cases Gestalt psychologists have failed to empirically define their main concepts, focusing on theoretical aspects of it alone.

On the whole Gestalt psychology as a system made several important contributions to modern psychology, for example its unique researches & experimentations in the field of perception.

Humanistic movement

Humanistic thinking emerged during the Renaissance in Europe. It held that art, laws, government & traditions must be measured in terms of their effect on people. Later in the U.S. a type of humanism called "transcendental humanism" developed from a literary movement in the nineteenth century exemplified by Waldo Emerson & Henry David Thoreau. This movement held that important truths develop from intuition rather than from objective evidence.

Psychoanalytic movement was the first to raise the question of the study of motivation & personality structure. It enriched the psychology with many important discoveries. But psychoanalytic approach ignored the study of such important characteristics as the qualitative features of the personality of each person, the ability to consciously & purposefully develop certain aspects of the "self-image" & so on. Scientists of the time were puzzled by the idea that the process of personal development ends in childhood, whereas the experimental data showed that the formation of personality occurs throughout life. Psychoanalysis was no longer satisfactory, as well as the approach to the study of personality, developed by behavioral trends. The scientists who developed this approach for some reason ignored questions of intrinsic motivation, personal experiences, as well as the study of those innate qualities, which were imprinted in the behavior. The shortcomings of traditional psychological trends led to the emergence of new psychological school, known as humanistic psychology. Humanistic trend, which appeared in the U.S. in the 40-s, was based on the philosophical school of existentialism.

Humanistic psychology as an established discipline began in the 1950s & formally came into being in the 1960s as a protest against the presumed unconscious forces that determine behavior according to psychoanalysis & against the presumed environmental forces that determine behavior according to behaviorism. Humanists called themselves "The Third Force." Its followers attempted to move away from the mechanistic conditioning of the behaviorists & from the deterministic instincts of psychoanalysis. They also negate the research methodologies & statistics that psychology had borrowed from the physical sciences. In their opinion laboratory experiments with rigorous controls & quantification of results missed what was important in human activity. Thus, experience & meaning rather than behavior must be the primary data of psychology. They also held that the study of so called lower animals, like rats will not lead to a full understanding of humans, since human beings make free choices & are not governed by reinforcements or unconscious forces. In making choices each individual has the responsibility to develop a set of values that will serve as a guide to finding meaningful life. Such an achievement in humanistic psychology is called self-actualization.

The development of humanistic psychology contributed to the situation that prevailed in the society after the Second World War. If the First World War demonstrated the unconscious cruelty & aggression of a man & shaky foundations of humanism, the Second World War introduced new aspects of the human psyche. It demonstrated that many people in extreme situations show resistance & preserve dignity in the most difficult situations. These facts, as well as data from individual psychology in the 30-50-s, have shown limited approach to the man, explaining the development of his motivations, his personal qualities solely by the desire to adapt. Man's desire to preserve & develop his spiritual uniqueness could no longer be explained in terms of the old psychology. While conventional psychology was concerned with rigorous experimental design humanistic psychology was problem centered. It maintained that conventional psychology lost the individual in a mass of statistics.

The principles of humanistic psychology

Gordon Allport's theory

Gordon Allport (1897-1967) is one of the founders of humanistic psychology, which he viewed as an alternative to mechanism of the behavioral approach & the biological, instinctual psychoanalytic approach. Allport objected to transfer of symptoms experienced by sick people, neurotics, on the psyche of a healthy person. Although he began his career as a psychotherapist, Allport very quickly moved away from medical practice, focusing on experimental studies of healthy people. He also considered it necessary not merely to collect & describe the observed facts, as was the case in behaviorism, but to systematize & explain them.

  Allport was born in Montezuma, Indiana, in 1897. His father was a country doctor, which meant that Gordon grew up with his father's patients and nurses and all the paraphernalia of a miniature hospital. Everyone worked hard. When he was 22 he traveled to Vienna to meet Sigmund Freud. Allport received his Ph.D. in Psychology in 1922 from Harvard. His career was spent developing his theory, examining such social issues as prejudice. Allport developed number of personality tests as well. He died in Cambridge Massachusetts in 1967.

In Western theoretical trends such as humanistic, factoral & structuralistic the conception of personality & its activeness at first glance appears to be diametrically opposed to the psychoanalytic tradition. In contrast to the psychoanalysis who seek the source of activeness in the subject's past & focus on child's early impressions & experiences displaced to the unconscious, humanistic psychology & other trends holding similar views see the main factor of personalities activeness in orientation towards the future, aspiration for the maximum possible self-actualization. Gordon Allport, one of the pioneers of humanistic psychology, like many investigators in the discipline, commended on the virtual impossibility of defining personality in precise terms. After reviewing definitions offered by theologians, philosophers, sociologists & psychologists, Allport presented his own version in his first book defining it simply "what man really is," but it was too brief, so he offered a more precise one; "the dynamic organization within the individual of those psychophysical systems that determine his characteristic behavior & thought."

Allport's systematic views on personality span a period of over thirty years. During this time he has been guided by two basic principles: To do justice to the complexity of personality compounded as it is of hereditary, temperamental, social & psychological factors; & to recognize the uniqueness of each individual personality. Allport's goal was to develop psychology of personality which recognizes the value of the nomothetic approach, especially in regard to the problem of the foundations of personality & its quantitative measurement, but eventually he recognized both the generalized nature of traits, in the sense that many traits in common by all adult members of a given culture, but at the same time provided for an individual functional autonomy in the actual operation of traits in a given personality.

Eventually Allport became less concerned with the traits & more elemental aspects of personality dynamics & increasingly interested in the foundations of personalistic psychology as a science. His choices for his papers on the nature of personality, as well as "Becoming" lean heavily in the direction of exploring the foundations of personality theory & at the same time show an increasing emphasis on the uniqueness of personality & what might be called "ego psychology."

Allport characterizes his definition of personality as a synthesis of contemporary definitions. By "dynamic organization" he means that personality is a developing, changing organization which reflects motivational conditions. By stressing an active organization, Allport avoids so called "sterile enumerations of the omnibus definitions." "Psychophysical" as Allport uses the phrase, refers to habits & traits. The choice of the term "psychophysical" is recognition of the fact that both mental & bodily factors must be taken into consideration in the description & study of personality. The inclusion of the term "determine" is a natural consequence of Allport's psychophysical point of view. The psychophysical systems that constitute personality are so called "determining tendencies" which, when set into motion by appropriate stimuli, give rise to those behavioral acts through which we come to know personality.

In Allport's theory, there are two types of functionally autonomous systems- perseverative & the propriate. Perseverative functional autonomy refers to physiologically based motivational systems which, once activated, can continue to function for a time without further environmental stimulation, which means that the process of habituation creates regular intervals of activeness & restlessness. Propriate functional autonomy higher order processes, such as interests, attitudes & the life style. In Allport's view interests tend to follow abilities, with people tending to do what they can do best. Such interests are functionally autonomous when the present reason for exercising the ability is no longer related to the original reason except in a historical sense.

Allport is in direct opposition to the psychoanalytic view of personality dynamics in which all present behavior must be traced to its genetic origins. According to Allport present motives are continuous with original motives, just as new is related to the old. He also separates his system from earlier instinct psychologies, such as McDougall's. Instincts may appear in the course of development, but once having appeared, are transformed under the influence of learning. The principle of functional autonomy is also in opposition to the behaviorist's theory of acquired drives.

Allport's concept of functional autonomy is also in opposition of homeostasis, since once a motive becomes functionally autonomous it is self-sustaining, whereas homeostasis implies the cyclic appearance of motivation dependent upon changes in psychological rhythms.

Allport favors the trait as the most valid concept for the description of personality. A trait is a neuropsychic structure that has the capacity to render many stimuli functionally equivalent, & initiate & guide equivalent forms of adaptive & expressive behavior. Allport's definition further implies that traits are consistent modes of behavior which are similar to habits but are more generalized. In principle, traits are more like attitudes than habits, since they are mainly determining tendencies rather than specific modes of behavior. Allport presents two types of traits; individual & common. In a sense every trait is an individual trait, since each personality is different from every other. However, such a view of traits, if taken quite literally, would make cross-comparisons between individuals impossible. Indeed, if such conditions prevailed there could be no science of personality. Since the members of a given culture are subject to common evolutionary & social influences, there many aspects of behavior on which members of a given culture can be compared. These are common traits.

Allport also recognizes cardinal, central & secondary traits. A trait which is dominant, outstanding & all-pervasive in the individual's life is a cardinal trait. Central traits are foci of personality, ordinarily measured by rating scales, mentioned in conversation, & described in letters of recommendation. Secondary traits are the less important or minor traits which usually escape notice except by the careful observer or close acquaintance. In some individuals a trait may be of such central importance as to be the dominant factor in life. For the most part the humanistic psychology is concerned with central traits which are the foundation of personality, & to a minor extent with secondary traits.

In Allport's theory the proprium corresponds to the traditional psychology terms like "self" & "ego." The proprium includes the bodily sense; self-identity, or the awareness of the continuity of self; ego enhancement; ego extension, or the identification of external objects with the self; rational & cognitive functions; the self image; & propriate striving, which is the most important in Allport's system. Accordingly propriate striving refers to that motivated behavior which is of central importance to the self as opposed to behavior which is peripheral to the self. Examples of propriate striving include all forms of behavior that serve self-realization. Propriate striving also represents growth motivation as opposed to deficiency motivation.

Man seeks new horizons & the freedom to explore, as well as relief from the irritations attendant upon deficiencies. Allport maintains that the essence of personality is the individual's way of living. The self eventually becomes the integration of the propriate functions that make up the unified style of life.

Allport characterizes Freud's theory of personality as a "strata" theory, because of its emphasis on the three levels of consciousness & the division of the personality into id, ego & superego. He believed that Freud developed too passive an ego theory, allowing too little room for self-determination. He also characterizes psychoanalytic theory as descriptive of neurotic as opposed to healthy personalities.

Allport demonstrates his individualism & humanism in maintaining that psychology cannot sever all links with philosophy. He believes that a purely psychological of the individual neglects the broader problem of human nature & man's place in cosmos.

Abraham Maslow's theory

Another follower of humanistic psychology Abraham Maslow (1908-1976) builds his theory of self-actualization by assuming that in each person there is an intrinsic nature that is good or neutral. He was born in Brooklyn, New York to a family of Jewish immigrants from Russia. Maslow was the eldest sibling in the family, & the family's culture expected him to care for his six brothers and sisters. Determined to succeed he turned to books. Maslow found himself immersed in the works of Freud, Jung, Pavlov and others. Psychology became his passion.

Maslow received his B.A. in psychology from the University of Wisconsin (1930). His thirst for knowledge, egged on by mentors such as Harry Harlow, led him to complete his Masters (in 1931) and later his doctorate (in 1934) in the same field. In Wisconsin Maslow became closely associated with Harlow's experiments on primates. He had himself pursued an independent line of research on primate dominance behavior and published a few papers. The papers produced by him from 1937 onwards manifest Maslow's shift towards social behavior, personality traits, self-esteem, and motivation theory.

Maslow moved to Brooklyn & began teaching psychology at Brooklyn College. In 1937 he published number of valuable works. Five years later his paper titled "A Theory of Human Motivation" was published in the Psychological Review. He also wrote "'Higher' and 'lower' needs", "Our maligned animal nature", "Resistance to acculturation", "The S-I Test (A measure of psychological security-insecurity)" & many more. Although Maslow borrowed ideas from other psychologists, the ideas, theories, postulates and insights that he built upon them were very original. He eventually became the leader of the humanistic school of psychology, which he referred to as the "third force".

In 1951, Abraham Maslow transferred to Waltham, Massachusetts-based Brandeis University, to serve as Chairman of the psychology department. He held this position till 1969. Washington, D.C.-based American Psychological Association elected him President for the year 1968. In 1969 Abraham Maslow accepted the resident fellowship of the Laughlin Foundation. He died of heart attack on June 8-Th 1970.

Maslow thought that healthy development is likely, only in a society that offers all necessary raw materials & then gets out of the way & stands aside to let the organism itself utter its wishes & make its choices. If the environment is restrictive & minimizes personal choice, the individual will develop in neurotic ways.

The main goal of Maslow's humanistic biology is to establish a scientific ethics, a natural value system for the determination of good & bad. In his opinion such an ethic is able to overcome the relativism inherent in traditional appeals to moral authority & provide a set of ideals that serves as a guide for human conduct.

Maslow recognizes two main groups of needs that are rooted in their biology. The first group is called deficiency or basic needs & the second; growth or Meta needs. According to Maslow basic human needs are more urgent than the growth needs. The Meta needs on the other hand are equally powerful & can be easily substituted one for another. In a way basic needs can be interpreted as psychological needs, for example love & safety needs. Maslow is convinced that the reconditions necessary to satisfy these needs are the freedom to speak, freedom to investigate & seek for information, the freedom to express oneself, justice, honesty & orderliness in the group. The lack of these freedoms, supposedly make the satisfaction of basic needs impossible. People deprived of physiological needs, such as sex tend to focus more & more of their attention on that deficiency. When such need is not satisfied, people give up their needs for love, safety; people give up their other needs for love, safety, esteem & belongingness, giving up their dream of self-actualization. Once people's physiological needs are satisfied, a set of safety needs emerges, including needs for security, protection, law, order, limits & freedom from fear. In Maslow's theory needs for safety is reflected in child's reference for an environment in which caregivers dispense reinforcement in a systematic & consistent manner. Adult's needs for safety are more subtle & difficult to detect.

According to Maslow the basic need for love is a selfish concern with seeking love from others. He termed it deficiency love (d-love). When this need is gratified, we supposedly become capable of loving others. Maslow called this being love (b-love), to distinguish it from the lower need to be loved. Being love, also known as mature love, becomes possible when the basic needs have been sufficiently gratified & the person is moving toward self-actualization. Esteem needs that the last of basic urges to emerge in Maslow's theory are divided into two groups; esteem based on respect for our own competence, independence, & accomplishments, & esteem based on others' evaluations. Esteem needs of the second group are best seen in striving for recognition from others & in attempts to secure status.

Man often seeks to find the destiny within him & strives toward the realization of his potentials. In majority of cases self-actualizing person is governed by growth needs such as striving for goodness by being altruistic & helpful to others. According to Maslow people fear their best side & talents. He called this fear Jonah complex. In women this fear emerges as a reluctance to make full use of their intellectual abilities, because achievement is considered in Maslow's theory to be unfeminine.

On the other hand the motives underlying men's fear of success differ, because success is considered gender-appropriate behavior for males, & does not bring with it a loss in masculinity or social rejection. Maslow thinks that man's fear of success may reflect a wish to avoid the responsibilities that continued success brings.

Maslow also maintained that poor socialization practices contribute to so called "desacralizing" attitude among young people, assuming that such an attitude emerges because many adolescents have parents whom they do not respect. As a result, the children despite their parents who never punish them or stop them from doing things that are wrong. Concluding that all grown-ups are like their parents, children eventually lose their respect for adults, becoming cynical & mistrustful. Thus Maslow finds that self-actualization is possible for such people only when they learn to "resacralize" their lives.

The complex process of actualization greatly depends upon good environmental conditions, including a socialization process that fosters equality & trust between people. The self-actualizing people claim that their parents more often used an authoritative disciplinary style to facilitate the personal growth. Such authoritative parenting style involves parental respect for their children, & consistent & firm discipline of them without resorting to physical or verbal abuse. According to Maslow parental firmness can be moderated by warmth, reason & flexibility.

The positive growth takes place in conditions where good socialization & willingness to take risks are present. Individuals begin to exist more & more in so called b-cognition state. In Maslow's theory d-cognition experiences include judging, condemning, & approving & disapproving people. Although self-actualizing people are more capable than ordinary people of b-cognizing, they cannot live in this state continuously, because continual existence in such a passive state would prove fatal.

Maslow called his theory of personal development universal, because in it individual must satisfy, the lower needs before higher ones can become operative. Environments that threaten the individual & hinder the satisfaction of basic needs are detrimental to growth. On contrary environments that support & gratify these needs promote growth toward self- actualization. Maslow held that environment can play an important role in the early stages of development when people are struggling to gratify basic needs. Such needs depend on cooperation of other people for cooperation of other people for gratification. When the higher needs emerge, people become less dependent on the environment & on rewards or approval of others.

Maslow used many different techniques in order to identify self-actualizing individuals. Among them was a selection technique named iteration. He collated his general belief concerning the meaning of self-actualization with other popular definitions & by gradually eliminating logical inconsistencies, arrived at a common definition. Using this definition, he divided a group of 3000 students into actualizers & nonactualizers. In the end Maslow's assessment procedures were fraught with ambiguities & imprecisions.

Carl Roger's theory

Another humanist psychologist Carl Rogers (1902-1987) based his psychology mainly on the analysis of subjective experiences of the individual. He was born in Oak Park, Illinois, a suburb of Chicago. His education started in the second grade, because he could already read before kindergarten. His first career choice was agriculture (University of Wisconsin, Madison) followed by history and then religion. At age 20 he started to doubt his religious convictions. Rogers switched to the clinical psychology program of Columbia University, and received his Ph.D. in 1931. He had already begun his clinical work at the Rochester Society for the Prevention of Cruelty to Children. At this clinic, he learned about Otto Rank's theory and therapy techniques, which started him on the road to developing his own approach.

In 1940 he was offered a full professorship at Ohio State. In 1942, he wrote his first book, Counseling and Psychotherapy. Three years later in he was invited to set up a counseling center at the University of Chicago, where published his major work, Client-Centered Therapy, wherein he outlines his basic theory.

Rogers returned to teach at the University of Wisconsin in 1957. In 1964, he was happy to accept a research position in La Jolla, California. He provided therapy, gave speeches, and wrote, until his death in 1987.

The subjective experiencing of reality serves as the basis for all of the individual's behavior. In Roger's opinion it is this subjective inner reality that determines the person's behavior. Inner experience in a sense is used to describe all of the events that occur within the organism at a particular moment. All this experience, conscious & unconscious makes up the person's phenomenal field. Conscious experience is the aspect of phenomenal field that can be symbolized, verbalized & imagined. On the other hand unconscious experience cannot be verbalized or imagined by the person. Therefore healthy individuals are those who can symbolize them & sense them fully.

According to Rogers self-actualizing tendency is an active drive toward fulfillment of potentials. He eased this concept on his varied & prolonged experience with troubled individuals. People constantly seek new experiences & avoid environments that lack stimulation. Rogers concludes that the actualizing tendency has both a biological & psychological aspect. The biological aspect includes drives aimed at the satisfaction of basic survival needs. The psychological aspect involves developing potentials that make us more worthwhile human beings. The actualizing tendency is thus selective, constructive & directional. Roger's view of human nature is overall optimistic, but he also held that human beings at times are immature & anti social, acting out of fear, ignorance & defensiveness. Such behavior is not in accordance with basic human nature, but is the result of wrong socialization practices.

Rogers held that infants receive their experiences as reality, interacting with their reality in terms of their basic actualizing tendency. Infants' behavior is directed toward satisfying their needs for self-actualization. In Rogers opinion infants are believed to engage in an organismic valuing process, during which they supposedly use their actualizing tendency as a criterion in judging the worth of a given experience. Unlike in infants, in adults valuing process is more complex, since adults tend to make complicated judgments about various issues. In this process two types of judgments arise, first; value judgments with tendency to change & second; judgments about friends, parents & acquaintances, which usually remain constant, but under certain circumstances may change as well.

The personal growth & will toward realizing potentials can be obtained through organismic valuing process. Rogers uses the term fully functioning to define people that fully realize their potentials. In his opinion such individuals have unique characteristics, like their creative nature, ability to live good lives, the openness to new experiences & so on. Eventually Rogers extended & amplified his view of the fully functioning person & applied it to what he called emerging person. He thought of them as honest, open, caring people indifferent to material goods. Rogers further held that emerging people are a small minority of the total population, but he believed that they are having an impact on society out of proportion to their numbers & will continue to exert significant influence in the future.

In Rogers' theory the social self is the organized set of characteristics that the individual perceives as being peculiar to him or herself. The social self is primarily acquired through contact with others. When people interact with significant people in their environment, they begin to develop a concept of self that is mainly based on the evaluations of others. Such people evaluate themselves in terms of what others think & not in terms of what they actually feel. The reason why people rely on the evaluation of others is that they have a strong need for positive regard. According to Rogers when we satisfy others needs, we satisfy our own need for positive regard. As a result, the desire for positive regard from others may be more compelling than our own organismic valuing process. People perceive experiences & behaviors as acceptable only if they meet with approval from others.

Rogers saw the ideal condition for developing a healthy self-concept & moving toward full functioning is in unconditional positive regard, which is a deep & genuine caring by others, uncontaminated by judgments or evaluations of human thoughts, or behaviors. With unconditional positive regard, the self-concept carries no conditions of worth, congruence exists between the true self & experience, & the person is psychologically healthy. All people have conditions of worth placed on their behavior & in the process of socialization they learn that some of their feelings are appropriate & others are not. When these normative rules are congruent with people's organismic evaluations, they get in touch with their true self & continue their movement toward self-actualization. In such conditions social selves & true selves are in harmony. Parents can establish creativity fostering environments, with rules that encourage children to be curious, self-reliant, & respectful. When people are guided by the expectations of others that run counter to their innate evaluations, problems occur. Congruence between the self & organismic experiencing leads to accurate symbolizing of experiences & positive growth; incongruence leads to inaccurate or distorted symbolization, psychological maladjustment, & vulnerability.

Rogers' self theory also suggests that self-accepting people should be more accepting of the behavior of others. If Rogers' theory about the relationship between the self & organismic experiencing is valid, it would mean that people who deny threats of their self-picture are more maladjusted than those who are non-defensive.

The members of humanistic movement are highly critical of continued reliance on the behavioristic approach to the study of man with its mechanistic, reductionistic & simplistic tendencies. However, they are also highly critical of the psychoanalytic approach. For example, Maslow has criticized Freud for studying only disturbed individuals. By focusing only on mental illness, Maslow asked, how can psychology ever know anything of man's positive qualities & characteristics? Humanists state that psychology has disregarded such attributes as kindness & generosity because it has focused only on the dark side of man, ignoring his great strengths & positive virtues.

It is against this incomplete psychology- the restricted, ahuman & sterile psychology put forth by both behaviorism & psychoanalysis- that Maslow & others propose an alternative- a new movement in psychology, a third movement.

Humanistic psychology desperately hopes to be a fresh orientation- a new framework of attitude toward psychology, rather than a new psychology per se. Its' followers insist that they do not wish it to be a new school of thought or a specific content area, but rather an attempt to reshape & supplement the existing form of psychology.

It is easier to state with clarity what humanistic psychology is against than to describe what they are for & how they hope to achieve their goals. Humanistic psychology seems to reflecting the kind of unrest & dissatisfaction currently being voiced against the mechanistic aspects of contemporary culture. Humanistic psychologists imply that behaviorism is antihuman, resisting the conception of man as an animal functioning mechanically & deterministically in response to his environment or his early years of experience.

Albert Ellis' Theory

Albert Ellis (1913-207) was an American psychologist who was best known for developing rational emotive behavior therapy (REBT). He is considered to be one of the originators of the cognitive revolutionary paradigm shift in psychotherapy & the founder of cognitive-behavioral therapies.

Albert Ellis was born in Pittsburgh, but he grew up in New York City. In 1934 he received a degree in business administration from the City University of New York. His first venture in the business world was a pants-matching business he started with his brother. In 1938, he became the personnel manager for a gift & novelty firm. Ellis spent most of his time writing short stories, plays, novels, comic poetry, essays & nonfiction books. By the time he was 28, he had finished almost two dozen full-length manuscripts, but had not been able to get them published.

In 1942 he returned to school, entering the clinical-psychology program at Columbia. He started a part-time private practice in family & sex counseling soon after he received his master's degree. In the late 1940s he taught at Rutgers & New York University, & was the senior clinical psychologist at the Northern New Jersey Mental Hygiene Clinic. He also became the chief psychologist at the New Jersey Diagnostic Center and then at the New Jersey Department of Institutions & Agencies.

By 1955 Ellis had given up psychoanalysis entirely, and instead was concentrating on changing people's behavior by confronting them with their irrational beliefs & persuading them to adopt rational ones. He published his first book on REBT called "How to Live with a Neurotic" in 1957. Two years later he organized the Institute for Rational Living, where he held workshops to teach his principles to other therapists. The Art and Science of Love, his first really successful book, appeared in 1960, and he has now published 54 books and over 600 articles on REBT, sex & marriage.

His REBT begins with ABC, in which A is for activating experiences, such as family troubles, unsatisfying work, early childhood traumas, & all the many things we point to as the sources of our unhappiness. B stands for beliefs, especially the irrational, self-defeating beliefs that are the actual sources of our unhappiness. And C is for consequences, the neurotic symptoms & negative emotions such as depression panic, & rage, that come from our beliefs. Ellis further adds D & E to ABC: The therapist must dispute (D) the irrational beliefs, in order for the client to ultimately enjoy the positive psychological effects (E) of rational beliefs. These beliefs take the form of absolute statements. Instead of acknowledging a preference or a desire, we make unqualified demands on others, or convince ourselves that we have overwhelming needs. There are a number of typical "thinking errors" people typically engage in, like ignoring the positive, exaggerating the negative & overgeneralizing.

Ellis also distinguished twelve irrational ideas that he believed cause & sustain neurosis. 1. The idea that it is a dire necessity for adults to be loved by significant others for almost everything they do -- instead of their concentrating on their own self-respect, on winning approval for practical purposes, & on loving rather than on being loved. 2. The idea that certain acts are awful or wicked, & that people who perform such acts, should be severely damned -- instead of the idea that certain acts are self-defeating or antisocial, & that people who perform such acts are behaving stupidly, ignorantly, or neurotically, & would be better helped to change. People's poor behaviors do not make them rotten individuals. 3.The idea that it is horrible when things are not the way we like them to be -- instead of the idea that it is too bad, that we would better try to change or control bad conditions so that they become more satisfactory, &, if that is not possible, we had better temporarily accept and gracefully lump their existence. 4. The idea that human misery is invariably externally caused & is forced on us by outside people and events -- instead of the idea that neurosis is largely caused by the view that we take of unfortunate conditions. 5. The idea that if something is or may be dangerous or fearsome we should be terribly upset & endlessly obsess about it -- instead of the idea that one would better frankly face it & render it non-dangerous and, when that is not possible, accept the inevitable. 6. The idea that it is easier to avoid than to face life difficulties and self-responsibilities -- instead of the idea that the so-called easy way is usually much harder in the long run. 7. The idea that we absolutely need something other or stronger or greater than ourselves on which to rely -- instead of the idea that it is better to take the risks of thinking. 8. The idea that we should be thoroughly competent, intelligent, & achieving in all possible respects -- instead of the idea that we would better do rather than always need to do well & accept ourselves as a quite imperfect creature, who has general human limitations & specific fallibilities. 9. The idea that because something once strongly affected our life, it should indefinitely affect it -- instead of the idea that we can learn from our past experiences but not be overly-attached to or prejudiced by them. 10. The idea that we must have certain and perfect control over things -- instead of the idea that the world is full of probability &chance & that we can still enjoy life despite this. 11. The idea that human happiness can be achieved by inertia & inaction -- instead of the idea that we tend to be happiest when we are vitally absorbed in creative pursuits, or when we are devoting ourselves to people or projects outside ourselves. 12. The idea that we have virtually no control over our emotions & that we cannot help feeling disturbed about things -- instead of the idea that we have real control over our destructive emotions if we choose to work at changing the masturbatory hypotheses which we often employ to create them.

Ellis maintained that religious restrictions on sexual expression are often harmful to emotional health. He also famously debated religious psychologists over the proposition that religion often contributed to psychological distress. Because of his forthright espousal of a nontheistic humanism, he was recognized in 1971 as Humanist of the Year by the American Humanist Association. Ellis was careful to state that REBT was independent of his atheism, noting that many skilled REBT practitioners are religious, including some who are ordained ministers. In his later days he significantly toned down & re-evaluated his opposition to religion. While Ellis maintained his firm atheistic stance, proposing that thoughtful, probabilistic atheism was likely the most emotionally healthy approach to life, he acknowledged & agreed with survey evidence suggesting that belief in a loving god can also be healthy.

In developing methods of psychotherapy & correction of deviations in personality development, all the representatives of humanistic psychology argued that each individual focuses on his "I" & that every attack on his "I" was considered as an attack on its existence. Supposedly this property

310

was common in humans & other living beings. In exploring the possibility of correcting behavior, representatives of humanistic psychology were guided by means of people developing awareness of their responsibility for their behavior, which in turn, was based on person's self-awareness of & his place in the world. Therefore, humanists' correction techniques differed significantly from those offered by psychoanalysts & behaviorists.

As we evaluate humanistic theories of personality, we should note that their developers for the first time closely studied not only the deviation, the difficulties & negative aspects of human behavior, but also the positive aspects of personal development. Humanists studied the achievements of personal experience & uncovered mechanisms of formation of personality & the way to its self-development & self-improvement.

Other Theories

William Stern's Theory

German psychologist William Stern (1871-1938) was educated at the University of Berlin, where he studied with Ebbinghaus. He was born in Berlin to a Jewish family. William Stern's grandfather was the German-Jewish reform philosopher Sigismund Stern. After receiving his doctorate, William was offered a position by the University of Breslau, where he worked as a professor of psychology until 1916. Stern also founded the Institute of Applied Psychology (1906) & simultaneously began publication of the Journal of Applied Psychology. In 1916 he was appointed Professor of Psychology at University of Hamburg, where he remained until 1933 as Director of the Psychological Institute. Stern left Nazi Germany & emigrated first to the Netherlands, then to the United States in 1933, where he became a Lecturer & Professor at Duke University. He taught at Duke until his death in 1938.

Stern was one of the founders of differential psychology. He argued that there exists not only common to all children normative, but also an individual normative that characterized a particular child. Among the most important properties of the individual Stern noted the rate of mental development, which was manifested in the speed of learning. He was convinced that violations of the individual's pace could lead to serious abnormalities, including neuroses. Stern was also one of the initiators of the pilot study of children & testing. Stern maintained that the potential of the child at birth was uncertain enough since he is not aware of himself & his inclinations. The environment helped the child to understand himself & organize his inner world, giving it a clear, conscious design & structure. The child tried to take everything from the environment, which corresponded to a potential disposition, the barriers to the influences that were contrary to his inner inclinations. The conflict between the external & the internal tendencies of the child had a positive significance, for it was the negative emotion that caused disparity in children, & served as a stimulus for the development of self-consciousness. Frustration made the child to look inside & into his surrounding in order to understand exactly what he needed for a good self-awareness. Thus, Stern argued that the emotions associated with environmental assessment, helped the process of socialization & the development of reflection.

In Stern's theory the integrity of the development was manifested not only in the fact that emotions & thinking were closely linked, but that the direction of development of all mental processes was the same. So first you have children develop contemplation (perception), then the representation (memory), & then thinking. He also believed that during the development of speech the child made a significant discovery; opened up important words & revealed that each item had its own name.

Stern was one of the first psychologists who was studying & analyzing the interest levels in children & child personality. The study of the whole person, the laws of its formation was the main objective of his theory called "personalism." This was especially important in the beginning of the century, as the study of child development at that time were limited mainly to the study of cognitive processes. Stern also paid attention to these issues, exploring the stages of development thinking & speech. However, he sought to explore not an isolated development of individual cognitive processes, forming a coherent structure, personalities of the child. Stern viewed personality as a self-determining unit, consciously & purposefully acting integrity, possessing a certain depth. By depth he meant conscious & unconscious layers. He held that psychological development was directed & determined by the environment in which the child lived. This theory was called the convergence theory, because it took into account the role of two factors in mental development; heredity & environment. The influence of these two factors Stern analyzed by some of the major activities of children, mostly games. He first identified the content & form of the game, arguing that the form was unchanged & was associated with innate qualities. He maintained that the game was not just for the exercise of instinct, but also for the socialization of children.

According to Stern development was a growth, differentiation & transformation of mental structures. He understood development (just like Gestaltists) as a transition from vague & indistinct images to more clear, structured & distinct gestalt of the world. This transition to a more clear & adequate reflection of the surrounding was in turn comprised of several phases, characteristic for all of the major psychological processes. Thus mental development was a tendency not only for self-development, but also for self-preservation, i.e. to preserve the inherent characteristics of each individual, especially the individual rate of development.

Thus, we can say without exaggeration that William Stern has affected virtually all areas of child psychology as well as the attitudes of many psychologists involved in child mental health studies.

Henry Murray's Personology

Henry Murray (1893-1988) was born in New York. His family was quite wealthy, so he entered Harvard to study history. Murray was a poor student but a good athlete. After Harvard he enrolled in Columbia College where he studied medicine. Apparently Murray was more interested in medicine; in 1919 he received his M.D. & also an M.A. in biology. For the next two years he was an instructor in physiology at Harvard. Murray received his doctorate degree in biochemistry at Cambridge, in 1927. The same year, he became assistant director of the Harvard Psychological Clinic.

Although Murray was trained in biochemistry, he eventually turned to psychology. He attributes this shift to his personal contact with Jung. When the World War II began, Murray left Harvard to work as lieutenant colonel for the U.S. Office of Strategic Services. He also acted as a consultant for the British Government in the setting up of the Officer Selection Board. Murray's extensive experience at the Harvard Psychological Clinic helped him to apply his theories in the design of the selection processes. In 1943 Murray helped the analysis of the personality of Adolf Hitler. He concluded that if defeat for Germany was near, Hitler would commit suicide. He also said that Hitler was impotent as far as heterosexual relations were concerned & that there was a possibility that Hitler had participated in a homosexual relationship.

In 1947 Murray returned to Harvard to teach psychology. Later he founded the Psychological Clinic Annex. Towards the end of his career Murray was a chief researcher at Harvard. When Murray became emeritus professor at Harvard, he earned the Distinguished Scientific Contribution Award from the American Psychological Association & Gold Medal Award for lifetime achievement from the American Psychological Foundation.

Perhaps Murray's most distinctive contribution to psychology was his theory of motivation. He held that the full understanding of human motivation must rest upon a system that employs relatively large number of variables to reflect the tremendous complexity of motives. In addition he attempted to provide empirical definitions for his variables. The result of these efforts was a set of concepts that was designed to affiliate the demands of empirical research with clinical description. Murray was also the cofounder of the so called Thematic Appreciation Test (TAT).

Without a doubt, need was the main concept of Murray's motivational theory. He called need a force which organizes perception, apperception, intellection, connation & action in such a way as to transform in a certain direction an existing, unsatisfying situation. Murray was convinced that needs make the person to become active. He recognized twenty basic human needs;

1. Abasement- to accept injury, blame, punishment, criticism, to surrender, to become resigned to fate, to seek & enjoy punishment & so on.

2. Achievement- to accomplish something difficult, to master, manipulate, or organize physical objects, human beings, or ideas, to increase self-regard by the successful exercise of talent & so on.

3. Affiliation- to adhere & remain loyal to a friend, to please & win affection of a desired person & so on.

4. Aggression- to fight, to overcome opposition forcefully & so on.

5. Autonomy- to break free, to resist coercion & restriction, to defy convention & so on.

6. Counteraction- to obliterate humiliation by resumed action, to overcome weaknesses, to repress fear & so on.

7. Defendance- to defend the self against assault, criticism & blame, to vindicate the ego & so on.

8. Deference- to admire & support the superior, to praise honor or eulogize & so on.

9. Dominance- to influence or direct the behavior of others by suggestion, seduction, persuasion or command, to control one's environment & so on.

10. Exhibition- to make an impression, to be seen & heard, to excite, amaze & fascinate, to intrigue, shock, amuse & so on.

11. Harmavoidance- to avoid pain, physical injury, death, to take precautionary measures & so on.

12. Infavoidance- to refrain from action because of the fear of failure, to avoid humiliation & so on.

13. Nurturance- to give sympathy & gratify the needs of a helpless object, to assist an object in danger & so on.

14. Order- to put things in order, to achieve cleanliness, arrangement, organization, balance, neatness, precision & so on.

15. Play- to like to laugh & make jokes, to participate in games, sports, dancing & so on.

16. Rejection- to exclude abandon, expel or remain indifferent to an inferior object, to snob an object & so on.

17. Sentience- to seek & enjoy sensuous impressions & so on.

18. Sex- to form & further sexual relationship & so on.

19. Succorance- to be nursed, supported, sustained, surrounded, protected, loved, advised, guided & so on.

20. Understanding- to ask or answer general questions, to speculate, to formulate, to analyze & so on.

In Murray's theory needs are closely connected with various environmental events. He called these events "press." A Press, according to Murray, is a property or attribute of something or someone in the environment that facilitates or impedes a person's efforts to achieve a certain goal. Murray used the term "thema" to describe the correlation of need & press. However, Murray did not view the person's behavior as a product of unrelated themas. He described personality with the help of so called "unity thema," which was a single pattern of related needs & press that gave meaning to the largest portion of the person's behavior.

Jean Piaget's Developmental Theory

Jean Piaget (1896-1980) was born in Neuchâtel, Switzerland. He published his first "paper" when he was ten years old. He began publishing in earnest in high school on his favorite subject, mollusks. He worked part time at the Nuechâtel's Museum of Natural History. Eventually his work became well known among European students of mollusks. Studying various philosophers & the application of logic, he dedicated himself to finding a "biological explanation of knowledge."

First he attended the University of Neuchâtel. Constantly studying and writing, he became sickly, & had to retire to the mountains for a year to recuperate. When he returned to Neuchâtel, he decided he would write down his philosophy. In 1918, Piaget earned his Doctorate in Science from the University of Neuchâtel. He worked for a year at psychology labs in Zurich & at Bleuler's famous psychiatric clinic. During this period, he was introduced to the works of Freud, Jung, & others. One year later he taught psychology & philosophy at the Sorbonne in Paris. In 1921, his first article on the psychology of intelligence was published in the "Journal de Psychologie." In the same year, he accepted a position at the Institute of J. J. Rousseau in Geneva. Here he began with his students to research the reasoning of elementary school children. This research became his first five books on child psychology.

In 1929, Piaget began work as the director of the International Bureau of Education, a post he would hold until 1967. In 1940, he became chair of Experimental Psychology, the Director of the psychology laboratory, & the president of the Swiss Society of Psychology. In 1942, he gave a series of lectures at the Collège de France, during the Nazi occupation of France. These lectures became The Psychology of Intelligence. Also during this period, he received a number of honorary degrees. He received one from the Sorbonne in 1946, the University of Brussels & the University of Brazil in 1949, on top of an earlier one from Harvard in 1936. In 1952, he became a professor at the Sorbonne. In 1955, he created the International Center for Genetic Epistemology, of which he served as director the rest of his life. And, in 1956, he created the School of Sciences at the University of Geneva. He continued working on a general theory of structures and tying his psychological work to biology for many more years. By the end of his career, he had written over 60 books and many hundreds of articles.

During his researches Piaget noticed that infants had certain skills in regard to objects in their environment. These were certainly simple, sensor-motor skills but they directed the way in which the infant explored his or her environment. These skills, which Piaget called schemas, further controlled how they gained more knowledge of the world & more sophisticated exploratory skills. He proposed that children's thinking did not develop entirely smoothly: instead, there were certain points at which it "took off" & moved into completely new areas & capabilities. He saw these transitions as taking place at about 18 months, 7 years & 11 or 12 years. This has been taken to mean that before these ages children were not capable of understanding things in certain ways. Piaget also was known for proposing several new interpretations of the terms & ideas that were never used before in psychology. For example, Adaptation was a process of adapting to the world through assimilation & accommodation. Assimilation, in turn, was a process by which a people took material into their mind from the environment. Accommodation was the difference made to one's mind or concepts by the process of assimilation.

Classification was the ability to group objects together on the basis of common features. Class inclusion was the understanding, more advanced than simple classification, that some classes or sets of objects were also sub-sets of a larger class. Conservation was the realization that objects or sets of objects stayed the same even when they were changed about or made to look different.

Piaget further noted that there were periods where assimilation dominated, periods where accommodation dominated, & periods of relative equilibrium, & that these periods were similar among all the children he looked at in their nature and their timing. And so he developed the idea of stages of cognitive development.

1. Sensorimotor stage (birth - 2 years old) -- Child interacts with environment through physical actions. These interactions build the child's cognitive structures about the world & how it functions or responds. Object permanence is discovered.

2. Preoperational stage (ages 2-7) -- Child is not yet able to form abstract conceptions, must have hands-on experiences & visual representations in order to form basic conclusions. Experiences must occur repeatedly before the child grasps the cause and effect connection.

3. Concrete operations (ages 7-11) -- Child is developing considerable knowledge base from physical experiences. Child begins to draw on this knowledge base to make more sophisticated explanations & predictions. Still understands best when educational material refers to real life situations.

4. Formal operations (beginning at ages 11-15) -- Child's knowledge base & cognitive structures are much more similar to those of an adult. Ability for abstract thought increases markedly.

Piaget's theory held that people develop schemas (conceptual models) by either assimilating or accommodating new information. These concepts can be explained as fitting information in to existing schemas, & altering existing schemas in order to accommodate new information.

Piaget's proposed an interesting theory of morality was quite radical when his book, "The Moral Judgment of the Child," was published in 1932. He was among few scientists to use the philosophical criteria to define morality. Piaget also opposed the equation of cultural norms with moral norms. Piaget, drawing on Kantian theory, proposed that morality developed out of peer interaction & that it was autonomous from authority mandates. In his theory, peers were a key source of moral concepts such as reciprocity, justice & equality.

Piaget attributed different types of psychosocial processes to different forms of social relationships, introducing a fundamental distinction between different types of said relationships. Where there is constraint because one participant holds more power than the other the relationship is asymmetrical, &, importantly, the knowledge that can be acquired by the dominated participant takes on a fixed & inflexible form.

Kelly's Theory of Personal Constructs

George Kelly (1905-1967) was born on a farm near Perth, Kansas. After high school Kelly received a bachelor's degree in physics & mathematics from Park College, followed with a master's in sociology from the University of Kansas. Later he moved to Minnesota, where he taught public speaking to labor organizers & bankers. He moved to Sheldon, Iowa, where he taught and coached drama at a junior college. Kelly's graduate work was as varied as his earlier schooling, leading him to study at the Universities of Kansas, Minnesota, & Edinburgh (Scotland) before graduating with a Ph.D. in psychology from the University of Iowa in 1931. Kelly's later logical, propositional framing of the psychology of personal constructs, his use of dramaturgical procedures in therapy, & his iconoclastic intellectual style can be viewed as outgrowths of this diverse educational background. During the depression, he worked at Fort Hays Kansas State College, where he developed his theory and clinical techniques. During World War II, Kelly served as an aviation psychologist with the Navy.

Following the war, he taught briefly at the University of Maryland before being hired to direct the clinical psychology program at the Ohio State University, where he was to make his most important theoretical contributions. Kelly began to fashion a unique perspective that grounded human attempts at meaning making firmly in the social realm.

Kelly sees man as scientist whose major concern is to interpret his world. His theory contains no concept of learning, motivation, emotion, stimulus-response, ego or unconscious. Kelly proposes a concept of constructive alternativism, which states that all of us are able to change or replace our present interpretation of the events. According to this concept behavior is rarely predetermined, so people are always free to some extent to re-interpret their experiences. Kelly believed in the primacy of individuals as responsible agents who make their own choices. Certain thoughts & behavior are determined by other phenomena which represents a joint base of freedom & determinism. According to Kelly determinism & thoughts are inseparable. The behavioral theorists oppose Kelly's free choice of goals, arguing that latter is determined by previous experiences.

Kelly held that since people are inclined to use their own personalized view of reality to make judgments constructs cannot be objectively defined. In his opinion scientists & their theories rarely meet the criteria set by the conventional science.

When people build personal constructs they assemble the interpretation & meaning of events through the abstraction process. This process entails placing constructions upon their experiences. Eventually these constructions are used to deal with new information from the environment. Such interpretations are the part of reality since they determine how the person acts in a given situation. The constructs are the ways of organizing experience, which in turn are formed & used to deal with new experiences. In Kelly's theory construct is a way in which at least two elements are similar & contrast with third. Constructs are considered bipolar because they contain at least there elements.

Kelly finds the so called "core" constructs to be the most important in man's life. Core constructs are very resistant to change, unlike "peripheral" constructs. A primitive belief in God, for instance, is a core construct, whereas a belief in superiority & brilliance of a monarch is a peripheral construct, since it is reluctant to change. Kelly describes constructs as preemptive, constellatory & propositional. A construct that includes only its own elements & precludes from being part of other constructs is called a preemptive construct. For instance, a person may argue that all Marxists hate capitalists. A constellatory construct allows its elements to belong to other realms at the same time fixing their realm memberships. Once we identify persons or objects as members of a given category, we then attribute to them a cluster or constellation, of other characteristics or traits. The propositional construct is a whole whose elements are open to construction in every respect. For example any round object (among other things) can be considered to be a ball. Under this construct a ball can also be worn or small. Thus, propositional thinking is flexible. It allows a person to be open to new experiences. In Kelly's view, the person best equipped to deal with the environment is one who knows the circumstances under which propositional or preemptive thinking is appropriate.

Kelly finds it unjust that psychologists attribute motivations to their subjects that are different from their own motivations, since the most important thing about people, in his opinion, is their need to predict & control.

Kelly further organized his theory into a fundamental postulate & its eleven corollaries, according to which person's processes were psychologically channelized by the ways in which he anticipated events. By processes, Kelly meant human experiences, thoughts, feelings, behaviors & so on. All these things were determined by person's efforts to anticipate the world, other people & himself.

In Kelly's theory person's construction system varied as he successively construed the replication of events. So when things change people begin to adapt & reconstruct. Adopted new experiences alter person's future anticipations. The so called construction corollary consisted of Kelly's belief that a person anticipates events by construing their replications.

The individual corollary lays the groundwork for the study of individual differences. People anticipate events in different ways. They differ because they take different approaches to anticipation of the same event. It is safe to say that the construct systems people generate are idiosyncratic in many respects.

Another type of corollary called organization, states that each person characteristically evolves, for his convenience in anticipating events. People differ in their constructs in the way in which they organize them. The more significant constructs are called superordinate. The less important ones are called subordinate.

Kelly's dichotomy corollary suggests that human constructs are bipolar & consist of similarity & contrast ends. Kelly also held that much of the language as well as everyday thinking implies contrast that it does not explicitly state. Our understanding of people's constructs, thus, is enhanced by this assertion.

In proposing the choice corollary, Kelly thought that people make choices that will allow them to deal most effectively with ensuing events. People tend to chose alternatives designed to increase their confidence in their interpretations of the world. We are biologically predisposed to make the elaborative choice to take risk, to try out new constructs, so that we can increase our understanding.

The range corollary states that constructs also vary in their range of convenience. This means that a given construct has relevance for some constructs but not for others. Another important moment of construct's range of convenience is its permeability. A construct is permeable if it allows new elements to be construed within its framework. Construct systems are in a continual state of flux. Within these systems there are many subsystems that are inferentially incompatible with one another. However, our construct systems are not always mutually consistent & we may sometimes show behaviors that are inconsistent with our most recent experiences. According to Kelly this is the fragmentation corollary.

In Kelly's individuality corollary people who differ in their construction of events behave differently. On contrary in his commonality corollary those who interpret events similarly behave alike. This means that to the extent that one person employs a construction of experience which is similar to that employed by another, his psychological processes are similar to those of the other person. This means if the two constructs are similar people act alike, even though they have been exposed to different stimuli.

In Kelly's system the development of each person revolves around attempts to maximize understanding of the world through the continuing definition & elaboration of his or her construct system. He held that the person's interaction with the environment plays a major role in moving the individual toward personal growth.

George Kelly is also well known for his unique method of Repertory Grid interview, designed as a means of getting people to show their construct systems.

Victor Frankl's Theory

Victor Emil Frankl (1905-1997) was born in Vienna, Austria to a middle class Jewish family. From an early age Frankl was involved in Socialist youth organizations & became interested in psychiatry. He finished his high school years with a psychoanalytic essay on the philosopher Schopenhauer, a publication in the International Journal of Psychoanalysis. At age 16 he began writing to Freud. He received a medical degree from the University of Vienna in 1930. Later he was assigned to work with suicidal women.

Frankl opened his own practice in neurology & psychiatry in 1937. In 1938 Nazi regime took over Austria. Frankl had plans to move to U.S. but concerned for his elderly parents he stayed. In 1940, Frankl was made head of the neurological department of Rothschild Hospital. Rothschild was the only Jewish hospital in Vienna at the time.

In 1942 Frankl, his wife & his parents were arrested & sent to the Theresienstadt Concentration Camp. At first Frankl worked as a general practitioner in a clinic. Later he worked at the unit that helped newcomers of the camp to overcome shock. Eventually Frankl's entire family was killed in various concentration camps. When he was moved to Auschwitz, his writings were discovered & destroyed. Frankl's strong desire to complete his work, & his hopes that he would be reunited with his wife & family someday, kept him from losing hope.

In April of 1945, Frankl's camp was liberated. Upon returning to Vienna he was given the position of director of the Vienna Neurological Policlinic. He also reconstructed his lost book & published it. It was translated into English in 1959, & in a revised & enlarged edition appeared as "The Doctor and the Soul." By the time of his death, Frankl's book, Man's Search for Meaning, had been translated into 24 languages and reprinted 73 times and had long been used as a standard text in high school and university courses in psychology & philosophy.

Frankl received his Ph.D. in philosophy in 1948. His dissertation was called "The Unconscious God." That same year, he was made associate professor of neurology and psychiatry at the University of Vienna. In 1950, he founded and became president of the Austrian Medical Society for Psychotherapy. Frankl was awarded Oskar Pfister Prize by the American Society of Psychiatry.

In 1992 Frankl's friends & family members established the Viktor Frankl Institute. Five years later he published his final work, "Man's Search for Ultimate Meaning," based on his doctoral dissertation. Frankl's 32 books, all of them successful, have been translated into 28 languages.

In Frankl's theory, which was born in concentration camps, there are three basic psychological reactions; shock, apathy & reactions of depersonalization, moral deformity, bitterness, & disillusionment. In this theory, the meaning of life is in every moment of living. Thus, the inner hold a prisoner has on his spiritual self relies on having a faith in the future.

Frankl was the founder of the so called logotherapy (study of meaning). Unlike Freudian will to pleasure or Adlerian will to power, Frankl's logotherapy is about will to meaning.

Another major topic for discussion for Frankl was conscience, which he viewed as a sort of unconscious spirituality. He held that the conscience was not just an ordinary factor but it was the core one's being & the everlasting source of personal integrity.

Victor Frankl was the first to use the term existential vacuum. He held that one of the most common signs of existential vacuum was boredom. Frankl argued that existential vacuum was a widespread phenomenon of the twentieth century. Every person attempts on way or the other to fill this existential vacuum because it provides some satisfaction. It develops when one's life is empty of meaning. It is as if existence has a large hole in it that cannot be filled.

According to Frankl finding meaning can make a person happy. He saw three ways of doing it. The first was through so called experiental values. Person truly understands the value of something by experiencing it. He further held that the most important experiential value was love. The second way of discovering meaning was through creative values, the traditional existential idea of providing oneself with meaning by becoming involved in one's projects. It also includes the creativity involved in art, music, writing& so on. In Frankl's theory views creativity was a function of the spiritual unconscious.

His third way of finding meaning was through attitudal values, which include such virtues as compassion, bravery, a good sense of humor, and so on. Finally, Frankl held that meaning can be achieved through suffering.

Frankl was also well known for introducing the method of paradoxical intention. This method was used to breaking down the neurotic vicious cycles brought on by anticipatory anxiety. Paradoxical intention consisted of wishing the very thing that one was afraid of. He also used a technique called dereflection. Since Frankl believed that majority of problems stem from an overemphasis on oneself, he thought that by shifting attention away from oneself & onto others, problems can simply vanish.

Rollo May's Neo Existentialism

Rollo May (1909-1994) was born in Ada, Ohio. May studied at the Michigan State University for a brief period of time. He was asked to leave because of his involvement with a radical student magazine. He received his bachelor's degree at the Oberlin College (Ohio). After graduation, he went to Greece, where he taught English at Anatolia College for three years. During this period, he also spent time as an itinerant artist and even studied briefly with Alfred Adler. He returned to U.S. & received a bachelor of divinity degree at the Union Theological Seminary. He even practiced for two years as a Congregationalist minister.Psychology, however, was the supreme calling for May, so he resigned from the ministry. May began his studies in psychology at Columbia University in New York. While working on his doctorate, he contracted tuberculosis, a life-threatening disease, &, out of this traumatic experience, May developed a new passion for existential philosophy. He later studied psychoanalysis at White Institute, where he met Harry Sullivan & Erich Fromm. In 1949 he went to Columbia University in New York, where he received the first PhD in clinical psychology that institution ever awarded.

His career in psychology included a position on the faculty of the William Alanson White Institute of Psychiatry, Psychology, and Psychoanalysis and a position as lecturer at the New School for Social Research, as well as being a visiting professor at Harvard, Yale, Princeton, and other universities. He spent the last years of his life in Tiburon, California.

Rollo May is the best known American existential psychologist. He was opposing those who use only the objective & subjective views of the reality in their formulations, thus targeting Rogers & Skinner. He criticized Rogers for supposedly overemphasizing the subjective side. In May's opinion Rogers was wrong in formulating that people are inherently good & exquisitely rational. He also criticized Skinner for placing too much emphasis on the objective side of human behavior. May held that the both views of human nature were necessary for psychology, because people were faced with the dilemma of living in both worlds. May combined Freudian theory with existentialism. In his efforts at reconciling Freud & the existentialists, he turned his attention to motivation. His main motivational construct was the so called daimonic. The term daimonic was used by May to describe the entire system of motives, different for each individual. It was composed of a collection of specific motives called daimons (means little god translated from Greek). These daimons can be either good or bad. They include lower needs, such as food & sex, as well as higher needs, such as love. According to May when the balance among daimons is disrupted, they should be considered evil. May considered eros (which represents love) to be one of the most important daimons in person's life.

In existential analysis there are three modes of being in the world; unwelt, mitwelt & eigenwelt. Unwelt is the natural, biological environment for animals & humans. It includes drives, instincts & biological needs. The second mode mitwelt is the world of interrelationships. It contains the meanings of things that people share with each other. The eigenwelt is person's own world. It contains self-awareness & self-relatedness. In May's opinion person lives in all three worlds simultaneously.

May recognized two types of ontological anxiety; normal & neurotic. He thought that feelings of anxiety stem from loneliness & emptiness. Anxiety was the human beings basic reaction to a danger to his existence. In his opinion ontological anxiety was a threat to values. Normal anxiety was proportionate to the threat of one's values, whereas neurotic anxiety was a reaction that was disproportionate.

May was convinced that, the more conscious of our being we are the more, the more capable we will be in reaching our goals. He held that individuals cannot fulfill their potentialities if these are mainly unconscious. Thus each person must strive to increase his consciousness. In May's theory, the sense of being that needs to be rediscovered is the capacity to see ourselves as beings in the world who can successfully deal with the problems of our existence. Such a fundamental sense of being had many similarities with the Freudian ego, yet it was different in its level of strength & activeness. According to May the shift toward realization begins with the sense of awareness of potentialities. Awareness, in turn, makes it possible for potentialities to become active.

Person's developmental process, in May's opinion, was closely connected with physical & psychological ties between him & his parents. The physical dependence on mothers, for example, tends to subside with years, but the psychological often remains strong. May saw this as a serious problem, since the way in which person deals with this dependence determines his level of maturity & personal growth. He thought that there was a conflict between every person's struggle toward enlarged self –awareness, & his tendency to remain a child. May's reinterpretation of the dependency struggle had many similarities with Freud's oedipal conflict. People constantly strive to establish autonomy in their relationships with more powerful people. There were three stages for this battle of freedom. During the first stage person was innocent having no consciousness or self. Second stage was all about rebellion, during which person was trying to establish his inner strength & potentials. The third stage signified the simple consciousness of the self. During this period person was able to fully understand his errors, learn from mistakes & assume responsibility for certain actions. Eventually May added another stage which signified maturity. He called this additional stage the creative consciousness of self. Supposedly person reaches maturity only when he experiences this moment of creative consciousness.

May thought that myths give expression to the universal truths of human nature & guide human existence. He described them as unique narratives that make sense in a senseless world. Myths were viewed as sources of universal themes to the individual regarding birth, death, love & so on. Thus memory & myth were inseparable. Myths gave a person a sense of personal identity & a sense of community, as well as supported moral values & allowed a person to deal with the mysteries of creation.

In the process of assembling his theory May was greatly influenced by a Danish existentialist philosopher Soren Kierkegaard. Kierkegaard was known for opposing Hegel's monumental efforts to comprehend reality by identifying it with abstract thought & logic.

Julian Rotter's Social Learning Theory

Julian B. Rotter was born in October 1916 in Brooklyn, NY. His interest in psychology began when he was in high school & read books by Freud and Adler. Rotter attended Brooklyn College, where he began attending seminars given by Adler & meetings of his Society of Individual Psychology.

After graduation, Rotter attended the University of Iowa. Here he took classes with Kurt Lewin. Rotter minored in speech pathology & studied with the semanticist Wendell Johnson, whose ideas had an enduring influence on Rotter's thinking about the use and misuse of language. Upon finishing his master's degree, Rotter took an internship in clinical psychology at Worcester State Hospital in Massachusetts. In 1939, he started his Ph.D. work at Indiana University. He completed his dissertation on level of aspiration & graduated in 1941. During the World War II Rotter became an adviser to the U.S. Army. He then joined the Ohio State University where he taught & served as the chairman of the clinical psychology program. At Ohio State, Rotter was influenced by George Kelly. Rotter then went to the University of Connecticut, where he remained for the rest of his career. Rotter has served as president of the American Psychological Association's divisions of Social & Personality Psychology & Clinical Psychology. In 1989, he was given the American Psychological Association's Distinguished Scientific Contribution award.

Rotter's theory of personality was based on the process of learning. When he developed this theory, the dominant perspective in clinical psychology at the time was Freud's Psychoanalysis. Unlike Freudians, Rotter found it necessary to probe the individual's past experiences in order to predict behavior adequately. He stressed the importance of past events only to the extent that they help to predict current behavior. Rotter emphasized the unity & interdependence of personality, in which a person's experiences & interactions continually influence one another. In developing Social Learning Theory, Rotter departed from instinct-based Psychoanalysis & drive-based behaviorism, arguing that a true psychological theory should have a psychological motivational principle. In Rotter's theory personality insured the interaction of the individual with the environment. In addition he described personality as a relatively stable set of potentials for responding to situations in a particular way.

According to Rotter past experiences are able to influence current influences & current experiences change the things learned in the past. Thus, he saw personality as changing, because the individual is constantly exposed to new experiences & stable because previous experiences affect new learning.

In Rotter's theory human behavior is goal directed & motivated to minimize punishment. This means that Rotter, just like Skinner endorsed the empirical law of effect. In his opinion any stimulus complex has reinforcing properties to the extent that it influences movement toward or away from a goal.

Rotter's unique social learning approach was based on 4 major concepts: behavior potential, expectancy, reinforcement value & the psychological situation.

Behavior potential was the likelihood of engaging in a particular behavior in a specific situation. In other words, what is the possibility that the person will exhibit a particular behavior in a situation? In any given situation, there are multiple behaviors one can engage in & for each possible behavior, there is a behavior potential. Accordingly the individual will exhibit whichever behavior has the highest potential. Behavior Potential (BP), Expectancy (E) and Reinforcement Value (RV) were combined into a predictive formula for behavior:

$$BP=f (E \& RV).$$

According to Rotter's formula the likelihood of a person exhibiting a particular behavior is a function of the probability that that behavior will lead to a given outcome and the desirability of that outcome. If expectancy & reinforcement value are both high, then behavior potential will be high. If either expectancy or reinforcement value is low, then behavior potential will be lower.

Expectancy was considered to be a cognition or belief about the property of some object or event. Expectancies varied in magnitude & were subject to modification by experience. Rotter's social learning theory had three kinds of expectancies: simple cognitions or labeling of stimuli, expectancies for behavior reinforcement outcomes & expectancies for reinforcement sequences. Any behavior that has been associated with reinforcement gives rise to expectancy. Rotter held that expectancies vary in terms of their generality; meaning a person may acquire generalized expectancies or expectancies specific to a given situation.

Reinforcement was another name for the outcomes of behavior. It referred to the desirability of these outcomes. The things that are attractive have a high reinforcement value. Things we don't want to happen, that we wish to avoid, have a low reinforcement value. If the likelihood of achieving reinforcement is the same, we will exhibit the behavior with the greatest reinforcement value. Reinforcement value refers to the importance we attach to different activities.

When it comes to expectancy, reinforcement value is subjective, meaning that the same event or experience can vastly differ in desirability, depending on the individual's life experience.

In Rotter's theory the least amount of reinforcement that still has a positive value is called a minimal goal. When a person achieves an outcome that equals or exceeds his minimal goal, he will feel that he has succeeded, but when the level of reinforcement falls below an individual's minimal goal, that reinforcement feels like failure. Naturally people differ in their minimal goals. Thus, the same outcome may represent success to one person (with a lower minimal goal) while it feels like failure to another person (with a higher minimal goal).

Finally Rotter's psychological situation is the situation as it is defined from the individual's personal perspective. This concept plays an important role in the determination of behavior, since traditional theories, according to Rotter, focus mainly on an inner core of personality, within which certain motives or traits are considered to control behavior. He also held that on the basis of a complex cues in a particular situation, the person develops expectancies for behavior-reinforcement outcomes & also for reinforcement-reinforcement sequences.

Rotter also introduced an important dimension of personality theories, called the "generality versus specificity," in which general constructs were broad & abstract, while specific constructs were narrow & concrete. Of course both constructs have their advantages. A theory with general constructs allows one to make many predictions, across situations, from knowing only a small amount of information. The disadvantage of general constructs, though, is that they are harder to measure. Specific constructs, on the other hand, are easier to measure, & they can be used to make more accurate predictions, but these predictions are limited to being situation-specific.

Rotter was against the medical model of conception of mental disorders as being diseases. Instead, he considered psychological problems to be maladaptive behavior brought about by faulty or inadequate learning experiences. For him, the symptoms of pathology, like all behavior, were learned. That is why Rotter viewed treatment in a same context as learning situation where adaptive behaviors & cognitions are taught, & the therapist-client relationship is viewed as being similar to a teacher-student relationship. He argued that pathology can develop due to difficulties at any point in his predictive formula. Therefore the behavior could be maladaptive, simply because the individual never learned more adaptive behaviors.

Hans Eysenck's theory

Hans Eysenck (1916-1997) was born in Berlin. He moved to England as a young man in the 1930s because of his opposition to the Hitler's regime. In England, he continued his education & earned his Ph.D. in Psychology from the University of London. During World War II Eysenck served as a psychologist at an emergency hospital, where he began conducting his research on the reliability of psychiatric diagnoses. The results led him to a life-long antagonism to traditional clinical psychology.

Eysenck was Professor of Psychology at the Institute of Psychiatry for 28 years. He was a major contributor to the modern scientific theory of personality & a brilliant teacher. He discovered treatments for several mental illnesses. Also in 1951 Eysenck published his first empirical study into the genetics of personality. He conducted an experiment in which identical & fraternal twins (ages 11 & 12) were given tests that were to do with neuroticism. Eysenck concluded that the factor of neuroticism was not a statistical artifact, but a unique factor which makes up a biological unit which, in turn, was inherited as a whole.

Being a behaviorist, Eysenck based his theory mainly on physiology & genetics. He considered personality differences as growing out of person's genetic inheritance. In addition, Eysenck was a research psychologist. In his researches he often used methods involving purely statistical techniques. One his favorite techniques were called factor analysis. It was used to extract a number of "dimensions" from large masses of data.

Eysenck used the term "neuroticism" to describe the shift from normal, calm state of mind to inadequate unstable behavior. His studies indicated that these nervous people tended to suffer more frequently from a variety of "nervous disorders" we call neuroses, hence the name of the dimension. Eysenck was convinced that, since everyone in his data-pool fit somewhere on this dimension of normality-to-neuroticism, this was a true temperament, i.e. that this was a genetically-based, physiologically-supported dimension of personality. Eysenck postulated that some people have a more responsive sympathetic nervous system than others. For instance, some people remain very calm during emergencies; some people feel considerable fear or other emotions; & some are terrified by even very insignificant incidents. He stated that this latter group had a problem of sympathetic hyperactivity.

He concluded that people with phobias & obsessive-compulsive disorder were introverted, whereas people with conversion disorders or dissociative disorders tended to be more extraverted. Eysenck thought that the latter was related to neurotic's responsiveness to fearful stimuli. If a person is introvert, he will eventually learn to avoid the situations that cause panic. On the other hand, highly neurotic extravert is good at ignoring & forgetting the things that overwhelms him. He often engages in the classic defense mechanisms, such as denial & repression.

Some of his studies Eysenck were conducting at the mental institutions of where he made an interesting discovery, a phenomenon which he called psychoticism. Psychotocism was rather an indication of one's inclination to become psychotic or exhibit psychotic behavior under certain circumstances. Just like neuroticism it did not mean that one is doomed to become psychotic. Later the concept of psychoticism was viewed by Eysenck more as a trait, eventually becoming a part of his famous P-E-N model (psychoticism, extraversion and neuroticism) model of personality. High levels of this trait were believed by Eysenck to be linked to increased vulnerability to psychosis. He also believed that blood relatives of psychotics would show high levels of this trait.

Albert Bandura's Cognitive theory

Albert Bandura was born on December 4, 1925, in Mundare, Canada. His parents immigrated to Canada when they were adolescents; his father from Krakow, Poland, & his mother from the Ukraine. Bandura received his elementary & high school education at his hometown. After gradua-tion he went to the University of British Columbia in Vancouver. Almost instantly Bandura became attracted to psychology. Within three years he graduated with the Bolocan Award in psychology. In 1952, he earned his Ph.D. from the University of Iowa, where he later developed the social learning theory. Bandura held that psychological research should be con-ducted in a laboratory setting, which helps to control factors that deter-mine behavior. In 1953, Albert Bandura accepted a position as a psychol-ogy professor at the University of Stanford.

Throughout his career Bandura has written several books & articles that have been widely used in psychological research. In 1959, Bandura wrote his first book in collaboration called "Adolescent Aggression." In 1973, he wrote Aggression: A Social Learning Analysis. Four years later, he pub-lished one his most popular books called the "Social Learning Theory."

In 1972, he received a distinguished achievement award from the Ameri-can Psychological Association & a Scientist Award from the California State Psychological Association. In 1974, Bandura was elected the president of the American Psychological Association. In 1980, he was also elected the president of the Western Psychological Association.

According to Albert Bandura human behavior cannot be influenced by inner & environmental forces alone. In his view it occurs as a result of a complex interplay between inner processes & environmental influences. These internal processes Bandura interprets as measurable covert events that are based on previous experiences. In Bandura's tragic reciprocal determinism all cognitive factors, behavior & environmental influences operate interactively as determinants of one another. Thus person does not just react to environmental events, he creates his own environments & attempts to change them. Bandura's cognitive events predict which en-vironmental events will be perceived, interpreted or organized. He also held that people represent external events symbolically & later use verbal & imaginal representation to guide their behavior. Hence people can solve their problems symbolically without having to resort to actual behavior. Bandura maintains that most of human behavior is not controlled by immediate external reinforcement, but is regulated by the so called anticipated outcomes. Thus, behavior can be acquired through observational learning without the administration of external reinforcement.

According to Bandura modeling plays a prominent role in person's life. He maintained that learning occurs when the person observes & imitates others' behavior. He distinguished 4 component processes influenced by the observer's behavior following exposure to models; attention, retention, motor reproduction & motivation. A person cannot learn by observation unless he perceives & attends to the significant features of the modeled behavior. Also, In order to reproduce the modeled behavior, one must code the information into long-term memory for later retrieval. In motor reproduction the observer must be able to reproduce the model's behavior. At the same time person must learn & posses the physical capabilities of the modeled behavior. Motivation is a very important part of the observational learning. In it the observer expects to receive positive reinforcements for the modeled behavior.

Albert Bandura is best known for his Bobo doll experiment, in which he had children watch a video of a model aggressively attacking a plastic clown (named Bobo). After the video, the children were placed in a room full of toys, but they could not touch them. The process of retention had occurred. Therefore, the children became angry & frustrated. Then the children were led to another room where there were identical toys used in the Bobo video. The motivation phase was in occurrence. Bandura witnessed that 88% of the children imitated the aggressive behavior. Eight months later, 40% of the same children reproduce the violent behavior observed in the Bobo doll experiment. Bandura believed that aggression must explain three aspects: 1,how aggressive patterns of behavior are developed; 2, what provokes people to behave aggressively, & 3, what determines whether they are going to continue to resort to an aggressive behavior in the future.

Personality characteristics & the gender of an observer play a major role in modeling. Bandura proved that boys tend to show more aggressive behavior after watching an aggressive male model than a female one. Girls tend to imitate the aggression of a female model more often than those of a male. Also, observers imitate the behavior of the competent model more rapidly than the behavior of an incompetent one. In this experiment models which are similar in personal background have a greater influence on the observers.

In Bandura's theory the cognitive mechanism of self-efficacy plays a major role. In fact modeling is viewed as a necessary procedure that helps to instill the level of self-efficacy. Efficacy expectations are person's beliefs that he can produce certain behaviors. According to Bandura, people who perform effectively acquire high, realistic efficacy expectations that guide their actions. Efficacy expectations, argues Bandura, should not be compared or equated with person's actual skills, because a person who knows what to do in a situation & has the skills required to do it will not necessarily perform well. Different people with same skills or the same person on different occasions may perform poorly, adequately or extraordinarily. Thus appropriate functioning requires not only skills but the judgment of self-efficacy to allow their effective use.

Bandura held that efficacy expectations affect people's choices of activities & environmental settings. For example people with low efficacy expectations are likely to avoid threatening situations that they believe to exceed their coping skills. On contrary people with high efficacy expectations opt for challenging tasks where they have an opportunity to develop skills. In such conditions, they are likely to expend maximum effort to engage in a minimum of harmful self criticism.

In Bandura's theory the acquisition of high or low efficacy expectations has 4 major sources: performance accomplishments, vicarious experiences, verbal persuasion & states of physiological arousal.

Success experiences suppose to create high expectations, whereas failure experiences generate low expectations. When a person has strong high efficacy expectations, occasional failures cannot alter his judgment of his own capabilities. The same is true with low expectations, except that low expectations can change as a result of repeated successes fueled by determined effort on the part of a given person.

It is safe to say that the actual accomplishments are the most powerful source of efficacy expectations, but vicarious experiences can also influence the acquisition of efficacy expectations. Thus, witnessing other people performing successfully can instill high self perceptions of efficacy in observers.

According to Bandura verbal persuasion is a powerful tool which is used to convince people that they have the adequate capabilities to accomplish a given goal.

As we know stressful situations can generate high states of arousal in most people. People often use this arousal to judge their capabilities.

Since high arousal usually lowers the quality of a performance, people experience low efficacy expectations when they are aroused.

Without a doubt Albert Bandura has had an enormous impact on personality theory. He also has lectured & written on many different topics such as deceleration of population growth, transgressive behavior, substance abuse & so on. He has traced the psychosocial tactics by which individuals & societies selectively disengage moral self-sanctions from inhumane conduct. His straightforward, behaviorist oriented thinking is acceptable for most people.

About Russian School of Psychology

The methodological approach employed by Russian school of psychology was based on the understanding of human psyche from the standpoints of Marxist interpretation of man, his affairs & his place in the society. An attempt was made to transform Marxist concepts of psychology & science in general into a meaningful & real discipline. Within one decade, from 1920 to 1930, the new social order was installed, causing the idealist psychology of consciousness to lose its previously accepted place. Perhaps the first novelty declared by the forerunners of the early Soviet psychology was their statement regarding the key role of activity in determining the conscious processes. The psycho-physiologists of the time stressed the importance of the activity deployed by the subject in labor processes, at the same opposing the theories which were based on the idea that labor altered the conditions for physiological processes in a negative way. The Soviet thinkers held that the labor activity caused the energy resources of the system to increase, rather than to fall. The notions of the organism's energy potential were advanced in opposition to the assumption that the individual's energy reserves were immutably fixed, & that his life acts were predetermined by biological constants. Therefore the development of the behavior meant not only the appearance of new conditioned connections between signals & responses, but the appearance of new motivations as well. This new approach soon opened up a way for labor to be interpreted as a form of creativity. The concept of motive was significantly reevaluated in consequence of the studies made of working process. The category of action also underwent some notable changes. In 19th century the only determinist interpretation of action was that based on the reflex system & when that was updated, the presentation of change from the supposedly rigid reflex-arc model to one of dynamic connection between external impulse & the response. The traditional category of action was given a new content by such concepts as activity, prevision, pretuning of the organism & so on. Action as a category was considered as a sort of basic unit in the human form of interaction between living human beings & the objective world, but soon it was denoted as object related activity.

The psychologist Mikhail Vladislavlev (1840-1890) was well known in Russia for translating & popularizing the views of the German psychologists, notably Kant. Vladislavlev was born in 1840, the son of a village priest. He studied first in the Novgorod Seminary & then in St. Petersburg Theological Academy. Eventually he was sent abroad to prepare for a professorship. After receiving his master's thesis Vladislavlev was elected full-time assistant professor of philosophy at St. Petersburg University, & thereupon took the chair of philosophy at the Institute of History & Philology. Moreover, he spent several years teaching the same science at the University for Women. In 1868 Vladislavlev earned a Ph.D. with a dissertation on Philosophy of Plotinus, the founder of Neo-Platonic school. In 1879 he received the rank of professor supernumerary. Six years later, in 1885 he was appointed a dean of History & Philology faculties. In 1887 he was became the rector of the St. Petersburg University.

In his theory Vladislavlev sought to combine the experiment with an idealistic view of the soul. Applying the energy law to psychology, which was a novelty in the 70-80-ies of the XIX century, Vladislavlev tried to link the energy theory of forgetting & playing, convinced that unconscious & forgetfulness were characterized by a minimum of energy. He shared the voluntarist approach of Wundt. In his textbook "Psychology" (1881) he introduced the interpretation of faith & its role in mental development rights. The combination of ethics & aesthetics was one of the main distinguishing features of Vladislavlev's psychology. Based on his concept of psyche, Vladislavlev considered art as a practical psychology & as a school of morality. He gave a detailed description of the difference in emotional impact of art, music, poetry & prose.

The theories of intuitivism & ideal realism were first introduced by Nikolai Lossky (1870-1965). He was born in the village of Kreslavka, Dinaburg region, Vitebsk province of Russian Empire Lossky first enrolled at the department of physics & mathematics In St. Petersburg University. He eventually transferred to the historical-philological faculty of the same University. From 1901-1903 he studied under Wundt. In 1922 was sent abroad as a member of the Kadet party. He worked in Berlin, Prague & Bratislava. Lossky became a Professor at the Russian University of Prague at Bratislava, in Czechoslovakia. In 1947 he took a position teaching Eastern Orthodox theology at Saint Vladimir's Orthodox Theological Seminary, a Russian Orthodox seminary in New York. In 1961, after the death of his son Lossky went to France, where he died in 1965.

Lossky argued that knowledge was an experience comparable to other experiences. He held that experience reflected the essence of objects of the world, directly & indirectly. The objects of knowledge, experiences were primarily aesthetic, religious, moral & legal norms. Lossky viewed freedom of will in connection with his theory of ideal-realism, proving that man as the bearer of a concrete ideal being was above the laws of nature & the manifestation of his own spiritual forces were made only according to his needs & interests. Lossky's gnosiology was similar to Hegelian dialectical approach of first addressing a problem in thought in terms of its expression as a duality. Lossky also followed & developed his ontological & gnosiological interpretation of objective reality from Christian Neo-Platonism. He was also greatly influenced by Leibnitz's "Monadology". In his "The World as an Organic Whole," Lossky introduced a neo-Leibnitzian, neo-Platonic theory based on monads. These monads were radically free to choose their own destiny. Some choose the way of divine righteousness & God's Kingdom, while others didn't.

In Lossky's theory intuition was the direct contemplation of objects, & furthermore the assembling of the entire set of cognition from sensory perception into a complete and undivided organic whole. He maintained that intuition functioned without rational or logical thought. Rational or logical thought via the nous then worked in reflection as hindsight to organize experience into a comprehensible order. Once knowledge was abstracted from conscious experience it was then stored in an ontological format in the mind.

One of the most loyal supporters of Lossky & his ideal-realism was professor Semen Frank (1877-1950). His most notable work was the psychological writing "Human Soul" (1917). In it he tried to restore the psychology of the concept of the soul. Frank believed that the basis of psychology was philosophy, not science, because psychology did not study the actual processes of objective being to their cause, or other natural laws. He held that psychology provides a general logical explanation of the ideal nature & structure of the psychic world & its relation to the same ideal other objects of existence. In his writings Frank discussed such concepts as psychic life, soul & mind. Frank maintained that, under a thin layer of solidified forms of rational culture is smoldering fire of great passions, dark & light, which can break through the dam & get out, sweeping away everything in its path, leading to aggression, rebellion & anarchy. He further argued that in the game & in art man reflects his vague, unconscious mental life & thus complements his narrow range of conscious experiences. It is the unconscious, according to Frank, the main subject of psychological research, as the main characteristics of psychic life is its formlessness, fusion, meaning timelessness. The union of the multiple heterogeneous & competing forces, emerging under the influence of sensual & emotional & volitional supra-sensuous aspirations, Frank placed in the soul. Vague spiritual life, associated with emotions & feelings, was the lowest level of the soul, which was associated with the body.

Another influential figure of the time was academician, Alexei Ukhtomsky (1875-1942). He was born in the ancestral estate in the village Vosloma Rybinsk district of Yaroslavl province.

In 1888 without completing the full course of the classical school, Ukhtomsky enters the Novgorod Cadet Academy. Here he becomes interested in scientific disciplines. Ukhtomsky was especially driven to philosophy, ethics & psychology. He was influenced by Spinoza, Descartes & James. In 1894 he enters the linguistic department of Moscow Theological Academy. Ukhtomsky was an idealist. His first scientific thesis was titled "Cosmological proof of the existence of God."

Ukhtomsky along with Pavlov & Bekhterev was attempting to transform the theory of reflexes in such a way that it would include the idea if activity of living beings. The existing opinion of the organism being preset to respond to an external stimulus, which he had discovered, was now viewed from another angle. Ukhtomsky presented his theory of the dominant which included a special systematic reflex that corresponded to a temporarily predominant seat of excitation in the central nervous system. On the biological level it corresponded to readiness for activity. Ukhtomsky also was preoccupied with the concept of functional system, or functional organ. An organ, as a working unit was considered as a systematic formation which united different components of the nervous system in order to achieve the particular result. According to Ukhtomsky dominant was a vector variable, meaning that fused together the energy aspect of the motive & its concentration upon its object.

He also maintained that perception is an integrated whole image, dependent upon motivation. Ukhtomsky's theory contained ethical psychological & physiological doctrines designed to bring together the psychological fields of cognition, motivation, personality & communication.

The overall structure of scientific understanding was undergoing major changes. The switch from bio-anthropological understanding of the action to a socio-historical one was in progress for a whole decade. This process was taking place when the main scientific trends in the country were "reflexological." The founder & leader of one such trend was Pavlov, while another was headed by Bekhterev. Pavlov's teachings greatly affected the development of psychology. Aside from defining the different types of higher nervous system, Pavlov was also in search of specific human characteristics of higher nervous activity. As result, Pavlov came to the conclusion that in the so called human phase brain acquired a special supplement which replaced first signals coming from physical environment by a second signaling system which was speech. He called the human type of higher nervous activity "artistic," because it showed the pre-dominance of sensual images, while the type which had a predominance of abstract concepts was called "thinking" type. In behaviorism, before Pavlov's inventions, the term speech was noted as a special kind of stimu-lus which regulated human thinking. However, Pavlov did not share the view that the words were a pure signal devoid of mental content & mean-ing, because the acceptance of the latter would mean that the subjective world was a reality.

Pavlov's concept of conditioned reflexes was included by all Soviet psy-chologists as an integral part of their general conceptions of their sub-ject.

Another brilliant psychologist of the time, Bekhterev (1857-1927), was known for his huge organizational work to bring into being a new dis-cipline-reflexology. Vladimir Bekhterev was also neurologist & the pio-neer of Objective Psychology. He was born in small village of Sorali, Rus-sia. Bekhterev attended Vyataka gymnasium in 1867, one of the oldest schools in Russia as well as the Military Medical Academy in St. Peters-burg in 1873. He also studied at the Medical and Surgery Academy of St. Petersburg. Bekhterev's was especially interested in neuropathology & psychiatry. He became best known for noting the role of the hippocam-pus (a key component of the brain) in memory, his study of reflexes & Bekhterev's Disease.

In 1877 Bekhterev took time off from his studies in order to help the war (between Russia & Ottoman Empire) effort by volunteering with an am-bulance detachment. After the war, he returned to his studies. Bekhterev worked as a junior doctor in the clinic of mental & nervous diseases at the Institutes of Medic's Improvement. He graduated from the Medical & Surgery Academy of St. Petersburg with a degree equal to a Bachelor of Medicine in 1878. After graduating, Bekhterev worked at the Psychiat-ric Clinic in St. Petersburg, where he was inspired to begin studying the anatomy and physiology of the brain.

Bekhterev's dissertation for the medical doctorate, introduced in 1881, dealt with the possible relation between body temperature & some forms of mental illness. He was awarded a fellowship to study and conduct re-search abroad. In 1884-1885 he worked with the Wundt. In 1895 at the University of Kazan Bekhterev introduced his famous superior vestibular nucleus. He also conducted several clinical researches into mental disor-ders & completed investigations of the role of the cortex in the regulation of the functions of the internal organs.

In 1907 Bekhterev founded a psycho neurological institute, which eventually was made into the State Psycho-neurological Academy. At first Bekhterev was the institute's director, but later he was forced to resign, despite the fact that this institute was originally sponsored by him. Later he established the State Institute for the Study of the Brain. He was restored to favor following the Russian Revolution. Bekhterev was the head of the department of psychology & reflexology at the University of Petrograd from 1918 until his death.

Bekhterev developed a theory of conditioned reflexes, studying both inherited & acquired reflexes in the laboratory. He also accumulated a considerable volume of data on skeletal reflexes.

Bekhterev's most valuable work was his research on brain morphology & his original description of several nervous symptoms & diseases. He also described numbness of the spine (Bekhterev's disease) and new forms of syphilitic-sclerosis & motor ataxia.

Bekhterev was a faculty colleague of Ivan Pavlov, with whom he was frequently in open conflicts. Pavlov believed work from Bekhterev's laboratory was poorly controlled & sloppy at best. This criticism was probably not quite unjust, as Bekhterev seemed to accept his assistant's experimental findings too readily & uncritically.

The subject-matter of reflexology was the human personality studied from a strictly bio-social standpoint. The concept of psyche was intentionally replaced by so called correlative activity which was a new term used to describe the connection between the responses of the organism & external stimuli. Bekhterev's reflexological methods were nearly universal at the time. The supporter's of this school of thought were convinced that it will help to provide a materialist explanation of human behavior, which in turn would transform people in the interests of the society. Eventually reflexology embraced a very heterogeneous data on behavior- from biochemistry to the highest forms of creative activity of the personality. During the 1920s the reflexology determined the general character of studies in Soviet psychology.

The assembly of the well defined theory which is intact with the philosophy of the time is not an easy task. Various versions of such a theory were put forward throughout years, but Konstantin Kornilov's (1879-1957) theory was the first which gained acceptance as a true embodiment of the principles of Marxism in psychology.

He was a member of the Academy of Pedagogical Sciences & served as president from 1944 to 1950. Earlier he had been director of the Institute of Psychology. He developed the idea of a reaction psychology (rather than the simple reflexology proposed by Bekhterev), in which reaction referred to all the response movements of an organism & not simply the reflex of a single organ. Reactions were considered biosocial. This involved all the phenomena of the living organism, from the simplest responses to the most complex forms of human behavior.

Kornilov often used various methods of Leipzig & Wundtian schools of psychology, yet he was highly critical of both of these schools. At first Kornilov was studying the reaction times, but towards the end of his career he was more focused on the studies of the dynamic aspect of the reaction. He was convinced that the thought & external movement were in an inverse relationship, meaning the greater the intensity of thought the less intensive is the reaction. This was the beginning of the "unipolar" principle, according to which intelligence is nothing other than a slowed-down process of will which is not converted into action. In this sense Kornilov was a follower of "energism"- the view that the mental process was energy of a particular kind. Gradually Kornilov's concept of response widened & became the foundation of a general conception which became known as reactology. The key concept in Kornilov's reformed psychology was the reaction, which was seen as a prime element in life-activity, comparable to the reflex, but differing from it in that it had a psychic aspect. He defined the psychic as that which is subjectively experienced, & accessible to the subject through internal observation. At one point Kornilov looked to the dialectical method for help in finding the key to the problem of the relationship between his psychology & the introspective-behavioral psychology. He held that the dialectical psychology must become the synthesis of the two. This attempt for synthesis advanced on the level of theoretical declaration, & ended up as a compromise at the level of practical research work.

Kornilov distinguished psychology from physiology, which dealt with simple human reactions but ignored social relations. He was one of the earliest Soviet psychologists to build a psychology based on Marxist philosophy. His theory of the reaction has been considered an eclectic combination of Marxist principles, including mechanical & energy propositions. He stressed the application of the reaction to both biological and social phenomena. He believed that humans had as many instincts as animals, but that human instincts were masked by socially acquired reactions.

The new generation of Soviet psychology

The determination of young Soviet psychologists to create a new view, differing from that of the reactologists, on the interaction between the personality & the social environment was the factor that begun the new era of Soviet psychology. One of the forefathers of the new Soviet school was Mikhail Basov (1892-1931) begun his professional career in Bekhterev's Psychoneurological institute & went on to work in the institute for the study of the brain & psychiatric activity. Basov was convinced that it was possible to make objective observation of processes within the psyche. As we know the reflexologists considered the subject matter of psychology the correlative activity. The internal aspect of it they left to introspection. Basov on the other hand was looking for objective means of gaining knowledge. He often used the term behavior to describe his own field of psychology, in which every separate behavioral act showed its full significance to the psychologist only when it revealed the inner essence, that is the definite experience of a particular person. For Basov the essence of a behavioral act was that it was experienced by an individual personality, yet for the reflexologists this statement was useless. Basov essentially was concerned with the question of deterministic explanation of the psychic activity. His views were sometimes functionalistic, especially when he stated that the activity of consciousness must be seen as rooted in its adaptive function.

Eager to draw distinction between his approach & that of reflexologists, Basov replaced the term behavior with the word activity. In defining the characteristics of the concept of activity he followed the model of Marxist concept of labor. What was new in Basov's position was that human psychic processes were being placed with a socio-historical system of coordinates. He also found the idea of conditioned reflex to be the basic structural element in activity, viewing reflexes as joined, organized & integrated whole.

In Basov's theory environment was seen as a source of stimuli which had ecological significance for the organism, not as a mass of physical-chemical agents all of equal indifference to it. According to Basov activity is a modeling link which carries within the objective logical content taken from reality. Because of this content human becomes an active agent within the environment. Thus the environment evokes action responses from the subject not directly, but through the mediation of science. With the help of the ideas of science as a factor organizing human activity Basov put foundations under the notion of cultural determination of activity-science, after all is a product of cultural history.

Pavel Blonsky (1884-1941) was a historian of philosophy, a teacher, psychologist & a founder of the Academy of Social Education in Moscow. He was born in Kiev, Ukraine. After graduating from the Moscow University in 1907, Blonsky began his career as an instructor, teaching pedagogic & psychology in various schools throughout Moscow. Blonsky was the first to introduce the behaviorist approach in Russian psychology. In 1919 he was a professor at the Moscow University. Blonsky was one of the organizers & directors of the Academy of Social Education. He is an author of over 200 scientific works & essays. Before revolution Blonsky's work was of historic-philosophical character. His post revolution work however, was more focused on the study of the mind.

Like his contemporaries, Blonsky saw the behavior as the subject matter of psychology. Later he equated human behavior with human movements. Blonsky eventually changed the subject matter of his psychology, giving the concept of behavior a new content which served to distinguish it from the behaviorist model. Eventually he made drastic changes in the direction of his studies, abandoning the attempts to explain in which way the society determines the development of consciousness. Instead Blonsky focused on biological foundations of behavior. The topics of his works varied from biological interpretations to sociology. Blonsky was also known for creating a new theory of memory, in which he distinguished four stages; motor, affective, image-forming & verbal. The integration of biological & socio-cultural knowledge enabled Blonsky to present a picture of evolution, not only the evolution of memory but that of behavior as a whole.

Unlike the rest Lev Vigotsky (1896-1934) did not have a specialized training in psychology. He was a law student at Moscow University. Lev Vigotsky was born into a middle-class Jewish family in Orsha, Russia. He entered the Moscow University in 1913, where he studied law. He simultaneously attended Shaniavsky University to study social sciences. Later Vigotsky was invited to join the research staff at the Psychological Institute in Moscow, where he met Alexander Luria.

In 1925 he wrote a study called "The Psychology of Art." His other work

"The Techniques of Reflexological & Psychological research" was very critical of Pavlov's & Bekhterev's reflexology. He spoke of a classical technique for building up a conditioned reflex & the complete misfit between such a technique & the task of finding a scientific, determinist explanation of human behavior as a whole. The forefathers of reflexology did not deny that behavior included consciousness, but they maintained that the latter was the business of another science. Vigotsky, on the other hand, demanded the objective investigation of consciousness. According to him consciousness was a reflex of reflexes. Thus it meant that he was a pure reductionist, bringing the psyche down to reflex. But for Vigotsky the speech reflex was qualitatively different from the salivary reflex which was the basis of Pavlov's work. He viewed the speech as a unique world of culture with its structures of sign & symbol. In his theory reflex was inseparable from the social consciousness that inspired it.

Reflexologists considered that psychology was beyond the reach of objective method, on the grounds that its facts were only accessible to self-observation. Vigotsky, on contrary, held that such facts could be comprehended, though only by indirect methods. Significant changes came about in Vigotsky's theory under the influence of practical work he did in the field of defectology. The concept of sign, which was central to Vigotsky's thinking, was brought into being through a rethinking of a theory of conditioned reflexes, in the context of behavior in the handicapped child. Vigotsky was the first Soviet psychologist to define the cultural & natural levels of organization. In the behavior of the handicapped children Vigotsky saw an experiment set up by nature, which discloses the divergence in development of the cultural & the natural. Thus, nature, by performing a cruel excising operation upon the normal human psychophysiological apparatus, provided a means of testing the forces of which society could bring to bear. The supposedly effective power of those forces made itself apparent on two planes; 1 provision of bypasses, that is the use of signs enabling the child to understand meanings common to people in general, & 2 stimulation of the personality's motivational energy.

Vygotsky's theory was one of the foundations of constructivism, consisting of three major themes: 1.Social interaction plays a fundamental role in the process of cognitive development. Vigotsky thought that every function in the child's cultural development appears twice: first, on the social level, & later, on the individual level. The first, interpsychological, was between people & the second, intrapsychological was inside the child. 2. The More Knowledgeable Other (MKO) referred to anyone who had a better understanding or a higher ability level than the learner, with respect to a particular task. 3. The Zone of Proximal Development (ZPD) was the distance between a student's ability to perform a task under adult guidance, & the student's ability solving the problem independently.

Lev Vigotsky is also known for proposing the development of a particular branch in science that would concern itself with working out a specific scientific methodology for psychological investigation. He viewed the history of science as an experimental apparatus, in which one could trace the mutual relationship between theory & fact. Vigotsky's basic premise was the distinction to be drawn between two levels of psychic processes-the natural & the cultural. That which was contributed to culture was seen as the human element in the psyche. Vigotsky was the first psychologist in the world to represent the use of working tools & sign systems as playing the main part in forming the entire structure of human consciousness. The principle that cultural artifacts are mediators for the Individual psyche brought about a radical change in the methods used to study psychic functions.

He also attributed the function of instrument of labor to words. He perceived the similarity between the tool & the word to lie in fact that both of these transform direct links, between an organism's psychic structure & the world, into mediated links. It is necessary to mention that the idea of interiorisation had become accepted long before Vigotsky's time: efforts had been made to elucidate the ways in which an organism's relationships with the external world form its internal, psychic environment. Basically Vigotsky's work responded to the need for a transformation of psychology into something based upon socio-determinism, historicism & a systems approach.

Toward the end of 1920 a new school of thought emerged in Soviet psychology, its founder was Georgian psychologist Dmitri Uznadze (1886-1950).He was born in the small village of Sakara in Georgia. He was expelled from Kutaisi high school for taking part in the 1905 revolution. The same year he went to Switzerland & then to Germany, where he entered the philosophy faculty of Leipzig University. Uznadze received his PhD in 1910 at the University of Wittenberg. He returned to Georgia in 1909 & from then until 1917 he taught history at the Kutaisi Gymnasium. He was also a headmaster of the Sinatle girls' school from 1915 – 1917.

Uznadze helped establish the Tbilisi State University. In 1935 he received Doctor of Science degree in Psychology. In 1941 he co-founded the Georgian Academy of Sciences. In 1941 - 1950 he was the first Director of the Institute of Psychology of the Georgian Academy of Sciences.

Uznadze was the author of the so called theory of "Attitude & Set."The theory of set was not a new category in psychology it was used in many shades of meaning. Although it was already an existing phenomenon, which needed to be characterized, it was not just a matter of adding the knowledge gained of it to the sum of total of empirical information. The implications of the discovery of this phenomenon, set, were more important since they involved a whole system of theoretical ideas of psychology. If this new fact to be fully comprehended some principles, that had been taken as fundamental to the whole structure of psychic activity, had to be abandoned. The notion of set came into being in consequence of the earliest achievements of experimental psychology, in the area of study devoted to reaction times & sensitivity thresholds. In reaction time studies the speed of mental processes was measured. An assumption was made that a simple reaction was a constant quantity in each individual.

The clear understanding of the subject-matter & the task of psychology was the guiding factor in the studies made by Uznadze. Putting his trust in the hypothesis that psychology could only become a true science when it took as its point of departure the individual as conditioned by the life-process, Uznadze reached the conclusion that the business of psychology was to study the living reality of human activity. Uznadze, just like the rest was focused on human activity, the only difference was that his main theme was not activity & consciousness, but activity & unconscious. At the same time Uznadze rejected Freud's interpretation of psyche, the irrationalism was alien to him. He also rejected the attempts to conjoin Marxism with Freudianism. In Soviet Union Uznadze was the only psychologist who studied the unconscious psyche from the scientific, materialistic standpoint, interpreting it in terms of the interaction between the subject & the situation in which his needs could be satisfied. It was in this interaction, he considered, the set was brought into being. When there is a need, & a situation in which it may be satisfied, a specific state arises within the subject, which is described as a tendency towards a performance of an act that can satisfy the need.

Uznadze was against the functional psychology instead he was favoring the Marxist doctrine of real activity. In Uznadze's theory the individual is not a reagent, whose behavior begins only when stimuli are consciously recognized & then connected either with one another or with muscular response. A real subject is always "set" in advance, & upon his set depend the nature of both his perception & his motor action. Set, as a real modus of the individual, exists independently of consciousness & may not be represented within it.

Basically, Uznadze's conceptions were evolved in opposition to the introspectionist dogma that the psyche & consciousness are one & the same, & were based on the interpretation of activity & personality, of the psyche & consciousness which is accepted in Marxist philosophy.

Nikolai Bernstein (1896-1966) a self taught, but well respected neuro-physiologist was best known for his biological motor control researches. In 1922 Bernstein, along with other researchers, were invited to study movement during manual labor in Moscow's Central Institute of Labor. The objective of the study was to optimize productivity, & Bernstein's analysis focused on cutting metal with a chisel. He incorporated cyclo-graphic techniques to track human movement. His observations showed that most movements, like hitting a chisel with a hammer, were com-posed of smaller movements, so any one of these smaller movements, if altered, could affect the movement as a whole. Inspired by this new experience Bernstein started a series of experiments that examined hu-man walking. At first he was aiming to with the engineering of pedestrian bridges. He studied the development of walking as humans matured & aged.

In 1935 Bernstein received a Doctor of Science degree, although he did not submit a thesis. In 1948 he was awarded the Stalin Prize for science. Bernstein was also one of the first members of the prestigious Academy of Medical Sciences of USSR.

Bernstein formulated many of the key issues in movement coordination. He conducted numerous researches on the degrees of freedom problem, motor equivalence & non-univocality of motor commands & peripheral effects. Due to political reasons, his 1947 book, "Coordination & Regula-tion of Movements" was not translated until 1967. He held that perfor-mance of any kind of movement results from an infinite variety of pos-sible combinations, or degrees of freedom, of neuromuscular & skeletal elements. Thus, the system, according to Bernstein, should be considered as self-organizing, with body elements coordinated in response to specific tasks. In Bernstein's theory motor development was dependent not on brain maturation, but adaptations to constraints of the body (changes in the growing infant's body mass and proportions) & to exogenous condi-tions (gravity, surface, specific tasks to be performed).

Alexander Luria (1902-1977) was born in Kazan, Russian. He enrolled in Kazan University at the age of 16. Luria obtained his degree in 1921 at the age of 19. While still a student, he established the Kazan Psychoanalytic Association, & planned on a career in psychology. His earliest research sought to establish objective methods for assessing Freudian ideas about abnormalities of thought.

His use of reaction time measures to study thought processes in the context of work settings won him a position at the Institute of Psychology in Moscow. Here he developed a psycho-diagnostic procedure he referred to as the "combined motor method" for diagnosing thought processes. In this method subjects were asked to carry out three tasks simultaneously. One hand was to be held steady while the other was used to press a key in response to verbal stimuli presented by the experimenter, to which the subject is asked to respond verbally. Preliminary trials were presented until a steady baseline of coordination was set. At this point, "critical" stimuli which the experimenter believed to be related to specific thoughts in the subject were presented. Luria's method was applied to a variety of naturally occurring and experimentally induced cases, providing a model system for psycho-diagnosis that won widespread attention in the west. In 1924 Luria met Vigotsky, with whom he sought to establish an approach to psychology that would enable them to discover the way natural processes such as physical maturation & sensory mechanisms become intertwined with culturally determined processes.

In the early 1930's he led two expeditions to Central Asia where he investigated changes in perception, problem solving & memory associated with historical changes in economic activity. During this same period he carried out studies of identical and fraternal twins raised in a large residential school to reveal the dynamic relations between phylogenetic & cultural-historical factors in the development of language.

The onset of World War II made Luria's specialized knowledge of crucial importance to the Soviet war effort. The tragic widespread availability of people with various forms of traumatic brain injury provided him with voluminous materials for developing his theories of brain function. It was during this period that he developed the systematic approach to brain and cognition which has come to be known as the discipline of neuropsychology. After the war Luria returned to his work in neuropsychology. He was fired from the Institute of Neurosurgery during a period of anti-Semitic repression. Eventually Luria was permitted to return to the study of neuropsychology, which he pursued until his death.

Luria was using an experimental approach that has its closest parallel in studies contained in the nature of human conflicts, but with a conceptual structure that grew directly out of the basic principles of the socio-historical school & a language that was predominantly Pavlovian.

Alexei Leontiev (1903-1979) was the founder of the activity theory, which was concerned with providing a mental evolutionary account of the continuity & discontinuity between human and animal psy-

350

chological existence. His early scientific work was done in the framework of Vygotsky's cultural-historical research program. Leontiev's main goal was to develop a Marxist psychology valid enough to oppose behaviorism. In 1931 Leontiev left Vygotsky's group in Moscow, to join Kharkov University. He returned to Moscow in 1950 as Head of the Psychology Department at the Faculty of Philosophy of Moscow State University. In 1966, Leontiev became the first ever Dean of the newly established Faculty of Psychology at the Moscow State University, where he worked until his death.

Leontiev held that activity was comprised of those processes that realize a person's actual life in the objective world by which he was surrounded & his social being. According to Leontiev's theory human processes can be examined from the perspective of three different levels of analysis. The highest level was that of activity & motives that drove it. At the intermediate level were actions & their associated goals & the lowest level was the analysis of operations that serve as means for the achievement of the higher-order goals.

Soviet developmental psychologist Pyotr Zinchenko (1903-1969) was born in Nikolayevsk Russia. Zinchenko was a disciple of Lev Vigotsky & Alexei Leontiev. In 1969 he was the head of the department of psychology at the famous Kharkov University.

Zinchenko spent most of his time in Kharkov studying so called involuntary memory. Involuntary memory is a conception of human memory in which cues encountered in everyday life evoke recollections of the past without conscious effort. It is the complete opposite of voluntary memory. Zinchenko's goal was to prove that the recall of material to be remembered mainly depends on the kind of activity directed on the material. He further concluded that the motivation performs the activity & the level of interest in the material. He was trying to prove that following the task of sorting material in experimental settings, human subjects demonstrate a better involuntary recall rate than in the task of voluntary material memorization. Zinchenko's superb research on involuntary memory prompted the development of Leontiev's activity theory. Many consider Zinchenko to be the founder of the new era of Soviet developmental psychology.

Conclusion

Essentially the theory of personality is an attempt to successfully organize the great variety of human thinking, feeling & behavior around some basic principles that will explain the similarities & differences of human character. Ideally the theory should be able to explain exactly which characteristics are important along with the most likely patterns of relationships among characteristics. It also must provide the way in which these patterns are established & the way in which they can be changed. It should be mentioned that personality theories are the most difficult & complex fields in psychology. The main reason for the variety of theories is that many of them emerged out of clinical observations of various patients with different cultural & social backgrounds. Some theories have grown out of studies of learning & individual differences One of the substantial differences in the theories of personality is the emphasis which in some cases is biological, in others psychological & in some socio-cultural. Because of this, theories are in constant contradiction with each other, which makes it difficult to study or summarize this field. It is safe to say that all of the theories have something useful to offer but none of them is entirely satisfactory.